ECONOMISTS OF THE TWENTIETH CENTURY

General Editors: Mark Perlman, *University Professor of Economics, Emeritus, University of Pittsburgh* and Mark Blaug, *Professor Emeritus, University of London, Professor Emeritus, University of Buckingham and Visiting Professor, University of Exeter*

This innovative series comprises specially invited collections of articles and papers by economists whose work has made an important contribution to economics in the late twentieth century.

The proliferation of new journals and the ever-increasing number of new articles make it difficult for even the most assiduous economist to keep track of all the important recent advances. By focusing on those economists whose work is generally recognized to be at the forefront of the discipline, the series will be an essential reference point for the different specialisms included.

A list of published and future titles in the series is printed at the end of this volume.

Industrialization, Inequality and Economic Growth

Jeffrey G. Williamson

Laird Bell Professor of Economics, Harvard University, USA

ECONOMISTS OF THE TWENTIETH CENTURY

Edward Elgar
Cheltenham, UK • Brookfield, US

© Jeffrey G. Williamson, 1997.

Published by
Edward Elgar Publishing Limited
8 Lansdown Place
Cheltenham
Glos GL50 2HU
UK

Edward Elgar Publishing Company
Old Post Road
Brookfield
Vermont 05036
US

3 2280 00609 0807

A catalogue record for this book is available from the British Library

Library of Congress Cataloging-in-Publication Data
Williamson, Jeffrey G., 1935-
Industrialization, inequality, and economic growth / Jeffrey G.
Williamson.

    (Economists of the twentieth century)
    Includes bibliographical references and index.
    1. Industrialization—History. 3. Income distribution—History.
2. Industrialization—History. 3. Income distribution—History.
Britain—History. 4. Income distribution—Great
development—History. I. Title. II. Series.
HD2329.W544 1997
338.941—dc20

96-38308
CIP

ISBN 1 85898 396 7

Printed and bound in Great Britain by
Hartnolls Limited, Bodmin, Cornwall

Contents

Acknowledgements

The author and publishers wish to thank the following who have kindly given permission for the use of copyright material.

Academic Press for articles: 'Was the Industrial Revolution Worth It? Disamenities and Death in 19th Century British Towns', *Explorations in Economic History*, **19**(3) (July 1982), pp. 221–45; 'Growth Equality and History' (with Peter H. Lindert), *Explorations in Economic History*, **22**(4) (October 1985), pp. 341–77.

Blackwell Publishers for article: 'English Workers' Living Standards During the Industrial Revolution: A New Look' (with Peter H. Lindert), *Economic History Review*, **XXXVI**(1) (February 1983), pp. 1–25.

Cambridge University Press for article and excerpt: 'Why Was British Growth So Slow During the Industrial Revolution?', *Journal of Economic History*, **XLIV**(3) (September 1984), pp. 687–712; 'Coping with City Growth', in R. Floud and D.N. McCloskey (eds), *The Economic History of Britain Since 1700, Volume 1: 1700–1860*, 2nd edn, Chapter 13; 1994, pp. 332–56 and references.

Journal of Japanese Studies for article: 'Saving, Accumulation and Modern Economic Growth: The Contemporary Relevance of Japanese History' (with Leo J. de Bever) **4**(1) (Fall 1977), pp. 125–67.

The Population Council for articles: 'The Historical Content of the Classical Labor Surplus Model', *Population and Development Review*, **11**(2) (June 1985), pp. 171–91; 'Population Growth, Industrial Revolutions, and the Urban Transition' (with Allen C. Kelley), *Population and Development Review*, **10**(3) (September 1984), pp. 419–41.

University of Chicago Press for articles: 'Inequality, Accumulation and Technological Imbalance: A Growth-Equity Conflict in American History?', *Economic Development and Cultural Change*, **27**(2) (January 1979), pp. 231–53; 'Capital Flows to the New World as an Intergenerational Transfer' (with Alan M. Taylor), *Journal of Political Economy*, **102**(2) (April 1994), pp. 348–71; 'What Explains Wage Gaps Between Farm and City? Exploring the Todaro Model with American Experience 1890–1941' (with Timothy J. Hatton), *Economic Development and Cultural Change*, **40**(2) (January 1992), pp. 267–94.

Introduction

Our economic knowledge about the Third World has undergone great leaps since the 1970s. The World Bank tapes, the Penn World Tables, new trade flow data, comprehensive surveys documenting the behaviour of poor households, lengthening time series – all of these and others have made it possible to explore questions about economic performance in the industrializing Third World which would have been impossible in 1966 or 1976. Indeed, such data has: nurtured the new growth theory and released a flood of conditional growth equations; nurtured a new theory of household behaviour and released a flood of cross-sections; and nurtured an explicit political economy of rational choice and released a flood of empirical efforts to endogenize policy. In spite of these advances, economists still fight over the same questions that classical economists did when writing almost two centuries ago about the British Industrial Revolution – accumulation, distribution and industrialization. The trilogy still stands, and it serves to organize this book too.

The eleven essays which follow were written between 1977 and 1994, 17 years which saw some exciting developments in our thinking about the Third World. Closed-economy models of autarkic import substitution have been replaced by open-economy models of export-led growth: a paradigm switch reflecting profound changes in policy. Labour surplus models, where distribution drives savings and thus accumulation, have been replaced by models in which investment demand drives accumulation: a paradigm switch consistent with the globalization of world capital markets. Hysteria about the costs of Third World urbanization has been replaced by a more sober view stressing the benefits of city growth. Malthusian pessimism about Third World population growth has been replaced by academic ambiguity and policy indifference. Thus, our thinking about the Third World has undergone a dramatic evolution since 1977 when the first of these essays was written.

All of the essays included in this book deal with economic history, but the agenda in each one is explicitly moulded by contemporary debate about Third World development. The questions were posed that way on purpose since I wanted then, as I still do, to use history to speak to these Third World debates. Some economic historians may object to writing economic history backwards in this fashion, but for me it is the only way to justify what economic historians do and to try to make our voices heard.

I believe that Third World analysts ignore economic history at their peril. I also believe that these historical essays still speak with fresh voices to the modern Third World issues of accumulation, distribution and industrialization. The chapters are organized into three parts based on these issues, and so is this Introduction. I start with accumulation, move on to distribution and end with industrialization. The partition is, of course, artificial, as even the simplest general equilibrium model should immediately expose. But since the artificial partition does little harm, I keep it for the sake of organization and to acknowledge an intellectual tradition almost two centuries old.

Capital accumulation: crowding, demography, inequality and technological events

I start here with the First Industrial Revolution. Chapter 3, 'Why Was British Growth So Slow During the Industrial Revolution' (1984), was motivated by a puzzle suggested by the title. New evidence confirms that there was little that was revolutionary about British economic growth from the 1760s or 1780s to the 1820s. Hardly any capital deepening took place, investment shares in national income averaged only a little more than a tenth (net shares were far lower), per capita income growth registered not much more than 0.3 per cent per annum, real wages stagnated, industry's share of output rose at a snail's pace, and trade was certainly no engine of growth, nor even a 'handmaiden' (Kravis, 1970). What kind of revolution was this? The First Industrial Revolution looks very odd indeed. In contrast, Britain underwent an impressive boom from the 1820s to the 1870s. Real wages rose at an annual rate close to 2 per cent per annum. Investment shares in national income and the rate of accumulation both nearly doubled, and the rate of capital deepening increased by eight times. Exports boomed and the rate of industrialization surged, so much so that Britain became the 'workshop of the world' by the mid-nineteenth century. Why the regime switch?

One answer to this puzzle is that the dating of the First Industrial Revolution is simply wrong (Cameron, 1985). Maybe this is so, but who cares about labels? Debate over labels and dates serves only to deflect our attention from the important (and harder) question: why the regime switch around 1820? A second answer is that it took Britain time to develop the institutions and policies which would accommodate her unrequited growth potential – like shedding a mercantilist legacy, an event not unlike modern Third World nations finally 'getting the prices right' (Rodrik, 1996). A third answer is the one which I favour: Britain tried to do two things at once during the six decades prior to the 1820s, industrialize *and* fight expensive wars. During the 60 years following 1760, Britain was at war for 36; in the three decades following the late 1780s Britain went from a peacetime economy to a level of wartime commitment that had no parallel until World War I. The war debt swelled, a substantial share of the civilian labour force was mobilized, a fifth of national income was siphoned off by taxes, while the contraction of trade shares – reflecting an increasingly closed economy – drove up the relative price of agricultural (and raw material) importables and drove down the relative price of manufacturing exportables.

Debt, taxes, mobilization and relative price shocks: which of these mattered most in accounting for the peculiar slow growth during the First Industrial Revolution? Or was it instead something else such as sluggish rates of technical progress or factor market failure? Chapter 3 offered an answer and it provoked subsequent debate which has yet to be stilled. I argued that in a war-torn environment of segmented world capital markets Britain had to go it alone on the financing, and that the enormous war debt issues crowded out private accumulation. I also argued that the war-induced relative price shock reinforced the accumulation slow down.

The modern debate provoked by Robert Barro's (1974) famous paper had its counterpart in the nineteenth century as the views of David Ricardo and John Stuart Mill often took centre stage in academic exchanges. While I offer reasons for supporting the time-dependent assumptions underlying strong crowding out, Chapter 3 has a different strategy. It only asks the reader to imagine what Britain's world would have been like without the wars if one assumes crowding out, indeed, if ones assumes *one-for-one* crowding out. Subsequent critics have made it appear that I believe one-for-one crowding out, but I do not. I only believe that the assumption can explain an enormous share of what was peculiar about the First Industrial Revolution. Other hypotheses may do as well, but, in my opinion, they have yet to come forward.

These hypotheses are tested using a five-sector, open economy, small country, computable general equilibrium model (CGE), a mode of analysis I have found extremely useful in untangling knotty problems in economic history. Reassured by the ability of the model to replicate the peacetime period 1821–1861, I then proceed with the counterfactual analysis of the earlier wartime period 1760–1820. How would Britain's performance have differed in the absence of wars? That is, how would it have differed without crowding out, without mobilization and without the trade disruptions? The bottom line which emerges from the counterfactual is that almost all of the acceleration after 1820 can be explained by the switch from war to peace. The acceleration in the trend after 1820 seems to have had little to do with the underlying fundamentals of capitalist development. Furthermore, the poor standard of living performance between 1760 and 1820 can be explained mostly by the tiny rates of capital deepening endured by crowding out. Indeed, the low investment share in national income cannot be explained by profligate consumption of potential savers since the gross *private* savings rate – including new private-sector holdings of government debt – were almost twice as high as the national investment shares.

Slow accumulation and thus slow rates of job creation (especially high-wage jobs in the cities) account for most of the poor performance of living standards up to the 1820s, but war-induced price distortions played a major role too. The war-induced price distortions (and trade suppression) explain even more of the disappointing rates of industrialization Britain experienced up the 1820s.

Chapter 2, 'Inequality, Accumulation and Technological Imbalance' (1979), deals with an important industrial follower in the New World, the USA. Here the puzzle is not slow growth, but fast growth. More than 40 years ago, W. Arthur Lewis argued that the central problem of development theory was to explain

the process by which a community which was previously saving and investing 4 or

> 5 per cent of its national income or less, converts itself into an economy where voluntary saving is running at about 12 to 15 percent of national income or more ... We cannot explain any 'industrial' revolution ... until we can explain why saving increased relative to national income. (Lewis, 1954, p. 155)

The USA seems to fit this quote admirably. The early nineteenth century launched the US economy along a sharply rising accumulation path. Prior to 1805, the rates of (non-human) capital deepening were very modest. The pace quickens up to 1835, but the really big leap took place between the 1830s and the late 1860s. The acceleration in the trend continued thereafter, but at a slower rate.[1] Investment and savings shares boomed: the net investment share more than doubled, from 6 per cent in 1839 to 15 per cent in 1897, more or less confirming Lewis' central problem of development. Most of the drama, however, was packed into the four decades from the 1830s to the 1870s.

Since the appearance of my paper and a similar one by Paul David (1977), the debate has provoked some scholars to diminish the size of Lewis-like doubling by expanding the asset portfolio being considered. But for the non-human capital accumulation that matters most to us, the dramatic rise in the US savings and investment rates persist. What accounts for the doubling in investment rates? It cannot be some increased dependence on foreign capital that released the constraints on accumulation. Even though there is evidence that the global capital market in the 1890s was at least as well integrated as in the 1980s (Zevin, 1992), and even though the USA was part of that assessment, her dependence on foreign capital fell throughout the century (Williamson, 1964). Thus, the presence of foreign capital leads to an even *bigger* accumulation puzzle, not smaller.

English nineteenth century economists thought rising savings rates could be explained by rising inequality. Confusing marginal with average rates, they thought any redistribution which worked in favour of the rich (who saved a lot) and against the poor (who saved little) would raise overall savings rates. They also thought that industrialization bred inequality. I will have more to say about this in the next section, but for the present I simply note that back in 1979 it appeared that there was unambiguous evidence supporting the nineteenth century English economists in that nineteenth century USA was tracing out the rising portion of the Kuznets Curve (Kuznets, 1955; Lindert and Williamson, 1976). If so, does the correlation support a growth-equity trade-off, or instead is the correlation spurious?

There are, of course, other plausible explanations. One appeals to unbalanced productivity advance. Suppose fast technical progress in the nineteenth century was centred exactly where it is in the Third World today, on the modern sectors – manufacturing, transport, communications – where capital and skill intensity were and are high. To the extent that technical progress was biased by sector in this fashion, it would have served to raise the demand for skills and machines. Skill premia would have risen, producing rising earnings inequality. Rates of return would have risen also, reinforcing the rise in inequality. Rising inequality might have augmented savings rates through the classical distribution hypothesis, but it would do the same if the savings rate was at all responsive to rates of return. In short, unbalanced technical progress by sector in the nineteenth century should have acted as if it were capital-cum-skills-using and labour-saving, events that would have contributed to rising inequality and rates of return, both of which would have served to drive up the savings rate between the 1830s and 1890s.

There is another possibility. The data document a greater rise in constant-price than in current-price investment rates, the reason, of course, being the decline in the relative price of investment goods in the USA. In fact, the relative price fell by 31 per cent between the 1840s and the turn of the century, but most of it was compressed between the 1840s and the 1870s – coinciding with the period when the investment rate underwent the most dramatic rise. Furthermore, the relative price decline was even greater for producer durables, a finding which is consistent with the more recent work of Delong and Summers which focuses on that component of capital formation (Delong and Summers, 1991; Delong, 1992). Chapter 2 argues that such relative price trends, presumably induced by unbalanced productivity advance favouring the producer durables sector, should help account for the rise in those investment shares across the nineteenth century.[2]

Finally, there are the varied influences of improved domestic financial institutions and policy to consider.

Chapter 2 uses a simple general equilibrium model of the investment funds market, a model which tries to identify shifts in savings supply and investment demand from movements along both. Thus, it tries to identify the underlying fundamentals that might explain Lewis' central problem of development. The answers appear to be unambiguous. Rising inequality, by raising savings rates, can explain only a modest portion of the doubling in the investment share, no more than a fifth and probably a lot less. The decline in the relative price of capital goods can explain much more, perhaps a third. The surge in investment demand driven by a capital-using bias can explain even more, perhaps a half and probably more. Savings mobilization explains none of the nineteenth century surge, perhaps because the impact of improved domestic mobilization capabilities on domestic savings was almost exactly offset by a reduced dependence on foreign capital.

Chapter 1 on 'Saving, Accumulation and Modern Economic Growth' (1977; written with Leo de Bever) confronts much the same problem, but in a very different context – Meiji and Taisho Japan between the 1880s and the 1930s. The chapter begins by pointing out a fact that seems to have been forgotten by modern growth analysts familiar only with the late twentieth century – typically, non-human capital accumulation contributes far more to growth during early stages of industrialization than during later stages. This fact is manifested most starkly by total factor productivity growth calculations. It was true of nineteenth century USA (Abramovitz and David, 1973), it has been true of late twentieth century Asia (Krugman, 1994) and it was true of Meiji and Taisho Japan. Between 1887 and 1922, capital deepening accounted for half of labour productivity growth, and between 1908 and 1938, it accounted for almost two-thirds. In short, while human capital accumulation may be a more important growth determinant in later stages of modern development, non-human capital accumulation is central to understanding growth in the early stages.

So, what explains the rising investment shares in Japan between 1887 and 1937? In constant prices, the share rose from 5 per cent in 1887, to 10 per cent in 1907, and to 17 per cent in 1937. Thus, the 50-year rise between 1887 and 1937, 12 percentage points, was not unlike the 55-year rise in the USA between 1839 and 1894, almost ten percentage points. What accounts for Japan's experience? Rising rates of labour force growth? A drift towards inequality? Heavier reliance on foreign capital? A switch from war to peace? A decline in the relative price of capital goods? Rising rates of capital-using technical change?

Once again, we found it useful to apply simple general equilibrium to the problem, thus identifying the underlying fundamentals driving up the investment share in Japan. Again the model was used to identify key forces that were causing the savings supply and the investment demand functions to shift to the right. Some of these forces repeat what we have found for Britain and the USA, but some offer surprises.

We start with a surprise: the impact of labour force growth. The standard view of the demographic transition has it that early development tends to diminish infant mortality, and since fertility rates only decline with a long lag, youth cohorts become glutted. Eventually, these fat cohorts cause a quickening in the rate of labour force growth and the problem of equipping, housing and commuting these young workers increases investment demand. There is abundant evidence to confirm this demographic thesis for the contemporary Third World – and especially for Asia (Higgins and Williamson, 1996), and the conventional historical literature implies that the same was true for Japan. The surprise is that the thesis fails for Meiji and Taisho Japan. There are complexities that the essay reveals, but the key finding is that the rate of labour force growth *fell* between the decades prior to 1907 and the decades afterward. The thesis even fails to explain the shorter run investment spurt following 1905 over which so much fuss has been made (Ohkawa and Rosovsky, 1973).

The second surprise deals with capital-using technical progress, events which appear to have accounted for so much of the nineteenth century US investment boom. True, buoyant rightward shifts in investment demand driven by capital-using technical progress mattered greatly during the short run boom between 1907 and 1917, just as Ohkawa and Rosovsky predicted. But it did *not* play a role for the 30 years as a whole up to 1937. This is a surprise, and scholars should give it more attention.

In contrast to these two surprises, the declining relative price of capital goods *did* help account for a big share of the surge in Japan's investment rate, just as it did for the USA between the 1830s and 1870s. That relative price drifted downward at 0.7 per cent per annum between 1907 and 1937, a downward drift just a little faster than that which the USA experienced between 1839 and 1874. It accounts for about a quarter of Japan's investment surge between 1907 and 1937. Since the relative price decline was about the same between 1887 and 1907 it must have played a similar role in the late nineteenth century. Given that the relative price decline of capital goods was more than double that rate between 1953 and 1971 (1.7 per cent per annum), perhaps a comparable share of the even bigger post-war investment boom can be explained by these relative price movements. Economic historians should have communicated this fact to modern macro growth empiricists much earlier, but at least it has received attention recently in the work of DeLong and Summers.

Finally, shifts in the savings function appear to account for an enormous share of the measured rise in net private savings rates over the three decades prior to 1937 even though it is difficult to find compelling evidence supporting significant inequality trends. This finding seems to be consistent with the post-war literature on Japan's savings-rate-boom puzzle. Economists interested in Japan's post-war miracle ought to add pre-war twentieth century savings experience to their agenda, it would appear.

The chapter then looks to the earlier accumulation experience from 1887 to 1907, a period with less comprehensive evidence and thus with a high opinion to fact ratio. But three findings are worth stressing. First, in the absence of government-induced instability associated with the Russo-Japanese and Sino-Japanese wars followed by peace, the investment spurt from 1905 to World War I would have disappeared. The switch from war to peace explains all of that boom which Ohkawa and Rosovsky thought was driven by the 'wave of foreign technology which washed up on Japan's shores'. Second, and in contrast to the post-1907 period, there *was* an investment boom driving up the savings and investment rates in the pre-1907 period, and much of that boom was driven by the exceptionally favourable decline in the relative price of industrial raw materials. The price of industrial raw materials relative to agricultural products fell by almost 50 per cent between 1887 and 1902, and by about 35 per cent relative to manufactures. Surely this price shock favoured industrial profitability and urban-based accumulation (just as it impeded them in Britain prior to the 1820s). Third, and in sharp contrast with Britain's experience up to 1820, the burdens of war did *not* suppress Meiji accumulation. Why not? The answer has two parts. The first part had to do with global capital markets: Japan was able to rely on net foreign lending in the 1880s and 1890s (prior to the breakdown of world capital markets in the inter-war period), while Britain could not during her conflict almost a century earlier. The link with the modern literature started by Feldstein and Horioka (1980) is clearly relevant here. The second part has to do with Japanese luck: she won the conflicts and the indemnities were enormous. Without those indemnities, the Japanese government would have had to increase her reliance on domestic borrowing, thus crowding out private capital formation.

Contemporary economists have pondered at length the sources of rising investment and savings rates in East Asia since the 1950s, including Japan. The answers have not always been satisfactory. Perhaps it is time they paid more attention to accumulation experience in the region prior to World War II.

The final chapter in Part I. 'Capital Flows to the New World as an Intergenerational Transfer' (1994; written with Alan Taylor), offers a new twist on an old problem, and extends the connection with the Feldstein-Horioka literature. The capital flows from Europe to the New World were simply enormous during the *belle epoque* from 1870 to World War I. About two thirds of British investment abroad headed in that direction, and at her peak British net foreign investment was about half of her annual savings. With the exception of the USA, most of these resource-abundant and labour-scarce New World countries were heavily dependent on foreign investment: through the 40 years prior to 1910, 30–50 per cent of Canadian annual investment was financed by foreign capital; the figure for Argentina was about 50 per cent; and the figure for Mexico was even bigger, about 75 per cent. The New World can be characterized by dual scarcity – scarce in labour and capital. Foreign capital chased after the emigrants, and both were pulled to the New World by abundant resources.

All of this is well known. What is not well known is why the flow was so enormous. As a share of the economies involved, these late nineteenth century flows were far bigger than were the capital flows to the Third World during the 1970s prior to the debt crisis, or even in the 1990s among the new Asian tigers. What were the underlying fundamentals that pushed those flows to such heights? Chapter 4 appeals to demography and the life cycle model. The demography is straightforward. Labour scarcity in the New World encouraged both early marriage and big families within marriage. It also implied good nutrition, good health, low infant mortality and high youth survival. These forces combined to create very large youth dependency rates, even though European immigration – heavily selecting young adults (Hatton and Williamson, 1994) – tried to offset those native-born effects. Thus, the New World manifested an elastic long run labour supply response to the labour scarcity, but it created high youth dependency rates. The opposite was true of labour-abundant Europe. Dependency rate differentials between the capital-exporting Old World and the capital-importing New World were big in the late nineteenth century.

The chapter then estimates the impact of dependency rates on savings and finds the effect powerful for Argentina, Australia and Canada. These estimates are then used to answer the question: how much of these enormous capital flows can be explained by the dependency rate differentials? The answers are stunning: between one-third and all of the New World net inflows may have been due to these demographic effects; and about three-quarters of British overseas investment may have been due to dependency-induced pull at the periphery.

In the late nineteenth century decades of capital market globalization, foreign investment by the Old World in the New can be viewed as an intergenerational transfer. Would the same apply to the late twentieth century when the Third World has been beset with dramatic demographic transitions, ones not muted by mass migrations? Apparently so. It appears that a very large share of Latin American (Taylor, 1995) and Asian (Higgins and Williamson, 1996) experience with capital inflows can be explained by exactly the same intergenerational forces. History seems to have repeated itself.

Standard of living debates, inequality and labour surplus models

Perhaps no other debate in economic history has persisted longer or has been so politically charged than that involving living standards during early industrial revolutions. It all started in Britain. The liberal pessimists argued that there was no trickling down to the working poor during the First Industrial Revolution, and started pushing for pro-poor reform in the 1830s. The optimists argued that there was trickling down, and further that smaller real wage increases today implied bigger real wage increases tomorrow, since it allowed faster accumulation. Thus, the conservative optimists tried to block pro-poor reform. Economic historians of Britain have continued this debate between optimist and pessimist, sometimes with the same intensity as was true of the 1830s!

Be assured that there is more than simply some academic squabble at issue here. British economists writing in the first half of the nineteenth century developed models of growth and distribution which focused on the events which they *thought* were going on around them. They were a little fuzzy about the facts since this was, after all, the *First* Industrial Revolution and they had not yet accumulated enough experience with modern economic growth to develop the stylized facts that we carry in our heads today. Indeed, they did not have anything like the evidence necessary to perform tests of their models then. We do now.

The British economist thought he saw stable real wages for the working poor, and developed what we now call classical explanations for it. Marx explained the event by appealing to technological forces. He developed labour-saving explanations by appealing to enclosures on the land and industrial dynamics in the city. Malthus offered a demographic explanation: his model pointed to labour supply explanations, an elastic labour supply response which, in the long run, ensured an equilibrium wage at some subsistence floor. Others appealed to 'disguised unemployment' in the Irish and English countryside to get elastic labour supplies.

British economists lost interest in these classical paradigms somewhere during the second quarter of the nineteenth century, partly because they thought the real wage was rising dramatically. In effect, they seemed to think that the British economy had passed through what more than a century later Fei and Ranis (1964) called the 'turning point'. Their neoclassical models implied that labour surplus notions were no longer relevant. But as post-World War II development in the Third World began to attract economists' attention, W. Arthur Lewis (1954) asked us to look again at those classical models and his celebrated 'labour surplus' model emerged as a result. It underwent refinement and elaboration in the 1960s. Fei and Ranis (1964) formalized the model and applied it to Japan and South Asia. Sen (1966) then showed us exactly what assumptions were required to make the labour surplus model operational, and by the early 1970s Dixit (1973) had placed it in mainstream growth theory. By the late 1970s, the fixed-real-wage paradigm was even being embedded in large-scale macro models (for example, Taylor et al., 1980), where policy debates were explicitly at issue.

Chapter 7, 'The Historical Content of the Classical Labor Surplus Model' (1985), offers this recitation to remind us that the modern labour surplus model has its roots with the classical economists, and that they developed their paradigms to account for the events they *thought* were taking place around them in the late eighteenth and early nineteenth century. Were they right?

Chapter 5, 'English Workers' Living Standards During the Industrial Revolution: A New Look' (1983; written with Peter Lindert), sought an answer to this question. Since Peter Lindert and I had so much better data than previous scholars, we naively thought the essay would settle the issue once for all. It generated instead an enormous outpouring of debate (led by Crafts, 1987 and Feinstein, 1988), but after almost 15 years of shouting, the central fact of pre-1820 real wage stability still stands (even in the eyes of Feinstein, 1996).

Chapter 5 also helped generated active interest in exploiting a completely, new data base, anthropometric information on heights and weights (Fogel, 1994; Komlos, 1995; Steckle, 1995). While the new anthropometric data are a welcome addition to the standard of living debate, they have not eliminated some very old problems. How do you add up changes in the quality and length of life when the two are connected? How do you measure the role of nutrition and housing when the disease environment deteriorates? When workers opt to locate in the high-wage but low-quality city, rather than in low-wage and high-quality countryside, what weights should be used to reflect the changing mix? How do we value those attributes of workers lives which fail to pass directly through the market place? As we shall see, these are old issues which provoked the creation of the World Bank Living Standards Study in the 1970s, many studies on Third World poverty (such as van der Gaag and Lipton 1993), and writings by some very able modern theorists (such as Dasgupta 1993; Dreze, Sen and Hussain, 1995).

The debate has also helped provoke comparable research for other early industrializers at other times. After all, British experience between 1780 and 1820 may have been the exception to the rule. True, Britain was first and her experience had an enormous impact on economic thought since so much of that thought was formed by nineteenth century British economists. For example, there has never been comparable hot debate for the USA during its *ante bellum* experience with early industrialization (Gallman and Wallis, 1992). Why? On the other hand, there *has* been hot debate for Meiji and Taisho Japan (Fei and Ranis, 1964; Minami 1968; Kelley and Williamson, 1974). Why? The point is that we need to document the behaviour of real wages of the working poor for far more early industrial revolutions before the debate can be put to bed.

What Chapters 3 and 5 failed to do, however, was to generate an equally vibrant literature on the *causes* of stable real wages during early industrial revolutions, or its absence. Clearly, that should be the agenda for the future, especially in light of the current debate about the global economy in the 1990s. If globalization holds down wages of the working poor in rich industrial countries (for example Freeman, 1995), then should it not raise their wages in poor agrarian countries just starting their industrial revolutions (Wood, 1994; Williamson, 1996b)? Thus, should not experience with real wages during industrial revolutions depend, at least in part, on whether a country's experience takes place in a world environment of global openness (for example 1820–1913 or 1970–1996) or in an environment of global autarky (for example 1780–1820 or 1913–1970)?

So much for introductions. What, then, did Chapter 5 on living standards during the First Industrial Revolution find? After labouring over a nominal wage data base representing many occupations, and after constructing better cost of living deflators that even included housing, we then aggregated up to five groups: farm labourers (with the lowest wages), urban unskilled workers, urban skilled artisans and white collar employees (the highest wages); blue collar wages were a weighted average of the first three. The bottom lines were that real wages were stable up to about 1820, that real wages increased smartly over the three decades up to 1851, and thus that there was a 'turning point' around 1820. The cost of living estimates in Chapter 5 were attacked by Crafts (1985), but the repairs made in response (Lindert and Williamson, 1985) did nothing to alter these bottom lines. The white collar series was attacked by Feinstein (1988), but this did nothing to alter the blue collar series or even the all worker series (since white collar workers were a relatively small share of the total labour force). Thus, his criticism also did nothing to alter these bottom lines (Feinstein, 1996).

In a sense, both the optimist and pessimist can find solace in these numbers. But the pessimists were not happy with a finding that showed significant real wage increases after 1820, especially since it offset the poor late eighteenth and early nineteenth century real wage performance. Like Frederick Engels and other critics of British capitalism, the modern pessimist could point to the probable rise in unemployment and the probable fall in the unmeasured components of the quality of life – poor health, greater pollution, broken marriages, numbing work discipline, crowded housing, rising crime, violence and social injustice. The remainder of the chapter turns to these issues to find that they simply do not matter much. Unemployment did not rise after 1820 and a declining quality of life implied only a modest reduction in those measured real wage gains. The reader will want to look at those details, but the most important offset – the poor quality of urban life – was pursued in two companion papers (Williamson, 1981a; 1981b) and a third which appears here as Chapter 6 – 'Was the Industrial Revolution Worth It? Disamenities and Death in 19th Century British Towns' (1982).

From the perspective of the 1990s, it is hard to form a proper appreciation of just how ugly nineteenth century cities really were in the industrializing countries of just that time. It was only around World War I that the relative quality of life began to favour the city over the countryside. In the industrializing Third World today, the differential favouring the city is, of course, quite marked (Lipton, 1976; Williamson, 1981b; Williamson, 1990). But in the 1830s, when city reformers began to generate angry rhetoric, the cities were noisy, crowded, dirty, polluted, poorly supplied with water, poorly supplied with toilets, and with no significant public health delivery system. Thus Frederick Engels viewed migration into the cities as 'social murder'.

Chapter 6 illustrates how debate over the quality of urban life during the First Industrial Revolution can be quantified, although the work has since provoked more detailed assessments for the same period (Brown, 1990; Williamson, 1990). The hedonic technique was motivated by the work of Nordhaus and Tobin (1972) who, in the early 1970s, were responding to the challenge of the 'green' pessimists – Ehrlich, Meadows, Forrester and the Club of Rome. First, I estimated for 1905 the value which workers of that time placed on urban life qualities: that is, it estimated the marginal bribe required to get the workers into cities which had a marginally worse environment. It turned out that city size, city density and infant mortality were the best proxies for environmental quality, an econometric finding that supported the intuition of knowledgeable social reformers of that time. Second, I selected some small rural towns with high quality of life – calling them 'Sweet Auburn', and some large cities with low quality of life – one standard deviation above mean quality levels – calling them 'Sheffield'. Third, I calculated the cost of the wage bribe to get the marginal worker to move from 'Sweet Auburn' to 'Sheffield' in 1905. The bribe was biggest in the northern counties, 3–7 per cent, but even inflating that adjustment to 15 per cent did little to damage inferences about booming real wages and living standards between 1820 and 1850.

But did the workers of 1835 place a higher value on the quality of life (and a lower value on commodities, which the real wage purchased) than did the worker of 1905? Furthermore, was the quality difference between 'Sweet Auburn' and 'Sheffield' bigger in 1835 than it was in 1905? The answer to the second question is definitely yes: the largest and nastiest cities underwent enormous environmental improvements after the 1840s, and infant mortality differences between city and countryside dropped sharply between 1871 and 1906. The answer to the first question is also yes: the marginal wage bribe was bigger in 1834 than it was in 1905. The total wage bribe in the northern counties in the 1830s and 1840s was therefore higher than in 1905 on two counts, perhaps 7–13 per cent rather than 3–7 per cent. Now apply this total wage bribe to what we know about the rising share of those exposed to the ugly cities between 1820 and 1850. The inference is that the measured real wage boom overstates the true standard of living improvement by perhaps 3–4 per cent, a trivial amount.

The pessimists are wrong. The deteriorating quality of life associated with the rural to urban move did not matter much since the workers placed far lower weight on it than did the social reformers. Furthermore, the argument that there was, in addition, a deterioration in the quality of life within cities does not alter the conclusion much either. It turns out that nineteenth century pessimists among the social reformers and twentieth century pessimists among the economic historians have both assumed a very different trade-off between private consumption and communal life quality in the debate over living standards, just as they tend to do today.

Let us now return to the issue raised at the outset of this section: what have we learned thus far about the classical model? The classical economists were right that real wages were stable up to 1820. They were wrong in treating the economic performance of the period as revolutionary. Growth and accumulation were very slow. We do not need a classical model with elastic labour supplies to get stable real wages up to 1820; a neoclassical model that takes account of war will do just fine. But what about the boom after 1820? Does the classical model work there? This is precisely the question pursued in Chapter 7.

While wages were hardly stable after 1820, it is true that unskilled wages lagged behind, as Chapter 5 has shown. Furthermore, there is some evidence supporting a more comprehensive rise in inequality during these three decades of Pax Britannica (Lindert and Williamson, 1983, 1985; Williamson, 1985). Those supporting the classical model have often pointed to Irish immigration as confirmation of the elastic labour supply hypothesis, and thus lagging unskilled wages, rising inequality and, presumably, rising savings, investment and accumulation rates. Chapter 7 reports experiments with a CGE model which would have shown that the Irish simply cannot have had the effect attributed to them.

The essay applies the *coup de grace* to the labour surplus model: it cannot find any historical evidence from the British industrial revolution to support the inequality-accumulation trade-off that is so central to the model. Real wages were certainly stable up to 1820, but the investment share only rose by four percentage points – hardly the 7–11 percentage point surge which Lewis labels the 'central problem in development theory'. And while inequality seems to reveal a modest upward drift after 1820, the investment share failed to rise at all! The lack of correlation between inequality and accumulation during the British industrial revolution does not bode well for the classical paradigm. There is very little historical content to the classical labour surplus model, it seems, and I suspect the same has been true of the Third World since 1950.

Part II ends with 'Growth, Equality and History' (1985; Chapter 8), a paper which Peter Lindert and I used to survey what we knew about the Kuznets Curve more than a decade ago. When it was written, inequality was no longer a popular topic, and the Kuznets Curve itself was under seige, considered by some to be a non-fact. Things have changed a bit since 1985. The enormous rise in income inequality in the USA since the early 1970s has suddenly been discovered by economists, and the debate between the effects of globalization and technological change on inequality has broken out, sometimes with very hot rhetoric. Oddly, this debate is being carried on by a new generation of economists who seem to be unaware of the fact that it (and the hot rhetoric) is very, very old.

The chapter tries to be cautious about Kuznets Curves. More than 40 years ago, Simon Kuznets (1955) noted that income inequality had declined across the mid-twentieth century in much of Europe and North America, and cautiously guessed that it had risen earlier. The early (and crude) cross section evidence which emerged from the World Bank almost two decades later (Ahluwalia, 1976) suggested good reasons for Kuznets' caution: the variance around any estimated Kuznets Curve is greatest from low to middle income levels; the correlation is tight from middle income levels upwards. Thus, the debate about the downside has been quiet, while the debate about the upside has been noisy. All industrial revolutions need not generate rising inequality, and the severity of the rise need not be the same among all who experience it. It depends on the starting points. History matters, and there is path dependence. The farther away any country gets from that starting point, the less important history is and the more important are the common shared features of industrialization.

Historical research confirms these World Bank cross-section inferences. There was indeed a common egalitarian trend in Europe and the USA after World War I, and it continued until the 1970s. The rise in inequality during the nineteenth century is, however, harder to document. First we think we see it in Britain and America (Williamson and Lindert, 1980; Williamson, 1985), and then we wonder (Grosse, 1982; Feinstein 1988; Lindert, 1991). The current status of the Kuznets Curve is thus somewhat like that of the Phillips Curve around 1970: now you see it, now you don't. The important inference of that fact, however, is *not* to reject the Kuznets Curve, but to ask why we sometimes see it and sometimes do not.

Chapter 8 argues that we must look to factor markets and factor returns in seeking answers. Inequality cannot be explored with models which have little to say about evolving factor demand and supply. Classical economists knew this well enough when developing their models of growth and distribution which focused on returns to land, labour and capital. Modern human capital theory knows the same by its focus on the skill premium. So, factor markets are the place to look for the origin or absence of the Kuznets Curve, and labour markets in particular. Thus, there is a reason why economic historians and development economists have spent so much time pondering how labour markets respond to the disequilibrating shocks of industrial revolutions, demographic transitions (or lack of them), and, more recently, globalization (or lack of it). The chapter then lists the factor-demand and factor-supply forces that seem to us most likely to account for the presence or absence of the Kuznets Curve in any country's historical record. The central forces are: unbalanced sectoral productivity advance yielding aggregate (unskilled) labour-saving early before abating late in the industrial revolution; demographic transitions which glut the labour market early before abating late in the industrial revolution, all of which can be modified greatly by mass migrations (Williamson, 1996a); human capital accumulation responses, modest early and robust late in the industrial revolution; and the potential globalization offset. Globalization can be an offset if a trade boom raises the wage of abundant (unskilled) labour early in the industrial revolution, while lowering it late in the industrial revolution (Williamson, 1996b).

The reader will want to look carefully at these arguments in Chapter 8, but it seems clear that the debate is hardly over. Mainstream economists were guided for two centuries by the Smithian belief that redistribution to the poor cut into the surplus available for accumulation. Rejection of the Smithian trade-off gained strength world-wide only in the early 1970s with the support of rising suffrage, national independence, and World Bank leadership. Now the debate has received a new boost in the USA and Europe by the argument that globalization has produced rising inequality there, undoing all the egalitarian gains accumulated since World War I. This debate is unlikely to die simply because it is highly politicized and also because the issue is exceedingly difficult to resolve with evidence. As the quality and coverage of that evidence continues to improve, we can only hope that it will provoke questions about the causes of inequality trends or their absence, not whether all countries, or even the majority of countries, have experienced the Kuznets Curve.

Industrialization, urbanization and migration off the farm

Modern economic growth is not simply about coarse aggregates like GDP per capita growth and capital-deepening. It is far more than that. It is also about structural transformation: after all, it *is* an industrial revolution we are talking about. It is also spatial: it is about the relative demise of village-based agriculture, about emerging town-based industry, about the rise of great cities, about emigration from farm to factory, and about societies coping with sometimes spectacular rates of urbanization. This section contains three essays that deal with these spatial aspects of industrialization. The essays also offer what I hope are good illustrations of how economic history can inform contemporary Third World debates, and, in turn, how the development literature can sharpen the agenda for economic history. We start with an analysis of the sources of Third World city growth when it reached a peak – during the 1960s and 1970s. We then explore how Britain coped with city growth during her industrial revolution. The section concludes with an assessment of US experience with rural–urban migration and wage gaps between 1890 and 1940, an epoch which, oddly enough, offers a perfect historical laboratory to test contentious debate about Third World labour markets.

Third World city growth and urbanization have both been spectacular since the early 1960s, although the rates have slowed down a little bit by now. What were the underlying fundamentals driving this transition? Quite naturally, demographers tend to favour pessimistic demographic hypotheses: unusually rapid rates of population growth have pushed landless labourers into the cities (with ugly social consequences). Economists, on the other hand, tend to favour optimistic economic hypotheses which stress the pull of the city: cheap city-based energy favouring the growth of energy-intensive and city-based activities; the diffusion of technology from the developed world which favours urban industry; foreign capital availability which makes possible more city infrastructure; policies that distort domestic prices to favour city activities; and liberal global trade environments which stimulate demand for city-based manufacturing exports. Which mattered most during the two decades when Third World city growth was fastest, 1960–1979?

Chapter 9, 'Population Growth, Industrial Revolutions, and the Urban Transition' (1984; written with Allen Kelley), reports the answers which emerge when a multi-sector CGE model is applied to the problem. Allen Kelley and I developed this model of the urban transition in which rural-urban migration is endogenous and responsive to various macroeconomic and macrodemographic forces. The reader will want to judge the model with a careful reading of the paper, but upon simulation it was able to replicate closely most of dimensions of Third World performance that we care about, including urbanization, city growth and rural–urban migration. Both the city immigration rate and the city growth rate reach their peaks in the early 1970s, falling off thereafter. I refer to an average Third World performance here, although each region exhibits considerable individuality: for example, East Asia leads the pack and South Asia lags behind. The model simulates a conventional logistic curve, with rising then falling city growth and immigration rates. It predicts that the Third World will have passed through about 85 per cent of the urban transition by the year 2000. When written in 1984, the essay also predicted that urban growth problems would be far less severe by the end of the century, that we would hear far fewer complaints from urban planners, that the much-abused term 'overurbanization' would have begun to disappear from our lexicon, and that the pessimists' stress on urban environmental decay would have lost some of its urgency. Furthermore, the model predicted a long-run decline in the relative importance of migration as a source of urban population growth, from about 45 per cent in the 1960s to about 35 per cent in the 1990s. As we enter the late 1990s, it appears that the model was about right.

But which exogenous shocks mattered most in driving city immigration and city growth, and in accounting for the turning point in the early 1970s? Was rural land scarcity an important ingredient? No. Did foreign capital availability play a dominant role? No. What about overall population growth? Two decades ago, a World Bank team stated that rapid population growth was 'the single most important factor distinguishing present [relatively fast] and past [relatively slow] urbanization' rates (Beier et al., 1976, p. 365). Theory shows them to be wrong regarding the urban share of the population or labour force, to the extent that urban activities are more capital-intensive than rural activities. Fact shows them to be wrong regarding city immigration and city growth. The facts are that the rates still would have been very high by historical standards even if the Third World had had the low rates of population growth typical of the post-World War II industrialized OECD.

Population growth mattered, certainly, but it definitely was *not* the 'single most important factor'.

So, what *were* the most important factors driving Third World city growth in the 1960s and 1970s? Chapter 9 shows unambiguously that two events mattered most. The first was relative price trends in world markets – for example, fuel, manufacturing intermediates and Third World manufactured exports. The favourable effect of globalization in world markets was therefore one key to the unusually rapid rates of city growth in the Third World. The second was productivity advance, but not so much economy-wide rates as the imbalance in those rates favouring urban sectors at the expense of agriculture. In particular, rapid improvements in urban export competitiveness was another key to unusually rapid city growth in the Third World. In short, it was the pull of favourable economic events not the push of demographic burdens that mattered most.

Economic success breeds problems of adjustment and they certainly seem severe in the Third World. In spite of the success, analysts have written at length about the failure of Third World cities to absorb the flood of rural emigrants into urban labour markets, about the difficulties which municipal planners face in improving or even maintaining the quality and availability of social overhead, about densely packed urban slums without adequate social services, about rising pollution and falling quality of the city environment. None of this would have been news to Victorians coping with British city growth in the middle third of the nineteenth century. They too were overwhelmed by the same economic success, and they didn't have World Bank loans and foreign technical advice to help them cope.

Since British macro performance in the early nineteenth century was slower than in the late twentieth century Third World, why is it so important to understand that history? Chapter 10, 'Coping with City Growth' (1994), shows that it wasn't even a particularly fast rate of city growth. Even compared with the rest of Europe who followed in Britain's footsteps, the rate of city growth was average. Yet, it *was* first. This is an important qualification since that fact makes it possible to see how Britain solved (or chose not to solve) her urban problems on her own. Nevertheless, there *was* one fact that made urban problems more severe for Britain than for the Third World – high city mortality rates. Chapter 6 showed that high urban mortality risk (by itself or as a proxy for urban environmental bads) required wage compensation to get rural workers to emigrate cityward and to keep them there. But this fact had more profound implications. Rural death rates exceed urban death rates in the Third World; the opposite was most definitely true of Britain. Rural rates of natural increase never exceed urban rates by much in the Third World; they exceeded urban rates by a lot in Britain. The demographic dimensions of British experience a century and a half ago were thus very different from those of the Third World today. The higher rates of natural increase in the countryside must have placed far greater stress on Britain's rural–urban labour market adjustment. Although Third World economies have certainly grown faster than did Britain, they never had to cope with

xxvi *Industrialization, Inequality and Economic Growth*

Britain's poor demographic match between excess city labour demands and excess rural labour supplies. Perhaps this is the reason why city immigration and rural emigration rates were so high, even compared with the Third World.

Events of the industrial revolution tend to augment the demand for labour and capital in the city far more than in the countryside. Labour and capital supplies tend to be far more abundant, at least initially, in the countryside. One of the fundamental problems created by industrial revolutions is, therefore, purely spatial: How do factor markets – which are unaccustomed to such shocks – reconcile excess factor demands in the cities with excess factor supplies in the countryside? There is a traditional literature that views the English farm labourer as conservative and reluctant to move, thus creating a rural England full of 'a vast, inert mass of redundant labour [who were] immobile' (Redford, 1926, pp. 84 and 94). This tradition is like other 'irrational peasant' views that were destroyed some time ago by Theodore Schultz (1964) and others. This one can be easily destroyed too. By the 1820s, rural emigration rates in England were higher than they were in the Third World in the 1960s, and by the 1860s they were twice as high! So much for inert British farm labour. On the other hand, there was a larger demographic-ally-induced disequilibrium to erase in Britain.

High city death rates implied high immigration rates to fill the gaps (and wage bribes to make the immigrants stay). They also implied that a far larger share of the city population increase in Britain should have been accounted for by immigration than has been true of the Third World. This appears to have been the case. The share averaged 61 per cent between 1776 and 1816 in Britain (45 per cent in the 1960s in the Third World), and 43 per cent between 1816 and 1871 (projected to 35 per cent in the 1990s in the Third World). The demographic mismatch between rural and urban labour markets also implied big rural–urban wage gaps, partly because of the disamenity premium associated with those high city death rates and partly because of the big gap between excess city labour demand and excess country labour supply. This prediction is apparently fulfilled: by the 1830s, nominal city wages were 73 per cent higher than farm wages. But have we measured those wage gaps properly?

Wage gaps have been commonly observed during industrial revolutions ever since Britain experienced the first, and the last essay in this book explores them at length. But it is the *size* of the 73 per cent gap in the 1830s that is striking. I know of no case, past or present, where there have been gaps of comparable magnitude. Why were farm labourers in the 1830s willing to accept so much lower wages than those available in city and town? It was due to a combination of factors: the cities were more expensive, there was a better social safety net in the countryside and the cities were ugly and required disamenity compensation. Taking everything into account the true wage gap was probably closer to 33 per cent, still significant but far smaller than the nominal 73 per cent.

Did these wage gaps matter? Contemporary development economists think so, and they have been central to debates over development strategy since World War II. The subject is discussed further below, but for now we simply note that the urban transition can be slowed down or curtailed if inelastic urban labour supplies drive up the nominal cost of labour facing urban firms. Based on the wage gaps recorded between the 1820s and the 1860s, British city growth and industrialization must have been curtailed some during the First Industrial Revolution. In this sense, Britain witnessed 'under' urbanization, not, as hysterical rhetoric suggested, 'over' urbanization.

That large wage gap includes a compensation for urban bads, and the latter was big enough to confirm the views of Victorian reformers that the cities were an environmental mess which needed to be cleaned up by more active policy intervention. Why were the cities such a mess? Some scholars argue in favour of ignorance, that is, there was an absence of the public health knowledge which would have made an attack on urban mortality and morbidity possible. I disagree. Chapter 10 argues instead that those cities were ugly due largely to a shortage of infrastructure (housing, sewers, water supplies, street paving, lighting, refuse removal and so on). Investment in housing and public works simply failed to keep pace with the rest of the economy. Indeed, it appears that dwelling stocks per capita were lower in 1860 than they had been in 1760! In short, while actual investment requirements may have been modest during the First Industrial Revolution, they would not have been so modest had investment in social overhead kept pace. It had its price: the cities became ugly, crowded and polluted, breeding high mortality and morbidity.

What was the reason for the infrastructure shortage? A large share of the answer lies with wartime crowding out, as argued in Chapter 3. The rest of the answer lies with a complex political economy yet to be unravelled. Until we understand the political economy, we will not know whether Britain's environmental ugliness was the most efficient path to industrialization.

By 1958, the early pioneers in development economics (Meier and Seers, 1984) had a full appreciation of wage gaps, and they were central to policy debates about state intervention. Everett Hagen published a paper in 1958 which offered an economic justification of protection. Hagen's priorities were strong. He felt that these wage gaps were due to disequilibrating forces and to labour market distortions. Since those wage distortions tended to price domestic manufacturers out of their own markets (by raising costs artificially), state intervention was warranted to offset the distortion. Hagen's view of wage gaps was important since it helped force him and many other economists into a policy position which favoured a protected economy, isolated from world markets. Like the new view of history offered by Nurkse, Myrdal, Prebisch and Singer, Hagen's view was to de-globalize.

Was Hagen right? Is it possible to develop an equilibrium view of labour markets, where the wage gaps did not reflect distortion? By focusing on expected rather than current wage gaps, Michael Todaro (1969) developed exactly such a framework almost thirty years ago. The thesis was simple and elegant: the first ingredient was an asymmetry between rural and urban labour markets, the former with flexible wages and no unemployment, and the latter with sticky wages and overt unemployment or underemployment in the low-wage urban informal sector; the second ingredient was the premise that migrants respond to expected wage differentials (the marginal employment rate representing the chance of getting the good urban job), not simply actual wage differentials.

Oddly enough, when Timothy Hatton and I published 'What Explains Wage Gaps Between Farm and City?' (Chapter 11) in 1992, none of these propositions had been formally tested. Even more surprising was our discovery that, while the Todaro model was constructed to explain a contemporary Third World problem, it had its intellectual roots with agricultural economists who in the 1940s were writing about the US inter-war wage gap. This was sufficient motivation for us to use a Hagen-Todaro time series model to ask: what drove the wage gap between city and countryside in the USA between 1890 and 1941?

The important fact is that the wage gap in the USA was not stable over the five decades between 1890 and World War II. On the contrary, nominal farm wages were catching up dramatically on nominal unskilled urban wages up to World War I, but they collapsed afterwards, from something like 65 to 35 per cent of urban wages. This huge plunge in the farm/non-farm wage ratio (an enormous rise in the wage gap) does not disappear when it is adjusted by unemployment rates and living costs: the fall in the adjusted ratio is from something like 80 to 55 per cent. So, what explains this behaviour? When Todaro's migration equation is embedded in a two-sector model, fundamental forces like the intersectoral terms of trade, the urban real wage, and total labour supplies are all shown to matter in accounting for those five decades of variable wage gap experience. True, the model must take account of the sluggish response of migration to these shocks, but in the long run it was those fundamental shocks to the economy which served to drive the urban unemployment rate and the wage gap, just as Todaro suggested.

Final remarks

These, then, are the ties which bind these essays together. Although written some time ago, the issues embedded in them have not disappeared from our agenda. I hope the reader will find enough fresh insight in these essays to provoke new thinking on these old problems.

Notes

1. In the twentieth century, the rates fell.
2. According to Robert Gordon (1961), the relative price of capital goods stops falling in 20th century America, coinciding with a decline in the non-human capital accumulation rate.
3. It was not true of Britain between 1780 and 1820 only because the rate of accumulation was suppressed by war, as I have argued.

References

Abramovitz, M. and P. David (1973), 'Reinterpreting Economic Growth: Parables and Realities', *American Economic Review*, **58**, 428–39.

Ahluwalia, M.S. (1976), 'Inequality, Poverty and Development', *Journal of Development Economics*, **3**, 307–42.

Barro, R.J (1974), 'Are Government Bonds Net Wealth?', *Journal of Political Economy*, **82**, 1095–117.

Beier, G., A. Churchill, M. Cohen and B. Renaud (1976), 'The Task Ahead for the Cities of the Developing Countries', *World Development*, **4**, 363–409.

Brown, J.C. (1990), 'The Condition of England and the Standard of Living: Cotton Textiles in the Northwest, 1806–1850', *Journal of Economic History*, **50**, 591–614.

Cameron, R. (1985), 'A New View of European Industrialization', *Economic History Review*, 2nd series, **38**, 1–23

Crafts, N.F.R. (1985), 'English Workers' Living Standards During the Industrial Revolution: Some Remaining Problems', *Journal of Economic History*, **45**, 139–44.

Crafts, N.F.R. (1987), 'British Economic Growth 1700–1850: Some Difficulties of Interpretation', *Explorations in Economic History*, **24**, 245–68.

Dasgupta, P. (1993), *An Inquiry into Well-Being and Destitution*, Oxford: Oxford University Press.

David, P. (1977), 'Invention and Accumulation in America's Economic Growth: A Nineteenth-Century Parable', in K. Brunner and A.H. Meltzer (eds), *International Organization, National Policies and Economic Development*, Amsterdam: North-Holland.

DeLong, J.B. (1992), 'Productivity Growth and Machinery Investment: A Long-Run Look, 1870–1980', *Journal of Economic History*, **52**, 307–24.

DeLong, J.B. and L. Summers (1991), 'Equipment Investment and Economic Growth', *Quarterly Journal of Economics*, **106**, 445–502.

Dixit, A. (1973), 'Models of Dual Economies', in J.A. Mirrlees and N.H. Stern (eds), *Models of Economic Growth*, New York: Wiley.

Dreze, J., A.K. Sen and A. Hussain (1995), *The Political Economy of Hunger*, Oxford: Oxford University Press.

Fei, J.C.H. and G. Ranis (1964), *Development of the Labor Surplus Economy: Theory and Policy*, Homewood, Ill.: Irwin.

Feinstein, C.H. (1988), 'The Rise and Fall of the Williamson Curve', *Journal of Economic History*, **48**, 699–729.

Feinstein, C.H. (1996), 'Invited Lecture', *II Congress of the European Association of Historical Economics*, Venice (January 19–20).

Feldstein, M. and C. Horioka (1980), 'Domestic Saving and International Capital Flows', *Economic Journal*, **90**, 314–29.

Fogel, R.W. (1994), 'Economic Growth, Population Theory, and Physiology: The Bearing of Long-Term Processes on the Making of Economic Policy', *American Economic Review*, **95**, 369–95.

Freeman, R. (1995), 'Are Your Wages Set in Beijing?', *Journal of Economic Perspectives*, **9**, 15–32.

Gallman, R.E. and J. Wallis (1992), *American Economic Growth and Living Standards Before the Civil War*, Chicago: University of Chicago Press.

Grosse, S.D. (1982), 'On the Alleged Antebellum Surge in Wage Differentials: A Critique of Williamson and Lindert', *Journal of Economic History*, **42**, 413–18.

Hagen, E.E. (1958), 'An Economic Justification of Protection', *Quarterly Journal of Economics*, **72**, 496–514.

Hatton, T.J. and J.G. Williamson (1994), 'International Migration 1850–1939: An Economic Survey', in T.J. Hatton and J.G. Williamson (eds), *Migration and the International Labor Market 1850–1939*, London: Routledge.

Higgins, M. and J.G. Williamson (1996), 'Demography and Foreign Capital Dependency: Asia from this Century into the Next', *NBER Working Paper* No. 5560, Cambridge, Mass.: National Bureau of Economic Research (May).

Kelley, A.C. and J.G. Williamson (1974), *Lessons from Japanese Development: An Analytical Economic History*, Chicago: University of Chicago Press.

Komlos, J. (1995), *The Biological Standard of Living on Three Continents: Further Explorations in Anthropometric History*, Boulder, Col.: Westview Press.

Kravis, I.B. (1970), 'Trade as a Handmaiden of Growth: Similarities Between the Nineteenth and Twentieth Centuries', *Economic Journal*, **80**, 850–72.

Krugman, P. (1994), 'The Myth of Asia's Miracle', *Foreign Affairs*, **73**, 62–78.

Kuznets, S. (1955), 'Economic Growth and Income Inequality', *American Economic Review*, **45**, 1–28.

Lewis, W.A. (1954), 'Economic Development with Unlimited Supplies of Labour', *Manchester School of Economic and Social Studies*, **22**, 139–91.

Lindert, P.H. (1991), 'Toward a Comparative History of Income and Wealth', in Y.S. Brenner et al. (eds), *Income Distribution in Historical Perspective*, Cambridge: Cambridge University Press.

Lindert, P.H. and J.G. Williamson (1976), 'Three Centuries of American Inequality', in P. Uselding (ed.), *Research in Economic History*, Vol. 1, 303–33.

Lindert, P.H. and J.G. Williamson (1983), 'English Workers' Living Standards During the Industrial Revolution: A New Look', *Economic History Review*, 2nd Series, **36**, 1–25.

Lindert, P.H. and J.G. Williamson (1985), 'English Workers' Real Wages: A Reply to Crafts', *Journal of Economic History*, **45**, 145–53.

Lipton, M. (1976), *Why Poor People Stay Poor: Urban Bias in World Development*, Cambridge: Cambridge University Press.

Meier, G.M. and D. Seers (1984), *Pioneers in Development*, Washington, D.C.: The World Bank.

Minami, R. (1968), 'The Turning Point in the Japanese Economy', *Quarterly Journal of Economics*, **82**, 380–402.

Nordhaus, W. and J. Tobin (1972), 'Is Growth Obsolete?', in National Bureau of Economic Research, *Economic Growth: Fiftieth Anniversary Colloquium V*, New York: Columbia University Press.

Ohkawa, K. and H. Rosovsky (1973), *Japanese Economic Growth: Trend Acceleration in the Twentieth Century*, Stanford: Stanford University Press.

Redford, A. (1926), *Labour Migration in England 1800–1850*, ed. and rev. by W.H. Chaloner, New York: Augustus Kelley.

Rodrik, D. (1996), 'Understanding Economic Policy Reform', *Journal of Economic Literature*, **34**, 9–41.

Schultz, T.W. (1964), *Transforming Traditional Agriculture*, New Haven, Conn: Yale University Press.

Sen, A.K. (1966), 'Peasants and Dualism With or Without Surplus Labor', *Journal of Political Economy*, **74**, 425–50.

Steckle, R.H. (1995), 'Stature and the Standard of Living', *Journal of Economic Literature*, **33**, 1903–40.

Taylor, A. (1995), 'Debt, Dependence and the Demographic Transition: Latin America into the Next Century', *World Development*, **23**, 869–79.

Taylor, L., E.L. Bacha, E.A. Cardoso and F.J. Lysy (1980) *Models of Growth and Distribution for Brazil*, New York: Oxford University Press.

Todaro, M.P. (1969), 'A Model of Labor Migration and Urban Unemployment in Less Developed Countries', *American Economic Review*, **59**, 138–48.

van der Gaag, J. and M. Lipton (1993), *Including the Poor*, Washington, D.C.: The World Bank.

Williamson, J.G. (1964), *American Growth and the Balance of Payments, 1820–1913: A Study of the Long Swing*, Chapel Hill, North Carolina: University of North Carolina Press.

Williamson, J.G. (1981a), 'Urban Disamenities, Dark Satanic Mills and the British Standard of Living Debate', *Journal of Economic History*, **41**, 75–84.

Williamson, J.G. (1981b), 'Some Myths Die Hard – Urban Disamenities One More Time: A Reply', *Journal of Economic History*, **41**, 905–7.

Williamson, J.G. (1985), *Did British Capitalism Breed Inequality?* London: Allen and Unwin.

Williamson, J.G. (1990), *Coping with City Growth During the British Industrial Revolution*, Cambridge: Cambridge University Press.

Williamson, J.G. (1996a), 'Globalization, Convergence and History', *Journal of Economic History*, **56**, 1–30.

Williamson, J.G. (1996b), 'Globalization and Inequality Then and Now: The Late 19th and Late 20th Centuries Compared', *NBER Working Paper No. 5491*, Cambridge, Mass.: National Bureau of Economic Research (March).

Williamson, J.G. and P.H. Lindert (1980), *American Inequality: A Macroeconomic History*, New York: Academic Press.

Wood, A. (1994), *North-South Trade, Employment and Inequality: Changing Fortunes in a Skill-Driven World*, Oxford: Clarendon Press.

Zevin, R.B. (1992), 'Are World Financial Markets More Open? If So Why and With What

Effects?', in T. Banuri and J. Schor (eds), *Financial Openness and National Autonomy*, Oxford: Oxford University Press.

PART I

CAPITAL ACCUMULATION: CROWDING, DEMOGRAPHY, INEQUALITY AND TECHNOLOGICAL EVENTS

JEFFREY G. WILLIAMSON AND LEO J. DE BEVER

Saving, Accumulation and Modern Economic Growth: The Contemporary Relevance of Japanese History

1. On Exhuming Old Fashioned Views of Capital Accumulation

The publication of *Asia's New Giant* has focused the attention of Western and Third World economists once more on Japanese contemporary growth, and the contributions of Edward Denison and William Chung are likely to attract the most interest. In a companion volume, they tell us *How Japan's Economy Grew So Fast*. Between 1953 and 1971, the nonresidential business sector grew at the rate of 10.04 per cent per annum (Denison and Chung, 1976, Table 4–6, p. 38). We are told that the increase in nonresidential capital stocks directly accounts for 2.19 percentage points, or only about one fifth of the total. Growth in output per unit of input, or "crude" total factor productivity growth, accounts for 5.86 percentage points. The remainder is explained by labor force growth, both in quantity and quality. Their finding that one half or more of output growth is attributable to total factor productivity growth coincides with earlier studies of postwar Japan and with numerous studies of other postwar economies.

If we accept the literature critical of "sources of growth" ac-

* The authors are, respectively, Professor of Economics at the University of Wisconsin and Economist at the Bank of Canada. We wish to acknowledge the support of the Bank of Canada, the Guggenheim Foundation and the University of Wisconsin Graduate Research Committee. However, the views expressed are those of the authors and no responsibility for them should be attributed to these supporting institutions. We gratefully acknowledge the comments of Moses Abramovitz, Susan Hanley, Allen Kelley, Peter Lindert, Hugh Patrick, Kozo Yamamura, Kunio Yoshihara, and seminar participants at the University of Washington, the University of British Columbia, and the Stanford Food Research Institute.

125

counting, capital's contribution is most certainly understated. First of all Denison and Chung use the gross rather than theoretically preferable net capital stock concept. Using net capital stocks, in combination with a more careful treatment of intermediate inputs and sectoral aggregation, Nishimizu and Hulten (1976) conclude that 73 per cent of real output growth performance can be explained by capital accumulation and intermediate input use. Second, any plausible "embodiment" view of technological progress would assign a far greater role to capital formation than the Denison and Chung arithmetic would suggest. Some of the very high total factor productivity growth simply could not have been achieved without high rates of capital formation (Abramovitz, 1977). This is certainly true of "improved resource allocation" which, as it turns out, refers primarily to the relative demise of low-wage employment in agriculture and urban self employment, a demise which could hardly have taken place without the rapid rates of capital formation which produced the more attractive job vacancies elsewhere in the economy. In the same way "economies of scale" is a benefit which must have been achieved by the capacity expansion induced by capital formation itself. Since these two sources of crude total factor productivity growth account for 3.51 out of 10.04 percentage points, it hardly seems unreasonable to conclude that capital's contribution is understated by Denison and Chung.

Suppose, however, we were to accept the Denison-Chung accounting without qualification. It would then seem relevant to ask whether the postwar period is unique. Has the contribution of conventional capital accumulation always been such a small share of total output growth performance in Japan, namely, a modest fifth of output growth? Can secular variations in output growth over the past century always be explained by corresponding variations in "crude" total factor productivity growth rates? Research over the past two decades offers two competing views. On the one hand, the literature on other postwar economies suggests that conventional capital accumulation has been a relatively minor actor in the growth dramas of the mid-twentieth century. The major actors in these modern histories, we are told, are human capital accumulation, scale economies, learning-by-doing, improved resource allocation, and disembodied technological forces. On the other hand, Kazushi Ohkawa and Henry Rosovsky (1973) have stressed the role of accelerating rates of total factor productivity growth in accounting for Japanese trend acceleration in the twentieth century. Their evidence is persuasive, and it implies a corollary: conventional capital accumulation must have been a more important vehicle of growth early in the present century. To the extent that developing countries draw their "lessons" from Meiji and Taisho history, it seems wise to probe the Ohkawa-Rosovsky position a bit deeper before accepting postwar Japanese experience as the norm.

Table 1 presents some evidence taken from the period 1887–1938. Consider first the thirty-five years of early modern growth, stretching from the late 1880s to shortly after World War I. Economy-wide labor productivity growth rates, averaging almost 2.2 per cent, were already impressive by international standards. Paul Bairoch (1976, Table 5, p. 283) estimates GNP per capita to have grown at slightly less than one per cent in Europe between 1860 and 1910, the highest rate being Sweden at 2 per cent per annum. Furthermore, there was already evidence of trend acceleration since the rate rose from 1.9 to 2.6 per cent between the two periods 1887–1907 and 1907–1922, predating the twentieth century trend acceleration documented so well by Ohkawa and Rosovsky. What were the "sources" of that impressive early growth? For the thirty-five years as a whole, capital's contribution to labor productivity growth was 1.32 percentage points, or just about half. The moral of the story is that conventional capital accumulation was a far more important vehicle of growth early in Japan's growth experience.[1] Furthermore, this result is consistent with the Ohkawa-Rosovsky interwar accounting for the private nonagricultural sector reproduced in Table 1. There we see that capital accounted for 65 per cent of labor productivity growth between 1908 and 1938.

In summary, while sources of growth accounting has well-known flaws, our use of it serves to point out that the postwar finding of enormous "crude" total factor productivity growth rates, and correspondingly low contributions of conventional capital accumulation, are not reproduced in the first six decades following the 1880s. The

---

1. Similar results have been reported recently for the U.S. Moses Abramovitz and Paul David (1973, p. 253) have found that in nineteenth century America "the pace of increase in real gross domestic product was accounted for largely by that of traditional, conventionally defined factors of production: labor, land, and tangible reproducible capital." In contrast with twentieth century findings, they have shown that the "crude" total factor productivity growth accounted for less than two-fifths of per capita output growth, and only 45 per cent of labour productivity growth between 1855 and 1905 (Abramovitz and David, 1973, p. 254). These results appear to be quite similar to those reported in Table 1 for 1887–1907, where "crude" total factor productivity growth accounted for 52 per cent of labor productivity growth.

TABLE 1

"CONVENTIONAL" SOURCES OF GROWTH ACCOUNTING, JAPAN, 1887-1938

Per Annum Growth Rates In:	de Bever-Williamson			Ohkawa-Rosovsky	
	1887–1907	1907–1922	1887–1922	1908–1917	1908–1938
1. ECONOMY-WIDE					
Real Gross Product: $\dot{Y}^*$	2.81	3.76	3.22		
Labor Force (FTE): $\dot{L}^*$	0.90	1.21	1.04		
Agricultural Land Stock: $\dot{R}^*$	0.35	0.57	0.44		
Capital Stock (Net, "Productive"): $\dot{K}^*$	4.72	5.13	4.90		
Labor Productivity: $(\dot{Y}-\dot{L})^*$	1.91	2.55	2.18		
Total Factor Productivity: $\dot{T}^*$	1.00	1.49	1.21		
Capital's Contribution to $\dot{Y}$: $\beta_K \dot{K}$	1.21	1.47	1.32		
Capital's Contribution to $(\dot{Y}-\dot{L})$: $\beta_K(\dot{K}-\dot{L})$	.98	1.12	1.04		
2. PRIVATE NON-AGRICULTURAL					
Real Net Product: $\dot{Y}^*$				5.07	4.17
Labor Force (Gainful Employed): $\dot{L}^*$				2.19	2.00
Capital Stock (Gross, "Productive"): $\dot{K}^*$				6.46	5.41
Labor Productivity: $(\dot{Y}-\dot{L})^*$				2.88	2.17
Total Factor Productivity: $\dot{T}^*$				0.95	0.76
Capital's Contribution to $\dot{Y}$: $\beta_K \dot{K}$				2.93	2.24
Capital's Contribution to $(\dot{Y}-\dot{L})$: $\beta_K(\dot{Y}-\dot{L})$				1.93	1.41

Source: Panel 1 is from de Bever and Williamson [1977, Table 1.3]. All figures are based on 1934–36 prices where relevant; labor force refers to full-time equivalents (revised LTES); capital stocks are net, and exclude both military and residential stocks (revised LTES; see Table 5 below); and land stock is restricted to agriculture (revised LTES). The share weights, averaged over the denoted periods are:

	β_K	β_R	β_L
1887–1907	.257	.121	.622
1907–1922	.286	.098	.616
1887–1922	.269	.112	.619

Panel 2 is from Ohkawa and Rosovsky (1973). The 1908–1917 figures are taken directly from Table 3.1, p. 47. The 1908–1938 figures are computed from Tables BST-4, BST-15 and BST-16, pp. 284, 310 and 312. Labor force is gainfully employed; capital stock is net private, excluding dwellings; and output is net domestic product. The $\beta_K = .414$ weight is an average of 1908–1938 taken from Table BST-17, p. 316.

exercise thus offers further motivation for improving our under-standing of accumulation in Japanese secular development.

2. *The Postwar Accumulation "Miracle": Can We Model the Sources of Japanese Accumulation?*

The capital accumulation magnitudes which "accounted for" a fifth of postwar growth are documented in Table 2. The post 1960 rates have been extraordinary. What, then, explains these high rates of capital accumulation? Alternatively, which economic model best accounts for the unusual private (nonresidential) saving rates sum-marized in Table 3?

This paper is motivated by the view that a comprehensive analy-sis of competing models of Japanese saving and accumulation has not yet been performed adequately. Furthermore, the profession has yet to make very good use of long historical time series available for Japan. While there has been considerable effort to estimate saving functions using postwar data (see the useful survey by Henry and Mable Wallich in Patrick and Rosovsky, 1976, pp. 258–59), very little work of similar quality has been done on the interwar years and the pre-World War I period. This is unfortunate and it has caused some distortion in our view of postwar Japanese growth. Certainly the pre-World War II data is of sufficient quality to pursue the long term analysis, and, as we shall argue at length, to ignore it is folly. This seems especially true given the wide variance in most poten-tially relevant explanatory variables—income growth, rates of re-turn, wealth stocks, the rate of issuance of new government debt, and the distribution of income and wealth—a variability whose ab-sence so often bedevils the econometrician's analysis of time series. Furthermore, the pre-World War II data offer exciting possibilities

TABLE 2

CAPITAL STOCK GROWTH PER ANNUM,
EXCLUDING DWELLINGS, CONSTANT PRICES: 1887–1971

Period	Gross			Net		
	Total	Private Non-Primary	Govern-ment	Total	Private	Govern-ment
1. Pre World War I						
1887–1907				4.72	5.18	3.85
1907–1922				5.13	5.64	4.94
1887–1922				4.90	5.36	4.30
2. Interwar						
1908–1917	5.20	6.46	6.87			
1917–1931	4.55	5.14	6.10			
1931–1937	4.02	4.39	4.64			
1908–1937	4.64	5.39	6.03			
3. Post World War II						
1953–1956		4.04			4.58	
1956–1960		7.29			8.60	
1960–1967		10.92			10.62	
1967–1971		13.29			12.54	
1956–1962	9.43	10.89	9.02			
1953–1961		6.49			6.10	
1961–1971		11.86			11.15	

Sources: Panel 1 is from de Bever and Williamson (1977), Table 1.1 and Appendix C. Panel 2 is from Ohkawa and Rosovsky (1973), Table BST-16. Panel 3 is from Denison and Chung (1976), Table 1-2, pp. 220-1, except for 1956-1962 which is from Ohkawa and Rosovsky.

for testing propositions at the heart of the saving and accumulation debate. How stable have Japanese structural parameters been over the twentieth century? To what extent has there been a shift in those structural parameters, and what form has it taken? After all, Table 2 suggests that private accumulation rates have been high in Japan for a century, not just since the 1950s. Can we supply an endogenous explanation for the long term trend acceleration which Ohkawa and Rosovsky have so effectively documented? Or rather, must we abdicate to *ad hoc* forces to account for the surge in saving ratios and private nonresidential accumulation rates between the 1930s and the 1950s?

Econometric studies of postwar Japanese private saving behavior have pursued five key hypotheses. First, it has been argued that high rates of growth may have induced high saving rates among households. If expected income and expected rates of return are

TABLE 3
SAVING RATES AND RELATIVE INVESTMENT GOODS PRICES, 1905–1971

	Share of Gross Domestic Fixed "Productive" Capital Formation in GNP		Relative Price of Investment Goods (1934-36 = 100)
	(1) Current Price	(2) Constant Price	(3)
1905–1909	.128	.099	131
1910–1914	.142	.124	114
1915–1919	.160	.133	122
1920–1924	.154	.145	107
1925–1929	.145	.148	98
1930–1934	.126	.128	99
1935–1939	.178	.170	105
1952–1954	.181	.156	121
1955–1959	.215	.178	120
1960–1964	.290	.262	111
1965–1969	.277	.286	97
1970–1971	.298	.331	90

Source: Residential and military investment are excluded throughout, both from GNP and gross fixed investment. Constant price series uses 1934–36 base pre World War II and 1965 base postwar. All data are taken from LTES-1, Tables 1, 1-A, 4, 4-A, 18, 18-A, and 21A. Col. (3) is derived from the implicit price deflators underlying cols. (1) and (2).

relevant to the consumption decision of individual households, lags in the adjustment of expectations may cause consumption to grow more slowly than income during a period of rapid expansion. If this is so, one can expect increased savings ratios from growth trend acceleration. (See, for example, the early studies of Williamson, 1968; Shinohara, 1970; and Yoshihara, 1972.) The growth hypothesis appears to help explain high saving rates, although Odaka (1974) has shown that there have been many other forces at work. In short, the growth hypothesis is too naive, *ad hoc*, and convenient. The models which yield these results imply long lags in the revision of expectations, and very myopic household behavior, assumptions which are unlikely to be very relevant in accounting for a century of private saving and accumulation experience. The present authors suspect that "growth rates" may be serving as proxies for something else, perhaps rates of return to wealth holding.

The second hypothesis that has been suggested is that inequality levels and trends might account for the high saving rates. While such "growth vs equity" conflicts are central to conventional development models, they fail in the Japanese postwar case. Japan does *not* have high inequality by international standards, and furthermore there is no evidence to support inequality trends following the late 1950s (Pechman and Kaizuka in Patrick and Rosovsky, 1976, p. 370; Ono and Watanabe, 1976). Third, while Shinohara (1959) argued that the large proportion of self-employed in Japan might account for the high saving rates, Mizoguchi (1970) and Komiya (1966) have shown that such influences have been marginal. Fourth, "institutional" factors have been offered as an explanation for saving rates. These include bonus schemes, low social security benefits, and limited credit for housing. Fifth, the life-cycle hypothesis has been applied to Japanese age distributions, but with little success in accounting for the high aggregate saving rates.

This brief summary of hypotheses should be useful in pointing out some additional directions that the postwar econometric literature might explore, and also will aid us here as we look at the pre-World War II accumulation experience. The questions raised in our minds by the above hypotheses are as follows: First, if the "growth" thesis explains postwar saving rates, it should do equally well in accounting for "trend acceleration" in the pre-World War II period. We doubt that it does, however, and our alternative approach will incorporate this skepticism. Second, we feel that it may well be a serious mistake to put too much emphasis on household saving behavior. David and Scadding (1974) have shown joint analysis of household and corporate savings to be more fruitful in accounting for American twentieth century experience, and the approach is central to the remaining sections of this paper. Third, where is the "rate of return" in this accounting of postwar accumulation performance? Surely an economy which has produced extraordinarily high and apparently accelerating rates of total factor productivity growth since 1905 may be characterized by similar trends in rates of return on nonresidential reproducible capital. Indeed, this issue seems likely to be central to any understanding of Japanese trend acceleration during the twentieth century and the likelihood of high saving rates in the future. Fourth, what about the relative price of capital goods? Table 3 indicates that it declined sharply in the postwar period, but no more rapidly than in the two decades following 1905–1909. Denison and Chung make much of these trends since they clearly imply that the same level of current saving will have a more potent impact on physical accumulation rates when prices of capital goods are declining over time, presumably because total factor productivity growth is relatively rapid in the capital goods sector. But might not this price decline also have an impact on saving behavior as well? Fifth, it is necessary to consider the behavior of such exogenous variables as the rate of government issuance of money and bonds. Surely monetary and fiscal policy must play a role in any accounting of Japanese private accumulation experience whether post or pre-World War II. Finally, we cannot disregard war-induced or legislated changes in the distribution of income and wealth, or in war-distorted portfolio mixes.

Most of these larger issues we have outlined here have been virtually ignored by previous literature, perhaps because of a pervading hypnotism with the disequilibrating impact of rapid income growth on current saving ratios.

Nevertheless, we must not expect econometric estimation to uncover the answers to all of these questions. It may be wise at the same time to pursue counterfactual simulations with macro models that are designed to help uncover the sources of the accumulation performance. Central to that exercise, in view of the incomplete historical data, is the development of plausible theoretical models that allow the evaluation of the impact of alternative government tax-expenditure-debt policy, alternative monetary strategies, alternative commercial policies and alternative experience with demographic variables on the rate of Japanese saving and accumulation, both public and private.

The analysis we advocate must also confront explicitly the two competing views of saving. The first argues that saving is a passive respondent to investment demand, a position most recently stated by Martin Bronfenbrenner (1977). The other views saving as a binding constraint on accumulation performance which no amount of "price incentives" (e.g., rising rates of return) will augment. Truth lies somewhere between these two extremes, but a quantitative documentation of where it in fact lies is absolutely essential to any understanding of contemporary saving and accumulation performance. These two competing views of saving can best be evaluated by using multi-equation macro models which confront the elasticity of saving response to the rate of return.

These comments have presented the reader with a very ambitious menu which our kitchen cannot yet deliver. This paper is a start, however. Section 3 develops a simple framework for decomposing the "sources" of Japanese accumulation. It then applies that framework to the period from 1905 to 1940. Section 4 examines the late Meiji and early Taisho accumulation experience in some detail. It reports some ongoing research on modelling this crucial early era of accumulation. Section 5 returns to the postwar themes introduced above, and offers some suggestions regarding future research directions.

3. *Saving, Accumulation and Growth: A Framework and an Interwar Application*

3.1 *Decomposing the Sources of Rising Private Saving Rates.* Models of saving and accumulation can be classified according to three attributes. First, is saving viewed as an "active" constraint on accumulation or does it passively respond to investment demand? Second, if saving is viewed as an active constraint, how elastic is private saving to rates of return, if at all? Third, does the supply of investment goods play a significant role as an additional influence on the rate of physical accumulation? The literature often takes an extreme position on each of these attributes. Some, like Bronfenbrenner, adopt a "one sword" or "Marshallian blade" view. Figure 1 offers an eclectic position which we believe is more consistent with Japanese trends, at least in the twentieth century.

The "private" saving rate in Figure 1 is written on the horizontal axis where it is to be understood that net real saving (or investment)

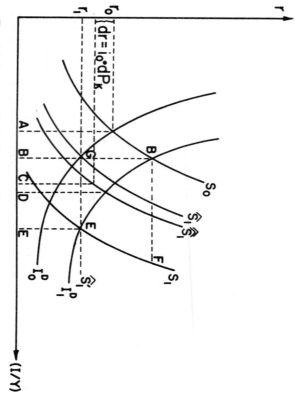

FIG. 1.   Decomposing the Sources of Rising Twentieth-Century Net Investment Rates

ratios are being measured. The rise from A to E roughly corresponds to the historic increase in net private saving rates between 1905 and 1940. Excluding military and residential investment, the gross "private" saving rate in constant 1934–36 prices rose from 9.9 to 17.1 per cent between 1905–1909 and 1934–1940 (Table 3). The net rate increased from 5.1 to 9.8 per cent over the same period, and it is this near doubling over these three decades which is documented by points A and E. The net rate of return on reproducible capital is written along the vertical axis, and the decline from r_0 to r_1 roughly corresponds to the observed fall from 23.8 per cent in 1905–1909 to 16.2 per cent in 1934–1940 (Table 4).[2] These are the long run historical "observables" which if explained will supply a clearer understanding of Japanese trend acceleration and accumulation performance.

The precise shapes of the investment demand and saving supply functions need not detain us at this point. It should suffice to point out that some positive slope on the saving function is allowed so that a rise in net rates of return induces additional saving. The long term investment demand function is drawn for given rates of labor force growth, land expansion, and technical change, including its bias. Under such *ceteris paribus* conditions, higher rates of investment drive down the rate of return through successful capital accumulation. The downward slope of the investment demand function is therefore conventional growth theory, and debate over the actual numerical values of the negative slope will be postponed for section 3.2.

There are two basic forces which can cause the long-term investment demand function to shift to the right. First, the rate of labor force growth may rise. This would serve to shift investment demand to the right, raise the rate of return on capital, and thus induce increased net saving rates and trend acceleration in capital accumulation. While there is abundant evidence that trend acceleration in both nineteenth century America and contemporary Third

2. Yasuba (1976, Table 12, p. 281) supplies rate of return estimates based on a 1932/1933 industry sample. An unweighted average across establishment class sizes yields a figure of 19.2 per cent, quite close to our 1934–1940 estimate (16.2 per cent) when it is recognized that smaller firms had higher rates of return and that larger firms utilized the majority of industrial capital by the early 1930s. That is, a *weighted* average rate of return would be somewhat lower than the unweighted figure of 19.2 per cent. Firms with asset values 50,000 yen or smaller had rates of return ranging between 18.0 and 25.3. Firms with asset values in excess of 50,000 had rates of return ranging between 11.5 and 19.0. Unfortunately, Yasuba's article does not report the necessary data to perform the weighted average calculation.

World nations can be explained in part by accelerating labor force growth, there is little to substantiate such a thesis for Japan when the half century following 1887 is scrutinized. Indeed, while the gainfully employed labor force grew at 0.87 per cent per annum between 1887 and 1907, the rate *declined* to 0.63 percent between 1907 and 1937 (Hundred Year Statistics of the Japanese Economy, 1966, pp. 56–57; hereafter abbreviated as HYSJE). This contrast between Japanese and early modern growth experience elsewhere is worth stressing. The rise in capital formation shares early in the twentieth century may well be explained by a drift to the right in investment demand after the turn of the century, but higher rates of labor force growth had nothing to do with that result.[3] In the absence of this retardation in labor force growth between 1887–1907 and 1907–1937, the shift in long-run investment demand to the right would have been even more dramatic. The result deserves note, since it leaves *more*, rather than less, of any alleged "episodic" shift in investment demand around the turn of the century to be explained.

Our focus in this section, however, is on long run saving and accumulation performance between 1905–1909 and 1934–1940. Can we document any rise in labor force growth which might have served to shift investment demand to the right and thus to have raised capital formation shares over these three decades? Apparently so, since the per annum rates of labor force growth increased from 0.48 per cent early in the century to 0.90 per cent by 1934–1940 (HYSJE, 1966, pp. 56–57). Whether this twentieth century trend acceleration in labor force growth made an important quantitative contribution to the rise in capital formation shares is a topic reserved for section 3.2 below. We can, however, conclude that changing rates of labor force growth contributed nothing at all to rightward shifts in investment demand during the investment "spurt" following 1905: the per annum rates of labor force growth were 0.48 per cent in the period 1905–1909 and 0.49 per cent in the period 1914–1920.

We must search for a second set of forces which could account

3. The *decline* in labor force growth rates between 1887–1907 and 1907–1937 contrasts with the apparent *rise* in population growth rates from 1.02 to 1.31 per cent per annum over the same period (HYSJE, 1966, pp. 12–13). While there is an ongoing debate regarding Meiji population growth, all of the competing estimates (Ohbuchi, 1976, p. 334) confirm a rise in population growth rates from the 1890s to the 1920s. The issues in the text, however, relate to the workforce, not to the population in general. Changes in the rate of labor force growth affect investment demand, while changes in the rate of population growth affect "productive" savings availabilities. We shall return to this second issue below.

for a rightward drift in investment demand. Japanese historians are almost unanimous in their view that the explanations are to be found in accelerating rates of labor-saving (capital-using) technical change. This is the position, for example, adopted by Kazushi Ohkawa and Henry Rosovsky (1973), as well as Yasukichi Yasuba (1976), in describing the early twentieth century Japanese economy. In their view, the investment spurt following 1905 is associated with the flood of borrowed technology which washed over Japanese industry at about that time. This had two effects. First, it raised rates of return in the short run and induced new investment. In addition, the investment spurt was reinforced by the "bonanza atmosphere" around World War I. Second, the new technology was more capital intensive thus inducing a larger volume of investment in the long run as well. While Ohkawa and Rosovsky prefer to stress exogenous labor-saving (capital-using) forces *within* firms and industries, we could also appeal to technological forces which shifted output mix in a direction which favored the demand for "machines" (and skills). The latter explanation seems to work well in accounting for similar patterns in early American growth (Williamson, 1977; Williamson and Lindert, 1977) where relatively high rates of productivity growth in modern industrial sectors were central to the mechanism of unbalanced output expansion favoring capital-intensive sectors. In a similar fashion, unbalanced rates of Japanese twentieth century total factor productivity growth may also have favored those sectors utilizing capital most intensively and unskilled labor least intensively. Such unbalancedness would have: (1) tended to foster inequality, and (2) raised the aggregate demand for investment goods as those sectors using machines intensively expanded.

Looking at the qualitative predictions of Figure 1, we see that first, private saving rates rise in response to the surge in net rates of return, induced by the initial rightward shift in the long term investment demand function. The investment ratio increases from A to B. Second, the saving function itself may have shifted to the right in response to any or all of the following forces: (1) Trending inequality, induced by labor-saving technological change, may have fostered higher aggregate saving if the rich tended to have higher marginal saving rates. While inequality explanations may have failed to account for any of the post-World War II saving experience, they may fare better in the pre-World War II period where inequality trends were apparently more in evidence, especially during the 1920s (Ono and Watanabe, 1976; Yasuba, 1976). In any case, this potential distribution impact on saving appears in Figure 1 as an induced shift in the private saving ratio from B to C. (2) The private saving rate may also have risen in response to declining relative prices for capital goods. While a similar decline has been noted for the post World War II period, the pre World War II relative price drift has been almost ignored. In fact, the relative price of investment goods drifted downwards from an index of 131 in 1905–1909 to 105 in 1935–1939 (Table 3). This decline was not quite as rapid as the rate since the mid 1950s, but it is sufficiently large to warrant attention. How would the mechanism work? Suppose cost improvements in the investment goods sector serve to lower the relative price of capital goods, especially producer durables.[4] Let r be the net rate of return to capital in constant prices, P_K be the price of capital goods relative to GNP, and i be the rate of return to equity capital or "the" interest rate. In equilibrium, $r = \frac{\partial Y}{\partial K} = P_K \cdot i$, but that equilibrium is now disturbed by the decline in investment goods prices. Since the capital stock is fixed in the short run, r must also be constant in the short run, so

$$dr = P_K \cdot di + i \cdot dP_K = 0 \text{ or } \frac{di}{i} = - \left(\frac{dP_K}{P_K} \right).$$

Thus, in the short run returns to equity capital must rise at a rate equal to the per cent by which relative capital goods prices decline. At the same net rate of return on capital, we would observe more saving since returns to equity are higher. This effect is captured by a shift in the saving function from $\hat{S}_1$ to $\hat{S}_2$, thus fostering a rise in the saving ratio from C to D.

Finally, we have three other forces which might have caused the saving function to shift further to the right, producing an additional rise in the equilibrium private saving rate from D to E. These forces are as follows: (3) There may have been an exogenous shift in the private saving function due to changing attitudes towards thrift or improvements in savings mobilization; (4) Private saving may have been influenced by a whole range of government policies. It is con-

4. One could hardly argue that it was long-run demand forces which served to drive the relative price of capital goods in general or producer durables in particular. The output of producer durables increased its relative share of manufacturing output from the early 1890s, even in constant prices. Machinery output shares (in per cent) behaved as follows: 1887–1896, 2.13; 1892–1902, 2.82; 1897–1906, 4.40; 1902–1911, 6.00; 1907–1916, 8.46; 1912–1921, 13.54; and 1917–1926, 11.39. (Saxonhouse, 1976, Table 1, p. 98). In the short run, of course, demand may have mattered, especially during World War I.

ceivable that such policies tended to drift in favor of private accumulation after 1905. Indeed, our analysis of the Meiji experience in section 4 suggests that government tax, debt, and monetary policy may have been a critical influence on private saving; (5) A fall in the rate of population growth would also serve to augment the supply of "productive" savings since residential investment requirements would diminish and the surplus available for nonresidential capital formation would increase. This is in fact precisely what happened between 1905 and 1940. While the rate of labor force growth rose, the rate of population growth declined from 1.01 and 1.07 per cent in 1905–1909 and 1914–1920, to 0.66 per cent in 1934–1940.

In sum, Figure 1 offers a framework which can be used to decompose the source of Japan's saving and accumulation experience between 1907 and 1937. Which forces were dominant: an increase in private saving induced by thrift, government policy, population growth, or inequality trends; technological forces causing the shift in investment demand; or the downward drift in the relative price of capital goods?

3.2 The Sources of Rising Private Saving Rates: 1905–1940. The formal model underlying Figure 1 is simple enough. In rates of change (*), the functions can be written as

$$I_N^* = T^* + \epsilon \Gamma_N^*,$$
$$S_N^* = Z^* + \eta \Gamma_N^*,$$
$$I_N^* = S_N^*.$$

I (net real investment), S (net real saving), T, and Z are all written as shares in income. It can be shown that $\epsilon = -\sigma$, where σ is the elasticity of substitution in a CES production function.[5] Contempo-

---

5. Assume a CES production function of the following form:

$$Y = \{\alpha(E_L L)^{1-1/\sigma} + \beta(E_K K)^{1-1/\sigma}\}^{\frac{\sigma(1-\theta_L)}{\sigma-1}} \{E_R R\}^{\theta_R},$$

where L, K, and R refer to labor, capital and land, the E_i denote factor augmentation levels through technology, the θ_i denote factor shares, and σ is the elasticity of substitution between capital and labor. As Paul David has shown (1976, pp. 40 and 48), the ratio of net investment to output, I^D, can be written as

$$I^D = v(r)G$$

where v is the capital-output ratio. The capital-output ratio is related to the rental rate on capital by the expression

$$v = (\gamma E_K^{\sigma-1}) r^{-\sigma} = B r^{-\sigma}.$$

rary econometric estimates of the elasticity of substitution commonly range between $0.5 < \sigma < 1.0$. Accordingly, Table 4 reports the decomposition for both "extremes", $\epsilon = -0.5$ and $\epsilon = -1.0$. Nevertheless, some years ago Jorgenson's (1971, pp. 1130–34) review of the literature showed that estimates of the elasticity of substitution are not significantly different from unity, suggesting that the most appropriate description of technology for our purposes is the Cobb-Douglas form ($\epsilon = -1.0$). The alternative CES specification ($\epsilon = -0.5$) fails to alter substantially our basic conclusions by much.

We know far less about the "interest" elasticity of saving, η. What range of values should we consider here? A recent econometric study of the United Kingdom offers some guidelines here (Edelstein, 1977). Under various models of saving behavior, the long-run elasticities range between 0.11, 0.37, 0.60 and 0.70 for the period 1870–1965 as a whole. The three assumptions examined in Table 4 would appear to cover the relevant cases.[6]

Table 4 supplies a tentative accounting for the sources of rising private saving rates covering the three decades (1907–1937) as a whole, as well as the shorter "investment spurt" early in the century. Saving excludes military and residential investment, is net of depreciation requirements, and is in constant prices. Consider first the long term stretching from 1905–1909 to 1934–1940. If one be-

Thus,

$$G = (\overset{*}{L} + \overset{*}{E}_L)\left\{ \frac{\theta_L}{1 - \theta_K} \right\} + \overset{*}{R}\left\{ \frac{\theta_R}{1 - \theta_K} \right\}.$$

where B is a constant and

$$I^D = Br^{-\sigma}G,$$

Changes in rates of labor force or land stock growth ($\overset{*}{L}$ and $\overset{*}{R}$) will cause I^D to shift, as will changes in the rate of labor-augmentation through technological progress ($\overset{*}{\bar{E}}_L$). See Williamson (1977).

6. While the perfectly elastic saving schedule is excluded as a relevant case, it might be defended for some countries by an appeal to capital from abroad. Such an argument would be cast by reference to $\hat{S}_1$ and $\hat{S}'_1$ in Figure 1. The savings function $\hat{S}_1$ would represent the active *domestic* savings constraint, while $\hat{S}'_1$ would represent the function aggregated to include some postulated elastic supply of finance from Europe and North America. This characterization would attribute a significant portion of the rise in domestic investment ratios, (E − G) to be precise, to foreign capital. There is no evidence to support such an interpretation for Japan. Except for some brief critical episodes of war financing, foreign investment was always a small share of total domestic investment in Japan.

TABLE 4
THE SOURCES OF RISING "PRODUCTIVE" NET SAVING RATES IN PREWAR JAPAN,
c1907–c1937 (constant prices)

Decomposition	$\varepsilon = -0.5$			$\varepsilon = -1.0$		
	$\eta = 1$	$\eta = 0.37$	$\eta = 0$	$\eta = 1$	$\eta = 0.37$	$\eta = 0$
c1907–c1917						
1. Total Increase in Net Real Investment Share, of which due to	.0320	.0320	.0320	.0320	.0320	.0320
1.1 Investment Demand Shift	.0220	.0141	0	.0171	.0092	0
1.1.1 Due to Labor Force Growth	.0007	.0005	0	.0006	.0003	0
1.1.2 Due to Residual Demand Forces	.0213	.0136	0	.0165	.0089	0
1.2 Declining Relative P_K	.0035	.0032	.0025	.0066	.0058	.0049
1.3 Residual Saving Function Shift	.0064	.0147	.0294	.0083	.0170	.0271
c1907–c1937						
2. Total Increase in Net Real Investment Share, of which due to	.0470	.0470	.0470	.0470	.0470	.0470
2.1 Investment Demand Shift	.0260	.0166	0	.0154	.0083	0
2.1.1 Due to Labor Force Growth	.0290	.0185	0	.0205	.0118	0
2.1.2 Due to Residual Demand Forces	−.0030	−.0019	0	−.0051	−.0035	0
2.2 Declining Relative P_K	.0077	.0068	.0051	.0133	.0119	.0103
2.3 Residual Saving Function Shift	.0137	.0238	.0419	.0183	.0268	.0367

NOTES: See text and Williamson (1977) for a full description of calculating methods. The following data is utilized in these calculations:

	$\overset{*}{L}$	P_K (1934–36 = 100)	S_G (constant 1934–36 prices)	$S_N = I_N$ (constant 1934–36 prices)	r_N
1905–1909 (c1907)	0.48	130.6	.099	.051	.238
1914–1920 (c1917)	0.49	117.9	.138	.083	.248
1934–1940 (c1937)	0.90	104.4	.171	.098	.162

The underlying income and investment data is taken from the sources underlying Table 3. The relative price of capital goods, P_K, is from the same source, where implicit price deflators for gross domestic fixed capital formation and GNP are used. The net rate of return on reproducible capital is

$$r_N = \theta_K v^{-1} - \delta$$

where δ is the depreciation rate on capital excluding dwellings ($\delta = .10$; de Bever (1976); p. 277), v is the capital-output ratio, and θ_K is reproducible capital's share. The net reproducible capital stock (excluding dwellings) estimates are in 1934–36 prices and are taken from LTES-3, Table 1, while θ_K is from Ohkawa and Rosovsky (1973), BST-17. The labor force growth figures ($\overset{*}{L}$) are from HYSJE, 1966. pp. 56–57.

lieves that $\eta = 0$, then *all* of the upward drift in capital formation shares must be attributed to declining relative capital goods prices and shifts in the private saving function, especially the latter. At the other extreme, if one believes $\eta = 1$ is a more realistic characterization of interest elasticities, then approximately 33 per cent of the rise in the private saving rate would be explained by the investment demand shifts, 39 per cent by a shift in the savings function, and 28 per cent by the decline in investment goods' relative price. We favor the intermediate case where $\eta = 0.37$. Here we find investment demand explaining only 18 per cent of the rise in private saving rates, shifts in the saving function accounting for 57 per cent, and the relative price of capital goods contributing an impressive 25 per cent. Furthermore, Table 4 reports that for the three decades as a whole *all* of the rightward shift in investment demand can be traced to the rise in labor force growth.[7] It appears that "true" technological forces (the residual investment demand shift) had either a negative or a neutral impact on private saving rates over the three decades as a whole.

Four conclusions are forthcoming from this exercise, and all of them raise some interesting questions regarding our interpretations of a century of Japanese saving and accumulation. First, the declining relative price of capital goods plays a significant, positive role throughout. This result is somewhat surprising since the relative price of investment goods drifted downward at a per annum rate of

7. The "true labor force growth" impact on investment demand, call it $\overset{*}{T}_L$, can be derived from the expression for G in footnote 5. We have

$$I^D = Br^{-\sigma}G = Tr^\varepsilon$$

where B is a constant and

$$G = (\overset{*}{L} + \overset{*}{E}_L) \left\{ \frac{\theta_L}{1 - \theta_K} \right\} + \overset{*}{R} \left\{ \frac{\theta_R}{1 - \theta_K} \right\}.$$

Since our interest here is solely with changes in $\overset{*}{L}$, we may set $\overset{*}{E}_L = \overset{*}{R} = 0$, and

$$G = \overset{*}{L} \left\{ \frac{\theta_L}{1 - \theta_K} \right\}.$$

It follows that the "true labor force growth" (fixed-weight) impact on investment demand is simply

$$\overset{*}{T}_L = \overset{*}{G} = \frac{d\overset{*}{L}}{\overset{*}{L}}.$$

In Table 4, the residual investment demand shift impact is calculated by reference to $(\overset{*}{T} - \overset{*}{T}_L)$.

almost 60 per cent of the measured rise in net private saving rates over the three decades as a whole ($\eta = 0.37$). Obviously, if the reader leans towards elasticity "pessimism" (e.g., $\eta = 0$), then shifts in the saving function will play an even larger role in his accounting. Furthermore, if the supply of saving plays the dominant and active role in accounting for trend acceleration, what then explains the rightward drift in the saving function over the three decades? Furthermore, why was the shift so much more dramatic prior to 1917 than afterwards?

Finally, it appears that demographic changes may have played a very important role in accounting for long-term Japanese accumulation performance between 1905 and 1940. Ignoring some striking shorter term cycles, labor force growth rates appear to have risen between 1905–1909 and 1934–1940, inducing a rightward drift in investment demand, thus fostering a rise in nonresidential investment ratios. On the other hand, population growth rates apparently declined quite significantly over the same period. The latter influence surely served to diminish new residential investment requirements, thus inducing a rightward shift in private saving schedules net of residential investment. How much of these two demographic forces are cyclic and how much are trend? Are the labor force and population data of sufficient quality to support this kind of quantitative analysis, or will the trends disappear with future revisions? Can we in fact measure the contribution of population growth either to Japanese trend acceleration or to the uniquely high accumulation rates already obtained by 1900?

Questions such as these motivate our more detailed inquiry into the sources of Japanese private accumulation performance prior to World War I at the end of Meiji early modern growth.

3.3 Looking Backward: Saving and Accumulation from Meiji to Taisho. If determinants other than rates of return account for the majority of the rise in private saving rates after 1907, it seems likely that they were even more central in the late nineteenth century. After all, net rates of return were at extraordinarily high levels at the turn of the century (e.g., 24 per cent over the period 1905–1909), even after two or three previous decades of rapid capital accumulation. Now, it seems to us common sense that when rates of return approach levels as high as this, changes in those rates are unlikely to influence saving behavior by very much. To put it differently, interest elasticities diminish the more rates of return exceed "average" historical values. This view is shared by both Lockwood (1968, pp.

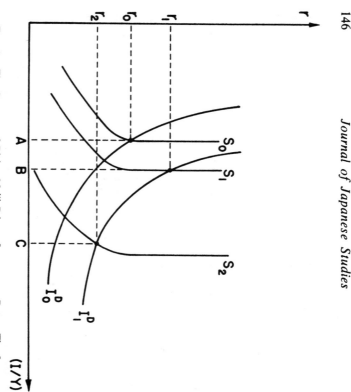

FIG. 2.   The Sources of Rising Meiji Private Investment Rates: The Interest-Inelastic Hypothesis

268–304) and Bronfenbrenner (1977, p. 4), and is depicted graphically in Figure 2. Under this interpretation, the Meiji era would fall between the private saving rates denoted by A and C. Early in the period rates of return are very high, between r_0 and r_1, saving is in the interest-inelastic range, and saving is the binding constraint on accumulation and growth. As the saving function drifts outward over the late nineteenth century, rates of return begin to decline so that by, say, 1907 the investment market is operating around the interest-elastic range on the private saving function (e.g., at r_2 and C).

If this interpretation of Meiji saving and accumulation is fairly close to the mark, then it follows that the saving supply function was the binding constraint on private rates of accumulation from the 1880s to shortly before World War I. What then determined the shift in that constraint over time? Was it a drift towards inequality? Was it simply the growth of income above subsistence? What role did government policy play in fostering shifts in the private saving constraint? And how important were demographic factors as an influence on residential investment and thus on the remaining "surplus" available for productive accumulation?

4. Late Meiji and Early Taisho Saving and Accumulation: Population Control, Militarism and the State

While Meiji Japanese accumulation and saving performance may appear modest by post-1960 standards, they were certainly impressive by the standards of the late nineteenth century. Consider first the capital stock growth rates presented in Table 5. The net "productive" capital stock grew at 4.9 per cent per annum over the period from 1887 to 1922 as a whole. By comparison, the rate in the United States from 1869 to 1907 (Abramovitz and David, 1973, p. 431) was 5.0 per cent, and the latter had a population growth rate (2.1 per cent per annum) far greater than that of Japan (1.0 per cent per annum). [9] There is also some evidence that trend acceleration was already apparent in Japan since the pre 1907 rate was 4.7 per cent per annum while the post 1907 rate was 5.1 per cent per annum. But this trend acceleration is quite modest, and it should be emphasized that the economy-wide accumulation rates achieved during the 1887–1907 period, 4.72 per cent, are comparable with those achieved during the 1908–1937 period, 4.64 per cent (Table 2). Indeed, the rate of accumulation of net private capital stocks between 1887 and 1922, 5.36 per cent, was not very far below the rate which prevailed between 1953 and 1961, 6.1 per cent (Table 2). Public and private capital stock growth rates were both large during the three decades or so prior to 1922, with the former, 4.3 per cent, somewhat less than the latter, 5.4 per cent. Furthermore, the growth performance was characterized by a lack of balance, since the rate in agriculture, 1.5 per cent, was far below that in either manufacturing (8.1 per cent) or services (5.7 per cent). Low rates in housing (1.2 per cent) were consistent with the modest population growth typical throughout the period.

Table 6 supplies the saving rates that made the "productive" accumulation rates possible. Excluding military and residential investment, the current price share of gross fixed capital formation in GNP rose from .090 in 1885–1889 (1887) to .154 in 1920–1924 (1922). Because of the downward drift in relative investment goods' prices

9. The competing estimates for the period 1885–1920 range between 1.0 and 1.18 per cent per annum (Ohbuchi, 1976, Table 1, p. 330), with the "best" estimate (Yasukawa) being 1 per cent per annum.

TABLE 5
NET CAPITAL STOCKS, CONSTANT PRICES,
1887–1922 (REVISED DE BEVER-WILLIAMSON ESTIMATES)

Year or Period	Agriculture	Manufacturing	Services	Total	Public	Private	Housing
			Stocks				
1887	53.4	13.9	32.6	100.0	31.5	68.5	100.0
1892	56.1	23.7	42.7	122.5	35.8	86.6	106.5
1897	59.0	51.6	61.1	172.0	42.8	129.1	112.4
1902	63.4	63.9	75.6	203.1	54.8	148.1	119.8
1907	68.2	93.0	93.5	254.9	66.9	187.8	124.7
1912	74.9	142.4	124.0	341.3	91.5	249.7	132.4
1917	81.0	185.1	159.4	425.5	112.7	312.8	143.1
1922	89.1	239.2	235.6	563.9	137.8	426.1	154.1
		Per Annum Growth Rates (in percent)					
1887–1922	1.46	8.13	5.65	4.90	4.30	5.36	1.24
1887–1907	1.22	9.50	5.27	4.72	3.85	5.18	1.11
1907–1922	1.78	6.29	6.16	5.13	4.94	5.64	1.42

NOTES: Total and Housing 1887 stocks set equal to 100. Five year averages centered on indicated years. See de Bever and Williamson (1976, Table 1.1 and Appendix C).

TABLE 6

SAVING RATES AND RELATIVE INVESTMENT GOODS PRICES, 1887–1922

	Gross Domestic Capital Formation Share in GNP Excluding Military and Residential Investment		Relative Price of Investment Goods (1934–36 = 100)
	(1) Current Price	(2) Constant Price	(3)
1887	.090	.053	169
1892	.107	.063	171
1897	.128	.078	165
1902	.098	.069	142
1907	.128	.099	131
1912	.142	.124	114
1917	.160	.133	122
1922	.154	.145	107

NOTES: All entries use five-year averages centered on the date indicated. See Table 3 for sources.

through 1912,[10] presumably induced by relatively rapid total factor productivity growth in the capital goods sector in Japan and abroad, the rise in "productive" capital formation or saving shares up to World War I was even more impressive in constant prices. This seems a point worth stressing since it appears throughout the past century of Japanese accumulation experience. It also seems apparent that growth was at times irregular. Some have argued that these "long swings" in investment behavior and development performance had their source in private sector investment demand. While a neo-Keynesian interpretation may seem plausible, it would appear unwise to ignore capital supply constraints associated with war related "stop-go" monetary expansion and government demands on domestic capital markets in accounting for observed growth instability. Indeed, our analysis in section 3 suggested the importance of shifting private saving constraints on investment shares even during the short term "spurt" 1905–1909 to 1915–1919.

How is this accumulation and saving performance to be explained? What role did government policy play, and in what way was private accumulation influenced by public policy and militarism?

The sources of early Japanese economic growth have been the subject of analysis for almost a century. Reference to the "Meiji

10. The downward drift is much more pronounced for producer durables than for investment goods as a whole (LTES-1, Tables 30 and 31, pp. 232–234). We already noted problems with this price data for the 1905–1920 period in footnote 8 above.

model of development'' can be found in almost any discussion of policy options confronting modern less developed countries. This is true despite the far from unanimous evaluation of the sources of Japanese growth, and a complete absence of analytical effort to sort out the role of the state during the period prior to the 1920s. On the other hand, an extensive descriptive literature stretching over three-quarters of a century from Ono (1890) to Landes (1965) emphasizes institutional factors, the unique Japanese culture, and, most important, the role of the state in accounting for Japan's growth performance. This literature most frequently relies on gross correlation between active state involvement and impressive economic performance to clinch the case in favor of intelligent and effective policy. The relevant questions are infrequently posed and quantitative answers are even rarer: Did policy really matter? Did the policies implemented foster accumulation or hinder it? Were there far more effective courses of action available to Meiji and Taisho Japan? On the other hand, while recent attempts to write analytical histories of Japan have had considerable success in isolating the sources of growth, neither Jorgenson (1966) nor Fei and Ranis (1966) nor Minami and Ono (1972), nor Kelley and Williamson (1974) have made any explicit attempt to introduce the state into their historical models of growth.

The authors recently attempted to bridge this gap (de Bever, 1976; de Bever and Williamson, 1976) by providing an integration of public and private sector saving and accumulation behavior in a multi-sector model which was applied to three and a half decades of Meiji and Taisho accumulation experience. The period of analysis extended over the years 1887 and 1922, the starting date partly a pragmatic matter since reliable macro data contained, for example, in the impressive recent volumes of *Estimates of Long Term Economic Statistics of Since 1868* (LTES) and the Bank of Japan's *Hundred-Year Statistics of the Japanese Economy* (HYSJE), are almost nonexistent for earlier years. Fortunately, the starting point has more to recommend it than that: By 1887, the financial and political framework which was to guide subsequent economic development was formalized with the Imperial Constitution. This law codified the articles which regulated government fiscal activity over the whole pre World War II period (Emi, 1963, p. 12) and marks the commencement of modern state activity in every sense. During the next thirty or forty years, output in the private sector grew at a rate which, if not approaching the contemporary post World War II experience, was nonetheless impressive by the international standards of the time.

The multi-sector model is relatively complex, and the present paper will make no effort to supply a full exposition of it but will instead simply describe its general attributes.[11] While it followed in the neoclassical dualistic tradition (Jorgenson, 1966; Kelley, Williamson and Cheetham, 1972; Kelley and Williamson, 1974), the model departed from that tradition in a number of distinctive ways. To begin with, we rejected the conventional two-sector classification which restricts analysis to agricultural and manufacturing commodity production. Instead, sectoral activities were expanded to include public and private services as well as housing. In addition, intermediate input costs had an impact on the prices of final manufactures. Three factors of production drove output in the system: land, labor and capital. Agriculture employed all three factors of production, while manufacturing and services did not use land. The aggregate labor force grew exogenously at its historic rates, but we made an explicit distinction between the population gainfully employed and full-time labor equivalents. These demographic distinctions turned out to be important in our analysis of Japanese growth. The agricultural land stock also grew at its exogenous historic rates, rates fully consistent with a highly inelastic land supply.

We adopted a putty-clay treatment of capital. Furthermore, capital took two generic forms. "Productive" capital was utilized in agriculture, industry and services while "nonproductive" capital was allocated to housing. We were motivated here by Ohkawa and Rosovsky (1973) who have drawn attention to the high proportion of residential construction in total capital formation. Since residential investment was a significant and variable share of total capital formation during the early years of Meiji growth, we thought it wise to treat new housing requirements as an explicit subsistence claim on investible private savings. The remainder of private investment was allocated by sectoral rates of return subject to the lagged constraints imposed by historical tradition. That is, we adopted Ronald McKinnon's (1973) "fragmentation" view of financial capital markets. Capital in each sector depreciated at fixed rates and was aug-

11. The November 1976 version of the de Bever and Williamson paper underlying this section is available upon request. So too is a revised 1977 version, as well as relevant appendices. Address requests to Professor Williamson, c/o Ms. Mary Hughes, Department of Economics, University of Wisconsin, Madison, Wisconsin, 53706.

mented by public and private purchases of investment goods from the manufacturing sector or from abroad. While public investment was treated as a policy instrument, the government could also influence private allocation by expanding bank loans to manufacturing.

Our focal point was public policy and its impact on economic growth. In our model the government could tax and spend, incur debts, and accumulate foreign exchange reserves. Government income and expenditure variables were taken to be exogenous policy instruments and much of our earlier paper (de Bever and Williamson, 1976) was devoted to an evaluation of their impact. In addition, the state controlled the money supply through the Bank of Japan. Following Patrick (1966) and McKinnon (1973), we took a revisionist position to the ''monetarist'' view of money in a developing economy. The public possessed a demand for real cash balances related to the volume of investment, the rate of price inflation and the level of non-farm consumption. Absolute price levels were determined by the demand for goods and services, the demand for cash balances, and the money supply. In addition, we introduced a financial framework in which government bonds financed long term debt. These alternative means of holding wealth introduced a relationship between the growth of physical capital and the availability of new financial assets, an approach which followed Tobin (1965), and Foley and Sidrauski (1971). Expansion in government debt and claims on foreigners both reduced savings available for private capital formation. Finally, our economy was open to trade but the government was assumed to control that trade through the Yokohama Specie Bank. Exports and imports were thus considered as policy targets. While raw material prices were determined by world market conditions, all other relative prices were determined endogenously at levels which balanced supply with domestic and foreign demand.

Dualism in demand parameters was not an attribute of our model. All private households were assumed to have the same consumption and savings function. However, the model allowed for sizable urban-rural differences in consumption patterns, differences attributable to higher urban reliance on the distribution system. This led to a higher urban cost of living, and differences between urban and rural relative prices, as Ohkawa has indicated. Private household spending and saving out of disposable income was described by a Stone-Geary linear expenditure system. Disposable income was defined net of direct taxes and after satisfying subsistence requirements at given prices, consumers allocate their remaining supernumerary income in fixed proportions to food, manufactured consumption goods, services, and savings.

Finally, factors of production were fully employed and paid their marginal value products. Labor migrated off the farm when real wage differentials exceeded migration costs, and in contrast with the conventional dualistic model nominal wage differentials were not an indicator of labor slack but rather of cost of living differentials. Similarly, rate of return differentials, even net of government taxes and subsidies, were allowed to persist due to lags in adjustment and barriers to capital mobility.

The model seemed to replicate reasonably well Japanese growth, accumulation as well as structural change over the thirty-six years as a whole (de Bever and Williamson, 1976, section 3). Encouraged by the model's ability to replicate history, a number of counterfactual experiments were then posed to establish the quantitative importance of various forces to the accumulation experience of Meiji and Taisho Japan. Some of these counterfactuals were designed to give quantitative answers to questions which have occupied students of Japanese history for decades. Others aimed to discover whether Japan's experience was atypical, and whether her growth strategy can or should be adapted to modern conditions. In contrast to the recent literature which focuses on Japanese total factor productivity growth performance, our approach was in an older tradition since our attention was riveted on accumulation and industrialization performance. Not only is this approach consistent with the findings of section 1 of this paper, but it also makes sense in terms of the professed objectives of national policy. It also conforms to an embodiment view of technological change.

What were the key findings of our tentative analysis?

First, we developed a plausible case which supplied an explanation for Japanese "long swings" in savings, accumulation and growth and which contrasted sharply with Kazushi Ohkawa and Henry Rosovsky's emphasis on private investment demand and cycles in aggregate demand. We assigned a far greater role to government "stop-go" policy associated primarily with exogenous fluctuations in wartime mobilization and postwar stabilization. In the absence of government-induced instability, Japan would have undergone, for example, a fairly smooth upward drift in the saving-income ratio from 1887 to 1922. In particular, the "investment spurt" from 1905 to World War I disappears. This result is consistent with the analysis in section 3 where we found that as little as 30 per cent of the investment surge from 1907 to 1917 (Table 3, $\epsilon = -1.0$,

$\eta = 0.37$) could be explained by a shift in private investment demands. There are a variety of public actions which induced instability in private accumulation rates, but the most important were sharp changes in the level of public borrowing in domestic capital markets to finance military-related variations in public outlays, instability in the rate of monetary expansion, and alterations in the composition of taxes. Each of these had an important impact on incentives for private "productive" capital accumulation and on the surplus available for doing so.

The second of our findings is that the Tokugawa legacy of population control appeared to be a prime candidate in accounting for Japan's impressive accumulation performance, and in our model all of these demographic influences on "productive" accumulation performance have their source from the saving availability side rather than the investment demand side. The role of the state and foreign events during the Meiji and Taisho regimes pale by comparison with these favorable demographic conditions. Indeed, demographic influences appear to have made a far more important contribution to successful industrialization and high rates of accumulation than the sum of nearly all the other exogenous forces combined which might be considered unique to late nineteenth century Japan. Furthermore, the Tokugawa legacy of population control had little or nothing to do with state policy. In fact, the government had no population policy, and little knowledge of demographic forces, until well into the twentieth century (Ohbuchi, 1976, p. 339).

The casual reader of Japanese economic history would hardly have reached this conclusion based on the conventional literature. Policy experimentation by Meiji and Taisho leaders receives prime attention while the extraordinary advantage of weak "population pressure" is hardly noted at all. Indeed, there seems to be some real confusion in the literature between the influence of *high population density* on low initial per capita incomes, on the one hand, and the impact of *low population growth* on high accumulation rates, on the other. Our focus is on the latter. The literature appears to focus on the former, that is it dwells on the consequences of "overpopulation." Perhaps this is explained by the participation of Japanese economists in the population debate during the 1930s, and by Western fears—apparently quite warranted—that "overpopulation" might lead to war.[12] While land scarcity and overpopulation may

---

12. This paragraph draws heavily on the excellent survey by Hiroshi Ohbuchi (1976, pp. 339–46).

have been very important political and social issues then *and* now, the fact remains that Japan was blessed by very low rates of population growth. And it is the *growth* in population which mattered most to Japanese accumulation performance during Meiji and Taisho.

Given low rates of population growth and low dependency rates, one is tempted to conclude that almost any policy, good or bad, would have been associated *ex post* with impressive accumulation and thus growth performance. Such a conclusion would be consistent with the common observation often repeated in *Asia's New Giant* that Japan's miraculous growth since the late 1950s can be explained in large part by having foregone residential housing and municipal overhead. We are told that when these "unproductive" investments are finally made in the near future, productive accumulation and thus growth will be partially choked off. A similar argument holds for the late nineteenth and early twentieth centuries: Low rates of population growth released resources for productive accumulation, and the size of that released margin was very large indeed. Our calculations show that had Meiji Japan lacked this demographic advantage and borne the demographic burdens of presently developing Asian nations instead, "productive" capital stocks *per worker* would have grown at 1.2 rather than 3.8 per cent per annum.

Third, favorable foreign events mattered a great deal to the high accumulation rates achieved during late Meiji, and they also contributed to the modest trend acceleration apparent even after government "stop-go" influences are removed. The most important of these foreign circumstances—the exogenous decline in foreign raw material prices—hardly plays a role in conventional histories either. It is generally agreed that the speed of Japanese industrialization and the rate of accumulation was critically influenced by the sufficiency of foreign exchange available for the purchase of imported capital goods and raw materials. Industrial export expansion and import substitution have therefore received much attention, the most recent and *correct* analysis, from our point of view at least, being that of Tuvia Blumenthal (1972). But we must also remember that successful industrialization required additional raw material imports, at prices over which Japan had little control. Hence, the rapid expansion of industrial exports must be evaluated simultaneously with the increased dependence on raw material (and food) imports. The question naturally follows: To what extent were raw material prices an engine-of-growth? The contemporary analogy is obvious. Recent OPEC activities have shown that a quadrupling of the price of oil can lead to severe adjustment problems for a resource poor nation. But what are the lasting effects of the relative price change? With no available substitutes, a lack of supply at any price would certainly bring industrial production and accumulation to a halt. But the issue now and in the Meiji period is price rather than supply. Watanabe (1975), for example, has argued that a reduction in the price of oil by 40 per cent from their 1975 levels would have increased, *ceteris paribus*, the growth rate in Japan after two years from 7.9 to 8.7 per cent. Of course, this analogy is not meant to imply that Japan at the turn of the century was heavily dependent on foreign fuels, or that fuels were a large share of total imports. On the contrary, imports were dominated by cotton and wool until very late in the period under study, while coal and crude oil were still small shares of the total import bill.

The fact remains that the price of raw materials relative to agricultural products declined by almost 50 per cent between 1887 and 1902, and by about 35 per cent compared to manufactures over the same period. These favorable price trends can be evaluated in our model by simply fixing the relative price of raw materials at the 1887 level, rather than allowing it to decline dramatically as it did in the late nineteenth century. This experiment suggests that the rate of ''productive'' capital accumulation over the period as a whole would have been only modestly suppressed, from 5.0 to 4.8 per cent per annum. Perhaps more revealing, however, is that trend acceleration in accumulation is reinforced in this counterfactual regime of stable relative raw material prices. Since the relative raw material price decline was in fact centered on the late nineteenth century, capital stock growth was fostered during the first two decades following 1887, not the last two. Stability in raw material prices would have served to lower capital formation rates in the first half of the period, and thus trend acceleration would have been more apparent without the favorable price trends.

One could easily imagine a world of greater raw material scarcity than the one just considered, for example, one in which the relative price of raw materials was twice as high in each year after 1887. If our study of Meiji Japan were motivated solely by a search for relevant ''models of development'' to guide contemporary policy in the Asian Third World, then this second experiment would be more to the point. After all, while Japan was favored by declining raw material prices early in her industrialization experience, contemporary less developed countries are confronted with a *rise* rather than stability in relative raw materials prices. If one wishes to compare Meiji Japan's performance with the contemporary Third World, then the doubling experiment may be far more instructive. Faced with the counterfactual doubling in raw material prices, our model suggests that the productive capital stock would have grown at the far lower rate of 4.2, rather than 5.0, per cent per annum.[13] Furthermore, the potential balance of payments gap would have required nominal industrial exports to rise above historical levels by one third. To repeat, a world of greater raw material scarcity would have produced even higher rates of industrial export growth (or rates of import substitution). The historian who views exports as the engine-of-growth would view this counterfactual world as confirmation of his thesis; that is, he would have observed a historical correlation between high accumulation rates, 4.2 per cent per annum, and high rates of export growth. He would have been quite wrong. The rapid growth in industrial exports would have been a sign of weakness, not strength.

The Tokugawa demographic legacy and the decline in raw material prices up to the turn of the century played a very important role in accounting for Japan's impressive accumulation performance following the 1880s. Furthermore, this accounting has made no effort to explore the independent influence of declining relative prices on imported capital goods in the late nineteenth century, an accounting which would further reinforce our view of the unusually rapid Japanese accumulation performance as purely fortuitous. Indeed, these highly favorable exogenous events made a far more important contribution to Japan's relatively rapid early industrialization than any policy variables subject to Meiji and Taisho control.

Our tentative analysis suggests a fourth conclusion: the drive toward trade in foodstuffs and the increased dependence on colonial

13. This experiment obviously deals with external terms of trade effects, and the counterfactual raw material price history could be (and implicitly is, by the model) translated into a counterfactual terms of trade history. Those readers who find our counterfactual doubling of raw material prices to be an outrageous experiment should read again the findings of Richard Huber (1971). From the 1850s to the 1870s, Huber (1971, p. 627) estimates that Japan's commodity terms of trade improved 3.5-fold and thus served to augment Japanese real income by as much as 65 per cent. That figure corresponds to an augmented annual growth rate of 2.02 per cent between 1850 and 1875! Huber's calculation for the pre 1880s may serve to cast more credence on our post 1880s counterfactual which assigns much of Japanese success to raw material import price trends. Huber's calculation relates, of course, to intelligent commercial policy since the earlier period was one of conscious movement from autarchy to free trade. The post 1880s relates instead to fortuitous forces completely out of the control of state policy.

"only" 0.7 per cent between 1907 and 1937 (Table 3). Contrast this with the more spectacular postwar experience, where from 1953 to 1971 the measured rate was 1.7 per cent per annum, almost all of which took place during the 1960s. One cannot help but believe that capital goods prices must account for an important part of Japanese twentieth century accumulation experience, including the extraordinary rates achieved since the 1950s compared with the interwar period. This seems all the more plausible, given our inability to gauge accurately the relatively rapid improvements in the quality of investment goods over time. Furthermore, such price behavior was not an international development either in the postwar period (Denison and Chung, 1976, p. 66) or during the 1907-1937 episode (Williamson, 1974, p. 108). The contrast between Japan on the one hand and Europe and North America on the other suggests that this unique relative price behavior has its source in the technological dynamics of Japan's domestic capital goods industry. It deserves far more attention than Japanese analysts have given it thus far.

The second conclusion is that this accounting does not vary greatly when applied to the "investment spurt" of the period 1907-1917. Here again, the saving function shift ($\epsilon = -1.0$; $\eta = 0.37$) accounts for over half of the observed rise in saving rates, and since interest elasticities are likely to be far lower over one decade than across three, it seems likely that we have overstated the role of shifting investment demand and understated the role of shifting saving supply.[8] This result is somewhat surprising given Ohkawa and Rosovsky's (1973) emphasis on long swings and cycles in aggregate demand. It also conflicts with Martin Bronfenbrenner's (1977) emphasis on high and rising marginal efficiency of domestic investment in Japan. Third, shifts in the saving function appear to account for

8. The residual saving shift would also be understated if the relative decline in P_K is overestimated for the c1907–c1917 episode. This may in fact be the case. Consider the following alternative P_K series:

	(1)	(2)	(3)
1905–1909	130.6	125.9	118.2
1914–1920	117.9	114.6	122.4
1934–1940	104.4	104.8	106.5

The first of these (1) is the ratio of LTES implicit price deflators, "investment goods," and "aggregate" (Table 4). The second (2) is from the same source, but uses implicit price deflators from series including military and dwelling investment. The last (3) is from Ohkawa and Rosovsky (1973, BST-5, 6, 7, 8 and 14) but uses the same concepts as in (2). We have not been able to reconcile these differences, and it matters a great deal.

Fifth, we conclude that expansive monetary policy did make a significant contribution to rapid accumulation in late Meiji. The descriptive literature attaches considerable importance to the inflationary growth hypothesis. According to this theory, capital formation was accelerated in Japan by allowing the money supply to expand at a faster rate than the growth in demand for real cash balances. Our model was constructed in such a way so as to give full vent to the inflationary growth thesis. Variations in the growth rate of the money stock have two influences on private accumulation in the model. First, monetary expansion initially influences the distribution of investment in favor of industry. Since Moulton (1931, pp. 423–24) and others have emphasized the advantage enjoyed by the zaibatsu and government-backed industrial ventures when it came to obtaining bank support, the model accepts the bias by allocating the resulting expansion in loans entirely to industry. Initially, the private sector responds passively by the proportionate reduction in their allocation of current saving to all other potential investment outlets. In a perfect capital market, such biases would be quickly eroded through compensating saving flows in response to the real rate of return differentials. If capital markets are fragmented, however, disequilibrium can exist for considerable lengths of time. While the model's specification argues that the size of equilibrating movements becomes stronger as the gap in sectoral rates of return widens, the adjustment need not be complete. Hence, the marginal impact of credit expansion on the sectoral distribution of new capital goods is not obvious when "capital mobility" is less than perfect.

While aggregate saving is initially left unchanged, it will rise in subsequent periods as inflation ensues. Inflation brings real money demand back into equilibrium with supply, but the process will have an additional impact on real accumulation rates. Inflation erodes the real value of wealth in government bonds and money (the "inflation tax"), and wealth holders are assumed to respond to fill the gap. Furthermore, the expectation of continued inflation diminishes the demand for cash balances, fostering a further portfolio shift into physical wealth accumulation.

Money may have had other contributions to growth other than those mentioned above. Nonetheless, does the model support the proposition that monetary expansion in late Meiji significantly fostered industrialization and accumulation? To explore this question, we posed a counterfactual which replaced the historic money supply expansion (9.75 per cent per annum) with a rate (5 per cent per annum) which would have produced "near stability" in price levels. That is, it produces a counterfactual annual inflation rate of 0.6 per cent rather than the historical rate of 5.4 per cent. This counterfactual rate of price inflation is in fact fairly close to the inflationary experience in North America and England over the same period.

Did the Meiji inflationary policy contribute to the high rates of private accumulation observed during the period? Without that policy, and with the "price stability" policy instead, the model suggests that the rate of accumulation would have been 4.6 per cent per annum rather than 5.0 per cent. The industrial capital stock would have suffered an even more dramatic reduction, and the rate of industrialization would have slowed, as would the rate of urbanization. It appears that both the aggregate rate of accumulation and the bias in favor of industrial accumulation were both augmented by Meiji monetary policy, the latter especially so.[14]

Sixth, our tentative results confirm some elements of conventional wisdom as well. Counterfactual experiments with the model suggest that the regressive tax system did make a significant contribution to accumulation and growth, but since the system is hardly unique to Japan one cannot appeal to the regressive tax structure in searching for explanations of the relatively high Meiji rates of accumulation. Nor is that system and its evolution over time likely to account for the upward drift in saving rates and accumulation performance from the late 1880s to the late 1930s.

Finally, some counterfactuals would appear to reject the basis for the "liberal-pacifist" critique. Namely, Meiji Japan's military adventurism did *not* retard development, unless, of course, one is prepared to argue that all of the resources released from her international military campaign would have been devoted to capital formation activities (an "investment biased" counterfactual). This position, while laudable on moral grounds, is likely to be politically naive since a strong and successful military was obviously an effective bribe to both the peasant and the urban worker who were as a result more willing to accept the foregone consumption. Instead, we posed a "consumption biased" counterfactual quite like that suggested by Harry Oshima (1965, p. 375) some years ago:

"If the military expenditures for the two wars are excluded, something like one-half of the total military spending of the entire Meiji

14. This experiment is likely to place a *lower bound* on our accounting of the quantitative impact of Meiji policy. The model introduces a naive treatment of price expectations, capital gains (losses) and portfolio response: inflation rates are poorly anticipated by holders of cash balances, and they have no impact whatsoever on attitudes towards holding government bonds. A more realistic specification of portfolio adjustment would almost surely raise the private accumulation rate of productive capital.

period remains. This might well have sufficed to keep Japan an independent nation, and the savings from such a reduction in military expenditures could have been used to reduce the burden of land taxes by one-half."

How would Meiji growth have been modified had the level of military expenditures, income from indemnities, and tax rates been altered in the manner suggested by Oshima? Would *long run* Meiji growth have been fostered? Apparently not, since the overall rate of accumulation would have been 4.8 per cent per annum rather than 5.0 per cent. Why is it that accumulation rates are *lower* under peacetime conditions? In large measure, this result reflects Japanese luck since she won the conflicts and the indemnities were enormous even as shares in GNP. Without those indemnities, the government would have had to increase her reliance on domestic borrowing which would have "crowded out" private capital formation, and this effect appears to dominate the augmentation of private accumulation that the tax relief would have fostered.

We conclude that Oshima's assertion is correct only when it is interpreted to hypothesize that accumulation would have been significantly augmented if taxes devoted to military expenditures had instead been used to increase public capital formation and retire the government debt, thereby enlarging the pool of investible saving relative to their historic levels. A comparable reduction in land taxes would have had the opposite effect, since the marginal private saving from augmented disposable incomes would not have offset the negative impact on saving associated with the loss in indemnities. It might be argued, therefore, that Meiji military luck explains some portion of the rapid accumulation rates prior to World War I. Furthermore, it has not passed unnoticed that the "investment biased" counterfactual is not unlike the policies in fact pursued by Japan after World War II. By systematically underestimating tax yields and keeping government consumption low, postwar public saving consistently accounted for 6 to 7 per cent of GNP, most of which was productively invested (Ackley and Ishi in Patrick and Rosovsky, 1976).

5. A Century of Accumulation—Good Fortune or State Policy?

This paper has offered some bold conjectures, several of which can be readily substantiated on the basis of our present knowledge. Some might better be labeled "working hypotheses" which must be tested by future quantitative research. One in this category is the interest-elasticity of the private saving function. In any case, before reviewing the conjectures made here, we wish to propose a new set of rules for theorizing about Japan's growth puzzle: *Ad hoc* theories tailored to specific historic episodes, Imperial Regimes, waves of innovation, and the American Occupation simply won't do. While such approaches make convenient and exciting historical narratives, they are not very useful additions to our body of economic knowledge regarding the determinants of secular rates of accumulation. This allegation applies equally well to late Meiji, interwar, or postwar historical analysis. Whatever theory seems to work well in accounting for post World War II experience, for example, should be sufficiently general to account for interwar and late Meiji experience as well. Using that rule as our guide, what factors appear to have been fairly consistent influences on Japan's accumulation performance over much of the past century? What explains the high rates of accumulation already reached by the 1880s, rates quite impressive when compared with the standards of the late nineteenth century or even with the contemporary Third World? To get answers with any quantitative content at all, Japanese economic historians must be more willing to model the accumulation process, to think in general equilibrium terms, and even to ask counterfactuals.

The availability of producer durables and intermediate industrial raw materials seems to have played a central role in accounting for rapid accumulation performance and even trend acceleration following the late 1880s. Of course, for some time now Japanese historians have stressed the availability of foreign exchange in ensuring a "ready" supply of imported industrial raw materials as well as foreign capital goods. Forces associated with balance of payments are obviously relevant in the short run, but we must dig deeper to account for long run trends in the "availability" of industrial raw materials and producer durables. In fact, what does account for the secular movements in the relative prices of these commodities? How much of their behavior can be attributed to endogenous forces and to pure chance? How much to state policy? We have found these relative price movements to have been very significant in accounting for Japanese accumulation experience over the past century, not just since the 1960s. Furthermore, while the behavior of raw material prices has never been subject to state control, we are less certain about the relative price of investment goods in general and producer durables in particular. Indeed, it would appear that the downward drift in the relative price of capital goods—apparently at an accelerating rate—must be explained primarily by forces indigenous to Japan.

This must be so since over the past century these critical price trends rarely coincided with trends elsewhere in North America or Europe. Unless state subsidies (in producer durables production relative to other sectors) mattered much more than the literature suggests, it must have been the relatively rapid and accelerating rate of total factor productivity growth in domestic producer durables production which matters in this accounting. But what accounts for this "unbalanced" rate of total factor productivity growth? Greater scope for scale economies? A larger scope for learning-by-doing?

Saving, not episodic changes in private sector investment demand, has always been the binding constraint on Japanese accumulation in the long run. What, then, explains the high rates of private saving in Meiji Japan and their secular rise over time? First and foremost are the unusual demographic conditions bequeathed from the Tokugawa period. Our analysis suggests that the high pre-World War II rates of private saving in the form of "productive" assets— that is, private wealth accumulation *net* of investment in dwellings—can be explained by the unusually low rates of population growth throughout the century, but especially in the late nineteenth and early twentieth centuries. To compare rapid Japanese accumulation with other developing countries, past or present, is a mistake unless the economies are standardized by a similar demographic yardstick. To make judgments about trend acceleration between 1890 and 1940 without similar demographic standardizations is also unwise.

What about the role of the state? To paraphrase Richard Rice (1977, p. 138), it has become increasingly fashionable in recent years to play down the role of the state, and one of the present authors may have appeared to have played a role in its demise (Kelley and Williamson, 1974). Lest the present paper be misinterpreted, we hasten to point out that there are three quite distinct questions raised here, and their answers suggest quite different evaluations of the "role of the state."[15] As far as macro policy goes, the volume of new

15. Recently, Martin Bronfenbrenner (1977, pp. 1–2) has characterized Japanese growth as an unstable process. He then cites previous work by one of the present authors (Kelley and Williamson, 1974) as a major example of "cliometric studies . . . [which] have come out strongly on the other side of the debate (p. 2)." The implication of his remarks is that we view Japanese growth as a stable historical process and that government policy mattered very little to that process. We believe he is wrong on both counts, and we hope the reader agrees upon careful examination of the present paper as well as the 1974 book by Kelley and Williamson. That we favor a different *model* than Bronfenbrenner is quite a separate issue.

government debt mattered a great deal to the rate of private accumulation in physical capital. We think that this statement holds true for the century as a whole, but thus far our research offers as concrete support only the first three decades following the 1880s. In any case, the three questions are as follows: (1) Can macro policy account for the "high" accumulation rates obtained in Japan throughout the past century? The answer is emphatically "No." Other forces were far more important and these were outside of state control. (2) Did macro policy influence accumulation performance, and was the influence positive? The answer here is emphatically "Yes." This is especially true of monetary policy prior to the 1920s, but tax-debt policy also had a role. (3) Did "state militarism" retard accumulation and growth? In the short run, it most assuredly did since war-related "stop-go" explains most of Japanese long swing experience and investment "spurts." In the longer run, at least during late Meiji, militarism appeared to *foster* accumulation. The explanation for this counterintuitive result, however, is hardly to be found among the "positive spillovers" listed recently by Kozo Yamamura.[16] Rather, they are to be explained by the enormous spoils awarded to Japan around the turn of the century.

UNIVERSITY OF WISCONSIN
BANK OF CANADA

16. Yamamura (1977) argues that the wars and "strong army" policy created arsenals, shipyards, and modern factories "which acted as highly effective centers for the absorption and dissemination of Western technologies and skills (p. 113)." In effect, Yamamura implies that these "unintended benefits of technological progress (p. 135)" were quantitatively significant. Yet, Yamamura supplies no such measurement, however tentative. Furthermore, the more relevant question is whether in the absence of wars and armament demand the heavy industrial sector might have grown even more rapidly in response to released private demand for producer durables. Indeed, why does the share of machinery production in total manufacturing output surge so dramatically *after* 1905 (footnote 4)? We think the answer is obvious—private sector accumulation.

REFERENCES

Abramovitz, M. "Rapid Growth Potential and Its Realization: The Experience of Capitalist Economies in the Postwar Period." Memorandum No. 211, Center for Research in Economic Growth, Stanford, California (March 1977).

Abramovitz, M. and David, P. "Reinterpreting Economic Growth: Parables and Realities." *American Economic Review* 58 (May 1973): 428–439.

Abramovitz, M. and David, P. "Economic Growth in America: Historical Parables and Realities." *De Economist* 121 (1973): 251–272.

Akino, M. and Hayami, Y. "Sources of Agricultural Growth in Japan: 1880–1965." Mimeographed. Tokyo: The Japan Economic Research Center, 1972.

Bairoch, P. "Europe's Gross National Product: 1800–1975." *Journal of European Economic History* 5 (Fall 1976): 273–340.

Bank of Japan. *Hundred-Year Statistics of the Japanese Economy*. Tokyo: 1966. Cited as *HYSJE*.

Blumenthal, T. "Exports and Economic Growth in Postwar Japan." *Quarterly Journal of Economics* 86 (November 1972): 617–631.

Bronfenbrenner, M. "A 'Marginal Efficiency' Theory of Japanese Economic Growth." Paper prepared for the Fifth World Congress of Economists (Tokyo, Japan: August-September 1977).

David, P. A. "Invention and Accumulation in America's Economic Growth: A Nineteenth Century Parable." Memorandum No. 199, Center for Research in Economic Growth, Stanford University, April 1976.

David, P. and Scadding, J. "Private Savings: Ultra Rationality, Aggregation and 'Denison's Law.'" *Journal of Political Economy* 82 (March 1974): 225–250.

de Bever, L. J. "The Role of the State in Early Japanese Growth." Doctoral Thesis. Department of Economics: The University of Wisconsin, 1976.

de Bever, L. J. and Williamson, J. G. "Accumulation and the State: Population Control, Militarism and Myths in Japanese History." Mimeographed. National Bureau of Economic Research: Stanford, California, 1976 and 1977 (revised).

Denison, E. F. and Chung, W. K. *How Japan's Economy Grew so Fast*. Washington, D.C.: The Brookings Institution, 1976.

Edelstein, M. "U.K. Savings in the Age of High Imperialism and After." *American Economic Review* 67 (February 1977): 288–294.

Emi, K. *Government Fiscal Activity and Economic Growth in Japan, 1868–1960.* Tokyo: Kinokuniya Bookstore, 1963.

Fei, J. C. H. and Ranis, G. "Agrarianism, Dualism, and Economic Development." In I. Adelman and E. Thorbecke, (eds.), *The Theory and Design of Economic Development.* Baltimore: The Johns Hopkins Press, 1966.

Foley, D. K. and Sidrauski, M. *Monetary and Fiscal Policy in a Growing Economy.* London: Collier-McMillan, 1971.

Hayami, Y. and Ruttan, V. *Agricultural Development: An International Perspective.* Baltimore: The Johns Hopkins Press, 1971.

Huber, R. "Effect on Prices of Japan's Entry into World Commerce after 1858." *Journal of Political Economy* 78 (May/June 1971): 614–628.

Jorgenson, D. W. "Testing Alternative Theories of the Development of a Dual Economy." In I. Adelman and E. Thorbecke (eds.), *The Theory and Design of Economic Development.* Baltimore: The Johns Hopkins Press, 1966.

Jorgenson, D. W. "Econometric Studies of Investment Behavior: A Survey." *Journal of Economic Literature* IX (December 1971): 1111–48.

Kelley, A. C. and Williamson, J. G. *Lessons from Japanese Development: An Analytical Economic History.* Chicago, University of Chicago Press, 1974.

Kelley, A. C., Williamson, J. G., and Cheetham, R. J. *Dualistic Economic Development: Theory and History.* Chicago, The University of Chicago Press, 1972.

Komiya, R. "Supply of Personal Savings." in R. Komiya (ed.), *Postwar Economic Growth in Japan.* Berkeley: University of California Press, 1966.

Landes, D. S. "Japan and Europe: Contrasts in Industrialization." In W. W. Lockwood (ed.), *The State and Economic Enterprise in Japan.* Princeton, N.J.: Princeton University Press, 1965.

Lockwood, W. W. *The Economic Development of Japan: Growth and Structural Change*. Princeton: Princeton University Press, 1968.

McKinnon, R. I. *Money and Capital in Economic Development*. Washington, D.C.: The Brookings Institution, 1973.

Minami, R. and Ono, A. "Economic Growth with Dual Structure: An Econometric Model of the Prewar Japanese Economy." Mimeographed. Tokyo: The Japan Economic Research Center, 1972.

Mizoguchi, T. *Personal Savings and Consumption in Postwar Japan*. Tokyo: Kinokuniya Bookstore, 1970.

Moulton, H. G. *Japan: An Economic and Financial Appraisal*. Washington, D.C.: The Brookings Institution, 1931.

Nakamura, J. I. *Agricultural Production and the Economic Development of Japan, 1873–1922*. Princeton, N.J.: Princeton University Press, 1966.

Nishimizu, M. and Hulten, C. R. "The Sources of Japanese Economic Growth: 1955–1971." Mimeographed. Department of Economics, The Johns Hopkins University, June 1976.

Odaka, K. "An Analysis of the Personal Consumption Expenditure in Japan, 1892–1967." Japan Economic Seminar, New Haven, Conn., April 27, 1974.

Ohbuchi, H. "Demographic Transition in the Process of Japanese Industrialization." In H. Patrick (ed.), *Japanese Industrialization and Its Social Consequences*. Berkeley, University of California Press, 1976.

Ohkawa, K. and Rosovsky, H. *Japanese Economic Growth: Trend Acceleration in the Twentieth Century*. Stanford: Stanford University Press, 1973.

Ohkawa, K., Shinohara, M. and Umemura, M. *Estimates of Long Term Economic Statistics of Japan Since 1868*. Vols. 3–12. Tokyo: Tokyo Keizai Shinpo Sha, 1966–72. Cited as *LTES*.

Ono, Y. "The Industrial Transition in Japan." *American Economic Association 5* (January 1890): 1–12.

Ono, A. and Watanabe, T. "Changes in Income Inequality in the Japanese Economy." In H. Patrick (ed.), *Japanese Industrialization and Its Social Consequences*. Berkeley, University of California Press, 1976.

Oshima, H. T. "Meiji Fiscal Policy and Agricultural Progress." In W. W. Lockwood (ed.), *The State and Economic Enterprise in Japan*. Princeton, N.J.: Princeton University Press, 1965.

Patrick, H. T. "Financial Development and Economic Growth in Underdeveloped Countries." *Economic Development and Cultural Change* 14 (January 1966).

Patrick, H. and Rosovsky, H. *Asia's New Giant: How the Japanese Economy Works*. Washington, D.C.: The Brookings Institution, 1976.

Rice, R. "Comment." *Journal of Economic History* 37 (March 1977): 136–38.

Saxonhouse, G. R. "Country Girls and Communication Among Competitors in the Japanese Cotton-Spinning Industry." In H. Patrick (ed.), *Japanese Industrialization and Its Social Consequences*. Berkeley, University of California Press, 1976.

Shinohara, M. "The Structure of Saving and the Consumption Function in Postwar Japan." *Journal of Political Economy* 67 (December 1959): 589–603.

Shinohara, M. "Causes and Patterns in the Postwar Growth." *The Developing Economies* 8 (December 1970): 349–68.

Tobin, J. "Money and Economic Growth." *Econometrica* 33 (October 1965): 671–84.

Watanabe, T. "Japan." In E. Fried and C. Schultze (eds.), *Higher Oil Prices and the World Economy*. Washington, D.C.: The Brookings Institution, 1975.

Williamson, J. G. "Personal Saving in Developing Nations: An Intertemporal Cross-Section from Asia." *The Economic Record* (June 1968): 194—210.

Williamson, J. G. *Late Nineteenth-Century American Development: A General Equilibrium History.* New York: Cambridge University Press, 1974.

Williamson, J. G. "Inequality, Accumulation, and Technological Imbalance: A Growth-Equity Conflict in American History?" Mimeographed. National Bureau of Economic Research. Stanford, California, 1977.

Williamson, J. G. and Lindert, P. H. *A Macroeconomic History of American Inequality.* Ongoing, 1977.

Yamamura, K. "Success Illgotten? The Role of Meiji Militarism in Japan's Technological Progress." *Journal of Economic History* 37 (March 1977): 113–33.

Yasuba, Y. "The Evolution of Dualistic Wage Structure." In H. Patrick (ed.), *Japanese Industrialization and Its Social Consequences.* Berkeley: University of California Press, 1976.

Yoshihara, K. "The Growth Rate as a Determinant of the Saving Ratio." *Hitotsubashi Journal of Economics* 12 (February 1972): 60–72.

Inequality, Accumulation, and Technological Imbalance: A Growth-Equity Conflict in American History?*

Jeffrey G. Williamson
University of Wisconsin

I. The Problem

Recent research on nineteenth-century America would appear to supply further confirmation of the classic correlation between accumulation and inequality. Indeed, the correlations among rising saving shares, accelerating accumulation rates, and trending inequality are sufficiently close to suggest support for the venerable interpretation of capitalist development which postulates conflict between growth and equity. Consider the evidence documenting both of these variables.

Table 1 establishes quantitatively that the early nineteenth century launched the American economy along a sharply rising trend in accumulation rates. Prior to 1805, nonhuman-wealth accumulation rates were very modest, at around 0.23% per annum in per capita terms. To be sure, the pace quickened up to 1835, but the biggest leap took place between 1835 and the end of the Civil War decade. The trend acceleration continued—but at retarding rates—until the turn of the century, after which the pace slowed down to a modest level not unlike the first 3 decades of the nineteenth century. Associated with this accumulation performance was a rise in current price gross saving rates in gross national product. By the early 1840s, the current price (gross) share was already 16%, but it surged to 28% by the end of the century. The rise was even greater in constant prices since the relative price of investment goods declined over the nineteenth century (table 2). Thus, whether measured in terms of gross domestic

* This paper was motivated by some of my previous work on American macrohistorical experience, but it has benefited considerably from criticisms supplied by my collaborator on American distribution research, Peter Lindert. The paper has also been improved by exposure to seminars at Berkeley, Stanford, and Wisconsin. In addition, the discussion contained in Section III owes much to Paul David's formulation of the problem. My thanks to all of these people.

Economic Development and Cultural Change

investment or gross domestic savings, capital-formation shares in constant prices rose by about 12 percentage points from the 1840s to the 1870s. Between 1839 and the turn of century, the rise was even more pronounced —about 18 percentage points—but it seems apparent that most of the drama was centered on the shorter period from the 1830s to the 1870s. In net terms, the rise was almost 10%, from 6% in 1839 to 15% in 1897.

How is this secular rise in capital-formation rates to be explained? English nineteenth-century economists thought the (alleged) inequality history of the Industrial Revolution supplied the ready answer. Simon Kuznets generalized on this theme in his celebrated article when he postulated that modern economic growth inevitably fostered inequality.[1] The accumulating inequality evidence on nineteenth-century America would appear to bear him out. Peter Lindert and myself have documented a surge in American inequality after 1820 measured by a whole range of (admit-

TABLE 1

WEALTH PER CAPITA AND CAPITAL PER WORKER
GROWTH RATES, 1685–1966
(% per annum)

Period	Private Physical Wealth per Capita (1967 $) (1)	Depreciable Capital per Laborer (1860 $) (2)	Reproducible Capital per Man-Hour (1840, 1860 $) (3)
1685–1805	.23	...	.77
1800–1835	...	...	1.60
1835–50	1.60	...	...
1805–50	...	2.17	...
1840–50	...	...	2.85
1855–71	...	2.63	...
1850–1900	1.90	...	...
1900–1966	1.20	1.00	...
1900–1958	...	...	...

SOURCES.—Col. 1 is based primarily on two sources. For 1774–1966, we use Alice Hanson Jones's "variant I" estimates ("Wealth Estimates for the American Middle Colonies, 1774," *Economic Development and Cultural Change* 18, pt. 2 [July 1970]: 135, table 53). These are economy-wide estimates, including land and structures, excluding cash, servants, and slaves. For 1685–1774, we use Russell Menard's eclectic estimates for Maryland and New England, applying population weights to derive an aggregate ("Comment on Papers by Ball and Walton," *Journal of Economic History* 36 [March 1976]: 124, table 3). Col. 2 is taken directly from Lance Davis et. al. (*American Economic Growth: An Economist's History of the United States* [New York: Harper & Row, 1972], p. 34, table 2.9), and excludes land. Col. 3 is derived from Moses Abramovitz and Paul David ("Reinterpreting Economic Growth: Parables and Realities," *American Economic Review* 58 [May 1973]: 431, table 2), net stock including land improvements.

[1] Simon Kuznets, "Economic Growth and Income Inequality," *American Economic Review* 45 (March 1955): 1–28.

Industrialization, Inequality and Economic Growth

Jeffrey G. Williamson

tedly imperfect) proxies.[2] Skill premiums rose sharply, wealth inequality surged, unskilled labor's share declined, and the real unskilled wage lagged behind overall economic growth (fig. 1).

American nineteenth-century history, therefore, supplies the classic evidence of a simultaneous rise in both inequality and accumulation rates. There is a venerable tradition in economic theory which appeals to this correlation to justify the conclusion that the investment requirements of early capitalist development can only be satisfied by the surplus generated by rising inequality. Indeed, such correlations from other countries and other times have suggested to many observers the operation of a "growth-equity trade-off." That is, increased inequality begot increased capital formation. Without the former, so the argument goes, the latter would never have followed, nor would modern economic growth have obtained

TABLE 2

GROSS AND NET REAL INVESTMENT SHARES, 1817–97
(in %)

YEAR OR PERIOD	GROSS INVESTMENT SHARE		D/Y	NET INVESTMENT SHARE		RELATIVE PRICE OF INVESTMENT GOODS
	Gallman (1)	Gallman-Davis (2)	(3)	Gallman (4)	Gallman-Davis (5)	Gallman (1860=100) (6)
1800–1835(1817)....	...	11	3.06	...	7.9	107.7
1834–43(1839)....	10	...	4.06	5.9	...	107.0
1839–48(1844)....	11	...	4.49	6.5	...	103.4
1844–53(1849)....	13	...	5.11	7.9	...	103.4
1849–58(1854)....	15	...	5.77	9.2	...	95.0
(1859)....	...	...	...	...	...	98.0
1869–78(1874)....	23	...	9.32	13.7	...	82.3
1874–83(1879)....	21	...	10.13	10.9	...	81.3
1879–88(1884)....	23	...	10.94	12.1	...	84.6
1884–93(1889)....	27	...	11.75	15.3	...	82.4
1889–98(1894)....	28	...	12.54	15.5	...	77.0
1890–1905(1897)....	...	28	13.03	...	15.0	73.3

NOTES AND SOURCES.—Constant 1860 prices, where cols. 1 and 2 refer to the U.S. gross domestic investment share in gross domestic product. Concepts include value added by home manufacturers and the value of farm improvements made with farm materials (Robert Gallman, "Gross National Product in the United States, 1834–1909," in *Output, Employment, and Productivity in the United States after 1800* [New York: National Bureau of Economic Research, 1966], p. 11, table 3, col. 3; and Paul David, "Invention and Accumulation in America's Economic Growth: A Nineteenth Century Parable," Memorandum no. 199 [Stanford, Calif.: Stanford University, April 1976], p. 25, table 4). The share of depreciation in gross domestic product, D/Y, is derived from $(D/Y = \delta\nu)$ linear interpolations on ν (the capital-output ratio) and δ (the depreciation rate) which David supplies for 1800–1835, 1835–55, 1855–90, and 1890–1905. Col. 6 is based on Gallman's implicit price deflators for gross investment in manufactured durables and new construction (p. 34, table A-3), and for gross national product (p. 26, table A-1). The observation for 1897 refers to 1894–1903.

[2] Peter H. Lindert and Jeffrey G. Williamson, "Three Centuries of American Inequality," in *Research in Economic History*, vol.1, ed. P. Uselding (Greenwich, Conn.: Johnson Associates, 1976). The evidence is supplied in far greater detail in our book, *A Macroeconomic History of American Inequality* (forthcoming), chaps. 2–5.

Economic Development and Cultural Change

the impressive rates now recorded in our history books. This paper will argue that such causal inferences are not only empirically unfounded but also probably totally wrong. If so, then the contemporary policy implications are embarrassingly obvious: The vast majority of historical analysts have written their histories of early capitalist systems assuming the presence of growth-equity conflicts when in fact such conflicts never really existed.

Sections II and III will present the theoretical framework which implements this controversial conclusion. The model is then utilized in Sections IV and V to decompose the sources of rising capital-formation shares in nineteenth-century America. The theme—the nonexistence of growth-equity conflicts in history—is resumed in a concluding section. Spurious correlation has been the villain of the piece far too long; the time has come to cast him out.

II. The Relative Price of Capital Goods and Unbalanced Total Factor Productivity Growth

The data document a greater rise in economy-wide investment shares when constant-price series are used in place of current prices. The explanation is

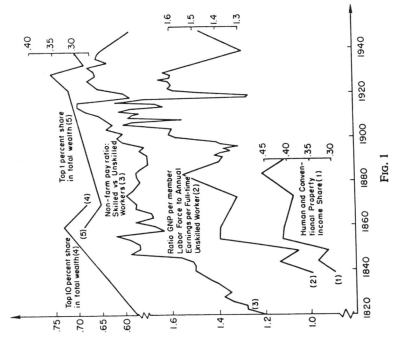

Fig. 1

Economic Development and Cultural Change

combination of two effects:[6] (1) a relatively dramatic downward shift in the supply function in the capital-goods sector due to technological discovery; and (2) the imposition of war tariffs which tended to raise the relative price of manufactured consumer goods compared to capital goods. Both of these effects would induce a decline in the relative price of producer durables, although the second of the two would tend to have the price decline concentrated later in the century during which the economy adjusted by induced capital formation over and above the antebellum rate. The first of these forces was likely to have been most fundamental.

Figure 2 should help clarify these technology-induced price effects emanating from the capital-goods sector.[7] The left-hand panel describes an asset market where capital is initially fixed in supply, at $K^*(0)$, and demand has its normal inverse relation to price, P_K. The market is assumed to be in equilibrium at $K^*(0)$ and $P_K^*(0)$. At this point, new capital goods are produced at a rate sufficient only to replace depreciated assets; that is, net investment is zero. The capital-goods sector is described in the right-hand panel. Now, let the supply function in the capital-goods sector shift downward due to relatively rapid total factor productivity growth there. If these shifts were sharp enough, a marked increase in investment would take place, as would the share of investment in GNP. The system would now be

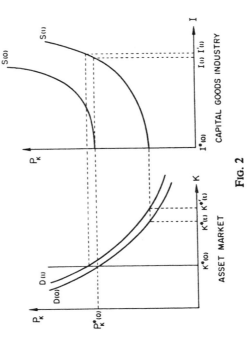

FIG. 2

[6] Williamson, *Late Nineteenth Century American Development*, pp. 106–7. As we shall see below, these relative-price trends account for much of the American nineteenth-century rise in accumulation rates. Recent work on Japan since the late Meiji suggests similar forces at work there (see Jeffrey G. Williamson and Leo J. DeBever, "Saving, Accumulation and Modern Economic Growth: The Contemporary Relevance of Japanese History," *Journal of Japanese Studies* 4 [Fall 1977]: 88–127, and "Accumulation and the State: Population Control, Militarism and Myths in Japanese History," mimeographed [Stanford, Calif.: National Bureau of Economic Research, November 1976]).
[7] Williamson, *Late Nineteenth Century American Development*, p. 108.

Jeffrey G. Williamson

in disequilibrium, and we would observe the following: The relative price of capital goods would decline over time; the "heavy-industry" (producer-durables) sector would enjoy relative expansion; the rate of capital accumulation would be high; and investment shares would be unusually large, especially in constant prices. If further downward shifts in the capital-goods sector supply function continued, the process might go on for some time. Obviously, the asset demand function could at the same time shift upward (to, say, $D[1]$), due either to an exogenous rise in saving rates or to a rise in profit rates on machines, or both. These additional forces will be examined shortly, but for the moment we note that the narrative is reinforced.[8]

Conventional neoclassical growth theory yields an explicit prediction regarding an economy's behavior in response to episodic changes in capital-goods prices. The equilibrium capital-labor and capital-output ratios rise. If for the moment we make the outrageous assumption of no subsequent technical progress and constant labor-force growth, then the rate of capital-stock growth declines from the initial high levels to a rate asymptotically approaching the constant labor-force growth. As a result, the rate of real output growth per worker must decline over time. Perhaps even more pertinent to our search for explanations of the nineteenth-century saving behavior, conventional growth theory would also predict a decline in the net rate of return to capital over time.

If the net rate of return to capital should decline over time in response to technology-induced cost improvements in the investment-goods sector, what about returns to equity capital and real interest rates? Following the initial shock, the rate of return to equity capital should rise to high levels. Economic intuition should suggest that result, but a little formalism may help that intuition along. Let r be the net rental rate on capital, $P = (P_K/P_Y)$ be the price of capital goods relative to GNP, and i be "the" interest rate. In equilibrium, $r = P \cdot i$. We propose to disturb that equilibrium by lowering capital-goods prices. Initially, interest rates (the nominal cost of funds) should rise in response to the decline in capital-goods relative price. This is so since holding the capital-labor ratio, and thus r, constant in the short-run yields $dr = P \cdot di + i \cdot dP = 0$, or $di/i = -(dP/P)$. Indeed, to maintain short-run equilibrium, interest rates must rise at a rate equal to the percent by which relative capital-goods prices decline. At the same net rental rate on capital, we would observe more saving to the extent that saving is responsive to the interest rate. There is abundant evidence to support the prediction of rising interest rates following precipitous declines in P. Consider two "blue chip" bonds. The average yield (adjusted for expected price

---

[8] There is a minor exception. If $D(i)$ shifted outward, the relative price of capital goods would first rise before undergoing its long-term secular fall. The relative stability of capital-goods prices through the 1840s would seem to be consistent with a rise in $D(i)$. Obviously, the cost reductions in the capital goods sector may be induced either by technological discovery or by scale economies.

Economic Development and Cultural Change

inflation) on federal bonds between 1845 and 1861 was 3.91%, while the comparable figure for 1867–78 was 8.85%.[9] New England municipal bonds exhibit a similar increase, from 4.08% to 9.82%. Those economic historians who hold to the plausible view that aggregate saving is positively influenced by real interest rates will welcome this evidence.[10] Their rise between the 1840s and the 1870s is certainly consistent with the observed discontinuity in the saving rate. Clearly, we must add the interest-rate hypothesis to our list of potential explanations for the episodic rise in nineteenth-century saving rates.

Recall, however, the long-run predictions of conventional growth theory *after* the initial capital-goods relative-price shock, when rising capital-formation shares begin to have their impact on the net rental rate on capital itself. With the subsequent capital accumulation, the net rate of return declines, as do interest rates. Indeed, the decline in both nominal and effective interest rates from the 1870s to the turn of the century is well known. The important issue, then, is what happened to the net rate of return from the early to the late nineteenth century. Paul David supplies an estimate: The average real net profit rate on conventional reproducible assets fell from 10.5% in the 1800–1835 period to 6.6% around the turn of the century.[11]

This discussion should be adequate to set the stage for what follows. We have the following nineteenth-century historical events to explain: a rise in the net real share of saving in real gross product from 6% or 8% to 15%, a fall (due to unbalanced rates of total factor productivity growth) in the relative price of investment goods by 31% and a fall in the net rate of return from 10.5% to 6.6%. A number of hypotheses have emerged from the discussion which, in concert, might account for the events enumerated. The next section will attempt to introduce those hypotheses into a consistent formal framework. We hope not only to isolate the causes of the nineteenth-century rise in accumulation rates but also to supply estimates of the role of trending inequality in accounting for the rise in saving. If the role can be shown to be minor, then we will have undermined empirical support for a growth-equity trade-off in America. We will also supply evidence along the way for an alternative endogenous explanation of accumulation which, in concert with rising accumulation rates, will appeal to other forces driving both variables.

[9] Williamson, *Late Nineteenth Century American Development*, p. 109.

[10] For an excellent review of the historical evidence on the interest (or rate of return) elastic saving hypothesis, see Michael Edelstein, "U.K. Savings in the Age of High Imperialism and After," *American Economic Review* 67 (February 1977): 288–94. We shall rely on some of Edelstein's econometric results below.

[11] Paul A. David, "Invention and Accumulation in America's Economic Growth: A Nineteenth Century Parable," Memorandum no. 199 (Stanford, Calif.: Stanford University, April 1976), p. 41.

III. Modeling Nineteenth-Century Accumulation

Models of saving and accumulation can be classified according to three attributes. First, is saving viewed as an "active" constraint on accumulation or does it passively respond to investment demand? Second, if saving is viewed as an active constraint, how elastic is aggregate saving to rates of return, if at all? Third, does the supply of investment goods play an active and systematic role as an additional influence on the rate of physical accumulation? While the literature often takes an extreme position on each of these attributes, figure 3 offers a more eclectic view which, we believe, is more consistent with nineteenth-century trends.

The saving rate, (I/Y), is written on the horizontal axis where it is to be understood that *net* real saving (or investment) ratios are being measured. The rise from A to E roughly corresponds to the near doubling in the net real savings rate in America, from 6% or 8% in the 1830s to 15% at the turn of the century. The decline in the net rate of return on reproducible capital, from r_0 to r_1, roughly corresponds to the observed fall from 10.5% to 6.6% over the same time period documented by David. We allow some positive slope to the saving function so that a rise in net rates of return induces additional investment. The elasticity is kept small intentionally since there is no econometric evidence supporting the alternative, elastic view.[12] Suppose the investment demand function shifts to the right in re-

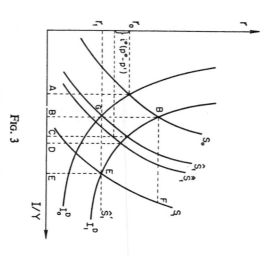

Fig. 3

[12] Contemporary evidence abounds, although these econometric results suffer from at least three flaws. First, the simultaneous equations bias insures an understatement of the estimated elasticity. Second, the independent variable used is the interest rate in money markets rather than rates of return to equity. Third, Edelstein's results suggest that nineteenth-century elasticities were far higher than those for the twentieth century at least in high-income economies (see Edelstein; Nathaniel Leff and Kazuo Sato, "A Simultaneous Equations Model of Savings in Developing Countries," *Journal of*

Economic Development and Cultural Change

sponse to two basic forces. First, the rate of labor-force growth rises. According to Lebergott, the total labor force grew at 2.67% per annum between 1800 and 1830.[13] The rate accelerated in the middle third of the century: The per annum rate was 3.3% between 1830 and 1860. The acceleration is even more striking for the free labor force which rose from 2.2% to 3.6% per annum between the same two periods. There is reason to believe, therefore, that this trend acceleration fostered a rise in accumulation rates during the first half of the century by shifting investment demand to the right, raising the net rate of return, and inducing increased net saving rates. Labor-force growth will not, however, help us explain the continued shift in investment demand later in the century since, as is well known, labor-force growth rates declined after the Civil War. Second, the investment demand function may shift to the right in response to an *increased* rate of labor-saving (capital-using) technical change. A number of forces can be documented that would yield this result, some appealing to labor saving within industries and some appealing to forces which shifted the output mix in a direction which favored skills and machines. Elsewhere Lindert and I have stressed one force in particular: Unbalanced rates of nineteenth-century total factor productivity growth can be shown to favor those sectors utilizing capital and skills most intensively and unskilled labor least intensively.[14] This form of unbalanced technological progress unleashed two forces: (1) it tended to foster inequality trends, and (2) it raised the aggregate demand for investment goods as those sectors using machines (and skills) intensively expanded. We shall be far more precise in identifying the shift in I^D below, but for the moment note the predictions of figure 3. First, saving rates rise in response to the rise in investment demand. The investment ratio increases from A to B. Second, the saving function shifts to the right in response to three forces: (1) the rise in inequality induced by labor-saving technical change and rapid unskilled labor-force growth, both exogenous forces; (2) an exogenous shift in the saving function due to changes in attitudes toward thrift and/or improvements in savings mobilization; and (3) the shift in the saving function in response to declining relative capital-goods prices. We shall have more to say about these three forces below, but they all in combination should contribute to a shift from B to F. Third, successful accumulation should drive down the net rate of return over the century, thus cutting the saving ratio back from F to E. It should be stressed that the rise in inequality is reinforced by two additional forces. Since producer durable production is itself capital-cum-skill in-

Political Economy 83, no. 3 [June 1975]: 1217–28; and Colin Wright, "Some Evidence on the Interest Elasticity of Consumption," *American Economic Review* 57 [September 1967]: 850–55).

[13] Stanley Lebergott, "Labor Force and Employment, 1800–1960," in *Output, Employment and Productivity in the United States after 1800* (New York: National Bureau of Economic Research, 1966), pp. 117–210.

[14] Williamson and Lindert, *A Macroeconomic History of American Inequality* (n. 2 above), chaps. 6 and 7.

tensive,[15] the rise in the investment share implies further unskilled-labor saving and inequality. In addition, the accumulation of machines induces a rising demand for skills, if skills and machines are complements in production, and thus skill premiums, wage differentials, and earnings inequality are given an added boost.

It should be noted, incidentally, that a perfectly elastic savings schedule cannot be defended by an appeal to nineteenth-century capital flows from abroad. Such an argument is cast by reference to $\hat{S}'_1$ and $\hat{S}_1$ in figure 3. The savings function $\hat{S}_1$ would represent the function aggregated to include the postulated elastic supply of finance from Europe. This characterization would attribute a significant portion of the rise in domestic investment ratios, $(E - G)$ to be precise, to foreign capital. There is no evidence to support such an interpretation. Except for some brief critical episodes in the first half of the nineteenth century, foreign investment was always a small share of total domestic investment in America, never exceeding 5% after the 1830s, and in any case the share declines over time.[16] Indeed, to use foreign capital to defend the elastic savings specification would place far more weight on the efficient operation of international capital markets than the historical evidence can support.[17]

Let us now elaborate the narrative suggested by figure 3. The model accounts for these six forces: (1) technical progress with a capital-deepening (labor-saving) bias; (2) an acceleration in the rate of labor-force growth for the first two-thirds of the century; (3) inelastic (but not completely) savings response to rates of return; (4) a distributive impact on saving; (5) a role for the decline in relative capital-goods prices, a phenomenon of which much was made in Section II; and (6) a role for exogenous savings mobilization and changing attitudes towards thrift. While figure 3 will be given empirical content in the following section, we shall deal now with its qualitative predictions. Following David's modern restatement of an older tradition, "the investment demand schedule was not elastic and therefore must have shifted to the right as a consequence of conventional capital-deepening bias in the progress of Invention during the nineteenth century."[18] We certainly have no argument with this general view, although

[15] Detailed evidence on direct and indirect factor intensity rankings of American output bundles can be found in ibid., chap. 8 and in Jeffrey G. Williamson, "Who Pays for the Services of the Working Poor?" Institute for Research on Poverty Discussion Paper no. 334–76 (Madison: University of Wisconsin, February 1976).

[16] Robert E. Gallman, "Gross National Product in the United States, 1834–1909," in *Output, Employment, and Productivity in the United States after 1800* (New York: National Bureau of Economic Research, 1966), pp. 14–15.

[17] Michael Edelstein, "The Determinants of U.K. Investment Abroad, 1870–1913: The U.S. Case," *Journal of Economic History* 34 (December 1974): 980–1007.

[18] David, "Invention and Accumulation in America's Economic Growth," p. 41. David has made much of the microeconomic sources of labor saving in his *Technical Choice, Innovation and Economic Growth* (Cambridge: Cambridge University Press, 1975). As the text indicates, our interpretation of aggregate labor saving relies instead on

Economic Development and Cultural Change

our rationalization of the unskilled labor-saving bias is quite different than his. We attribute the lion's share of the increased rate of labor saving after 1820 to two sources: a shift to capital-cum-skill-intensive sectors in response to a higher rate of total factor productivity there in general, and the shift within the nonfarm commodity-producing sector to investment-goods production, in particular producer-durables production, for the same reason. In addition, some of the shift in the investment demand function must also have been assigned to the acceleration in labor-force growth rates. A key point of departure, however, is this: If unskilled-labor saving plays a role in shifting I^p to the right, it must also do the same for the saving schedule. Surely the inequality induced by labor saving must have had some positive impact on savings. The question is, how much?

We can perform a simple calculation on the maximum potential impact of distribution on saving. We emphasize the word "maximum." We wish to err on the high side in the calculation since, if even then distribution is shown to have had a minor impact on aggregate saving, we shall have presented the strongest case against the growth-equity trade-off position. Assume that all saving in reproducible assets (we ignore human-capital formation here) has its source in nonlabor income. This is no more than the extreme Classical-Cambridge postulate which plays such an important role in contemporary growth and development models as well as in Kuznets's search for capital-accumulation theories.[19] Elsewhere

the endogenous determinants of shifting output mix. In contrast with David's approach, which is typical of the development literature, our general equilibrium approach offers an endogenous explanation for changes in the *rate* of labor saving economy-wide.

[19] Kuznets, *Capital in the American Economy* (n. 5 above). Kuznets would reject our Marxian, or modern Cambridge, assumption as far too extreme, although he looks with favor on the view that inequality may foster rising net saving rates economy-wide. Kuznets's empirical translation of the Marx-Ricardo-Robinson saving postulate can best be stated in his own words: "We might divide the whole body of personal savers into two groups: the overwhelming majority—say, the lower 95 percent classified by their relatively permanent income position—who perhaps account for 80 percent of income and 50 percent of total personal net savings; and the top 5 percent who account for the other 50 percent of total personal savings. A countrywide (net) savings-income rate of 10 percent under these conditions implies a savings-income ratio of about 6 percent . . . for the lower 95 percent, and of 25 percent . . . for the top 5 percent. The figures are illustrative, intended only to suggest the broad lines of the dichotomy" (p. 100). While the figures may have been used only to "illustrate" the impact of changing distribution on saving, the example has been repeated often enough to have gained the status of "fact." Some empirical confirmation of the postulate on contemporary data drawn from the Third World can be found in Hendrick S. Houthakker ("On Some Determinants of Savings in Developed and Underdeveloped Countries," in *Problems in Economic Development*, ed. E. A. G. Robinson [New York: Macmillan, 1965]) and Jeffrey G. Williamson ("Personal Savings in Developing Nations," *Economic Record* 44 [June 1968]: 194–210), although there has been further confirmation in studies done since the mid-1960s. In short, the assumptions used in the text must indeed be viewed as an upper bound on the impact of changing distribution on changing net saving rates in nineteenth-century America. This must be so, even if we recognize that the distribution of human- and nonhuman-property income itself became more unequal concomitant with the shift of income away from unskilled labor. After all, Allen Kelley's analysis of urban workers for the late nineteenth century has shown that saving rates out of average urban

Lindert and I have supplied some estimates of trends in unskilled labor's share in national income over the nineteenth century where it can be seen that labor's share (θ_L) declined by approximately 11 percentage points over the half century following 1839–40.[20] The vast majority of the decline took place by the 1880s. Indeed, the share fell by almost 16 percentage points up to 1879–88. Let the constant net saving rate out of property (human and nonhuman) income be denoted by s_p, the initial aggregate saving ratio by $\hat{s}_1$. Holding the rate of return constant, the primitive classical saving model would then predict

$$S_0 = \theta_L(s_L) + \theta_K(s_p)$$
$$= .704(0) + .296(s_p) = .08$$
$$\therefore s_p = (.08)(.296)^{-1} \cong .27$$
$$\hat{s}_1 = .593(0) + .407(.27) \cong .11 .$$

We would therefore estimate distribution at maximum to have raised aggregate net saving rates from .08 to .11 from the 1830s to the 1890s, ceteris paribus. It is an upper-bound statement about the shift in the saving function, not a statement about equilibrium values. Alternatively, we note that the rise in equilibrium net investment ratios was more or less complete by 1869–78, as was the inequality surge. Nonetheless, the calculations over the longer period will serve well enough for the moment: Section V will decompose the nineteenth century into shorter "episodic" parts. Now if the observed change in distribution was explained entirely by a labor-saving bias, the above calculation on $\hat{s}_1$ would indeed supply an upper-bound estimate of the "induced-distribution" shift in the aggregate saving function. To some readers the calculation may appear to understate the distribution influence since the initial inequality bias is offset in figure 3 by conventional accumulation, the subsequent decline in r from high disequilibrium levels, and the offsetting decline in θ_K which would inevitably follow. Indeed, this tale is consistent with the inequality facts (fig. 1) which show the surge in inequality arrested by the end of the 1870s and a very modest drift toward equality thereafter up to the turn of the century. It will be understood, therefore, that $\hat{s}_1$ refers to the net inequality trends which accumulate to the end of the disequilibrium period.

We are now equipped to decompose qualitatively the sources of rising nineteenth-century saving rates depicted in figure 3. Biased technological

workers' incomes were indeed far in excess of zero, negating the extreme class-saving characterization implied by our experiment (see Allen C. Kelley, "Demographic Changes and American Economic Development," in Research Reports of the Commission on Population Growth and the American Future: Economic Aspects of Population Change [Washington, D.C.: Government Printing Office, 1972]).
20 Williamson and Lindert, A Macroeconomic History of American Inequality, table 3.3, and fig. 1 above.

Economic Development and Cultural Change

progress and labor-force growth induces an increase in net saving ratios equal to $(D - A)$. This in turn is composed of three parts.

A. Impact of investment demand on saving. Labor-saving technological change and acceleration in labor-force growth shift the investment demand function to the right. If the saving function is held fixed, the net investment ratio would rise to B if some elasticity with respect to r is granted.

B. Induced distribution impact on saving. The same labor-saving technological progress tends to induce increased inequality and thus causes the saving function to shift to the right to $\hat{S}_1$. This shift in the investment ratio is forthcoming $(C - B)$. This must be viewed as an endogenous saving response to the same technological forces that are driving I^p. As we have argued above, the inequality effect may be in addition reinforced by the rise in investment-goods production and by capital-skill complementary forces.

C. Increased saving induced by declining capital-goods prices. Technological change was also biased in favor of the capital-goods sector. This lowered the relative price of capital goods and thus raised the level of saving forthcoming at any given r. The induced saving response amounts to $(D - C)$. The remaining shift in saving $(E - D)$ is the residual exogenous shift due to financial intermediation, mobilization, government debt-tax policy, external capital flows, and changing attitudes toward thrift.

The mechanism which translates the decline in the relative price of investment goods into a saving response requires some amplification. While Section II noted that this sharp decline has been appreciated for some time now, David has recently made the link more explicit (see n. 21 below). In equilibrium $r = P \cdot i$, so that $(r_0 - r_1) = P_1(i_0 - i_1) + i_0(P_0 - P_1)$. It is the second term in this expression, $i_0(P_0 - P_1)$, which motivates the saving response to declining relative capital-goods prices. In effect, the same saving would be forthcoming at $r_0 - i_0(P_0 - P_1)$ as would be forthcoming at r_0 prior to the decline in capital-goods prices. This induced effect is translated in figure 3 into a shift in the saving function from $\hat{S}_1$ to $\hat{\hat{S}}_1$, thus fostering a rise in the investment ratio equal to $(D - C)$.

IV. Decomposing the Sources of Rising Nineteenth-Century Net Investment Rates: The Long View

We require only two parameters to impart empirical content to figure 3: the saving and investment elasticities with respect to r. If we assume constant elasticities over relevant ranges for both functions, then we have (where I^p, S, T, Z are now written as *shares* in Y) in absolutes: $I^p = Tr'$, $S = Zr''$, and $S = I^p$; and in rates of change: $\dot{I}^p = \dot{T} + \epsilon'\dot{r}$, $\dot{S} = \dot{Z} + \eta'\dot{r}$, and $\dot{I}^p = \dot{S}$. It can be shown that $\epsilon = -\sigma$, where σ is the elasticity of substitution in a CES production function.[21] Since the twentieth-century econometric evidence supports unambiguously the assertion $0 < \sigma < 1$, we shall restrict our attention to experiments where $-1 < \epsilon < 0$. Initially, we set $\epsilon = -0.5$. Similarly, we insist that saving exhibits a fairly inelastic response to rates of return, so that our experiments are restricted to cases where $0 < \eta \leq 1$. Based on the contemporary econometric estimates in general and those applied to the Goldsmith data 1897-1949 in particular,[22] to explore cases where $\eta > 1$ would amount to an irrelevant exercise. Do we have any additional information about the magnitude of the "interest" elasticity of saving? A recent econometric study of the United Kingdom offers some guidelines.[23] Under various models of saving behavior, the long-run elasticities range between 0.11, 0.37, 0.60, and 0.70 for the period 1870-1965 as a whole. For the period 1870-1913, however, Edelstein finds η approximately equal to unity. The (admittedly limited) evidence suggests that nineteenth-century interest elasticities were higher than twentieth-century elasticities and thus we initially set $\eta = 1.0$.

We have the following data on (assumed) equilibrium values between the 1830s and the turn of the century: $\dot{r} = (.066 - .105)/.105 = -.371$, $\dot{I^D}(\equiv \dot{S}) = (.15 - .08)/.08 = +.875$. We can also solve for the shift in the investment demand schedule: $\dot{T} = \dot{I^D} - \dot{\epsilon^I} = +.6895$. In summary, for what we shall label case 1A, we have $\dot{r} = -.371$, $\dot{I^D} = +.875$, $\dot{T} = +.6895$, $\eta = +1.0$, and $\epsilon = -0.5$.

We can now decompose the rising net saving rate into its four components. First, the impact of investment demand shifts on saving in figure 3 $(B - A): \dot{S} = \eta[-\dot{T}/(\epsilon - \eta)] = +.4597, S(\equiv I)$ rises from .08 to .168, or $(B - A) = .0368$. Second, the (maximum) induced impact on

[21] Paul David's elegant statement in "Invention and Accumulation in America's Economic Growth" (n. 11 above) is useful at this point. Let the economy be characterized by the CES production function:

$$Y = [\alpha(E_L L)^{1-1/\epsilon} + \beta(E_K K)^{1-1/\epsilon}]^{\epsilon/(\epsilon-1)}[E_R R]^{\theta_R},$$

where the E_i refer to levels of factor augmentation through technical progress; L, K and R refer to unskilled labor, capital, and land, respectively; σ is the elasticity of substitution between K and L; and the θ_j are factor shares. If we focus on long-run equilibrium, then the ratio of net investment to output, I^D, can be written as $I^D = \nu(r)G$, where ν is the capital-output ratio and G is a constant. Influences on G can be seen in the expression,

$$G = (\dot{L} + \dot{E_L})[\theta_L/(1 - \theta_K)] + \dot{R}[\theta_R/(1 - \theta_K)].$$ The capital-output ratio is related to the rental rate on capital by $\nu = Br^{-\sigma}$. Thus, $I^D = Br^{-\sigma}G$, and so $\epsilon = -\sigma$.

[22] The reference is to Wright's (n. 12 above) estimates of positive but low interest elasticity of saving using Raymond Goldsmith's data for the United States, 1897-1949. For those who feel that this assumption embodies too much "elasticity optimism," recall that we are describing saving behavior, not just household saving behavior. There is reason to believe that firm reinvestment rates are far more sensitive to rates of return than households. This presumption has been confirmed by the more recent research reported by Edelstein.[23]

[23] Edelstein, "U.K. Savings in the Age of High Imperialism" (n. 10 above).

Economic Development and Cultural Change

saving due to distribution effects alone, $\dot{Z}_D$: $\dot{Z}_D = (.11 - .08)/.08 = +.375$, $\dot{S} = \epsilon \dot{Z}_D/(\epsilon - \eta) = +.125$, $S(=I)$ rises from .1168 to .1314, or $(C - B) = .0146$. Third, the impact of declining capital-goods prices on saving, $(D - C)$, can be easily determined when we recall $(P_1 - P_0) = (.69 - 1.00) = -.31$. Thus, $\dot{r}^* = -.31$ from the decline in capital-goods prices. It follows that its impact is $\dot{I}^\nu = \epsilon \dot{r}^* = +.155$, $S(=I)$ rises from .1314 at C to .1518 at D, or $(D - C) = .0204$. Fourth, the residual due to exogenous saving mobilization is -.0018. A summary appears in table 3.

What do we conclude from this experiment? Case 1A in table 3 suggests that the vast majority of rising saving rates in nineteenth-century America were technology or labor-force growth induced. The portion attributable to exogenous saving mobilization is trivial and negative, a result in sharp contrast with Ronald McKinnon's emphasis on the operation of capital markets in developing economies.[24] That the mobilization effect is negative may encourage some to reject the experiment as implausible. We hasten to remind the reader of two facts which can readily account for the negative residual. First, the distribution experiment is an *upper bound* (a maximum value for $\dot{Z}_D$ is assumed), and thus the residual saving mobilization component is a lower bound. Second, recall that the foreign investment share in American gross domestic capital formation *fell* over the nineteenth century. Foreign investment never did augment domestic savings by more than 5% or so in the most buoyant antebellum years, but the

TABLE 3

DECOMPOSING THE SOURCES OF RISING NINETEENTH-CENTURY NET INVESTMENT RATES: THE LONG VIEW

	CASE 1A	CASE 1B	CASE 1C	CASE 1D	CASE 2	CASE 3
	$\epsilon = -.5$ $\eta = 1.0$	$\epsilon = -.3$ $\eta = 1.0$	$\epsilon = -.7$ $\eta = 1.0$	$\epsilon = -.5$ $\eta = .5$	$\epsilon = -.5$ $\eta = 0$	$\epsilon = -.5$ $\eta = \infty$
Total increase in net saving ratio.........	.0700	.0700	.0700	.0700	.0700	.0700
1. Technology and labor-force induced..	.0718	.0708	.0828	.0676	.0471	.0762
A. Investment demand impact $(B-A)$.........	.0368	.0470	.0359	.0276	0	.0552
B. Distribution impact $(C-B)$......	.0146	.0110	.0179	.0202	.0300	0
C. Decline in capital-goods prices impact $(D-C)$.	.0204	.0128	.0290	.0198	.0171	.0210
2. Residual mobilization impact $(E-D)$.	-.0018	-.0008	-.0128	.0024	.0229	-.0062

SOURCE.—See text.

[24] Ronald I. McKinnon, *Money and Capital in Economic Development* (Washington, D.C.: Brookings Institution, 1973).

share declined over time so that by the turn of the century America became a net capital exporter. Thus, the negative residual in case 1A may simply reflect the drift towards self-financing over the nineteenth century. In any case, the maximum impact of changing inequality on rising saving rates is also quite modest, only one-fifth of the total increase. In contrast, the labor-saving bias in technical change along with labor-force growth tended to account for more than half the observed rise in net saving rates, while the technology-induced decline in relative capital-goods prices accounted for almost a third. The experiment suggests only the weakest support for the growth-equity trade-off, certainly much too weak to warrant the attention lavished on it in the historical and development literature.

Cases 1B-1D offer some alternative experiments with various values of $-1 < \epsilon < 0$ and $0 < \eta \leq 1$. How robust are the results of case 1A? In no case does the (upper bound) impact of distribution on saving ratios exceed one-quarter of the total increase in saving ratios over the nineteenth century. Once again, although the inequality trends were quite pronounced after the 1830s, they must have made a relatively minor contribution to the total rise in net saving ratios over the nineteenth century. In every case, at least 95% of the observed rise in saving rates can be attributed to the combined influences of the three effects induced by technology and labor-force growth. Exogenous savings mobilization, never plays a significant role in any experiment.

Table 3 also presents two additional cases which we view to be extreme. Case 2 allows the saving function to be completely inelastic with respect to r. We view this case to be wide of reality, not only because we believe that nineteenth-century firms did respond positively to rising net returns on equity, but also because the assumption predicts a rise in r in response to shifts in I^P which cannot be established by fact. That is, the rise in r prior to subsequent accumulation induced by distribution and mobilization would have been $\dot{r} = \dot{T}/(\eta - \epsilon) = +1.379$, or r should have risen from 10.5% to almost 25%! Although the specification ($\eta = 0$) seems grossly unrealistic, even here distribution changes account for only 40% of the total increase in net saving ratios. The key difference between case 2 and case 1A is that the labor-saving investment demand impact is zero and exogenous saving mobilization usurps its role completely. Case 3 assumes a perfectly elastic saving function with respect to r. Here, of course, distribution has no impact at all.

V. Decomposing the Sources of Rising Nineteenth-Century Net Investment Rates: Shorter-Run Episodic Phases

Table 2 suggests some difficulty in reconciling David's estimate of the 1800-1835 net investment share (7.9%) with Gallman's for 1834-43 (5.9%), but both record a comparable total increase across the nineteenth century as a whole. The advantage of Gallman's series is obvious: It supplies evidence on episodic phases of saving-rate experience. The net investment rate in America did not drift upward smoothly across the nineteenth century but rather surged upward in two apparently quite distinct phases. Between ca. 1839 and ca. 1854, it rose by 3.3 percentage points or by 0.22% per annum. During the late nineteenth century the rise was more modest, 1.3 percentage points up to 1897 or by 0.06% per annum. Were the sources of the rise more or less the same in each of these three episodes? More to the point of this paper, did the antebellum surge in inequality account for far more of the rise in net investment rates prior to the Civil War? While Section IV showed that inequality trends cannot account for a very large share of the quickening in accumulation rates across the nineteenth century as a whole, was it a far more critical influence in the first half of the century? Can a stronger argument be made for the growth-equity trade-off early in America's modern economic growth?

Using the assumptions and methodology of case 1A in Section IV, there is no reason why we cannot decompose the sources of rising net investment rates in each of these three nineteenth-century episodes. All we require are the estimates of r in table 4, and the results of the numerical experiment are reported in table 5. They are enlightening, to say the least.

The sources of the rise in Gallman's net investment rate for the 6 decades as a whole (ca. 1839–97) are more or less the same as those previously calculated in table 3 on slightly different data and for a somewhat longer period (ca. 1817–97). Once again, savings mobilization plays a trivial role, accounting for only a very small share of the total increase.

TABLE 4

IMPLIED NET RATES OF RETURN ON REPRODUCIBLE CAPITAL STOCK: ca. 1817–97

Year or Period	θ_K	v	δ	$\hat{r}$
1800–1835 (ca. 1817)......	.23	1.80	.0170	.1108
(1835)......	(.25)	(1.90)	(.0195)	(.1121)
1835–55......	.27	2.19	.0209	.1024
(1855)......	(.32)	(2.48)	(.0238)	(.1052)
1855–71......	.34	2.80	.0261	.0953
(1871)......	(.34)	(3.11)	(.0284)	(.0809)
1871–90......	.35	3.31	.0312	.0745
1890–1905 (ca. 1897)......	.37	3.62	.0360	.0662

SOURCES AND NOTES.—All figures in parentheses are linear interpolations, except for the 1855 estimate of θ_K. Judged by my research with Peter Lindert (*A Macroeconomic History of American Inequality* [forthcoming], table 3.3), almost all of the rise in θ_K between 1835–55 and 1855–71 must have been centered on the 1845–55 period. The 1855 estimate of $\hat{\theta}_K$ is adjusted accordingly. The net rate of profit on the reproducible capital stock can be written as $r = (\theta_K/v) - \delta$, where θ_K = the "conventional" reproducible capital share, taken from Moses Abramovitz and Paul David ("Reinterpreting Economic Growth: Parables and Realities," *American Economic Review* 58 [May 1973]: 431, table 2); v = the capital-output ratio; 1800–1835 and 1890–1905 are taken from Paul David ("Invention and Accumulation in America's Economic Growth: A Nineteenth Century Parable," Memorandum no. 199 [Stanford, Calif.: Stanford University, April 1976], p. 25, table 4); intervening dates derived from capital stock and output growth rates $(\overset{*}{K}, \overset{*}{Y})$ in Abramovitz and David (p. 431, table 2); and δ = the depreciation rate on reproducible capital from David, (p. 25, table 4).

Furthermore, the combined influence of rising investment demand and declining relative capital-goods prices accounts for the lion's share of the increase, 6.9 of the 9.1 percentage points. Rising inequality fails to play a very important role, 1.6 of the 9.1 percentage points, even though we continue to adopt the classical saving assumption which maximizes the potential impact of distribution. On the other hand, rising inequality does play a more important role in accounting for rising saving rates during the antebellum period when inequality was on an especially steep trend. Even here, however, a shifting distribution at a maximum accounts for only a third of the rise in net savings ratios (1.1 of the 3.3 percentage points). While some readers may wish to debate my interpretation, it seems to me that increasing inequality was hardly the main source of rising accumulation rates even very early in American modern economic growth when inequality was sharply on the rise.

Note, however, the changing sources of rising net real investment rates from period to period. The residual mobilization impact was apparently fairly important, although still not the dominant influence between the 1850s and the 1870s. This result is certainly comforting to this author, who recently argued that the Civil War was indeed a watershed in accumulation performance.[25] A portion of these relatively strong "mo-

TABLE 5

DECOMPOSING THE SOURCES OF RISING NINETEENTH-CENTURY NET INVESTMENT RATES: SHORTER-RUN EPISODIC PHASES

CASE 1A DECOMPOSITION ($\epsilon = -.5$, $\eta = 1.0$)	EPISODES			
	ca. 1839–54 (1)	ca. 1854–71 (2)	ca. 1871–97 (3)	ca. 1839–97 (4)
Total increase in net saving...	+.0330	+.0450	+.0130	+.0910
1. Technology and labor-force induced...	+.0363	+.0283	+.0088	+.0857
A. Investment demand impact...	+.0206	+.0029	+.0004	+.0525
Due to changing rate of labor-force growth...	+.0074	−.0201	+.0159	−.0029
Due to technology changes...	+.0132	+.0430	−.0155	+.0554
B. Decline in capital-goods prices impact...	+.0047	+.0077	+.0060	+.0169
C. Distribution impact...	+.0110	−.0023	+.0024	+.0163
2. Residual mobilization impact...	−.0033	+.0167	+.0042	+.0053

SOURCE.—See text.

NOTE.—Cols. 1, 2, and 3 should add to col. 4 only in the first line of the table. In effect, a Laspeyres weighting scheme is used throughout in the decomposition analysis. Thus, col. 4 need not correspond to the sum of the other three columns along any line. In fact, aggregating across lines yields the following: Technology and labor-force induced, +.0734; investment demand, +.0439; capital-goods prices, +.0184; distribution, +.0111; residual, +.0176, for a total of +.0910.

[25] Jeffrey G. Williamson, "Watersheds and Turning Points: Conjectures on the Long Term Impact of Civil War Financing," *Journal of Economic History* 34 (September 1974): 636–61 and *Late Nineteenth Century American Development* (n. 3 above), chaps. 1 and 5.

Economic Development and Cultural Change

bilization" forces may be attributable to accumulation response to South-ern war destruction and emancipation, a portion to federal debt manage-ment in the North and "catching up" after the war, and a portion to those financial intermediation developments which play such a dominant role in our conventional histories. The important insight which our experiment offers is that these mobilization effects were limited to the ca. 1854–71 period alone: They play no significant role elsewhere in the nineteenth century. Our second finding is that the declining relative price of capital goods had a consistent positive impact throughout, although its contribu-tion is more impressive after the 1850s than before. Nonetheless, it still ac-counted for a seventh of the rise in net investment shares between 1839 and 1854. (The comparable figures for 1854–71 and 1871–97 are, respectively, one-sixth and one-half). Finally, the investment demand impact associated with labor-saving technical change and rising labor-force growth is most pronounced in the antebellum period, accounting for six-tenths of the total increase. The result is consistent with other recent findings on nineteenth-century macroeconomic performance.[26] The rate of labor-saving economy-wide induced by changes in output mix was most dramatic prior to the Civil War; the unbalanced rate of total factor productivity growth was also most pronounced up to 1860; and the rate of labor-force growth reached its zenith between 1830 and 1860. Nevertheless, the investment demand impact is still striking during the 1854–71 episode, accounting for half the total increase in the net investment share. It is insignificant for the remainder of the nineteenth century when rates of total factor productivity and output growth were relatively balanced. Technological quiescence was consistent with inequality quiescence and with relatively stable net investment shares.

It might be worthwhile to report one additional calculation. Economic intuition tells us that episodes of accelerating rates of labor-force growth should, for that reason alone, have raised investment requirements and thus the net investment share. Indeed, it can be shown formally that the shift in the investment demand schedule, $\dot{T}$, can be decomposed into two parts: $\dot{T}_L$, the impact of rates of change in labor-force growth, and a re-sidual, presumably due to technological (and land expansion) forces. The labor-force impact on investment demand is written as[27]

[26] Williamson and Lindert, *A Macroeconomic History of American Inequality*, chaps. 7 and 9.

[27] In terms of the notation in the text, $I^D = \dot{T} + \dot{e}$, where (n. 21 above):

$$T = B \cdot G = B\{\dot{L}[\theta_L/(1 - \theta_K)] + \dot{R}[\theta_R/(1 - \theta_K)] + \dot{E}_L[\theta_L/(1 - \theta_K)]\} ;$$

B is a constant, and, as before, the θ's are factor shares economy-wide, $\dot{L}$ and $\dot{R}$ refer, respectively, to labor-force and land stock growth, and $\dot{E}_L$ denotes the rate of labor augmentation through technological change. Our interest here is in the impact of chang-ing labor-force growth rates on investment demand, and this component can be written

Jeffrey G. Williamson

$$T_L = \frac{dL}{L} + \frac{d[(\theta_L)/(1-\theta_K)]}{[(\theta_L)/(1-\theta_K)]}.$$

Since labor-force growth rates accelerated between the early and late antebellum periods, a positive contribution to investment demand from this source between ca. 1839 and ca. 1854 is to be expected. A tentative estimate is offered in table 5: the acceleration in labor-force growth rates served to raise net investment shares by 0.74 percentage points, or a little less than one-third of the total increase attributable to investment demand shifts and a little more than one-fifth of the total increase in net investment rates in the antebellum period. The share attributable to this source is even greater following the 1870s (ca. 1871–97). But for the nineteenth century as a whole, labor-force growth fails to account for any of the rise in the net investment ratio. The reason is obvious: The rate of labor-force growth in fact *declines* from 2.77% per annum between 1800 and 1840, to 2.60% per annum between 1880 and 1900. In short, labor-force expansion helps account for a modest portion of the expansion in savings rates during the first half of the nineteenth century but fails to account for any of the rise over the century as a whole.

Once again, we do not argue that the underlying data base is impeccable or that our parametric assumptions are unassailable. It seems to us unlikely, however, that any of our main conclusions would be overturned by subsequent improvement in either.

VI. The Gordian Knot Untied and Contemporary Analogies

This paper has shown that nineteenth-century America replicates the inequality and accumulation experience of most "successful" contemporary Third World economies.[28] The time-series evidence confirms a high

---

as $T_L = B[L\theta_L/(1-\theta_K)]$. It follows that $\dot{T}_L = (dL/L) + [d\theta_L/(1-\theta_K)]/[(\theta_L)/(1-\theta_K)]$. Stanley Lebergott (n. 13 above, table 1, p. 118) offers the following estimates of $\dot{L}$: 1800–1840 (ca. 1839), 2.77; 1840–60 (ca. 1854), 3.43; 1860–80 (ca. 1871), 2.27; and 1880–1900 (ca. 1897), 2.60. These plus the θ estimates supplied by Moses Abramovitz and Paul David ("Reinterpreting Economic Growth: Parables and Realities," *American Economic Review* 58 [May 1973], table 2, p. 431) and by table 4 yield:

APPROXIMATIONS OF COMPONENTS

Components	ca. 1839–54	ca. 1854–71	ca. 1871–97	ca. 1839–97
$d\dot{L}/\dot{L}$	+.238	−.338	+.145	−.061
$d[\theta_L/(1-\theta_K)]/[(\theta_L)/(1-\theta_K)]$	−.050	+.011	+.029	−.012
$\dot{T}_L$	+.188	−.327	+.174	−.073

* These estimates of $\dot{T}_L$ are utilized in table 5.

28 As Gustav Ranis has recently reminded us, there are some significant exceptions to "the old chestnut of an unequal distribution of income required to generate high savings rates" (Gustav Ranis, "Development Theory at Three-Quarters Century," in *Essays on Economic Development and Cultural Change*, ed. Manning Nash [Chicago: University of Chicago Press, 1977], p. 265). There are three well-documented cases which

Economic Development and Cultural Change

positive correlation between inequality, capital-formation shares, and accumulation performance. The correlation is certainly close enough to have suggested support for the classic view of capitalist development where growth and equity are in conflict. Indeed, the conflict was sufficiently obvious to nineteenth-century economists that their models of development were all built on the premise that accumulation rates could only be increased with shifts in income toward property-income recipients. That premise gained some support with early econometric work on the savings function.[29] A revisionist literature has accumulated since then, however, which tends to deflate the influence of distribution on saving performance.[30] Yet, even William Cline's oft-cited book fails to offer a true alternative to the classical model since it only confronts the impact of inequality on saving, ignoring the explanation of inequality itself.[31] The advantage of the classical model is that distribution and accumulation are both endogenous variables. Perhaps this explains why the Ricardian-Marxian systems are just as central to modern growth and distribution theory today as they were a century ago. One need not look far for examples of the tradition. Lance Taylor and Edmar Bacha offer such a framework in their efforts to model recent Brazilian growth experience.[32] Furthermore, Sir W. Arthur Lewis's model of surplus labor still reigns supreme as the central thesis underlying contemporary models of Third World development, and it is even used to explain post-World War II growth in Europe.[33] Modern dualistic models of development are applied systematically everywhere in the developing Third World and even play a central role in accounting for Japan's leap to modern economic growth. The theoretical tradition is alive, of that there is no doubt, and it is in large part based on correlations like those uncovered by American growth, inequality, and accumulation experience.

This paper has shown the growth-equity-conflict inference to be suspect in the American nineteenth-century case.[34] One would be hard pressed to find a more relevant and important example of the "identifica-

---

offer the simultaneous experience of high saving rates and relative equality, all from Asia: Japan, Korea, and Taiwan.

[29] Houthakker; and Williamson, "Personal Savings in Developing Nations" (n. 18 above).

[30] Franco Modigliani and E. Tarantelli, "The Consumption Function in a Developing Economy and the Italian Experience," *American Economic Review* 65 (December 1975): 825–42.

[31] William Cline, *Potential Effects of Income Redistribution on Economic Growth: Latin American Cases* (New York: Praeger Publishers, 1972).

[32] Lance Taylor and Edmar Bacha, "The Unequalizing Spiral: A First Growth Model for Belinda," *Quarterly Journal of Economics* 90 (May 1976): 197–218.

[33] Charles P. Kindleberger, *Europe's Postwar Growth: The Role of Labor Supply* (Cambridge, Mass.: Harvard University Press, 1967).

[34] The Japanese case from Meiji to Taisho is also being reappraised, with similar results (see Allen C. Kelley and Jeffrey G. Williamson, *Lessons from Japanese Development: An Analytical Economic History* [Chicago: University of Chicago Press, 1974]; DeBever and Williamson, "Accumulation and the State"; and Williamson and DeBever, "Saving, Accumulation and Modern Economic Growth" [both in n. 6 above]).

68   *Industrialization, Inequality and Economic Growth*

Jeffrey G. Williamson

tion problem'' or a stronger argument for the more extensive use of general equilibrium models in history. We have shown that increased inequality did not account for a significant portion of increased saving rates, and foreign capital never offered an easy means of accelerating accumulation performance either. Inequality may have been an inevitable by-product of modern economic growth, but modern economic growth was not dependent upon increased inequality in any important way for its survival.

Finally, this paper has offered a competitor to the classical model which seems to accord far better with the facts of American history. One cannot help but wonder whether it would do equally well when applied to the more recent experience in the Third World. The paper suggests that regardless of the model eventually adopted, all models must pay more serious attention to the endogenous influences of unbalanced rates of total factor productivity growth on both accumulation and equality.

253

[3]

Why Was British Growth So Slow During the Industrial Revolution?

JEFFREY G. WILLIAMSON

Although it has been labeled the "First Industrial Revolution," British growth and industrialization was slow between the 1760s and the 1820s. The explanation seems to lie with low capital formation shares in national income, low rates of accumulation, and thus little change in the capital-labor ratio. What accounts for the modest investment rates? Lack of thrift? Weak investment demand? This paper argues that the answer is to be found in the enormous debt issues used to finance the French Wars. The war debt crowded out civilian accumulation, inhibited growth, and contributed to the dismal performance in the workers' standard of living. Mobilization and war-distorted prices also played an important role. A general equilibrium model is used to factor out the quantitative impact of each of these three wartime forces on British economic performance up to the 1820s.

I. INTRODUCTION

WE understand the dimensions of the British industrial revolution far better now than a century ago when the debate over its causes and consequences began to heat up. Feinstein has presented pioneering estimates of accumulation rates from 1760 to 1860, and Wrigley and Schofield have offered a brilliant reconstruction of demographic events at the time. The early estimates of national income by Deane and Cole have been augmented by a steady revisionist stream, most recently by Crafts, Harley, Lindert, and me. Informed guesses on the rate of total factor productivity growth are now available; and even trends in the standard of living of workers have now been nailed down more securely.[1]

Journal of Economic History, Vol. XLIV, No. 3 (Sept. 1984). © The Economic History Association. All rights reserved. ISSN 0022-0507.

The author is Professor of Economics at Harvard University. Cambridge. Massachusetts 02138. The research underlying this paper has been supported by grants from the National Science Foundation (SOC76-80967 and SOC-7906869) and the National Endowment for the Humanities (RO-26772-78-19). I acknowledge with pleasure the research assistance of Bruce Flory, Patrice Robitaille, and Kenneth Snowden. Participants at Berkeley, Davis, Harvard, Northwestern, Stanford, and Wisconsin workshops, as well as at the Cliometrics Conference (Iowa City, Iowa: April 29–May 1, 1983), greatly improved the argument from early versions. My special thanks to Michael Bordo, Rondo Cameron, Nicholas Crafts, John Hughes, John James, Frank Lewis, Peter Lindert, Donald McCloskey, Frederick Mishkin, Joel Mokyr, Larry Neal, Martha Olney, Richard Sutch, and Nicholas von Tunzelmann. Alas, many of their best comments have been ignored.

[1] Charles Feinstein, "Capital Formation in Great Britain," in *The Cambridge Economic History of Europe: Volume VII: the Industrial Economies: Capital, Labour, and Enterprise*, ed. Peter Mathias and Michael Postan (Cambridge, 1978); E. A. Wrigley and R. S. Schofield, *The Population History of England, 1541–1871: A Reconstruction* (Cambridge, 1981); Phyllis Deane and W. A. Cole, *British Economic Growth, 1688–1959* (Cambridge, 1962); N. F. R. Crafts, "English

688

Williamson

The new evidence confirms what has come to be called "trend acceleration." Somewhere around the 1820s Britain passed through a secular turning point. Growth in national income was much lower before than after; for example, Harley estimates the growth in per capita income at 0.33 percent per year 1770–1815 and 0.86 percent per year 1815–1841.[2] The doubling of the growth rate is apparent, too, in the indices of industrial production, which grow annually at 1.5 or 1.6 percent before 1815 and at 3.0 or 3.2 percent afterwards.[3] Feinstein's estimate of the rate of capital formation also drifts upwards during the period: in constant prices, the share of gross domestic investment in national income rises from about 9 percent in the 1760s to almost 14 percent in the 1850s; the rate of capital accumulation rises from 1 percent 1761–1800 to 1.7 percent per year 1801–1860; the capital per worker growth rate rises from 0.11 percent per year 1761–1830 to 0.88 percent per year 1830–1860.[4] The turning point is even more dramatic in the standard of living: the adult, male, working-class real wage failed to increase between 1755 and 1819, but from 1819 to 1851 rose at an annual rate of 1.85 percent.[5]

British growth before the 1820s, then, was modest at best. By the standards of the many industrial revolutions to follow, Britain's annual growth in per capita income of 0.33 percent before 1815 is hardly impressive. Even during the uneven 1970s the Third World managed per capita income growth rates around 3.2 percent per year, ten times the British rate before the 1820s.[6]

Economic Growth in the Eighteenth Century: A Re-examination of Deane and Cole's Estimates," *Economic History Review*, 2nd ser., 29 (May 1976), 226–35, "National Income Estimates and the British Standard of Living Debate: A Reappraisal of 1801–1831," *Explorations in Economic History*, 17 (April 1980), 176–88, and "British Economic Growth, 1700–1831: A Review of the Evidence," *Economic History Review*, 2nd ser., 36 (May 1983), 177–99; C. Knick Harley, "British Industrialization Before 1841: Evidence of Slower Growth During the Industrial Revolution," this JOURNAL, 42 (June 1982), 267–89; Peter H. Lindert and Jeffrey G. Williamson, "Revising England's Social Tables, 1688–1812," *Explorations in Economic History*, 19 (Oct. 1982), 385–408, and "Reinterpreting Britain's Social Tables, 1688–1913," *Explorations in Economic History*, 20 (Jan. 1983), 94–109. On the rate of total factor productivity growth, see Feinstein, "Capital Formation," p. 86; Crafts, "British Economic Growth," p. 196; and Crafts and McCloskey in *The Economic History of Britain Since 1700. Volume 1: 1700–1860*, ed. Roderick Floud and Donald McCloskey (Cambridge, 1981), chaps. 1 and 6. A recent quantitative assessment of the standard of living can be found in Lindert and Williamson, "English Workers' Living Standards During the Industrial Revolution: A New Look," *Economic History Review*, 2nd ser., 36 (Feb. 1983), 1–25.

[2] Harley, "British Industrialization Before 1841," p. 286.

[3] Ibid., p. 276, Divisia Index.

[4] Feinstein, "Capital Formation," Table 3 (col. 10), and pp. 84 and 86. Crafts, "British Economic Growth," also offers new estimates for aggregate output growth, industrial output growth, and the investment rate. While his revisions may turn out to be superior, Crafts' choice of benchmark dates—1760, 1780, 1801, and 1831—are inconvenient for the analysis in this paper, where wars are at issue and the 1815 or 1821 benchmark is critical.

[5] Lindert and Williamson, "English Workers' Living Standards," Table 5, p. 13.

[6] International Bank for Reconstruction and Development, *World Tables*, 2nd ed. (Baltimore, 1980), p. 372.

British Growth and Industrialization   689

British growth before the 1820s looks odd when set beside the conventional dating of the industrial revolution. There is no evidence of improvement in the standard of living among the working classes until the 1820s. Indeed, stability in the real wage during the early industrial revolution has encouraged models of labor surplus, still popular today in the Third World.[7] Growth of income as a whole was also poor down to the 1820s. And even the rate of industrialization was quite slow during the alleged industrial revolution. Industrial output grew at 1.5 or 1.6 percent per year up to the 1820s, a rate which exceeded the national income growth rate of 1.3 percent only modestly. Furthermore, Britain was a low saver. A gross domestic saving rate of 9 or 10 percent is low compared with the contemporary Third World average of 20.1 percent in 1977 or Meiji Japan (14.8 percent, 1910–1916) or late nineteenth-century America (28 percent, 1890–1905).[8] The rate of capital accumulation was so modest that hardly any capital-deepening took place. The absence of capital-deepening has suggested that the new technologies sweeping England were capital-saving.[9] The suggestion is remarkable when set beside the voluminous work on labor-saving in nineteenth-century America and in the contemporary Third World. The First Industrial Revolution looks very odd indeed.

Why was British growth so slow in the six decades before the 1820s? One answer might be that the conventional dating of the industrial revolution is simply wrong. Another answer, however, is more plausible: that Britain tried to do two things at once—industrialize *and* fight expensive wars, and she simply did not have the resources to do both.

During the 60 years following 1760, Britain was at war for 36; in the three decades following the late 1780s Britain went from a peacetime economy to a level of wartime commitment that had no parallel until World War I. The war mobilized a good share of the civilian labor force, suggesting that labor scarcity might have been created in the civilian economy. The war debt grew to enormous size, suggesting that civilian capital accumulation might have been suppressed by crowding-out. Tax revenues surged to one-fifth of national income, implying that real private incomes after tax were eroded. Meanwhile, war, blockades, and embargoes diminished international trade, inflating the relative prices of agricultural and raw material importables in the home market while

[7] The classic labor surplus statement, of course, can be found in W. Arthur Lewis, ''Economic Development with Unlimited Supplies of Labour,'' *Manchester School of Economic and Social Studies*, 22 (May 1954), 139–92.

[8] International Bank for Reconstruction and Development, *World Tables*, p. 421; Allen C. Kelley and Jeffrey G. Williamson, *Lessons from Japanese Development: An Analytical History* (Chicago, 1974), p. 233; and Williamson, ''Inequality, Accumulation and Technological Imbalance: A Growth-Equity Conflict in American History?'' *Economic Development and Cultural Change*, 27 (Jan. 1979), 233.

[9] For example, see G. N. von Tunzelmann in *The Economic History of Britain*, chap. 8.

lowering the price of manufactured exportables deflected from world markets.

There has been no shortage of speculation on how the wars affected growth. The conventional wisdom on the standard of living, for example, is that the wars "almost certainly worsened the economic status of labor."[10] The same may perhaps be said of industrialization, capital formation, and export expansion. But we will not know until we make an explicit commitment to models capable of sorting out the influence of war.

II. WAR DEBT: CROWDING OUT CIVILIAN CAPITAL ACCUMULATION

Was Saving a Constraint on British Growth?

The "modest" rate of accumulation during most of the First Industrial Revolution could have been a result of limited saving (constrained perhaps by war) or merely a result of modest growth in investment demand.[11] The two views are portrayed in Figure 1, where the rate of return or interest rate appears on the vertical axis and the investment share in national income on the horizontal axis. Assume for the moment that prices were stable, so that the nominal and real interest rate are the same. If one believes, as most neo-Keynesians did in the 1950s and early 1960s, that investment demand is the critical variable, then the Elastic Saving Function will be attractive. Investment demand shifts and saving responds passively. If one believes, as most neoclassicists in the 1980s do, that saving is an active constraint, then the upward sloping saving functions will be more attractive. In such cases both investment demand and saving supply play a role. The modest rise in the investment ratio from 1760 to 1815 is driven in the diagram by the shift to Actual Saving in 1815 and by the shift to Investment in 1815. If the rise in the war debt competed with civilian accumulation, then Actual Saving in 1815 would be somewhere to the left of Hypothetical (No Wars) Saving in 1815, a counterfactual peacetime case in which the war debt is kept constant. Clearly the war debt helps explain the modest rate of accumulation up to 1815 if the saving function was inelastic. The war debt explains none of the modest rate of accumulation if, instead, the saving function was perfectly elastic. Judging from François Crouzet's *Capital Formation in the Industrial Revolution*, the active-investment-passive-saving belief dominated as late as 1972.

[10] T. S. Ashton, "The Standard of Life of the Workers in England, 1790–1830," this JOURNAL, 9 (Supplement 1949), 22–23.

[11] Deane and Cole (*British Economic Growth*, p. 276) call it a "modest" increase and in Peter Mathias's words ("Preface," in François Crouzet, *Capital Formation in the Industrial Revolution* [London, 1972], p. viii), the "modesty of rates of capital accumulation" is one profound difference between eighteenth-century England and contemporary Third World economies.

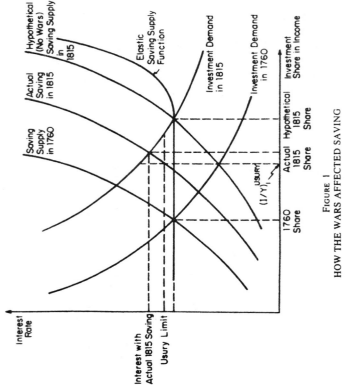

FIGURE 1

HOW THE WARS AFFECTED SAVING

Source: See text.

Contemporaries had some strong beliefs about forgone civilian accumulation and the cost of the wars, but most modern historians do not give them much weight. Deane and Cole's chapter on "Longterm Trends in Capital Formation" has no mention of the War, though they are puzzled by the modest rates of accumulation.[12] The same is true of von Tunzelmann's recent paper on the standard of living debate.[13] In his otherwise penetrating assessment of whether an enlightened policy could have done better for Britain's poor during the industrial revolution he makes no mention of the resource commitment to military conflict. Mokyr and Savin add crowding-out to their list of potential explanations of British economic performance between 1793 and 1815, but ignore crowding-out when they offer an assessment of what they call "stagflation."[14] Even Charles Feinstein's oft-cited "Capital Accumula-

[12] Deane and Cole, *British Economic Growth*, chap. 8, pp. 259–77.

[13] Von Tunzelmann, "The Standard of Living, Investment, and Economic Growth in England and Wales, 1760–1850," in *Technical Change, Employment, and Investment*, ed. Lars Jörberg and Nathan Rosenberg (Lund, 1982), 209–24.

[14] Joel Mokyr and N. E. Savin, "Stagflation in Historical Perspective: The Napoleonic Wars Revisited," *Research in Economic History*, ed. Paul Uselding, vol. 1 (Greenwich, 1976), 198–259.

tion and Economic Growth" ignores the issue, save for a suggestive reference to a "wartime dip" in the investment to GNP ratio.[15] And while Mathias and O'Brien tell us that "the ability of the British state to wage war effectively seems even more dependent upon the ability of governments to raise loans through the accumulation of a permanent National Debt than it was upon increasing revenues from taxation," their useful paper is devoted entirely to documenting the thesis that "the main economic impact of taxation in Britain fell upon consumption and demand, rather than upon savings and investment."[16]

The Mill-Ashton Hypothesis

Contemporary observers saw things quite differently. New war debt crowded out private debt and the usury laws were seen to deflect saving to government borrowing, much as funds in Third World financial markets are diverted to state-backed projects and government borrowing.[17] Writing on the state of the private capital market after the government borrowed £12 million in 1781, David Macpherson and George Chalmers saw the crowding out clearly:[18]

Such high interest with government security evidently makes it extremely difficult, if not quite impossible, for individuals to borrow any money, upon legal interest, either for the extension of commerce and manufacture, or the improvement of agriculture.

Every one must remember how impossible it was for individuals to borrow money on any security for any premium towards the end of 1784.

Writing after the French Wars had ended, but in the face of the immense debt, John Stuart Mill saw deflection and crowding-out as an important cause of relatively modest British progress:[19]

Did the government, by its loan operations, augment the rate of interest? . . . When they do raise the rate of interest, as they did in a most extraordinary degree during the French War, this is positive proof that the government is a competitor for capital. . . .

What was true of England was apparently true for Scotland as well:

A small amount of government securities first appeared in the accounts of the Bank of Scotland in 1766, but they did not become a permanent feature until the American Revolution. Such investments, including Bank of England . . . stock, shot up dramatically after 1792, quickly overshadowing ordinary lending. . . . [T]his policy, which was

15 Feinstein, "Capital Formation," p. 90.
16 Peter Mathias and Patrick O'Brien, "Taxation in Britain and France, 1715–1810," *Journal of European Economic History*, 5 (Winter 1976), 616 and 623.
17 Ronald I. McKinnon, *Money and Capital in Economic Development* (Washington, D.C., 1972).
18 David Macpherson, *Annals of Commerce* (London, 1805), vol. 3, p. 686; George Chalmers, *An Estimate of the Comparative Strength of Great Britain* (London, 1794), p. 186.
19 John Stuart Mill, *Principles of Political Economy*, 5th ed. (New York, 1909), vol. 2, p. 481.

apparently also followed by the other Edinburgh banks, drew criticism on the grounds that it deprived Scottish industry of capital . . .[20]

Mill had a view of crowding-out in which new war debt issues displaced private capital accumulation, one-for-one: "the government, by draining away a great part of the annual accumulations . . . subtracted just so much [capital] while the war lasted."[21] And Mill thought crowding-out was large enough to warrant the belief that the counterfactual peacetime rate of capital accumulation would have been "enormous":

the accumulation going on in the hands of individuals was sufficient to counteract the effect of that wasteful [military] expenditure, and to prevent capital from being diminished. The same accumulation would have sufficed, but for the government expenditure, to produce an enormous increase.[22]

A century later Ashton affirmed the crowding-out hypothesis, using it to explain the operation of capital markets in the eighteenth century.[23] The best statement of his thesis can be found in Chapter 4 ("Building and Construction") of his Economic Fluctuations in England:

much of the revenue needed for the prosecution of war had to be obtained from loans. The proportion was low at first, but mounted as the cost of maintaining the forces increased. . . . Some of the money subscribed must have come out of idle balances, but . . . a good deal of it was deflected from other channels, and in particular from investment in building and construction. The production of capital goods was relatively low in most years of war.[24]

Building and construction were the victims of crowding-out, and according to Feinstein they were 60 percent of total gross domestic fixed capital formation in the 1760s and 68 percent in 1801–1810.[25] Ashton has more to say about the operation of British capital markets during wartime, especially about usury and credit rationing. The banking system did not expand total credit when they purchased war debt, but it did ration what credit remained:

when the Bank of England increased its advances to the state it usually curtailed its loans and discounts to other clients. . . . Nor does the cautious policy of the Bank seem to have been offset by an expansion of credit elsewhere. There was no marked increase

[20] Rondo Cameron, "Scotland, 1750–1845," in Banking in the Early Stages of Industrialization, ed. Cameron (New York, 1967), pp. 81–82.

[21] Mill, Principles, vol. 2, pp. 481 and 483.

[22] Mill, "Observations on the Effects Produced by the Expenditure of Government During the Restriction of Cash Payments," The Westminster Review, 2 (July 1824), Art. II, p. 40.

[23] Ashton, An Economic History of England: The 18th Century (London, 1955), and Economic Fluctuations in England, 1700–1800 (Oxford, 1959).

[24] Ashton, Economic Fluctuations, p. 65.

[25] Feinstein, "Capital Formation," Table 7, p. 41.

in the number of private banks, and there is evidence that the London banks, at least, reduced their loans to private customers when they lent to the state.[26]

The civilian loan market was constrained by usury:

in the eighteenth century the range of possible rates on mortgages and bonds was limited. No instance has been found of a rate below 3 per cent.; and the Usury Laws prohibited borrowers from offering, or lenders from receiving, more than 6 per cent. until 1714 and more than 5 per cent. during the rest of the century. The existence of this upper limit is of the utmost importance to an understanding of the fluctuations of the period. Once the critical point had been reached further borrowing might become impossible.[27]

The usury laws are not essential to crowding-out, but they help Ashton explain the business cycle. Further, they make clear that the interest rate is not the sole index of scarcity in the civilian capital market:

It was not, then, simply through a rise in the cost of borrowing, but through interruptions to the flow of funds, that depression came to [building and construction].... When the rate of 5 per cent. had been reached builders and contractors might be getting all the loans they wanted or, on the other hand, many of them might be in acute need of more. If we want to know the degree of scarcity we must look for other sources of information.[28]

The Size of the War Debt

The first step in testing the Mill-Ashton hypothesis is to compute the size of the war debt. The calculation requires two pieces of evidence: national income and net additions to the war debt. The additions to the debt were available even to Mill, but national income estimates only became available with the appearance in 1962 of Deane and Cole's book. Table 3 summarizes the information using two different concepts of the real impact of the war debt. One estimate follows most economists in using the Department of Commerce National Income Accounts view, deflating the increase in nominal debt outstanding. Siegal, Dewald, Eisner, and others have recently argued that we should use instead Real Accrual Accounting, computing the real debt at the beginning and the end of the period, before the increase is calculated.[29] The accrual concept includes the impact of inflation on the stock of old debt, whereas the national accounts concept does not. Since these were

26 Ashton, Economic Fluctuations, pp. 65–66.
27 Ibid., p. 86.
28 Ibid., pp. 86–87.
29 Jeremy J. Siegal, "Inflation-Induced Distortions in Government and Private Saving Statistics," Review of Economics and Statistics, 61 (Feb. 1979), 83–90; William G. Dewald, "Federal Deficits and Real Interest Rates: Theory and Evidence," Federal Reserve Bank of Atlanta Economic Review, 68 (Jan. 1983), 20–29; Robert Eisner and Paul J. Pieper, "A New View of the Federal Debt and Budget Deficits," American Economic Review, 74 (March 1984), 11–29.

TABLE 1

CIVILIAN INVESTMENT IN REPRODUCIBLE CAPITAL AND NATIONAL INCOME PER YEAR, 1761–1860:
BASED ON FEINSTEIN, DEANE AND COLE

Decade	Y: National Income in Great Britain, £m		Investment and "Saving" in Great Britain, Current Prices, £m			Investment and "Saving" in Great Britain, 1851/61, Prices, £m			Implicit Price Deflators	
	(1) Current Prices	(2) Constant 1851/61 Prices	(3) Gross Domestic Fixed Capital Formation	(4) Gross Domestic Capital Formation	(5) Gross Domestic Saving in Reproducible Capital	(6) Gross Domestic Fixed Capital Formation	(7) Gross Domestic Capital Formation	(8) Gross Domestic Saving in Reproducible Capital	(9) Investment	(10) National Income
1761–1770	74.6	89.6	3.7	4.7	5.2	6.6	7.6	8.1	.55	.83
1771–1780	88.8	96.0	4.0	6.0	6.5	7.1	9.1	10.1	.57	.92
1781–1790	107.1	110.2	6.8	8.8	10.3	11.1	13.1	14.6	.61	.97
1791–1800	174.3	139.7	11.4	14.9	16.4	14.3	17.3	18.8	.80	1.25
1801–1810	266.6	172.1	20.4	21.9	18.9	16.6	17.6	15.6	1.23	1.55
1811–1820	296.1	212.2	26.5	29.5	37.0	20.5	22.5	27.5	1.29	1.40
1821–1830	315.5	291.6	31.3	35.8	44.3	28.3	32.3	39.8	1.11	1.08
1831–1840	396.2	396.9	40.5	44.0	48.5	38.6	42.1	46.6	1.05	1.00
1841–1850	487.8	495.7	50.5	55.0	61.5	49.4	54.4	60.9	1.02	.98
1851–1860	595.7	595.7	58.0	61.5	81.5	58.0	61.5	81.5	1.00	1.00

Sources: Cols. (1) and (2): Mid-decade averages, based on Deane and Cole, *British Economic Growth*, Tables 19 and 37, where Table 19 is converted into current prices by applying Gilboy's price index reported in Mathias and O'Brien, "Taxation in Britain and France," p. 605, and linking on 1801; Table 37 is converted into constant prices by applying Deane and Cole's (Table 72, p. 282) implicit national product price deflator, which is, in fact, the Rousseaux index.

Cols. (3) and (6): Gross domestic fixed capital formation, decade averages, in Feinstein "Capital Formation," Tables 6 and 7, pp. 40–41.

Cols. (4) and (7): Gross domestic capital formation, cols. (3) and (6) plus stockbuilding, in ibid., Table 16, p. 69.

Cols. (5) and (8): Gross domestic savings in reproducible capital, cols. (4) and (7) plus net investment abroad, in ibid., Table 16, p. 69.

Col. (9) = col. (3) ÷ col. (6).

Col. (10) = col. (1) ÷ col. (2).

food supplies had only a trivial impact on accumulation performance over the three or four decades following 1887 as a whole. One would have expected otherwise given the attention which the trade in grains has received in the literature. Perhaps the flow of articles in the two-sector tradition explains the overwhelming attention to trade in rice and the agricultural terms of trade, but the recent empirical work by Akino and Hayami (1972), Hayami and Ruttan (1971), and even Nakamura (1966) may help account for the attention to trade in food. Yet, almost all of the attention has been focused on the *ex post* expansion in net food imports rather than on an analysis of its impact on Meiji and Taisho performance. While the share of foodstuffs in total imports declined from 23 to 15 per cent between the early 1890s and World War I, the fact remains that net rice imports rose from 49,000 to 406,000 tons between 1895 and 1915. While this colonial supply must certainly have reduced the rise in rice prices at home, the fact remains that they still drifted upward over the period 1890–1915. The shift to a net rice import position after 1895 can be explained by two well-known forces. First, the growth and promotion of agricultural productivity at home, while impressive, was still neglected in comparison with attention given the modern sector. Second, acquisition of Korea and Taiwan made it possible to import foodstuffs from these territories on more advantageous terms than were available at home. Coercion played a role in procuring this colonial supply, particularly after 1918 when rice riots compelled the government to reduce the urban worker's cost of living quickly by colonial rice imports (Hayami and Ruttan, 1971, p. 221).

In spite of such documentary accounts, the importance of trade in foodstuffs to Japanese growth and accumulation still remains unclear. Our model supplies a tentative answer, however, since we need only observe how the modelled economy would have behaved had Japan been forced—or had chosen—to be self-sufficient in food for all thirty-six years. This counterfactual world of food self-sufficiency is, of course, one of higher relative prices of foodstuffs and thus industrialization is given a less dramatic incentive. It is also a world of deteriorated terms of trade. Furthermore, real wages would have suffered and distributional influences would have been quite inegalitarian. Nevertheless, the model tells us that the rate of accumulation would not have changed a whit from its actual values. While the availability of colonial food supplies had a significant impact on the composition of Japan's income and output, it did not have a significant impact on overall accumulation and growth performance.

Jeffrey G. Williamson

apparent when the relevant nineteenth-century price data are given even the most cursory look. Gallman's implicit price deflators in table 2 record a decline in the relative price of investment goods from an index of 108 in 1839 to 82 in 1869–78, while relative stability is the rule after the 1870s. To be more precise, the relative price of investment goods declined by 31% between the 1840s and 1899–1908. A roughly comparable pattern emerges when a similar index is constructed for textiles.[3] Thus, whether examined at the industry or national level, the average relative price of capital goods in the 1870s was far below that of the 1840s. Which component of gross domestic capital formation (GDCF) was undergoing the most dramatic price decline? Relative to buildings, the price of producer equipment underwent a dramatic plunge from the 1840s to the 1870s. Furthermore, the decline continued up to 1879–88, and it was only an offsetting rise in construction costs which produced stability in the relative price of capital goods after the 1870s.[4] Given these price trends, it comes as no surprise that the constant-price share of producer-durables investment in GDCF rose from 22% in 1854 to 45% in 1879–88. It also seems evident that the direction of causation went from relative-price change to invest-ment-mix change since the relative price of investment goods declined in spite of the enormous increase in capital-formation rates and the abrupt shift in its composition toward producer durables.

I have made much of these relative-price trends here and elsewhere for two reasons. First, they contrast sharply with Robert A. Gordon's influential paper which documented a long-term secular rise in the relative price of capital goods dating from the 1870s, although he emphasized the upward surge from the turn of the century.[5] The sharp decline in nine-teenth-century capital-goods prices is thus even more remarkable when viewed in terms of twentieth-century experience. But there is a second reason for stressing these trends: The relative price decline seems to offer one hypothesis capable of explaining the rise in nineteenth-century "con-ventional" saving rates. The decline may best be explained by one or a

[3] Jeffrey G. Williamson, *Late Nineteenth Century American Development: A General Equilibrium History* (Cambridge: Cambridge University Press, 1974), pp. 106–9. It should be apparent that the decline in the relative price of investment goods would be even steeper if adequate adjustment for differential rates of quality improvement were possible. Since such adjustments are not embodied in the price indices, we can safely infer that the relative price decline is understated.

[4] Ibid., p. 107.

[5] Robert A. Gordon, "Differential Changes in the Prices of Consumers' and Capital Goods," *American Economic Review* 51 (December 1961): 937–57. Kuznets noted the same phenomenon in *Capital in the American Economy: Its Formation and Financing Since 1870* (Princeton, N.J.: Princeton University Press, 1961), but Gordon's paper received more attention. In reference to twentieth-century trends, Kuznets said that "the price trend in capital formation . . . shows a somewhat greater long-term rise than that in national product as a whole" (p. 24).

TABLE 2
THE TAX BURDEN IN GREAT BRITAIN, 1761-1860

Decade	(1) Share of Direct Taxes in Total Tax Revenues: ϕ_t	(2) Share of Net Tax Revenue in National Income	(3) Share of Direct Taxes in National Income
1761-1770	.208	.128	.027
1771-1780	.188	.129	.024
1781-1790	.184	.140	.026
1791-1800	.168	.139	.023
1801-1810	.235	.180	.042
1811-1820	.258	.202	.052
1821-1830	.136	.165	.022
1831-1840	.088	.122	.011
1841-1850	.150	.102	.015
1851-1860	.199	.097	.019

Sources: Col. (1) calculated from Brian R. Mitchell and Phyllis Deane, *Abstract of British Historical Statistics* (Cambridge, 1962), pp. 387-88 and 392-93, where taxes on income and wealth include land and assessed taxes, property and income taxes. Central government only.

Col. (2) takes current price national income from Table 1, col. (1). Net tax revenues for 1760-1800 are from Mathias and O'Brien "Taxation in Britain and France," Table 2, p. 605, five-year averages, central government only, and for Great Britain. For 1801-1861, the United Kingdom gross tax revenues in Mitchell and Deane, *Abstract*, pp. 392-93, are adjusted downwards to get estimated net tax revenues for Great Britain, and refer to five-year averages.

Col. (3) = col. (1) × col. (2).

decades of inflation the two concepts may well yield quite different results.

Whether one favors the national income or the accrual concept, the size of the war debt issue was enormous, although the two concepts imply somewhat different timing in the real impact of war debt. While the national income concept in Table 3 (column 9) suggests a peak share in national income of 11.5 percent across the 1790s, the accrual concept (column 8) reduces this figure to 3.6 percent, removing the impact of rapid inflation on the outstanding stock of old war debt. Symmetrically, the price deflation across the 1810s raises the accrual share above the national income share, 14.9 versus 7.4 percent. The estimates are comparable over the long run: for the 1760-1820 epoch, the accrual and national income estimates averaged 5.8 and 6.8 percent of national income. Since it is used so commonly in the literature I shall use the national income concept in what follows.

Net additions to the war debt were 3.6 percent of national income as early as the 1760s (Table 3, NIA, column 9) about the same as the 3.7 percent America achieved during 1980-1982, when crowding-out and capital scarcity began to attract attention. The share had risen to 6.5 percent by the 1780s, a near doubling. It reached a peak of 11.5 percent

TABLE 3

PUBLIC DEBT ISSUE, GROSS DOMESTIC SAVING IN REPRODUCIBLE CAPITAL, AND GROSS PRIVATE SAVING: LEVELS AND SHARES IN NATIONAL INCOME, 1761–1860

Column groups:
- (1)–(3): debt levels at year points — (1) Government Debt Outstanding D (£m); (2) National Income Price Deflator (1851/61 = 1.0) P_y; (3) Real Debt Outstanding D/P_y
- (4) P_y (decade)
- Increase Per Year in Government Debt: (5) Nominal ΔD (£m); (6) Real: RAA $\Delta(D/P_y)$; (7) Real: NIA $\Delta D/P_y$
- Shares in National Income: (8) RAA $\Delta(D/P_y)$; (9) NIA $\Delta D/P_y$; (10) S/P_y
- Gross Private Saving Rate: (11) RAA $[S/P_y + \Delta(D/P_y)]$; (12) NIA $[S/P_y + \Delta(D/P_y)]$

Year	(1)	(2)	(3)	Decade	(4)	(5)	(6)	(7)	(8)	(9)	(10)	(11)	(12)
1761	103.2	.77	134.7										
1771	130.2	.90	144.9	1761–1771	.83	2.7	1.0	3.3	1.1%	3.6%	9.1%	10.2%	12.7%
1781	173.7	.95	183.2	1771–1781	.92	4.4	3.8	4.7	4.0	4.9	10.5	14.5	15.4
1791	243.6	1.00	244.9	1781–1791	.97	7.0	6.2	7.2	5.6	6.5	13.3	18.9	19.8
1801	443.1	1.50	295.6	1791–1801	1.25	20.0	5.1	16.0	3.6	11.5	13.5	17.1	24.9
1811	619.9	1.60	387.3	1801–1811	1.55	17.7	9.2	11.4	7.8	9.0	6.6	14.4	15.6
1821	838.8	1.19	703.6	1811–1821	1.40	21.9	31.6	15.7	14.9	7.4	13.0	27.2	20.4
1831	790.6	.97	813.4	1821–1831	1.08	−4.7	11.0	−4.7	3.8	−1.5	13.6	17.4	12.1
1841	790.9	1.02	773.1	1831–1841	1.00	0.0	−4.0	0.0	−1.0	0.0	11.7	10.7	11.7
1851	789.1	.95	835.0	1841–1851	.98	−0.2	6.2	−2.0	1.3	−0.0	12.3	13.5	12.3
1861	805.8	1.05	764.5	1851–1861	1.00	1.7	−7.1	1.1	−1.2	0.3	13.7	12.5	14.0

Sources: Col. (1): funded and unfunded government debt of the United Kingdom, where annual observations are five-year averages, centered, from Mitchell and Deane, Abstract, pp. 402–3.

Cols. (2) and (4) are described in the "Sources" to Table 1.

Cols. (6) and (7) offer two alternative estimates of the real increase in the war debt: RAA refers to "real accrual accounting"; = $\Delta(D/P_y)$; NIA refers to Department of Commerce "national income accounting" = $\Delta D/P_y$.

Cols. (8) and (9): cols. (6) and (7) divided by col. (2).

Col. (10) from Table 1, col. (8) divided by col. (2).

Col. (11) = col. (8) + col. (10).

Col. (12) = col. (9) + col. (10).

in the 1790s. The last figure approximates that for America during the Civil War (15.5 percent).[30] America generated a similar burden of war debt over five years or so of the Civil War decade, as did Japan over the decade 1894–1905 (during war with China and Russia).[31] But neither of these newly industrializing countries maintained the burden over six decades. Net additions to the British war debt continued at high levels throughout the first two decades of the nineteenth century, holding at 6.6 percent of national income in the 1800s and 7.4 percent in the 1810s.

The average burden of these net additions to the war debt was 6.8 percent between 1761 and 1820, and 8.5 percent between 1791 and 1820. To get an estimate of the *gross private saving rate*, civilian reproducible capital formation and new public war debt should be added. When they are, Britain's private saving rates during the First Industrial Revolution no longer seem so modest. Indeed, while domestic investment in reproducible capital averaged only around 11.4 percent of national income from 1761 to 1820 (Table 3, column 10), the gross private saving rate averaged 18.1 percent (Table 3, column 12).

It appears that Britain was not a "modest" saver during the First Industrial Revolution after all. What makes Britain unusual is that much of the potential saving went into the financing of war.

Crowding-Out and the Ricardian Non-Equivalence Theorem

Does the typical household view government debt issue as an increase in its own net wealth? It has been assumed that it does in some full employment models: an increase in government debt is assumed to imply an increase in perceived household wealth, inducing a rise in desired consumption, an increase in interest rates, and a decline in the share going to capital accumulation. While one-for-one crowding-out survived Franco Modigliani's tests on American data, and while David and Scadding thought that the "invariance [of the gross private saving rate in twentieth-century America] to changes in the size of the government deficit suggests that private debt and public debt are close substitutes in private portfolios," the debate over crowding-out has hardly been closed.[32]

A critical assumption of these models is full employment. If Britain is

[30] Williamson, "Watersheds and Turning Points: Conjectures on the Long Term Impact of Civil War Financing," this JOURNAL, 34 (Sept. 1974), Table 3, p. 643.

[31] Williamson and Leo J. DeBever, "Savings, Accumulation and Modern Economic Growth: The Contemporary Relevance of Japanese History," *The Journal of Japanese Studies*, 4 (Fall 1977), 125–67.

[32] Franco Modigliani launched this literature with his "Long-Run Implications of Alternative Fiscal Policies and the Burden of the National Debt," *Economic Journal*, 71 (Dec. 1961), 730–55, and his tests appear in "The Life Cycle Hypothesis of Savings, the Demand for Wealth and the Supply of Capital," *Social Research*, 33 (Summer 1966), 160–217. Paul A. David and John L. Scadding, "Private Savings: Ultrarationality, Aggregation, and 'Denison's Law'," *Journal of Political Economy*, 82, Pt. 1 (March/April 1974), 239.

better described by under-full employment, then the war debt issue may have crowded *in* private investment.[33] But the full employment assumption is the best description of Britain during the industrial revolution, certainly when attending to a period as long as three to six decades.

But even granting full employment, there were always strong opponents to one-for-one crowding-out. James Tobin thought such arguments implied "fiscal illusion": "How is it possible that society merely by the device of incurring a debt to itself can deceive itself into believing that it is wealthier? Do not the additional taxes which are necessary to carry the interest charges reduce the value of other components of wealth?"[34] Barro's 1974 paper ("Are Government Bonds Net Wealth?") showed that taxes can offset debt issue, but had to make two assumptions likely to be grossly inconsistent with the environment of the British industrial revolution.[35] For one thing, future tax liabilities were probably *not* fully capitalized. Bondholders probably did suffer fiscal illusion. As O'Driscoll pointed out, Ricardo thought fiscal illusion was the best characterization of bondholders' behavior in late eighteenth- and early nineteenth-century Britain:

In [theory], there is no real difference [between taxes and debt issue] . . .; but [in fact] the people who pay the taxes never so estimate them, and therefore do not manage their private affairs accordingly. We are too apt to think that war is burdensome only in proportion to what we are at the moment called to pay for it in taxes, without reflecting on the probable duration of such taxes.[36]

Ricardo wrote his analysis of the impact of the war debt in September of 1820, when crowding-out and sinking funds were being publicly debated, with the background of two decades of British accumulation under war finance.

For another thing, Barro was "willing to make the severely restrictive assumption that the source for the ultimate purchase of the government bonds is identical to the source from which the alternative taxes would be drawn."[37] Historians have always assumed the opposite, namely, that those receiving the interest on bonds were not the tax payers. Ignoring certain subtleties of tax incidence, Table 2 suggests that the historians have been right. The British central government tax system was highly regressive at this time. Direct taxes on income and wealth

[33] Benjamin M. Friedman, "Crowding Out or Crowding In? Economic Consequences of Financing Government Deficits," *Brookings Papers on Economic Activity*, 3 (1978), 593–641.

[34] James Tobin, *Essays in Economics: Vol. 1: Macroeconomics* (Amsterdam, 1971), p. 91.

[35] Robert J. Barro, "Are Government Bonds Net Wealth?" *Journal of Political Economy*, 82 (Nov./Dec. 1974), 1095–117; James M. Buchanan, "Barro on the Ricardian Equivalence Theorem," *Journal of Political Economy*, 84 (April 1976), 337–42.

[36] David Ricardo, *The Works and Correspondence of David Ricardo*, ed. P. Sraffa (Cambridge, 1962), vol. 4, pp. 186–87; see also G. P. O'Driscoll, "The Ricardian Nonequivalence Theorem," *Journal of Political Economy*, 85 (Feb. 1977), 207–10.

[37] Buchanan, "Barro on the Ricardian Equivalence Theorem," p. 339.

produced a very small share of total taxes (Table 2, column 1, φ.). Furthermore, the temporary direct taxes that *had* been imposed in the late 1790s and afterwards were quickly dismantled after the war, leaving tariffs and excise taxes on necessities the main source of revenue to make payments on the debt. Fiscal illusion was not illusory.

In short, the assumption of one-for-one crowding-out may be a rather good description of behavior during the British industrial revolution. It may be good enough, at least, to warrant its use to assess what the rate of accumulation might have been had the wars never been fought and had the debt never been issued.

Civilian Accumulation in the Absence of War: Counterfactual Conjectures

The next step is to explore the implications of the crowding-out when it is posed in its strongest, one-for-one form. The most difficult part of the exercise involves the redistributive effect of the war debt. The redistributive effect is a simple enough notion, with a long tradition in British historiography.[38] Since the war debt was held by high-income savers, and since taxes fell primarily on low-income nonsavers, a redistribution from nonsavers to savers is implied. The redistribution effect would not have had a favorable impact on the living standards of workers, but nonetheless would have served to augment the gross private saving rate. In other words, the redistribution effect might have offset the crowding-out effect, raising investment.

The question is how large the offset might have been. The answer depends in part on the size of the debt charges. They were large, exceeding the new debt issue itself in all but one decade, the 1790s. The answer also depends on the source of the tax revenue. Pitt had imposed an income tax on the rich, which lasted from 1799 to 1816. Of course, there were land and assessed taxes too, all of which imply thorny problems of tax incidence, ignored here. And the answer also depends on the marginal saving rates of the taxed poor against the debt-holding rich.

The set of assumptions underlying Table 4 can be stated briefly. Assume that ("direct") taxes on income and wealth fell on the top half of the income distribution. The assumptions are likely to make the estimate of the redistribution effect too large, which is the right direction of bias. While some of the direct taxes on wealth must have been shifted back on the poor, one would think that the shifting was trivial; more importantly, some of the regressive indirect taxes fell on the rich; on net the latter bias probably dominated the former.

[38] E. P. Thompson, *The Making of the English Working Class* (New York, 1963). p. 304; Sidney Pollard and D. W. Crossley, *The Wealth of Britain, 1085–1966* (London, 1968), p. 207; R. M. Hartwell and Stanley Engerman, "Models of Immiseration: The Theoretical Basis of Pessimism," in *The Standard of Living in the Industrial Revolution*, ed. A. J. Taylor (London, 1975), pp. 208–9.

TABLE 4

CONJECTURES ON THE IMPACT OF WAR DEBT ISSUE ON CIVILIAN SECTOR ACCUMULATION AND GROWTH, 1761–1860

Period	(1) Counterfactual Rise in I/Y	(2) Capital's Productivity Y/K	(3) Counterfactual Rise in the Rate of Accumulation, dK^*	(4) Counterfactual Rise in the Aggregate Growth Rate, dY^*
1761–1820	+4.84%	0.36	+1.74%	+0.61%
1791–1820	+6.38	0.38	+2.42	+0.85
1821–1860	−2.22	0.53	−1.18	−0.41

Sources and Notes: Col. (1) is a constant price estimate derived from $d(I/Y)_{CF} = [\Delta D - (\delta)(1 - \phi)(iD)] \div Y$. The NIA estimates of the real deficit, ΔD, are taken from Table 3, col. (7). The estimate of ϕ is taken from Table 2, col. (1), and the estimate for δ can be found in the text (.362). Average annual charges on the funded and unfunded government debt, iD, are taken from Mitchell and Deane, *Abstract*, pp. 390–91 and 396–97, Great Britain 1761–1800, and United Kingdom 1801–1860, deflated by P_Y in Table 1, col. (10). The constant price national income figure, Y, is taken from Table 1, col. (2).

Col. (2) assumes that a *net* capital-output ratio of 2.5 applies to the eighteenth and early nineteenth centuries as a whole (1760–1830); from Phyllis Deane, "Capital Formation in Britain Before the Railway Age," *Economic Development and Cultural Change*, 9 (April 1961), 356, an estimate which Floud and McCloskey (*The Economic History of Britain*, p. 8, fn. 2) also accept, and which Kuznets cites with favor (*Population, Capital, and Growth* [New York, 1973], pp. 143 and 149). Feinstein reports *gross* capital-output ratios which are much higher, but his estimated *trends* in capital productivity (Feinstein, "Capital Formation," Table 26, p. 87) are used here.

Col. (3) = col. (1) times col. (2).

Col. (4) = col. (3) times 0.35, the latter an estimate of capital's output elasticity from Floud and McCloskey (*The Economic History of Britain*, p. 8). See text.

If the average saving rate out of incomes in the lower half of the distribution was zero, and defining the average saving rate out of the top half to be s_H, then the economy-wide gross private saving rate can of course be written as $s = (s_H Y_H)/Y$, where by definition $Y_H/Y = .5$. The value for s in Table 3 (column 12) averaged 18.1 percent (1760–1820) implying that s_H was .362.[39] The differential between *average* saving rates may, of course, exceed the differential between *marginal* saving rates. If so, the assumption exaggerates the positive net saving associated with the redistribution effect and the impact of the war debt on civilian accumulation rates is, once again, understated.

The investment share can now be calculated in the absence of the

[39] If this estimate seems large, recall that it covers business reinvestment rates in a precorporate era. The estimate is very close to that favored for America by Simon Kuznets, *Shares of Upper Income Groups in Income and Savings*, National Bureau of Economic Research, Occasional Paper No. 35 (New York, 1950).

wars, reported in Table 4. Including the redistribution offset, the counterfactual rise in I/Y is calculated as:

$$d[I/Y]_{CF} = [\Delta D - (\delta)(1 - \phi_t)(iD)]/Y,$$

where ϕ_t is the share of income and wealth taxes in total tax revenue, ΔD is the deflated deficit, iD is the deflated interest charge on the debt outstanding, Y is total real income, and δ is the differential between saving rates. Using Harrod's identity (the rate of capital accumulation, K^*, equals the investment share divided by the capital/income ratio), it is a simple matter to compute the counterfactual change in the accumulation rate, dependent on the change in the investment share just calculated:[40]

$$d[K^*]_{CF} = (Y/K) \cdot d[I/Y]_{CF}$$

where Y/K is the income/capital ratio.

If the crowding-out assumptions are anywhere near correct, Table 4 suggests that war debt issue explains much of the peculiarities of the First Industrial Revolution. Between 1761 and 1820 the capital formation share would have been 4.84 percent higher in the absence of war, and the rate of accumulation would have been 1.74 percent per year higher. Assuming an output elasticity of 0.35, national income would have grown some 0.6 percent per year faster. The counterfactual calculations are even more striking for the decades in which the wars were most important, 1791–1820: the capital formation share would have been higher by 6.38 percent, the rate of accumulation would have been higher by 2.42 percent per year, and the rate of output growth would have been some 0.8 or 0.9 percent per year faster. In contrast, the post-1820 growth rates would have been lower in the absence of the wars. Thus, most of the trend acceleration from the pre-1820 war-distorted decades to the post-1820 *Pax Britannica* may well be explained by crowding-out rather than by some endogenous attribute of capitalist development.

While the counterfactual conjectures reported in Table 4 are useful, they are not enough. They ignore the potential impact of other war-induced economic influences—such as mobilization and labor scarcity, or food and resource scarcities induced by blockades and embargoes. And they only offer insight into the impact at the aggregate level. They tell us nothing about the standard of living of common labor or about industrialization.

---

[40] The counterfactual assumes that all of the rise would be allocated to domestic accumulation, implying one-for-one crowding-in. It should also be pointed out that I ignore the possibility that the rate of return to capital might have declined in response to the higher rates of accumulation. Unless capital rationing under usury continued to bind capital markets, rates of return would have fallen with more rapid accumulation.

III. MOBILIZATION AND WORLD MARKETS DURING THE NAPOLEONIC WARS

Major wars create a scarcity of unskilled labor, and the French Wars were no exception. Ashton's compilation from the *Parliamentary Papers* shows men in the armed forces rising from 98,000 in 1790 to 437,000 and 482,000 in 1795 and 1802.[41] Colquhoun estimated that men under arms number 501,000 in 1812.[42] By 1820, demobilization had reduced the figure back to a peacetime level of about 100,000. These estimates suggest that the share of the total labor force mobilized for the French Wars rose from about 2 to 10 percent, a mobilization rate that begins to approximate twentieth-century wars.[43]

Furthermore, mobilization had a predictable impact on the composition of the diminished civilian labor force: mobilization fell most heavily on the young, unskilled, rural male. The mobilization bias comes as no surprise—the same bias tended to breed scarcity of unskilled labor in the twentieth century. In America, for instance, both World Wars were ones of very steeply rising relative costs of unskilled labor, producing a leveling in earnings and a collapse in pay gaps between the skilled and unskilled.[44] Perhaps the collapse in pay gaps during the Napoleonic Wars can be explained in the same way.[45] These mobilization effects have in any case been documented for the 1790–1815 epoch.[46] They suggest that the growth of the civilian labor force was lowered from what it might have been, 1.25 percent per year, to what it was, 0.91 percent per year.

The relative price of agricultural goods rose sharply across the period, implying a deterioration in Britain's terms of trade, an erosion in aggregate real income, and a fall in the standard of living of the working classes. By reworking the Gayer-Rostow-Schwartz and Beveridge series, Glenn Hueckel estimated that, relative to manufactures, grain prices rose by 1.05 percent per year, 1790–1815, and I have estimated that the relative price of imported raw materials rose by even more, 2

[41] Ashton, *Economic Fluctuations*, Table 8, p. 187.

[42] Patrick Colquhoun, *A Treatise on the Wealth, Power, and Resources of the British Empire* (London, 1815), Table 1, p. 47.

[43] Mokyr and Savin ("Stagflation in Historical Perspective," p. 221) feel that these estimates of the mobilization effect are too high. They estimate that those mobilized went from 2 to 5 percent, rather than from 2 to 10 percent as reported in the text. My estimate covers the period 1790–1812, while the Mokyr and Savin figure covers the period 1800–1812. Furthermore, my estimate includes the navy and marines while the Mokyr and Savin estimate does not. I shall stick to my estimate in what follows, but if Mokyr and Savin are correct the impact of war on the standard of living, per capita income, and industrialization is understated in Section IV, the right direction of bias.

[44] Williamson and Lindert, *American Inequality: A Macroeconomic History* (New York, 1980), chap. 4.

[45] Williamson, "The Structure of Pay in Britain, 1710–1911," in *Research in Economic History*, ed. Paul Uselding, vol. 7 (Greenwich, 1982).

[46] Williamson, *Did British Capitalism Breed Inequality?* (London, forthcoming 1984), chap. 12, Table 12.1.

TABLE 5
CONJECTURES ON THE IMPACT OF WAR ON BRITAIN'S RELATIVE PRICE TRENDS

Price Variable in Per Year Rate of Change	(1) Actual Wartime, 1790–1815	(2) The Impact of War: Based on Hueckel 1790–1815	(3) The Impact of War: Based on Hueckel 1760s–1810s
Grains: P_A^*	1.57%	0.99%	0.49%
Manufactures: P_M^*	0.52	0	0
Imported Raw Materials: P_F^*	2.00	0.99	0.49
$P_A^* - P_M^*$	1.05	0.99	0.49
$P_F^* - P_M^*$	1.48	0.99	0.49

Sources and Notes: Col. (1): P_M and P_A from Hueckel, "War and the British Economy," Table 3, p. 388, who reworked the Gayer-Rostow-Schwartz and Beveridge series; P_F is based on Gayer-Rostow-Schwartz "imported commodities" in Mitchell and Deane, Abstract, p. 470, sugar, tea, cotton, wool, and raw silk. Cols. (2) and (3) are based on Hueckel's (p. 389) estimate that the wars raised P_A/P_M by 28 percent.

percent per year.[47] These relative price trends are somewhat less dramatic when the longer period from the 1760s to the 1810s is examined, but the drift towards greater scarcity of imported raw materials is still apparent. The question is how much of the drift was due to war.

Three supply-side forces have received attention. First, rapid technical progress in manufacturing tended to raise the relative price of all other goods, including grains. Second, harvest failures can account for some of the increased scarcity of food, but not for very many years.[48] Third, the French Wars affected trade.[49] Hueckel has estimated that the hostilities and blockades inflated 1812 wheat prices by some 25–40 percent due solely to higher freight and insurance costs. For the 1790–1815 period as a whole, Hueckel estimated that the wars raised the relative price of grains by 28 percent.[50] Table 5 summarizes his findings.

[47] Glenn Hueckel, "War and the British Economy, 1793–1815: A General Equilibrium Analysis," Explorations in Economic History, 10 (Summer 1973), p. 369. Williamson, Did British Capitalism Breed Inequality? Appendix D.

[48] J. D. Chambers and G. E. Mingay, The Agricultural Revolution: 1750–1880 (London, 1966), p. 113; E. L. Jones, Seasons and Prices: The Role of Weather in English Agricultural History (London, 1964); Hueckel, "War and the British Economy," pp. 367–68.

[49] Mancur Olson, The Economics of Wartime Shortage (Durham, 1963); Mokyr and Savin, "Stagflation in Historical Perspective," pp. 223–31.

[50] Hueckel, "War and the British Economy," p. 389. In "The 1807–1809 Embargo Against Great Britain," this JOURNAL, 42 (June 1982), 305, Jeffrey Frankel recently estimated that the American embargo raised British raw cotton prices by as much as 72 percent in English markets, and that it served to lower the British terms of trade at home (cotton twist relative to Sea Island cotton) by some 42 percent. Frankel's calculations are much too high to be applied to the Napoleonic Era as a whole. Furthermore, they cannot serve as a very effective proxy for the terms of trade between imported grains and raw materials relative to all manufactures.

IV. ASSESSING THE IMPACT OF THE WARS ON BRITISH ECONOMIC PERFORMANCE

Modeling the Industrial Revolution

A general equilibrium model is necessary to factor out the wars from the industrial revolution properly, as an early effort by Glenn Hueckel has shown.[51]

A simple model capturing the main features of the British economy in the early nineteenth century has five domestic factors of production:[52]

farm land (*J*), excluding improvements other than initial clearing for cultivation or pasture;

capital (*K*), consisting of all civilian nonhuman asset services in the private and government sectors, other than farm lands, and excluding dwellings;

unskilled labor (*L*), or total civilian manhours compensated at the unskilled wage rate, including own labor time utilized in owner-occupied farms and in nonfarm proprietorships;

skills (*S*), or all attributes of civilian labor inputs generating earnings in excess of the unskilled wage; and

intermediate resource inputs (*B*), used directly in the manufacturing sector or indirectly in the urban sectors facilitating manufacturing production.

In addition, the model needs one imported intermediate input:

imported raw material inputs (*F*), processed by manufacturing and unavailable at home.

The first four are determined exogenously; that is, primary factor endowments are given. Intermediate inputs (*F* and *B*), however, are determined endogenously in response to demand and supply, domestic and foreign.

These factor inputs are used in the production of four sectoral outputs:

agriculture (*A*), or all national income originating in agriculture, forestry, and fisheries;

manufacturing (*M*), or all national income originating in manufacturing, building, and construction;

the tertiary sector (*C*), or all national income originating in finance, trade, gas, electricity and water, private services, local and national government (excluding military), transport and communications; and

[51] Hueckel, "War and the British Economy."
[52] Hueckel's "War and the British Economy" was the pioneering application of such methods to the problem, but his approach differs from what follows. For example, there are only two sectors in Hueckel's model—agriculture and manufacturing, no raw material inputs to manufacturing, and no nontradables. The most important difference is that Hueckel did not offer a quantitative assessment of the impact of capital formation.

intermediate resources (*B*), or all national income originating in mining and quarrying.

The civilian economy is open to trade in all *final* consumption and investment goods, save the tertiary sector, which produces nontradable home services. The home-produced *intermediate good B* cannot be traded internationally (for example, coal) while the foreign-produced intermediate good *F* cannot be produced at home (for example, cotton). The model conforms to the reality that Britain was a net importer of agricultural goods and a net exporter of manufactured goods. The small-country assumption has prices of all tradables determined exogenously by commercial policy and events outside of Britain, such as blockades, embargoes, and international transport costs. That is, demands for exportables and supplies of importables are taken to be highly price elastic.

The production relationships can be summarized as:

$$A = A(L, K, J),$$
$$M = M(L, K, S, B, F),$$
$$C = C(L, K, S, B),$$
$$B = B(L, K).$$

Capital and unskilled labor are assumed to move freely among all sectors; skilled labor is mobile between the industrial and tertiary sectors to which its use is restricted; land is specific to agricultural production; the imported intermediate resource is an input to manufacturing only; and the home-produced intermediate resource (coal) is used in manufacturing and the service sector.

The six inputs and four produced outputs have nine prices, since one of the produced outputs is also an input. By the small-country assumption, P_A, P_M, and P_F are taken as exogenous. The remaining six prices are determined endogenously:

d = rent earned on an acre of cleared farm land under crop or pasturage;

r = rent (or rate of return) earned on reproducible nonhuman capital (and the return on equity $i = r/P_K$, where P_K = price of capital);

w = the wage rate (or annual earnings) for unskilled labor;

q = the wage for skills;

P_C = the price of tertiary services; and

P_B = the price of home-produced resources.

The first four of these prices are factor rents, central to understanding inequality and the standard of living. The share of wages is the ratio of $[wL + qS]$ to national income. Pay ratios are measured by q/w, and the distribution of earnings is approximated by unskilled labor's share, $wL/[wL + qS]$. The distribution of income among recipients of property income can also be explored by the behavior of rents (dJ) and profits (rK). The model is class-ridden, and capable, therefore, of telling explicit stories about the determinants of inequality in nineteenth-century Britain.

The prices in nominal values can be converted into real or relative prices. For example, the standard-of-living debate can be confronted by deflating the nominal wage of common labor by the cost-of-living index (P), the latter constructed by a weighted average of the various prices in the model, taking the weights on each to be the budget shares implied by the demand system elaborated below.

The model also predicts the following seven quantities:

A = home-produced agricultural goods;
M = home-produced manufactured goods;
C = tertiary services, home-produced and home-consumed;
B = home-produced resources;
A_M = imported agricultural goods;
M_X = exported manufactured goods;
F = foreign-produced intermediate goods, imported.

The mix of industrial output is determined endogenously in the model. Industrialization can be measured by the behavior of the value of manufactures, $P_M M$, as a share in national income. World market conditions and domestic supply can both play critical roles as engines of industrialization.

Final product demands are endogenous. The budget constraint serves to eliminate the demand equation for tertiary services, and the remaining two final demand equations take the form:

$$A + A_M = D_A (y/P)^{\eta_A} (P_A/P)^{\varepsilon_A} (P_M/P)^{\varepsilon_{AM}} (P_C/P)^{\varepsilon_{AC}} (Pop)$$

$$M - M_X = D_M (y/P)^{\eta_M} (P_A/P)^{\varepsilon_{AM}} (P_M/P)^{\varepsilon_M} (P_C/P)^{\varepsilon_{MC}} (Pop)$$

The market clearing condition is imposed, making sectoral supplies equal to final aggregate demand. The D_js are exogenous shift terms, y is nominal gross national product per capita, P is the cost-of-living index, Pop is total population, η_{ij} is the income elasticity of demand for j, and ε_j and ε_{jk} are own-price and cross-price elasticities of demand for j. Nominal income is defined as:

$$Y = P_A A + P_M M + P_C C + D$$

where resource output, $P_B B$, is excluded since it is an intermediate good, and D is the net trade deficit in nominal terms. A final equation insures that the trade account is in balance:

$$P_A A_M + P_F F = P_M M_X + D.$$

It is a simple matter to convert the model into annual rates of change, and it makes a lot of sense to do so. After all, the issues raised by debate over the First Industrial Revolution hinge on trends and growth performances, not the level of variables. Of the many exogenous variables driving the model, only five attract attention in the counterfactual analysis that follows (asterisks refer to annual rates of change): the impact of wars, embargoes, and blockades on the price of the three tradables—P_A^*, P_M^*, and P_F^*; the impact of mobilization on civilian unskilled labor supplies—L^*; and the influence of crowding-out on civilian capital accumulation—K^*. The important endogenous variables are:

the real wage of the common laborer: $\quad w^* - P^*$

real national income: $\quad Y^* - P^*$

sectoral output in constant prices:

agriculture $\quad A^*$

industry $\quad M^*$

"home" services $\quad C^*$

mining and quarrying $\quad B^*$

industrialization index: $\quad M^* - A^*$

export expansion: $\quad M_X^*$

All interpretations of history are fiction, of course, but some fictions are better representations of the past than others. This one has been estimated with data drawn from the early 1820s. The model was then asked to predict British trends between 1821 and 1861, a far better documented epoch than 1760 to 1820. It did extremely well.[53] Thus encouraged, we can proceed with confidence to the period before 1820.

How Would Britain's Performance Have Differed in the Absence of Wars?

One could image two counterfactuals, either of which would serve to factor out the wars from the industrial revolution. On the one hand, we could ask how the British economy would have performed in the absence of the wars. On the other, we could ask how Britain's performance would have *differed* in the absence of the wars. The second counterfactual is used here, for the sufficient reason that economic historians do not agree on what actually happened during the wars. Better to focus on the differences between wartime performance predicted by the model and a predicted peacetime counterfactual.

Table 6 reports the counterfactual. The last column supplies the total impact while the first three columns break the total into its three parts—crowding-out affecting capital formation, dK^*; mobilization affecting the growth of the unskilled labor force, dL^*; and trade disruptions affecting relative prices at home, dP_j^*. The counterfactual is reported separately for 1790–1815 (the worst of the war years) and for the 1760s—

[53] Williamson, *Did British Capitalism Breed Inequality?* chap. 9.

TABLE 6

BY HOW MUCH WOULD BRITAIN'S GROWTH HAVE CHANGED UNDER COUNTERFACTUAL PEACETIME CONDITIONS?
(annual growth rates)

Endogenous Variable (growth per year)	No War Debt Crowding-Out Effects, dK^*	No Mobilization Effects, dL^*	No War-Distorted Price Effects, dP_j	All Effects Combined
1. The 1790–1815 Period				
Real Wage: $d[w^* - P^*]$	.94%	−0.27%	0.59%	1.27%
Real Income: $d[Y^* - P^*]$	.93	0.13	0.46	1.51
Sector Outputs: dA^*	.40	0.34	−2.76	−2.05
dM^*	1.14	0.02	2.93	4.09
dC^*	1.13	0.09	0.70	1.93
dB^*	1.14	0.02	2.82	3.98
Industrialization Index: $dM^* - dA^*$	.74	−0.32	5.69	6.14
Export of Manufactures: dM_x^*	1.59	−0.56	11.92	12.95
2. The 1760s–1810s Period				
Real Wage: $d[w^* - P^*]$	.68	−0.13	0.30	.84
Real Income: $d[Y^* - P^*]$	.67	0.06	0.23	.96
Sector Outputs: dA^*	.29	0.15	−1.38	−.94
dM^*	.82	0.01	1.47	2.30
dC^*	.81	0.05	0.35	1.21
dB^*	.82	0.01	1.41	2.24
Industrialization Index: $dM^* - dA^*$	.53	−0.14	2.85	3.24
Export of Manufactures: dM_x^*	1.14	−0.28	5.96	6.82

Notes: The counterfactual civilian capital stock assumptions are taken from Table 4, col. (3). The counterfactual price assumptions are taken from Table 5, and the counterfactual civilian unskilled labor force assumptions are taken from the text in Section III: for the 1790–1815 period, $dL^* = 0.17$, $dP_A^* = -0.49$, $dP_F^* = -0.49$, and $dP_M^* = -0.98$, and $dP_M^* = 0$; for the 1760s–1810s period, $dL^* = 0.34$, $dP_A^* = -0.98$, $dP_F^* = -0.98$, and $dP_M^* = 0$.

1810s. Each panel reports the impact on the growth rates of eight endogenous variables: aggregate real income, output in four sectors, manufactured exports (in constant prices), an industrialization index (the difference between the growth of industry and of agriculture), and the real wage of common labor.

The effects on capital accumulation were the most important source of slow growth (0.67/0.96 = 60 percent of the combined effects of war from the 1760s to the 1810s). Yet the war-induced decline in the terms of trade (the dP_i^* effects) plus mobilization (the dL^* effects) were both sufficiently important that the effects of war in total exceeded the accumulation effects themselves. It appears that Britain's aggregate real income growth per year would have been higher by 1.51 percent from 1790 to 1815, and 0.96 percent per year higher from the 1760s to the 1810s, had peace prevailed.

If these calculations are even close to the mark they have important implications for the debate over British growth during the First Industrial Revolution. Harley has estimated that aggregate income growth per year accelerated from 1.3 to 2.3 percent between 1770–1815 and 1815–1841.[54] Table 6 suggests that almost all of the acceleration was caused by peace. In other words, the measured trend acceleration had little to do with the underlying forces of capitalist development.

Furthermore, the relatively slow rate of industrialization prior to 1820 appears to have been war-induced. Had peacetime conditions prevailed, manufacturing output would have grown 2.3 percent per year faster; that is, Harley's Divisia Index would have grown 3 or 4 percent per year, rather than the modest 1.5 or 1.6 percent actually achieved between 1770 and 1815.[55] Once again, if these calculations are even close to the mark, they imply that the doubling in the growth of industrial output that Harley measured can be explained entirely by the switch from war to peace.

In contrast, agriculture would have undergone far slower growth, perhaps some 0.94 percent per year slower, had not the wartime food scarcity encouraged domestic production. Since British agriculture grew annually no faster than 0.8 percent between 1770 and 1815, the counterfactual suggests that agricultural output might in fact have declined without war. And, of course, the great surge in Britain's exports would have been faster and sooner with peace, faster by some 6.8 percent per year.

One of the strangest features of the period is of course the failure of the standard of living of the working classes to rise much until the 1820s. Social reformers have argued for more than a century that British capitalism simply failed to let income improvements trickle down while others have stressed that supplies of labor were elastic. Table 6 suggests

[54] Harley, "British Industrialization Before 1841," p. 286.
[55] Ibid., Table 5, p. 276.

instead that most of the dismal standard of living performance before the 1820s can be attributed to the wars and their financing. Peace would have raised the growth in workers' living standards by 0.84 percent per year, or by 65 percent for the six decades as a whole. Once again, if this counterfactual result is even close to the mark, then it suggests that the evidence generated by the debate on the standard of living is of doubtful relevance for testing whether the gains from capitalism trickled down.

Crowding-out appears to have been the dominant force affecting the standard of living (0.68/0.84 = 81 percent of the total over the six decades as a whole). Slow accumulation and thus slow rates of job creation (especially in cities) account for most of the poor performance in living standards up to the 1820s, though war-induced price distortions played a major supporting role (0.30/0.84 = 36 percent of the total). As has been shown, crowding-out and forgone accumulation also account for most of the slow aggregate growth, but it does *not* account for a large share of slow industrialization. Prices and world markets played a far greater role.

V. SOME CONCLUDING REMARKS

Most of the increase in national income per worker during the First Industrial Revolution was caused by productivity advance, and little by accumulation and capital deepening. This has long been textbook wisdom. Now there is some evidence to support it. Feinstein, for example, estimates that total factor productivity growth accounted for almost nine-tenths of output per worker growth from 1761 to 1860.[56] McCloskey finds much the same, encouraging the conclusion that "ingenuity rather than abstention governed the industrial revolution."[57] Yet these findings seem inconsistent with most of what we know about other economies passing through the early stages of the industrial revolution. In the contemporary Third World, total factor productivity improvements explain only about 10 percent of growth.[58] Abramovitz and David have shown that total factor productivity improvements explain very little of antebellum American per capita output growth (about 27 percent). Ohkawa and Rosovsky suggest the same for Japan between 1908 and 1938 where total factor productivity improvements explain only a third of labor productivity growth.[59] Britain's industrial

[56] Feinstein, "Capital Formation," Table 26, p. 86.
[57] McCloskey, *The Economic History of Britain*, p. 108.
[58] Angus Maddison, *Economic Progress and Policy in Developing Countries* (London, 1970), Table 11.11, p. 53.
[59] Moses Abramovitz and Paul A. David, "Reinterpreting Economic Growth: Parables and Realities," *American Economic Review*, 63 (May 1973), Table 1, p. 430; Kazushi Ohkawa and Henry Rosovsky, *Japanese Economic Growth: Trend Acceleration in the Twentieth Century* (Stanford, 1973).

revolution seems odd: whereas other nations passing through early industrialization record high contributions for conventional capital accumulation and low contributions for total factor productivity growth, Britain prior to 1820 suggests the opposite. Why? The answer seems to be very simple: the rate of accumulation was suppressed by war well below what it would have been in peace.

The rate of accumulation in Britain up to the 1820s was so tiny that the capital-labor ratio hardly rose at all. The absence of capital-deepening is so striking that it has encouraged all manner of exotic speculation about the capital-saving attributes of the new technologies. Perhaps less exotic speculation is warranted: capital-deepening was modest because saving in reproducible capital out of national income was modest. Indeed, the surprising fact is the low saving rate. Deane and Cole called the level and increase in the conventional saving rate "modest," and Mathias thought the "modesty of rates of accumulation" was one profound difference between eighteenth-century England and the contemporary Third World.[60] The explanation for the apparent lack of thrift in eighteenth-century Britain is simply that savers were accumulating war debt. The gross private saving rate—which includ₅s increased holdings of war debt—was as high as 18.1 percent between 1761 and 1821, not so distant from the contemporary Third World estimates after all.

There are two morals to the story. First, wars *can* be factored out of the First Industrial Revolution, and the exercise appears to have a profound impact on our interpretations of early British growth. Second, the time seems ripe for economic historians to examine critically their single-asset view of thrift, saving, and accumulation. It makes more sense to think in terms of multi-asset, portfolio choices. The motive for saving can be served by accumulating government debt, foreign debt, irreproducible assets, capital gains on these (including rising land values), as well as real capital. While it is certainly true that investment demand will influence the extent to which savers favor capital formation, it is also true that any exogenous change in the *supply* of the other forms of accumulation will tend to crowd out capital formation. These two forces—investment demand and crowding-out—are likely to be far more important than thrift in accounting for the historical variety in growth.

60   Deane and Cole, *British Economic Growth*, p. 276; Mathias in Crouzet, *Capital Formation*, p. viii.

Capital Flows to the New World as an Intergenerational Transfer

Alan M. Taylor

Northwestern University

Jeffrey G. Williamson

Harvard University

The late nineteenth century saw international mass migrations of capital and labor from the Old World to the New. Factors chased each other and the abundant resources at the frontier. Demographic structure also contributed to the massive capital flows from Britain to the New World. The dependency hypothesis is confirmed by estimation of savings functions in three New World economies (Argentina, Australia, and Canada) in which high dependency rates may have significantly depressed domestic savings rates and pulled in foreign investment: in effect an intergenerational transfer from old savers in the Old World to young savers in the New.

I. The Problem

After 1492, the central problem for Old World Europe was to exploit the cheap natural resources in the New World. Since the resources were immobile, the exploitation could take the form of only imports

Jeffrey Williamson acknowledges financial support from the National Science Foundation, grant nos. SES-9021951 and SBR-9223002. Alan Taylor acknowledges financial support from the Harvard Academy for International and Area Studies, the Tinker Foundation, and the Committee on Latin American and Iberian Studies (Harvard University). The topic was in part stimulated by the recent work of Ian McLean at the University of Adelaide (Australia). With regard to the background data, we also acknowledge the help of M. C. Urquhart at Queen's University (Canada) and Roberto Cortés Conde and Gerardo Della Paolera at the Instituto Torcuato di Tella (Argentina). In addition, the paper has been improved by the comments of Lance Davis, James Foreman-Peck, Matt Higgins, Ken Kang, Peter Lindert, and seminar participants at the Harvard Economic History Workshop, the Instituto Torcuato di Tella, the Australian National University, the University of Adelaide, and the University of Melbourne. The usual disclaimer applies.

[*Journal of Political Economy*, 1994, vol. 102, no. 2]
© 1994 by The University of Chicago. All rights reserved. 0022-3808/94/0202-0008$01.50

of resource-intensive commodities. That trade, in turn, was economically feasible only with the introduction of the investment and technologies that lowered freight rates on such low-value, high-bulk products. By the late nineteenth century, freight rates had fallen far enough to have created a partial convergence of resource-intensive commodity prices between the two sides of the Atlantic. The problem for the New World was to augment its capacity to supply more resource-intensive exports so as to exploit the gains from trade. The economies of the New World were characterized by dual scarcity: dear labor, dear capital, and cheap resources. The problem was to augment the supplies of labor and capital that combined with the abundant resources. The Old World helped the process along with emigration and capital export, and this process reached a crescendo between 1870 and 1913 (Green and Urquhart 1976; Schedvin 1990).

Capital chased after the European migrants, but the reason has never been clear, and the correlation may have been spurious (Nurkse 1954). In the simple two-factor trade models, capital will not chase after labor. If labor was abundant in the Old World, capital must have been scarce. Thus emigration from the Old World would have gone hand in hand with capital imports, not capital exports. The ahistorical prediction of the simple model is repaired when we add the key third factor, natural resources. The resulting dual scarcity in the New World now makes it possible for Old World capital to chase after the emigrants.

But how, exactly, did it work? And why did those capital and labor flows reach such heights at the turn of the century, the years between 1907 and 1913 in particular? According to Paish (1914; cited in Kennedy [1987, p. 184]), Britain placed £1,127 million abroad during those seven years, 61 percent of it, or £689 million, in the New World regions of Canada, Australasia, Argentina, and the United States (table 1). Adding the rest of Latin America pushes those numbers up still further to £857 million, or 76 percent.

For some time now, economic historians have debated two questions: first, whether the "world" capital market was "well integrated"; and second, how much of the massive capital flows to the New World were pulled by an economic boom in the New World, and how much by an economic bust in Britain. This paper does not deal with the first question, although we note that the evidence certainly seems to confirm the well-integrated view. Indeed, the evidence suggests that world capital markets were at least as well integrated in the 1890s as they were in the 1980s and probably better (Zevin 1992), and that they were probably well integrated as early as the eighteenth century (Neal 1985). This paper assumes as much and focuses on the second question.

TABLE 1

BRITISH OVERSEAS INVESTMENT, 1907–13

Area	Amount (£ Million)	Share (%)
New World Empire	319	28
Canada and Newfoundland	254	
Australasia	65	15
United States	164	
Latin America	268	24
Argentina	118	
Brazil	88	
Mexico	34	
Chile	28	
Other Empire	163	14
China and Japan	50	4
Europe	49	4
Russia	46	4
Miscellaneous foreign	68	6
Total	1,127	100

SOURCE.—Kennedy (1987, p. 184); based on Paish (1914, p. 81).

Having dual scarcity, the New World countries needed both capital and labor to exploit fully their abundant natural resources. The problem, however, was that any effort to increase New World labor supplies served to augment still further their capital requirements. And they certainly did increase their labor supplies relative to those of the Old World. Figure 1 reports the simple correlation between population growth rates (the rate of change of $\log N(t)$ on the vertical axis) and the initial real wages in 1870 ($\log W_0(t)$ on the horizontal axis) for the period 1870–1913. Four New World countries are clustered to the right (Argentina, Australia, Canada, and the United States), the poorest Old World countries are clustered to the left (Italy, Sweden, Spain, Norway, the Netherlands, and Denmark), and the remaining richer Old World countries are clustered in the middle (France, Ireland, Belgium, Germany, and the United Kingdom). Labor scarcity produced the predictable labor supply response among these 15 countries, and the correlation is strong (slope coefficient 0.011, t-statistic 2.75).

Fast population and labor force growth in the New World implied high investment rates to equip the new workers. This view has become conventional wisdom, so much so that we now have come to talk about the importance of booms in population-sensitive investment demand in pulling capital from the Old World to the New (Green and Urquhart 1976; Edelstein 1982, pp. 198–208). Not only were investment booms in the New World driven in large part by population and labor force growth, but they tended to be centered on social

CAPITAL FLOWS

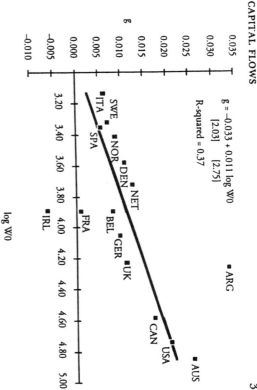

$g = -0.033 + 0.011 \log W_0$
[2.03]   [2.75]
R-squared = 0.37

FIG. 1.—Real wages and population growth, 1870–1913; g is the growth rate of the population, and W_0 is the real wage in 1870. (Source: Williamson 1994.)

overhead activities, which, being very capital intensive, tended to augment investment requirements even further (Lewis 1978; Williamson 1979). Thus labor force growth in the New World, responding to labor scarcity, raised capital scarcity, augmented investment requirements, and pulled in even more capital from the Old World. All of this is well known, although what role labor force growth played in accounting for the massive capital flows to the New World remains an open question.

Rapid population and labor force growth in the New World was achieved, of course, in two ways. First, the immigrants augmented labor supplies in the New World (while depleting them in the Old). In the United States, for example, immigrants accounted for 40.5 percent of the population increase between 1870 and 1913 (U.S. Bureau of the Census 1975, 1:8, 104–5). Second, New World residents augmented the labor supply by high fertility and low infant mortality rates. Such demographic forces had implications for labor participation and dependency rates (the share of the population dependent on adult workers); in this paper we focus on the latter. According to the life cycle model, economies full of very young households burdened with high dependency rates should save smaller shares of their income. Section II will elaborate on the argument and survey the relevant literature; we are certainly not the first to suggest that high dependency rates were likely to have choked off domestic savings rates in the New World full of younger generations, increasing their dependence on the Old World (full of older generations) to satisfy their investment requirements (Green and Urquhart 1976, p. 219). But no one to our knowledge has taken a close look at the size of the dependency rate gaps between the Old World and the New, and tried to assess the role that those gaps might have made in contributing to the massive capital transfer just prior to World War I.[1]

The paper poses the following counterfactual: What would New World domestic savings rates have been like prior to World War I had they been favored by the lower dependency rates then prevailing in Britain, the key capital exporter in the Old World? We then ask by how much foreign capital requirements in the New World would have declined and, thus, how much of Britain's capital exports can be explained by demographic forces. The bottom line is this: It appears that dependency rate gaps can account for a large share (roughly three-quarters) of late nineteenth century capital flows to the New World, and as a consequence, it is appropriate to view them as an intergenerational transfer.

II. Dependency Rate Gaps and the Life Cycle Model

First, we must establish whether there were dependency rate gaps between the Old World and the New, and whether they were big enough to have mattered. For this discussion we take the Old World to be the United Kingdom, which, after all, was the main source of capital exports. The New World includes Argentina, Australia, Canada, and the United States, a group that accounted for the vast majority of the New World capital imports from the United Kingdom and that includes those countries whose database makes it possible to implement a quantitative assessment.[2] Figure 2 should suffice to motivate the discussion. Figure 2a plots the dependency rate (D_{15}, equal to the share of the population aged under 15 years) from the mid–nineteenth century to the present. All the New World countries start with enormous dependency rates: the United States, in 1850, .415; Canada, in 1851, .560; Australia, in 1861, .367 (rising to .422 in 1871); and Argentina, in 1869, .452.[3] They did not stay that high, declining steadily to 1900 as these New World countries matured. Yet even in the 1890s, the dependency rates were still high by the

---

[1] An exception is Taylor (1992), which explores the retreat of British capital from Argentina around World War I.

[2] A statistical appendix is available from the authors on request.

[3] These dependency rates are very high even by the standards of the Third World in 1989—low-income economies, .355; the middle-income economies, .362 (World Bank 1991, p. 254)—where fertility and population growth have been so high, and where the dependency rate debate, as we shall see, had its origin.

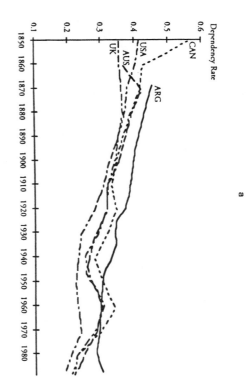

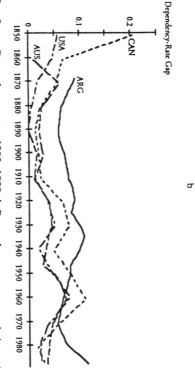

a

b

FIG. 2.—*a*, Dependency rates, 1850–1988. *b*, Dependency rate gaps relative to Britain, 1850–1988. The dependency rate is the share of the population aged 0–15 years. The dependency rate gap is the difference between each country's dependency rate and that in Britain. (Source: See our unpublished appendix.)

standards of the contemporary Third World, and they were equally high in New Zealand (.397) and in Latin America generally (.414). The important point, however, is the size of the dependency rate gap between the New World and the United Kingdom (fig. 2*b*). Between 1900 and 1913, they were still positive. Around 1900, the gap was 7.7 percentage points for Argentina, 2.7 for Australia, 2.0 for Canada, and 1.8 for the United States.[4] The issue now is whether these

[4] These gaps are smaller than those between the OECD countries and the Third World in 1989 (15–16 percentage points) according to the World Bank (1991), but between the 1850s and the 1870s, Canada and Argentina fell in that range (10–20 percentage points).

dependency rate gaps were big enough to matter, and the answer hinges on their estimated impact on New World savings.

High dependency rates imply low savings rates. This follows directly from the dependency hypotheses, a centerpiece in the economic-demographic literature for about two decades following the appearance of Coale and Hoover's highly influential *Population Growth and Economic Development in Low-Income Countries* (1958).[5] The dependency hypothesis reached its apex with Leff's (1969) paper, which offered very strong empirical support based on a cross section of 74 countries. Across the 1970s, however, better data and more careful analysis yielded more ambiguous results, and it looked as though the dependency hypothesis was about to be shelved as another plausible theory with no strong evidence to support it. In the 1980s, new life was breathed into the hypothesis by Mason (1981, 1987, 1988), Fry (1984), and Fry and Mason (1982). The new version recognized the importance of the growth environment in the form of what they called the variable rate-of-growth effect.[6]

The basic idea behind both the old and the new versions is the life cycle model popularized by Modigliani (1966) (see also Modigliani and Brumberg 1954; Modigliani and Ando 1957; Ando and Modigliani 1963).[7] The household is characterized as accumulating no wealth over its lifetime, with saving in midlife exactly offsetting dissaving in early and later life. Even so, economywide saving can vary considerably if the economy is growing fast, because of either population growth or per capita income growth. In early stages of high fertility and rapid population growth, the average household is likely to be very young and therefore able to obtain only low or even negative saving rates. In middle stages of declining fertility and maturing populations, the average household is likely to be middle-aged and therefore able to obtain high and positive saving rates. In late stages, older households may dominate, and therefore low saving rates may again characterize the economy. If, in addition, per capita income is growing fast, young households command a much greater lifetime income than older ones, and thus young households' consumption will increase, generating less aggregate saving. When the microeconomics is fully explored, Mason emerges with his variable rate-of-growth estimation equation, and his results using national panel data from 1965 to 1980 strongly support the model: "a higher dependency ratio

---

[5] For a survey of this literature, see Bilsborrow (1980).

[6] Mason has shown that it should apply with special strength in fast-growing environments—such as the New World between 1870 and 1913—and Schultz (1987) has shown how powerfully it can work through the educational delivery system.

[7] The brief exposition that follows relies heavily on Mason's (1987, pp. 530–39) extension of the model.

leads to lower saving, *particularly among countries with moderate to high rates of income growth*" (Mason 1987, pp. 549–50; emphasis added).[8]

Some economic historians have already found the dependency rate model useful for exploring various problems in the past. Although Kelley (1968) did not estimate a model for Australia, he used one to illustrate how important demographic effects might have been in late nineteenth century experience of that country. Lewis (1983) applied the life cycle model to identify successfully the role of the decline in the American dependency rate between 1830 and 1900. He approached the problem using child rearing costs implied by various household surveys from 1889–90, 1900, and 1935–36. He then estimated that the decline in the dependency rate could have accounted for perhaps a quarter of the marked rise in the aggregate domestic savings rate, a rise that so much has been made of by American economic historians (Gallman 1966; David 1977; Williamson 1979; Ransom and Sutch 1983), and a rise that helped wean America away from foreign capital as the late nineteenth century unfolded. Williamson (1990, pp. 34–39) applied the same dependency rate reasoning to help account for the higher savings rates in England's cities (compared with the countryside) during the Industrial Revolution. A lower dependency rate also raised city savings rates perhaps as much as three percentage points above those of the countryside, thus diminishing the rural-urban capital flows necessary to finance the urban-based industrial revolution.

The most recent application in economic history was offered by McLean (1991), who successfully applied a simple version of the dependency rate hypothesis to Australian and Canadian experience from the 1860s to the present. McLean's research has stimulated our own, but we have extended it in three directions: Argentina has been added to the analysis; McLean's version of the dependency rate hypothesis has been replaced by one that draws on Mason and Leff; and, most important, the results are used to explore the underlying sources of those massive capital flows from the Old World to the New just prior to World War I.

III.   Estimating the Impact of Dependency Rates on Domestic Savings

The demographic analysis of savings has been a common, if controversial, element of the empirical development literature since Leff's

---

[8] It should be stressed that the dependency rate need not just influence household saving. Its influence can also be felt indirectly through government saving. High dependency rates are likely to increase the load on poor relief and other current public expenditures, thus diminishing the funds available for capital expenditures. They may also raise the tax burden, thus lowering the disposable incomes of potential savers and contributing to lower household saving.

seminal work in the late 1960s. Leff (1969) analyzed savings rates in a large cross-section sample, including both developed and less developed countries, and found that high dependency rates had a significant negative impact on savings rates. The savings equations estimated by Leff typically took the form

$$\ln s_i = \beta_0 + \beta_1 \ln g_i + \beta_2 \ln\left(\frac{Y}{N}\right)_i + \beta_3 D_{1i} + \beta_4 D_{2i} + \epsilon_i,$$

where g denotes the rate of growth of real per capita income, Y/N the level of real income per capita, D_1 and D_2 the young (ages 0–15) and old (ages 65 and older) dependency rates, and s the aggregate savings rate. Leff's study generated much criticism based on its sample choice and omitted variables, and subsequent work revealed a great disparity in the magnitude and significance of the effect.[9]

In more recent efforts to explore the link between savings and dependency rates, panel data have been used to overcome such data restrictions. Mason (1987) exploited a three-period panel data set for a large group of post–World War II countries, including the growth rate interaction term in his savings functions. His typical regression takes the form

$$\ln c_{it} = \beta_0 + \beta_1 \alpha_{it} g_{it} + \beta_2 \alpha_{it} g_{it} \ln D_{it} + \beta_3 g_{it} + \epsilon_{it},$$

where c denotes the aggregate consumption share (net or gross) in income, g the rate of aggregate real income growth, D the young dependency rate (a proxy for the quantity of child rearing activities), and α a derived measure of the difference between mean ages of child rearing and other activities. The Mason model bears the stamp of Leff's pioneering approach yet reflects the subtleties of a thorough microanalysis of household saving and child rearing decisions, as noted above.

Given the eclectic nature of the literature, a hybrid model has been used in this paper to incorporate both direct effects of the dependency rate on savings, in the manner of Leff and his critics, and indirect effects operating via the growth rate, following Mason. Although data limitations preclude a time-series analysis for most of today's less developed countries, we were not similarly hampered when dealing with the New World economies, whose documented

---

[9] As Hammer (1986) points out, many variables in the development process are highly correlated, and, consequently, cross-country studies will generally suffer from collinearity problems and a lack of robustness with respect to alternative specifications. A better approach would be to use individual country time-series data that "would control for the country-specific variables which determine savings. However, since age distributions change slowly and population censuses are conducted relatively infrequently, data restrictions for such studies are severe" (Hammer 1986, p. 583).

macroeconomic experience stretches back to the turn of the century and beyond. National saving can be calculated from investment and the current-account identity, and savings rates can then be derived using an estimate of national income. Time series for real national income provide estimates of growth rates, and frequent population censuses allow the calculation of dependency rates using interpolation as necessary. In this way a complete time-series database was built up for four New World economies, comprising national aggregate savings rates (s), young dependency rates (D), and growth rates of aggregate real income (g).[10] The following hybrid savings equation was estimated for Argentina, Australia, Canada, and the United States with dummy variables included to account for wartime effects:[11]

$$s_t = \beta_0 + \beta_1 g_t + \beta_2 D_t + \beta_3 D_t g_t$$
$$+ \beta_4 (\text{dummy WW1})_t + \beta_5 (\text{dummy WW2})_t + \epsilon_t.$$

The results are presented in table 2 for various sample choices and for three New World countries in which dependency rates mattered: Argentina, Australia, and Canada. Columns 1–3 contain the basic results on individual country time series. In column 4, panel data results are shown for the three-country sample with corrections for autocorrelation and heteroscedasticity.[12] The results do not offer much support to the growth rate interaction theories, since neither g nor $D \times g$ enters with a significant coefficient. The key finding is that the direct dependency rate impact on savings rates is large and highly significant in all three cases, with an estimated coefficient of between -0.61 and -1.53 on the dependency rate, corresponding to the partial derivative $\beta_D = \partial s / \partial D$. Using sample averages, we obtain

---

[10] The records begin in 1897 for the United States, in 1900 for Argentina, in 1862 for Australia, and in 1871 for Canada. See our unpublished appendix.

[11] This approach was inspired by McLean (1991), who estimated savings functions for Australia and Canada. He used the proportion of the population aged 45–64 years as an explanatory variable and embedded it in a somewhat different interpretation of the life cycle hypothesis. In an effort to make our results comparable with the development literature, our model differs by using the dependency rate as an explanatory variable and admitting interactions with the growth rate. Furthermore, we prefer to use the autoregressive AR1 specification: although a lagged dependent variable (LDV) model could not be rejected using standard tests, it was found that the AR1 specification dealt more convincingly with serial correlation problems, particularly with the Australian data. Nonetheless, the conclusions of this paper apply with equal force if the LDV specification is adopted. On testing LDV versus AR1 models, see Griliches (1967) and Maddala (1977, pp. 141–48).

[12] For the panel data estimation, the individual country time series are p-differenced, and a residual variance series is constructed. The equation is then estimated by applying weighted least squares to the p-differenced series, a procedure outlined by Pindyck and Rubinfeld (1981, pp. 258–59). We are grateful to Ken Kang for suggesting this approach.

TABLE 2

SAVINGS FUNCTION ESTIMATES FOR THE NEW WORLD ECONOMIES

	Argentina, 1900–1988 (1)	Australia, 1862–1988 (2)	Canada, 1871–1988 (3)	Panel of Three, 1900–1988 (4)	United States, 1898–1988 (5)
	A. Regression Results				
Estimation method	AR1	AR1	AR1	Weighted least squares	AR1
Coefficients:					
Constant	.620*	.381*	.360*	.416*	.122
	(6.50)	(5.05)	(4.64)	(8.01)	(1.58)
g	.857	−.534	−.224	−.246	.508
	(.98)	(1.47)	(.76)	(1.10)	(1.16)
D	−1.53*	−.685*	−.613	−.834*	.0679
	(5.22)	(2.89)	(2.51)	(5.18)	(.25)
D × g	−2.17	2.05	.607	.887	−1.43
	(.85)	(1.95)	(.71)	(1.37)	(.97)
Dummy WW1	.0805*	−.0105	−.00926	...	−.0142
	(2.28)	(.39)	(.58)		(.71)
Dummy WW2	.0380	−.0657*	−.0177	...	−.0823*
	(1.27)	(2.51)	(1.12)		(3.85)
ρ	.416*	.755*	.838*	...	.696
	(4.08)	(12.78)	(15.80)		(8.86)

Continued overleaf

an estimate of the elasticity of the savings rate with respect to the dependency rate, $(D/s)(\partial s/\partial D)$, which ranges between -1.24 and -3.90. The panel data estimates fit somewhere within these bounds, as expected, but in all cases the elasticity estimates are large in the context of recent studies. For example, these figures are much larger on the whole than the estimates from contemporary international cross-section analysis reviewed by Hammer (1986, p. 584).

Broadly speaking, the analysis of saving in these three New World economies offers strong support for the dependency hypothesis. The exception to this rule is the United States, the New World country that, on the basis of previous microeconomic analysis, has the most supportive dependency rate and life cycle literature. Table 2 reports these unexpected findings: definitive support for the hypothesis that the changing U.S. age distribution has affected the macroeconomic aggregates has proven elusive.[13]

Of course, it is tempting to expect too much of the model. In the short to medium term, however, a dependency rate theory of saving is clearly unable to track long-swing and Kuznets cycle phenomena. Such phenomena include the typical long-wave, boom-and-bust variations in macroeconomic aggregates so clearly evident over this period. The dependency rate theory is much better suited to analysis over the medium to long term where such variations wash out: a sound motivation for the long time-series analysis pursued here.[14]

On a more positive note, table 2 suggests that the impact of dependency rates in the other three New World countries was highly sig-

[13] In some very recent work, Fair and Dominguez (1991) explored a time-series approach for the period 1954–88 and found that the age distribution enters as a significant determinant of U.S. aggregate saving. Their results have little to say, however, about dependency rates and savings rates in the late nineteenth and early twentieth centuries, a link that appears weak for the United States in our own tests. The ambiguity surrounding the link was highlighted in a recent discussion by Edelstein (1991), who found that the impact of declining dependency rates in the United States from 1890 to 1910 could translate into increases in the savings rate of 0.44, 1.69, or 4.08 percentage points, depending on whose estimates are used. Edelstein contrasted the large impact on savings rates arising from a Leff-type calculation with more modest figures derived from a Modigliani-Sterling (1983) formula.

[14] We return to this point in our concluding remarks, but it suffices to say that those wishing to test the life cycle or dependency rate theories of saving with macroeconomic data face frustration. The use of multicountry cross sections for short periods (or even a single year) raises the possibility of omitted variable bias, a typical criticism of Leff's original study. The use of long time series for a few countries (or only one country) raises the question of the structural stability of the savings equation and inclines the model to track poorly over the short to medium term. It may be that a panel of medium-length time series for groups of sufficiently similar countries offers the best compromise. For the United States at least, it will certainly require further research to reconcile the differences in the array of estimates arising from variations in the quality of the data, the length and scope of the time series, and the sensitivity of the hypotheses to alternative model specifications.

nificant and large in comparison to contemporary estimates: typically, a one-percentage-point rise in the dependency rate led approximately to a one-percentage-point fall in the aggregate savings rate.

IV. Capital Flows to the New World as an Intergenerational Transfer

What Is the Counterfactual?

What fraction of the capital flows were pulled from Britain by a demographically induced savings shortfall in the receiving regions? In an attempt to answer this question, a natural counterfactual suggests itself. As we have seen, the New World tended to have much higher dependency rates than Britain over the period. Yet what would national savings rates have looked like at the periphery had the demographic burden been absent? Would the New World have been self-sufficient in terms of accumulation given enough mature savers (or sufficiently few children)? We claim that the natural counterfactual, couched in these terms, is as follows. First, start with the imposition of the British age distribution on all New World regions receiving capital flows from the Old World, and calculate the implied decline in the dependency rate in each country. Second, use the savings function parameters estimated in table 2 to estimate the counterfactual rise in New World savings rates (excluding the United States, naturally). Third, use New World national income to estimate the rise in their aggregate national savings. Finally, assume a fixed investment demand to infer the crowding-out of foreign capital that would ensure by exploiting the current-account identity. The method is essentially a means to measure how much "demographic crowding-out" would be entailed by eliminating the dependency rate gaps between sending and receiving regions in the world capital market. The appropriate measure is[15]

[15] Let D^j denote the young dependency rate in country j, and ΔD^j denote the dependency rate gap in country j relative to Britain, written $\Delta D^j = D^j - D^{UK}$. The impact of changes in the dependency rate on savings rates for three New World capital importers operates through the partial derivative $\beta_D = \partial s/\partial D$. Let β_{D^j} denote the parameter estimate for country j. The current-account identity expresses the relation between national savings (S^j), investment (I^j), and net foreign investment (NFI^j) in each country: NFI$^j = I^j - S^j$. With invariant levels of domestic investment under counterfactual conditions, any increase in the total domestic savings level spills over into a one-for-one decrease in the current-account balance, crowding out foreign investment: ΔNFI$^j = -\Delta S^j$. To estimate the change in total domestic savings due to "demographic crowding-out," we first observe that the counterfactual change in the savings rate is given by $\Delta s^j = \Delta(S^j/Y^j) = -\beta_{D^j}\Delta D^j$. The implied change in the level of total domestic savings may be imputed using an estimate of country j's national income Y^j, and hence the implied spillover into the balance of payments, and thus the net foreign investment crowded out, is given by the formula that follows.

JOURNAL OF POLITICAL ECONOMY

demographic crowding-out $= -\Delta \mathrm{NFI}^j = \Delta S^j$

$$= Y^j \Delta_S{}^j = -Y^j \hat{\beta}_{Dj} \Delta D^j.$$

This crowding-out may be expressed in terms of its impact in either the sending or receiving region. For any receiving region j (a country or a group of countries), we may calculate the share of demographic crowding-out in total worldwide British net foreign investment (NFI $= \Sigma_j \mathrm{NFI}^j$), or we may calculate the share of the demographic crowding-out in total British net foreign investment *in that region alone* (NFI^j):

share of total British NFI crowded out in country $j = \dfrac{-\Delta \mathrm{NFI}^j}{\sum_j \mathrm{NFI}^j}$,

share of British NFI in country j crowded out in country $j = \dfrac{-\Delta \mathrm{NFI}^j}{\mathrm{NFI}^j}$.

If these measures are limited to only the three New World countries for which a dependency rate effect has been identified, then we have established a *lower bound* or minimum impact level for such demographic counterfactuals, since they assume no changes in the rest of the world capital market. If instead we assume that the rest of the New World behaved exactly like one or all of the three countries, then we have established an *upper bound* or maximal impact associated with demographic influences (e.g., "so goes Argentina, so goes Latin America"). In this way the analysis offers a variety of bounds for the analysis and, hence, some measure of sensitivity.

In what follows, four separate cases are explored, yielding a lower bound (MIN), two midrange estimates (MID1 and MID2), and an upper bound (MAX). Two different groups of receiving regions are used: the three New World economies (Argentina, Australia, and Canada) and a wider New World group (the former plus Brazil, Mexico, and Chile—three Latin America economies for which we have national income and dependency rate estimates). Each group's demographic crowding-out is examined from the point of view of both the sending and receiving regions. The results are presented in table 3.

Counterfactual 1: How Much of Total British Net Foreign Investment Would Have Been Crowded out in the Three New World Economies Alone (MIN Estimate)?

Part A of table 3 shows counterfactual demographic crowding-out in Argentina, Australia, and Canada during four periods between 1884 and 1913. The figures are cumulated and compared to Feinstein's (1972) and Edelstein's (1982, app. 1) estimates of total British capital outflows. The levels of crowding-out suggest that demographic influences at their peak may have been responsible for pulling as much as 46 percent of total British capital exports to these three countries alone between 1901 and 1906; the figure was 28 percent for 1907–13. The impact was much smaller before 1891, not because dependency rate gaps were smaller (they were larger), nor because elasticities were lower (they are assumed constant), but because national incomes and, thus, savings shortfalls in those three countries were modest in relation to total British capital export potential. Thereafter, demographic crowding-out in the three New World economies always amounted to at least 25 percent of total British NFI.

Part B of table 3 uses a different set of NFI estimates, comparing demographic crowding-out to Paish's (1914) figures for British overseas investment in the great surge just prior to the First World War.[16] This counterfactual implies that about 31 percent of total British capital exports would have been displaced by demographic crowding-out in the three New World economies alone (compared with 28 percent in part A of table 3); just 6 percent would have been displaced in the two Empire regions, Argentina itself being responsible for a massive 26 percent. The 31 percent figure is taken as our MIN estimate for the impact of demographic crowding-out.

Counterfactual 2: How Much of the Three New World Economies' Net Foreign Investment Would Have Been Crowded Out (MIDI Estimate)?

Part B of table 3 also explores the implications of a reduced dependency burden for the receiving regions. Had they had counterfactual British dependency rates, the three New World economies would have greatly reduced their dependence on foreign capital: Canada by 18 percent, Australia by 31 percent, and Argentina by an enormous 245 percent. In a dramatic illustration of the potential influence of the dependency burden, this latter figure suggests that, with a British dependency rate, Argentina would have been a net capital exporter around 1910. The average share of NFI crowded out in the three New World economies combined is estimated to have been 81 percent, our MIDI estimate.

16 Paish classifies British investment by destination over the period 1907–13, and, despite recent revisions, his estimates are still considered robust (Platt 1986; Feinstein 1990).

Continued overleaf

TABLE 3

A. DEMOGRAPHIC CROWDING-OUT IN THREE NEW WORLD ECONOMIES, 1884–1913

YEAR	COUNTERFACTUAL DEMOGRAPHIC CROWDING-OUT (£ Million, Annual Average)				ACTUAL BRITISH NFI (£ Million, Annual Average)	TOTAL DEMOGRAPHIC CROWDING-OUT AS A SHARE OF BRITISH NFI (Col. 4/Col. 5)
	Argentina	Australia	Canada	Total of Cols. 1–3		
	(1)	(2)	(3)	(4)	(5)	(6)
1884–90	5.3	1.3	1.2	7.8	82.7	9%
1891–1900	13.0	1.3	1.4	15.7	49.8	31%
1901–6	20.4	3.2	3.1	26.7	57.8	46%
1907–13	41.4	2.8	6.4	50.6	181.3	28%

B. Demographic Crowding-out in Six New World Economies, 1907–13

	Counterfactual Demographic Crowding-out (£ Million, Annual Average)	Actual British NFI (£ Million, Annual Average)	Total Demographic Crowding-out as a Share of British NFI in That Region	Total Demographic Crowding-out as a Share of Total British NFI in All Countries
Canada	6.4	36.2	18%	4%
Australia	2.8	9.3	31%	2%
Argentina	41.4	16.9	245%	26%
Brazil	30.1	12.6	239%	19%
Chile	4.5	3.9	115%	3%
Mexico	23.4	4.8	483%	15%
First three	50.6	62.4	81%	31%
Empire pair	9.2	45.5	20%	6%
Latin four	99.4	38.3	260%	62%
All six	108.6	83.8	130%	67%
All countries		161.1		

Source.—Panel A: British NFI from Edelstein (1982, app. 1). Panel B: Nominal national income estimates are obtained for Brazil, Chile, and Mexico using Maddison's (1989, p. 113) estimates of the real rankings of gross domestic product (in 1980 U.S. dollars) of these countries relative to those of the United Kingdom in 1913 and Mitchell's (1983) estimate of nominal national income in the United Kingdom. Dependency rates are also taken from Mitchell, by taking the nearest census and working out the dependency rate gap relative to that in the United Kingdom in that year. See our unpublished appendix for U.K. dependency rate sources. Census dates are 1920 for Brazil, 1907 for Chile, and 1910 for Mexico.

Counterfactual 3: How Much of Total British Net Foreign Investment Would Have Been Crowded out in the Six New World Economies Alone (MID2 Estimate)?

To extend our analysis to other New World countries (but, to repeat, *not* the United States), we now use the panel data estimate of the parameter β_D as a basis for estimating demographic crowding-out in other parts of Latin America ($\hat{\beta}_{Di} = -0.80$).[17] Part B of table 3 exploits crude estimates of national income and dependency rate gaps for Brazil, Mexico, and Chile around 1910 and compares the implied demographic crowding-out to actual British NFI. Once again the effects are large in Latin countries: the Brazilian counterfactual alone displaces 19 percent of British NFI, and Mexico and Chile add another 18 percent. Added to the already large Argentine figure, demographic pull effects in the four Latin American countries may have accounted for more than two-thirds of all British overseas investment in the period 1907–13. For the sample of six (Australia, Canada, and the four Latin economies), demographic crowding-out would have displaced about 71 percent of total British NFI, our MID2 estimate.

Counterfactual 4: How Much of the Six New World Economies' Net Foreign Investment Would Have Been Crowded Out (MAX Estimate)?

As a corollary to the calculations above, we now examine the impact of demographic crowding-out on foreign capital from the point of view of the six receiving New World countries. Part B of table 3 confirms that from a receiving region perspective the impacts were immense. With small dependency rate gaps and large capital inflows (relative to the size of the economy), the Empire pair would have reduced their foreign capital dependence by 20 percent. In Latin America, the influence was an order of magnitude higher: larger dependency rate gaps and smaller borrowing requirements offered a potential for massive crowding-out. All four Latin economies would have become self-sufficient in capital accumulation had they enjoyed the smaller counterfactual dependency burden. On average, 130 percent of British NFI would have been crowded out by augmented domestic savings in the six countries, our MAX estimate.

V. Conclusion

What prompted the huge capital export from Britain around the turn of the century? The scarcity of capital abroad, of course. But

[17] We could just as easily have used the Argentine parameter estimate ($\hat{\beta}_D^{ARG} = -1.60$), but that would have implied even larger effects.

was this scarcity induced by a buoyant investment demand boom or by a savings shortfall at the periphery? In some sense, both mattered. Yet the results above appear to favor the latter as a key difference between capital markets in the Old and New Worlds, and indicate that a sizable share of British overseas investment before World War I took the form of an intergenerational transfer. Consideration of a number of counterfactual alternatives has provided us with a range of estimates, including some plausible guesses about upper and lower bounds. Of course, the question still remains whether our estimates may in some way be biased, because of flaws either in the modeling or in the econometrics. We can think of two potential biases, but they operate in different directions.

On the one hand, since we estimate saving as investment plus the current account, our results may be biased if investment was correlated with the dependency rate and if the current account was a binding constraint. An obvious example is offered by the population-sensitive investment categories noted earlier. In this case, higher dependency rates would have been associated with augmented investment demand and diminished savings supply. If the New World economies were in any way savings constrained, these forces would have tended to offset each other, diminishing the measured dependency rate impact on aggregate saving. Such influences would tend to bias toward zero our estimate of the direct dependency rate impact on saving, since we are trying to estimate the direct impact of D on s with I held fixed. If demographic forces crowded in investment, then we have underestimated the influence of dependency rates on savings rates, and, hence, we have understated the potential for demographic crowding-out of foreign investment in our counterfactual.

On the other hand, by assuming a full pass-through of surplus savings into the current account, our analysis represents only a partial equilibrium approach. What would have been the impact of counterfactual increases in New World savings in the world capital market? Presumably, an excess supply of world capital would have lowered interest rates and, in general equilibrium, crowded in investment and crowded out saving in all countries. In general equilibrium, the demographic impact on savings would be muted compared to partial equilibrium: the counterfactually augmented world supply of savings would entail a price of capital adjustment that would have crowded out some of the rise in savings observed in the counterfactual. For example, if all supply and demand schedules in the capital market had elasticities of equal magnitude, our counterfactual estimates of demographic crowding-out would be reduced by half if we were to allow general equilibrium to operate. By this line of reasoning, we may have an overestimate of the dependency rate impact on savings and an overstatement of the potential for demographic crowding-out of foreign investment.

Since we do not wish to oversell the accuracy or completeness of the analysis, some words of caution are in order. The paper does not present a theory nor offer any explanation of Kuznets cycles or long swings, the pronounced yet enigmatic long waves observable in macroeconomic aggregates in New World and Old, and most markedly evident in the late nineteenth and early twentieth centuries. The interested reader is directed to the resurgent literature on this topic (Solomou 1987; Rowthorn and Solomou 1991). Our savings function estimates include no long-swing variables except the growth rate of real income, and this enters the equation insignificantly all the same. Thus our model was not designed to track savings booms and busts in the short to medium term.

Notwithstanding these caveats, there seems to be ample evidence that the dependency rate hypothesis was alive and well in three New World economies. It has been shown to have had especially potent force in the late nineteenth and early twentieth centuries, when the New World was burdened with a very high dependency rate. Furthermore, relatively low New World saving capacities implied large capital inflows from mature savers in the Old World, so much so that from one-third to all of the observed inflows of net foreign investment may have been attributable to such demographic effects. In the middle of this range, two of our counterfactual results suggest that about three-quarters of British overseas investment could be accounted for by dependency-induced pull at the periphery. We consider this persuasive evidence that foreign investment in the New World just prior to World War I should be viewed as an intergenerational transfer.

References

Ando, Albert, and Modigliani, Franco. "The 'Life Cycle' Hypothesis of Saving: Aggregate Implications and Tests." *A.E.R.* 53 (March 1963): 55–84.
Bilsborrow, Richard E. "Dependency Rates and Aggregate Savings Rates Revisited: Corrections, Further Analysis and Recommendations for the Future." In *Research in Population Economics*, vol. 2, edited by Julian L. Simon and Julie DaVanzo. Greenwich, Conn.: JAI, 1980.
Coale, Ansley J., and Hoover, Edgar M. *Population Growth and Economic Development in Low-Income Countries: A Case Study of India's Prospects.* Princeton, N.J.: Princeton Univ. Press, 1958.
David, Paul A. "Invention and Accumulation in America's Economic Growth: A Nineteenth-Century Parable." In *International Organization, National Policies and Economic Development*, edited by Karl Brunner and Allan H. Meltzer. Amsterdam: North-Holland, 1977.
Edelstein, Michael. *Overseas Investment in the Age of High Imperialism: The United Kingdom, 1850–1914.* New York: Columbia Univ. Press, 1982.
———. "Were U.S. Rates of Accumulation in the Twentieth Century Invest-

CAPITAL FLOWS

ment or Savings Driven?" In *Research in Economic History*, vol. 13, edited by Roger L. Ransom. Greenwich, Conn.: JAI, 1991.

Fair, Ray C., and Dominguez, Kathryn M. "Effects of the Changing U.S. Age Distribution on Macroeconomic Equations." *A.E.R.* 81 (December 1991): 1276–94.

Feinstein, Charles H. *National Income, Expenditure and Output of the United Kingdom*. Cambridge: Cambridge Univ. Press, 1972.

———. "Britain's Overseas Investments in 1913." *Econ. Hist. Rev.* 43 (May 1990): 288–95.

Fry, Maxwell J. "Terms of Trade and National Savings Rates in Asia." Manuscript. Irvine: Univ. California, 1984.

Fry, Maxwell J., and Mason, Andrew. "The Variable Rate-of-Growth Effect in the Life-Cycle Saving Model: Children, Capital Inflows, Interest and Growth in a New Specification of the Life-Cycle Model Applied to Seven Asian Developing Countries." *Econ. Inquiry* 20 (July 1982): 426–42.

Gallman, Robert E. "Gross National Product in the United States, 1834–1909." In *Output, Employment, and Productivity in the United States after 1800*. Conference on Research in Income and Wealth. Studies in Income and Wealth, no. 30. New York: Columbia Univ. Press (for NBER), 1966.

Green, Alan, and Urquhart, M. C. "Factor and Commodity Flows in the International Economy of 1870–1914: A Multi-country View." *J. Econ. Hist.* 36 (March 1976): 217–52.

Griliches, Zvi. "Distributed Lags: A Survey." *Econometrica* 35 (January 1967): 16–49.

Hammer, Jeffrey S. "Population Growth and Savings in LDCs: A Survey Article." *World Development* 14 (May 1986): 579–91.

Kelley, Allen C. "Demographic Change and Economic Growth: Australia, 1861–1911." *Explorations Entrepreneurial Hist.*, 2d ser., 5 (Spring/Summer 1968): 207–77.

Kennedy, William P. *Industrial Structure, Capital Markets, and the Origins of British Economic Decline*. Cambridge: Cambridge Univ. Press, 1987.

Leff, Nathaniel H. "Dependency Rates and Savings Rates." *A.E.R.* 59 (December 1969): 886–96.

Lewis, Frank D. "Fertility and Savings in the United States: 1830–1900." *J.P.E.* 91 (October 1983): 825–40.

Lewis, William Arthur. *The Evolution of the International Economic Order*. Princeton, N.J.: Princeton Univ. Press, 1978.

McLean, Ian W. "Saving in Settler Economies: Australian and North American Comparisons." Working Paper no. 91-7. Adelaide: Univ. Adelaide, Dept. Econ. 1991.

Maddala, G. S. *Econometrics*. New York: McGraw-Hill, 1977.

Maddison, Angus. *The World Economy in the 20th Century*. Paris: OECD, 1989.

Mason, Andrew. "An Extension of the Life-Cycle Model and Its Application to Population Growth and Aggregate Saving." Working Paper no. 4. Honolulu: East-West Population Inst., 1981.

———. "National Saving Rates and Population Growth: A New Model and New Evidence." In *Population Growth and Economic Development: Issues and Evidence*, edited by D. Gale Johnson and Ronald D. Lee. Madison: Univ. Wisconsin Press, 1987.

———. "Saving, Economic Growth, and Demographic Change." *Population and Development Rev.* 14 (March 1988): 113–44.

Mitchell, Brian R. *International Historical Statistics: The Americas and Australasia*. Detroit: Gale Res., 1983.

Modigliani, Franco. "The Life Cycle Hypothesis of Savings, the Demand for Wealth and the Supply of Capital." *Soc. Res.* 33 (June 1966): 160–217.

Modigliani, Franco, and Ando, Albert. "Tests of the Life Cycle Hypothesis of Savings: Comments and Suggestions." *Bull. Oxford Univ. Inst. Statis.* 19 (May 1957): 99–124.

Modigliani, Franco, and Brumberg, Richard E. "Utility Analysis and the Consumption Function: An Interpretation of Cross-Section Data." In *Post-Keynesian Economics*, edited by Kenneth K. Kurihara. New Brunswick, N.J.: Rutgers Univ. Press, 1954.

Modigliani, Franco, and Sterling, Artie G. "Determinants of Private Saving with Special Reference to the Role of Social Security—Cross-Country Tests." In *The Determinants of National Saving and Wealth*, edited by Franco Modigliani and Richard Hemming. New York: St. Martin's (for Internat. Econ. Assoc.), 1983.

Neal, Larry. "Integration of International Capital Markets: Quantitative Evidence from the Eighteenth to Twentieth Centuries." *J. Econ. Hist.* 45 (June 1985): 219–26.

Nurkse, Ragnar. "International Investment To-day in the Light of Nineteenth-Century Experience." *Econ. J.* 64 (December 1954): 744–58.

Paish, Sir George. "Export of Capital and the Cost of Living." *Statist, Suppl.* (February 14, 1914), pp. i–viii.

Pindyck, Robert S., and Rubinfeld, Daniel L. *Econometric Models and Economic Forecasts.* 2d ed. New York: McGraw-Hill, 1981.

Platt, Desmond C. M. *Britain's Investment Overseas on the Eve of the First World War: The Use and Abuse of Numbers.* New York: St. Martin's, 1986.

Ransom, Roger, and Sutch, Richard. "Domestic Saving as an Active Constraint on Capital Formation in the American Economy, 1839–1928: A Provisional Theory." Manuscript. Berkeley: Univ. California, Dept. Econ., 1983.

Rowthorn, Robert E., and Solomou, Solomos N. "The Macroeconomic Effects of Overseas Investment on the UK Balance of Trade, 1870–1913." *Econ. Hist. Rev.* 44 (November 1991): 654–64.

Schedvin, C. B. "Staples and Regions of Pax Britannica." *Econ. Hist. Rev.* 43 (November 1990): 533–59.

Schultz, T. Paul. "School Expenditures and Enrollments, 1960–80: The Effects of Income, Prices, and Population Growth." In *Population Growth and Economic Development: Issues and Evidence*, edited by D. Gale Johnson and Ronald D. Lee. Madison: Univ. Wisconsin Press, 1987.

Solomou, Solomos N. *Phases of Economic Growth, 1850–1973: Kondratieff Waves and Kuznets Swings.* Cambridge: Cambridge Univ. Press, 1987.

Taylor, Alan M. "External Dependence, Demographic Burdens, and Argentine Economic Decline after the *Belle Époque*." *J. Econ. Hist.* 52 (December 1992): 907–36.

U.S. Bureau of the Census. *Historical Statistics of the United States, Colonial Times to 1970.* Bicentennial ed. 2 vols. Washington: Government Printing Office, 1975.

Williamson, Jeffrey G. "Inequality, Accumulation, and Technological Imbalance: A Growth-Equity Conflict in American History?" *Econ. Development and Cultural Change* 27 (January 1979): 231–53.

———. *Coping with City Growth during the British Industrial Revolution.* Cambridge: Cambridge Univ. Press, 1990.

———. "The Evolution of Global Labor Markets in the First and Second World since 1830: Background Evidence and Hypotheses." *Explorations Econ. Hist.* 31 (1994), in press.

CAPITAL FLOWS

371

World Bank. *World Development Report.* New York: Oxford Univ. Press, 1991.

Zevin, Robert B. "Are World Financial Markets More Open? If So, Why and with What Effects?" In *Financial Openness and National Autonomy: Opportunities and Constraints,* edited by Tariq Banuri and Juliet B. Schor. New York: Oxford Univ. Press, 1992.

PART II

STANDARD OF LIVING DEBATES, INEQUALITY AND LABOUR SURPLUS MODELS

Degrees of freedom	81	119	110	3.27	84
R^2	.603	.749	.836	.089	.601
Standard error	.052	.036	.021	1.04	.027
Durbin-Watson	1.96	2.33	2.26	2.09	1.75

B. Statistics for the Data Series

s:				
Mean	.129	.161	.159	.152
Standard deviation	.080	.070	.052	.068
g:				
Mean	.031	.032	.038	.034
Standard deviation	.052	.053	.053	.053
D:				
Mean	.329	.317	.323	.322
Standard deviation	.038	.054	.047	.042

C. Implied Long-Run Coefficients

Partial derivative: $\partial s/\partial D$	−1.60	−.62	−.59	−.80
Elasticity: $(D/s)(\partial s/\partial D)$	−4.08	−1.21	−1.20	−1.70

SOURCE.—See our unpublished appendix.

NOTE.—The dependent variable is the savings rate s. Absolute t-statistics appear in parentheses. The AR1 estimations utilize the Cochrane-Orcutt procedure. In the panel regressions, all variables are transformed by ρ-differencing, and a residual variance series for each country allows use of weighted least squares to correct for heteroskedasticity; but the statistics in panel B still refer to the untransformed data.

* Significant at the 1 percent level (one-tail test).

[5]

THE ECONOMIC HISTORY REVIEW

SECOND SERIES, VOLUME XXXVI, No. 1, FEBRUARY 1983

SURVEYS AND SPECULATIONS, XVII

English Workers' Living Standards During the Industrial Revolution: A New Look*

By PETER H. LINDERT AND JEFFREY G. WILLIAMSON

The politically charged debate over workers' living standards during the Industrial Revolution[1] deserves renewal with the appearance of fresh data or new perspectives. This paper mines an expanding data base and emerges with a far clearer picture of workers' fortunes after 1750. While optimists and pessimists can both draw support from the enterprise, the pessimists' case emerges with the greater need for redirection and repair. The evidence suggests that material gains were even bigger after 1820 than optimists had previously claimed, even if the concept of material well-being is expanded

* This article is part of a larger research project on 'British Inequality since 1670', supported by grants from the US National Science Foundation (SOC76-80967, SOC79-09361, SOC79-06869) and the US National Endowment for the Humanities (RO-26772-78-19). The authors gratefully acknowledge the able research assistance of George Boyer, Ding-Wei Lee, Linda W. Lindert, Thomas Renaghan, Ricardo Silveira, Kenneth Snowden and Arthur Woolf, as well as the helpful comments of G. N. von Tunzelmann, Stanley L. Engerman, two anonymous referees, and seminar participants at the University of California (Berkeley, Davis, UCLA), Harvard University, Northwestern University and the University of Wisconsin.

Readers are referred to the fuller display of evidence in the discussion paper, 'English Workers' Living Standards during the Industrial Revolution: A New Look', September 1980, available either from the Department of Economics, University of California, Davis, 95616 USA (Working Paper Series No. 144) or from the Graduate Program in Economic History, University of Wisconsin, Madison, 53706 USA. Hereafter this paper is cited as 'DP'.

[1] The historical literature is too vast to cite here. Readers who want a full bibliography could begin with sources cited below and in M. W. Flinn, 'Trends in Real Wages, 1750-1850', *Economic History Review*, 2nd series, XXVII, 3 (1974), pp. 395-413; A. J. Taylor ed., *The Standard of Living in Britain in the Industrial Revolution* (1975); Stanley L. Engerman and P. K. O'Brien, 'Income Distribution during the Industrial Revolution', in R. C. Floud and D. N. McCloskey eds., *The Economic History of Britain since 1700* (Cambridge, 1981). For heated eloquence, the best twentieth-century clash is that between T. S. Ashton ('The Treatment of Capitalism by Historians', in F. A. von Hayek ed. *Capitalism and the Historians* (Chicago, 1954)) and E. P. Thompson (*The Making of the English Working Class* (Harmondsworth, 1968)).

2   PETER H. LINDERT AND JEFFREY G. WILLIAMSON

to include health and environmental factors. Although the pessimists can still find deplorable trends in the collective environment after 1820, particularly rising inequality and social disorder, this article suggests that their case must be shifted to the period 1750 to 1820 to retain its central relevance.

1

Which occupations and social classes are of the greatest relevance to the debate? It seems unlikely that we would get full agreement from the participants, but there are a few groups whose fortunes have been of prime concern, both to the historical standard of living debate and to the contemporary debate over Third World growth and distribution.[2]

Following established conventions in the literature, each group listed in Table 1 refers to adult male employees: the self-employed and permanently unemployed are excluded. Our lowest earnings group consists of hired farm labourers, who represent the bottom two-fifths of all workers. Next come the non-farm common labourers and their near-substitutes, a low-skilled "middle group". Artisans, whose organizational efforts and sizable wage gains have caused them to be singled out as the "labour aristocracy",[3] fall roughly between the 60th and 80th percentiles in the overall distribution of earnings. "Blue collar" workers include each of these groups, and define "the working class" most closely, at least within the debate over living standards.[4] The list is completed by the addition of a diverse white-collar group.

These "class" rankings changed little across the nineteenth century, at least between 1827 and 1851. However, since the relative growth of group incomes was rarely the same over the century following 1750, each will be documented in the sections which follow. Furthermore, later in this paper we shall explore just how much of the real wage trends for the blue collar labourer can be explained by shifts into higher paid work and how much by wage gains among all blue collar workers. Table 1 simply establishes who the workers were and where they fit in the size distribution of earnings in the early nineteenth century.

II

Quantitative judgements on workers' living standards have always begun with time series on rates of normal or full time pay.[5] This was certainly the

[2] On the debate over the 'bottom 40 per cent' in the Third World, see H. B. Chenery et al. *Redistribution with Growth* (Oxford, 1974); W. R. Cline, 'Distribution and Development: A Survey Article', *Journal of Development Studies*, 11 (1975), pp. 359-400; M. Ahluwalia, 'Inequality, Poverty, and Development', *Journal of Development Economics*, 2 (1976), pp. 307-42; and Simon Kuznets, *Growth, Population and Income Distribution* (New York, 1979).

[3] See T. S. Ashton, *An Economic History of England: The 18th Century* (1955), ch. VII; idem., 'The Standard of Life of the Workers in England, 1790-1830', *Journal of Economic History*, Supplement IX (1949), as reprinted in A. J. Taylor ed., *The Standard of Living*; E. J. Hobsbawm, *Labouring Men* (New York, 1964), esp. chs. 15 and 16; and Harold Perkin, *The Origins of Modern English Society, 1780-1880* (1969), pp. 131, 143, 395-7, 417.

[4] On the changing nuances of the term 'working class', see in particular Asa Briggs, 'The Language of "Class" in Early Nineteenth-Century England', in Asa Briggs and J. Saville eds. *Essays in Labour History* (1967), and R. J. Morris, *Class and Class Consciousness in the Industrial Revolution, 1780-1850* (1979).

[5] We follow past authors in referring to earnings or 'pay' as though these represented all pre-transfer income, either gross or net of direct taxes. This simplification is valid for English workers before this century. Only a tiny share of blue-collar employees owned their own homes or significant amounts of other non-human property, and only a tiny share paid any direct taxes. The heavier indirect taxes – excises, import duties, and the local rates on property – were reflected in the prices and rents workers paid, which are measured below.

Table 1. Adult-Male Employee Classes and Their Approximate Mean Positions in the Nineteenth-Century Earnings Ranks for England and Wales

Occupational Class	"Representative" Mean-wage Series used here	Approximate Mean-wage Percentile Positions in the Earnings Ranks	
		1827	1851
(1) Farm Labour (Bottom 40%)	(1L) farm labour	13th	14th
(2) Middle Group	(2L) non-farm common labour	38th	35th
	(5L) police and guards		50th
	(6L) colliers	55th	51st
	(5H) cotton spinners	62nd	58th
(3) Artisans ("Labour aristocracy")	(2H) shipbuilding trades	67th	62nd
	(3H) engineering trades	77th	77th
	(4H) building trades	74th	63rd
	(6H) printing trades	75th	71st
(4) Blue-Collar Workers = (1)+(2)+(3)			
(5) White-Collar Employees	(3L) messengers and porters	78th	71st
	(4L) other government low-wage	65th	62nd
	(1H) government high-wage	87th	80th
	(7H) clergy	90th	81st
	(8H) solicitors and barristers	95th	100th
	(9H) clerks	88th	80th
	(10H) surgeons and doctors	86th	79th
	(11H) schoolmasters	75th	70th
	(12H) engineers, surveyors and other professionals	89th	94th
(6) All Workers = (4)+(5)			

Notes and Sources: The sources for the group earnings averages are discussed in Section II below, and at greater length, in Jeffrey G. Williamson, 'The Structure of Pay in Britain, 1710-1911', in P. Uselding ed. Research in Economic History, 7 (1982). The overall earnings distributions for 1827 and 1851 on which these group means are ranked are reported in Jeffrey G. Williamson, 'Earnings Inequality in Nineteenth-Century Britain', Journal of Economic History, XL (1980), pp. 457-75.

These size distributions refer to employee earnings only, excluding incomes from property, self-employment, pensions or poor relief.

starting point for the pioneering contributions by Bowley and Wood, Gilboy, Phelps Brown and Hopkins, and others. We also begin in the same way, adding several new pay series along the way.

An essential first step is to select appropriate annual pay rates. Most pay series are constructed from daily or weekly rates, and we still have only the sketchiest evidence documenting the average number of days or weeks worked per year. It seems sensible to exploit the normal or full-time pay rates first, and then turn to clues about unemployment or underemployment trends (Section V) to infer movements in true annual earnings. Daily and weekly normal pay rates are aggregated up to a 52-week year, using various estimates of normal days per week in different occupations.[6] These annual earnings

[6] The choice of numbers of weeks per year is arbitrary and matters little to what follows. Arthur L. Bowley thought that six weeks was the average 'lost time' per year (Wages in the United Kingdom in the Nineteenth Century (Cambridge, 1900), p. 68). The choice of weeks per year matters only if the number of weeks 'lost' varied greatly over time, due to movements in true involuntary unemployment and not just due to marginal shifts in employment rates by persons valuing their time about the same in and out of work. We doubt that the work year shifted in ways altering the conclusions of this paper, to judge from the unemployment evidence in Section V below and from M. A. Bienefeld's exploration of trends in normal annual industrial hours: Working Hours in British Industry (1972), chs. 2, 3.

4 PETER H. LINDERT AND JEFFREY G. WILLIAMSON

figures generally exclude payments in kind, but this rule is violated for farm labourers, whose large in-kind payments have been included.

Eighteen nominal pay series are documented in Table 2. These series reflect a number of additions and revisions to the time-series literature on wage rates. The most conspicuous additions, though not the most crucial to the conclusions below, are the service occupations (Series 3L, 4L, 1H, and 7H to 12H inclusive). With the exception of clergy and teachers, our view of service-occupation pay leans heavily on the public salary figures reported in the "Annual Estimates" (printed in the House of Commons' Accounts and Papers

Table 2. *Estimates of Nominal Annual Earnings for Eighteen Occupations, 1755-1851: Adult Males, England and Wales (in current £'s)*

Occupation	1755	1781	1797	1805	1810	1815	1819	1827	1835	1851
(1L) farm labourers	17.18	21.09	30.03	40.40	42.04	40.04	39.05	31.04	30.03	29.04
(2L) non-farm common labour	20.75	23.13	25.09	36.87	43.94	43.94	41.74	43.65	39.29	44.83
(3L) messengers & porters	33.99	33.54	57.66	69.43	76.01	80.69	81.35	84.39	87.20	88.88
(4L) other government low-wage	28.62	46.02	46.77	52.48	57.17	60.22	60.60	59.01	58.70	66.45
(5L) police & guards	25.76	48.08	47.04	51.26	67.89	69.34	62.95	63.33	53.62	
(6L) colliers	22.94	24.37	47.79	64.99	63.22	57.82	50.37	54.61	56.41	55.44
(1H) government high-wage	78.91	104.55	133.73	151.09	176.86	195.16	219.25	222.95	270.42	234.87
(2H) shipbuilding trades	38.82	45.26	51.71	51.32	55.25	59.20	57.23	62.22	62.74	64.12
(3H) engineering trades	43.60	50.83	58.08	75.88	88.23	94.91	92.71	80.69	77.26	84.05
(4H) building trades	30.51	35.57	40.64	55.30	66.35	66.35	63.02	66.35	59.72	66.35
(5H) cotton spinners	35.96	41.93	47.90	65.18	78.21	67.60	67.60	58.50	64.56	58.64
(6H) printing trades	46.34	54.03	66.61	71.11	79.22	79.22	71.14	70.23	70.23	74.72
(7H) clergy	91.90	182.65	238.50	266.42	283.89	272.53	266.55	254.60	258.76	267.09
(8H) solicitors and barristers	231.00	242.67	165.00	340.00	447.50	447.50	447.50	522.50	1166.67	1837.50
(9H) clerks	63.62	101.57	135.26	150.44	178.11	200.79	229.64	240.29	269.11	235.81
(10H) surgeons & doctors	62.02	88.35	174.95	217.60	217.60	217.60	217.60	175.20	200.92	200.92
(11H) schoolmasters	15.97	16.53	43.21	43.21	51.10	69.35	69.35	69.35	81.89	81.11
(12H) engineers & surveyors	137.51	170.00	190.00	291.43	305.00	337.50	326.43	265.71	398.89	479.00

Sources and Notes: From Williamson, 'The Structure of Pay', Appendix Table 4. Some of these occupations need no elaboration. Those that do are explained as follows: (4L) – watchmen, guards, porters, messengers, Post Office letter carriers, janitors; (1H) – clerks, Post Office sorters, warehousemen, tax collectors, tax surveyors, solicitors, clergymen, surgeons, medical officers, architects, engineers; (2H) – shipwrights; (3H) – fitters, turners, iron-moulders; (4H) – bricklayers, masons, carpenters, plasterers; (6H) – compositors.

from 1797 onwards). This is a rich source for consistent time series on well-defined occupations. Annual earnings are reported there for large numbers of employees in each occupational category, spanning the whole earnings distribution over age, tenure, and skill within a given occupational group. The key issue underlying their use is whether trends in public "civil service" salaries replicated trends in the same private sector occupations. Elsewhere we have offered evidence confirming the correlation, at least for the nineteenth century.[7]

Service-sector pay, again for public posts, is also available for 1755 and 1781. For the latter year we have figures reported to the House of Commons.[8]

[7] See Jeffrey G. Williamson, 'The Structure of Pay in Britain, 1710-1911'.
[8] Report of 'Commission Appointed to Examine, Take, and State the Public Accounts of the United Kingdom', House of Commons Papers, 1782 and 1786.

John Chamberlayne's estimates supply figures for 1755, though for fewer employees and departments than is true at the later dates.[9] These eighteenth-century public pay data must, of course, be treated with care, since a truly baroque payments system prevailed in the upper echelons.[10]

For clergy and schoolmasters, we have made use of private pay series. Clergymen's mean annual earnings (including the rental value of the vicarage) can be estimated for the greater part of the nineteenth century by using *The Clerical Guide and Ecclesiastical Directory* and *The Clergy List*. A random sample of 550 clergymen, from all patronage sources (royal, ecclesiastical, university, and private), yields their pay for 1827, 1835, and 1851. For earlier benchmark years we had to use public pay rates for clergy, splicing these on to the private series at 1827. This procedure seems to have yielded plausible pay series for the average clergyman back to 1755, judging by the similarity in trend between public and private clergy salaries from 1827 on.

Schoolmasters had low monthly cash earnings, both because much of their income was in kind (rents and fuel), and because they often received supplementary fees and holiday bonuses. We have assumed that income in kind was a stable share of total income, so that the twelve-month cash-income series in Table 2 accurately reflects trends in total income. For 1755-1835, our estimates rely on schoolmasters' earnings in several Charity Schools in Staffordshire and Warwickshire. The 1851 figure refers to civilian schoolmasters in public pay, as reported in the Annual Estimates.[11]

For nineteenth-century manufacturing and building crafts (Series 2H to 6H inclusive), the well-known estimates of Bowley and Wood suffice.[12] The available series on eighteenth-century artisans' pay refer only to the building crafts, but Gilboy's data on these crafts offer the advantage of regional diversity. To give proper weight to the well-known regional variance in nominal wages, and to the shift in eighteenth-century populations, we have constructed an earnings average for building craftsmen that reflects changes in "regional mix" between 1755 and 1797.[13] The result is a steeper rise in

[9] John Chamberlayne, *Magnae Britanniae Notitia, Or the Present State of Great Britain*, 17th ed. (1755). Earlier editions, begun by Edwin Chamberlayne, date back to the 1680s. We are indebted to David Galenson for alerting us to the Chamberlayne almanacs.

[10] For example, department heads and high titled clerks were part of a patronage system. Often extremely high reported salaries were gross salaries out of which the recipient had to maintain his staff of clerks. We have ignored the pay of all officials for which this seemed to be the practice.

In other cases, salaries surely understated earnings. Customs officials, for example, received a portion of the taxes collected in addition to the reported incomes. These were excluded from our estimates. Also excluded were officials for whom the stated stipends were but partial political side-payments and heraldic perquisites. For example, in an earlier edition of *Magnae Britanniae Notitia* (1694 ed. p. 238), Edwin Chamberlayne listed the Lancaster Herald's pay as only £26 13s. 4d. per annum. The Herald in this case was Gregory King. Were this his only income, King would have been no better paid than a common seaman, a messenger or a porter.

[11] For a fuller discussion of all schoolmaster pay series, with comparisons to other available series on benchmark dates, see Williamson, 'The Structure of Pay'.

[12] Bowley, *Wages in the United Kingdom*, and the series of Bowley-Wood articles that appeared in the *Journal of the Royal Statistical Society* between 1898 and 1906.

[13] For the London area we used an unweighted average of wage series from Westminster, Greenwich Hospital, Southwark and Maidstone. The London area series is then combined with series from six counties: Oxfordshire, Gloucestershire, Devon, Somerset, the North Riding, and Lancashire. These county earnings estimates are combined using the regional population weights reported in Phyllis Deane and W. A. Cole, *British Economic Growth, 1688-1959* (Cambridge, 2nd ed. 1969), Table 24, p. 103.

6 PETER H. LINDERT AND JEFFREY G. WILLIAMSON

earnings in the building trades up to 1797 than that reported by Brown and Hopkins, whose series referred to southern England only.[14]

Three very large unskilled occupations remain: colliers, non-farm common labourers, and farm labourers. The colliers' earnings figures refer to underground mining by adult males. The 1851 figure is derived from Wood's wage series.[15] The 1835 figure is from Bowley, as are the 1810-19 estimates, the latter referring to southern Scotland. We have also used figures for 1755 to 1805 inclusive, and (again) 1835 from Ashton and Sykes, referring to colliers' daily wage rates in the northern counties, in Lancashire and in Derbyshire.[16] These diverse estimates are linked together at various dates and converted into annual earnings rates using the procedures sketched above. Non-farm common labourers' earnings are based on two sources. For the period 1797-1851, we have accepted the Phelps Brown-Hopkins estimates for labourers in the building trades. For 1755-97, their estimates have been set aside in favour of a multi-regional series based on Gilboy data for building labour, using the same procedure described for building crafts above. For farm labourers, the 1797-1851 figures are based on Bowley's wages for a "normal work week", taking account of both income in kind and seasonal wage-rate variation (but not seasonal employment variation).[17] Fifty-two "normal weeks" are arbitrarily assumed in constructing an annual full-time series. The 1781 figure also relies on Bowley, but here it is an unweighted average of the figures for Surrey, Kent, Hertfordshire, Suffolk, Cumberland, and Monmouth, spliced to the national series at 1797. The 1755-81 estimates are constructed from raw earnings data collected by Rogers.[18]

Table 2 represents our best interim view of trends in occupational earnings. It is confined to ten benchmark years simply because the data are more abundant for these years.

Table 3 reports average full-time earnings for the six groups identified in Section I. The employment weights used in the aggregation over our eighteen

[14] E. H. Phelps Brown and Sheila V. Hopkins, 'Seven Centuries of Building Wages', *Economica*, XXII (1955), pp. 205-6.

[15] As reproduced in Brian Mitchell and Phyllis Deane, *Abstract of British Historical Statistics* (Cambridge, 1971).

[16] Bowley, *Wages*; T. S. Ashton and J. Sykes, *The Coal Industry in the Eighteenth Century* (Manchester, 1929).

[17] A. L. Bowley, 'The Statistics of Wages in the United Kingom. Part I. Agricultural Wages', *Journal of the Royal Statistical Society*, LXI (1898).

Alternative estimates for the period 1790-1840 are also available for Kent, Essex, Dorset, Nottinghamshire, Lincolnshire, Hampshire, and Suffolk in T. L. Richardson, 'The Standard of Living Controversy, 1790-1840' (unpub. Ph.D. thesis, University of Hull, 1977), Pt. II. Richardson's nominal daily wages for 'fully employed agricultural day labourers' show somewhat less steep rises across the 1790s than do Bowley's national averages. The discrepancy may reflect the more rapid rise in wages in the north, an area given its due more fully in the Bowley averages. In any case, the Bowley and Richardson averages conform rather closely between 1805 and 1840.

[18] James E. Thorold Rogers, *A History of Agriculture and Prices in England*, VII (1902). Once again, we have tried to build an earnings average for England and Wales that reflects shifts in population between regions across the eighteenth century, this time for farm labour. The task is complicated by the paucity of time series data, and the resulting average is hardly definitive. Our average wage for southern England is a weighted average of Cambridgeshire and Gloucester, the only two counties for which Rogers supplies continuous daily wage series for adult male farm labourers. The north is represented only by Bramsby, Yorkshire, though the number of observations for this location is large. The northern and southern averages were weighted by population estimates from Deane and Cole, where the 'south' is defined by the twenty counties including, or south of, Gloucester, Oxford, Northampton, Cambridge, and Norfolk. The 'north' in this case consists of Lancashire and the three Ridings. The resulting average daily wage is then linked with the 1781 annual earnings estimate.

LIVING STANDARDS   7

occupations are very rough. Those for 1811 and earlier are based on work previously published, while those for later years are based on manipulations of the imperfect early census data on occupation.[19] Table 3 reveals the earnings history experienced by different classes of workers. The variety is striking. In the latter half of the eighteenth century, farm and non-farm common labourers gained ground on higher-paid workers, the labour aristocracy especially. From 1815 to the middle of the nineteenth century, on the other hand, the gap between higher- and lower-paid workers widened dramatically. Farm wages sagged below, while white-collar pay soared above, the wages for all other groups.[20] Table 3 also compares our results with earlier series that have shaped past impressions of wage trends and played a key role in Flinn's recent survey.[21] The new and old series exhibit both conformity and contrast. Where they diverge, we stand by the new series as improvements, and urge other scholars to harvest additional wage series from the archives.[22] The major

Table 3. *Trends in Nominal Full-Time Earnings for Six Labour Groups, Compared with Three Previous Series, 1755–1851*

(1851 = 100)

	(1)	vs.	(2)	vs.	(3)	vs.	(4)	(5)	(6)
Year	Farm Labourers	Bowley's Farm Labourers	Middle Group	Phelps-Brown-Hopkins Building Labourers	Labour Aristocracy	Tucker's London Artisans	All Blue Collar	White Collar	All Workers
1755	59·16		42·95	48·5	50·86	69·8	51·05	21·62	38·62
1781	72·62	75·5	54·88	57·6	57·38	69·8	59·64	26·42	46·62
1797	103·41	93·9	72·92	66·7	64·86	81·0	74·42	32·55	58·97
1805	139·12		98·89	83·3	79·44	87·0	96·58	38·88	75·87
1810	144·76		110·95	97·0	92·03	105·6	107·81	43·01	84·89
1815	137·88		105·55	97·0	95·28	112·1	106·18	46·55	85·30
1819	134·47		99·41	97·0	91·92	103·3	101·84	50·77	84·37
1827	106·89	100·8	98·89	97·0	93·55	105·1	97·59	55·09	83·11
1835	103·41	112·3	96·98	97·0	88·68	98·9	94·11	75·03	88·77
1851	100·00		100·00	100·0	100·00	100·0	100·00	100·00	100·00
52 weeks' earnings in 1851:	£29·04	£29·04	£52·95	£42·90	£75·15	n.a.	£52·62	£258·88	£75·51

Sources and Notes: The indices are aggregated from the finer groups listed in Table 1, using wage series from Table 2 and employment weights. The employment weights for 1755–1815 draw on Lindert, 'English Occupations, 1670–1811', Table 3, while those for 1815–1851 are derived from censuses. The derivations of the employment weights are described in DP, Appendix A.

For the three previous series, see Bowley, *Wages in the United Kingdom*, table in back; Phelps Brown and Hopkins, 'Seven Centuries'; Rufus S. Tucker, 'Real Wages of Artisans in London, 1729–1935', *Journal of the American Statistical Association*, 31 (1936), pp. 73–84. The conversion of the Phelps-Brown-Hopkins series from daily to annual wages assumed 312 working days a year.

[19] The occupational numbers for 1811 and earlier are estimated, with comparisons to contemporary estimates by Massie and Colquhoun, in Peter H. Lindert, 'English Occupations, 1670–1811', *Journal of Economic History*, XL (1980), pp. 685–712.

[20] For more details on these distributional changes, see Williamson, 'The Structure of Pay', and idem., 'Earnings Inequality in Nineteenth Century Britain', *J. Econ. Hist.*, XL (1980), pp. 457–76.

[21] M. W. Flinn, 'Trends in Real Wages'.

[22] Bernard Eccleston has assembled a new series on Midlands wage rates for building craftsmen, building labourers, estate workers and road labourers ('A Survey of Wage Rates in Five Midland Counties, 1750–1834', unpub. Ph.D. thesis, University of Leicester, 1976). Consistent with our findings is Table 3, for common labourers Eccleston finds the Phelps-Brown-Hopkins series rising too slowly between 1755 and 1815, and agrees that the Phelps-Brown-Hopkins series misses the slight postwar deflation as well. Eccleston

8   PETER H. LINDERT AND JEFFREY G. WILLIAMSON

conclusions of this paper are reinforced by, but not conditional on, our choice of these new nominal pay series.[23]

III

Several scholars have attempted to construct cost-of-living indices to deflate such nominal earning series. The period 1790 to 1850 has attracted particular attention. The four price indices most often cited are those offered by Gayer-Rostow-Schwartz (GRS), Silberling, Rousseaux, and Tucker.[24] These pioneering efforts can be criticized on three fronts: (1) the underlying price data; (2) the commodities included in the overall index; and (3) the budget weights applied to each commodity price series.

Wholesale prices are used by GRS, Silberling, and Rousseaux. GRS, in fact, used wholesale prices collected by Silberling who, in many cases, chose not to use them. Rousseaux also borrowed from Silberling, as well as from Jevons and Sauerbeck. Silberling's chief source was the *Price Current* lists "issued by several private agencies in London for the use of business men".[25] Tucker's chief sources were the contract prices paid by three London institutions: Greenwich, Chelsea, and Bethlem Hospitals. Other writers have criticized these series for relying on wholesale and institutional London prices, rather than on retail prices actually paid by workers' families across England and Wales.[26] As Flinn has argued,[27] however, wholesale prices are a fair proxy for consumer prices over the very long term. In most cases, there is no alternative anyway. An exception is clothing, for which we have used a GRS cotton-textile export price series instead of Tucker's institutional London prices, leading to a slightly more optimistic view of the cost-of-living trend between 1790 and 1850.

The commodities included in the cost-of-living index also need revision. We have added more relevant working-class commodities, especially potatoes. Some irrelevant industrial raw materials, included in the GRS series, have been removed. But the most important change is the addition of house rent. Past impressions about the cost-of-living,[28] While the classic indices all omitted this important part of the cost-of-living.[28]

[23] For fuller documentation of the points made in this section, see DP, Section 4 and Appendices B and C.

[24] A. Gayer, W. W. Rostow, and A. J. Schwartz, *The Growth and Fluctuations of the British Economy, 1790–1850* (Oxford, 1953); N. J. Silberling, 'British Prices and Business Cycles, 1779–1850', *Review of Economics and Statistics*, 5 (1923), pp. 223–61; P. Rousseaux, *Les mouvements de fond de l'économie anglaise* (Louvain, 1938); and Tucker, 'Real Wages of Artisans in London'.

[25] Silberling, *British Prices*, p. 224.

[26] T. S. Ashton, 'The Standard of Life of the Workers in England', p. 48; Deane and Cole, *British Economic Growth*, p. 13.

[27] Flinn, 'Trends in Real Wages', p. 402.

[28] House rents have been measured for parts of England covering slightly shorter or more recent periods: see G. J. Barnsby, 'The Standard of Living in the Black Country during the Nineteenth Century', *Econ. Hist. Rev.*, 2nd ser. xxiv (1971), pp. 220–39; and R. S. Neale, 'The Standard of Living, 1780–1844: A Regional and Class Study', *Econ. Hist. Rev.* 2nd ser. xix (1966), p. 666, giving rents for Bath, 1812–1844.

finds faster wage advances for craftsmen between 1755 and 1815 than Phelps Brown-Hopkins or the present estimates, which also show faster nominal gains than Tucker's sluggish series. Eccleston's results serve to emphasize a geographic contrast already suggested by past writers: nominal wage gains were considerably greater in the midlands and north than in London and the south, at least up to 1815. Past impressions about the late eighteenth century and the war years have underestimated nominal wage gains by relying too heavily on southern series.

ours includes a rent series based on a few dozen cottages in Trentham, Staffordshire (just outside Stoke-on-Trent). While the data base is narrow, it does apply to a housing stock of almost unchanging quality.[29] The rent series implies that the cost of housing (at a fixed location) rose relative to other consumer items throughout the Industrial Revolution, thus offering some new support to the pessimists.[30]

Finally, the cost-of-living index should use commodity weights which reflect workers' budgets shares. Past series do not fully satisfy this requirement. All exclude any weight for housing, some include industrial inputs, and others are simply vague about their weights. One set of workers' household budgets stems from the pioneering work of Davies and Eden on the rural poor in the late eighteenth century.[31] Another is a miscellaneous group of urban workers' budgets from the late eighteenth and early nineteenth centuries.[32] The urban workers' budgets reveal a lower share spent on food, and a higher share spent on housing, than do the rural poor studied by Davies and Eden.

[29] We were able to hold the quality of the cottages virtually constant by (a) splicing together subseries that followed fixed sets of cottages and (b) conducting hedonic rent regression tests on detailed Trentham cottage surveys of 1835, 1842, and 1849. The regressions quantified the impact of cottage qualities and attributes of the tenants on the rent charged. It turned out that the rents fetched by the best and worst cottages differed very little for given types of tenants. See DP, Appendix C.

It has not been possible to pursue the issue of quality variation for other consumer items. Perhaps the quality of clothing and bedding rose, and perhaps the quality of meat declined, in ways not revealed by prices. The quantitative relevance of such possible quality drifts is doubtful given what we know about expenditures among workers' households. If, for example, the quality of meat fell by half between 1780 and 1850, the hidden extra cost to workers would still be only $.50 \times .111 = 5.5\%$ since $.111$ is the share of meat expenditures in the average budget (DP, Appendix B). The true net drift in quality was almost surely far less than this.

[30] The importance of adding rents, and of replacing institutional prices with market prices for clothing, can be seen from the following calculations, using "southern urban" budget weights (see Table 4 and DP, Section 4 and Appendix B):

Cost of Living

	Percentage change over the period		
	1790-1812	1812-1850	1790-1850
With Tucker's institutional clothing prices, and without rents	96.4	−56.0	−13.0
With export price of clothing, without rents	81.0	−62.3	−31.7
With export price of clothing, with rents (Table 4, "Best Guess")	87.2	−57.6	−20.6

The net effect of the two cost-of-living revisions is to tip the trend toward optimism (towards declining living costs) but the inclusion of rents by itself adds eleven per cent to the net cost-of-living increase between 1790 and 1850.

Readers should be warned, however, that the small Trentham sample may give too pessimistic an impression about trends. Across the nineteenth century the Trentham series has the same trends as two urban series (Barnsby, 'Standard of Living', p. 236; and H. W. Singer, 'An Index of Urban Land Rents and House Rents in England and Wales, 1845-1913', Econometrica, 9 (1941), p. 230). If rural cottage rents rose more slowly across the nineteenth century, then the Trentham series overstates the rise in a national average residential rent index using fixed locational weights. (As for the migration from low- to high-rent locations, see Section VI below). From about the 1770s to about the 1840s, the Trentham series rises much faster than two other rural series (T. L. Richardson, 'Standard of Living', pp. 245-8; and Sir James Caird, English Agriculture in 1850-1851 (New York, 1967), p. 474). The difference in trend is so great as to imply an unreasonably rapid rise in urban rents if Trentham were taken as a national (rural-and-urban) average index. So for both the Industrial Revolution era and the nineteenth century, the Trentham series rose faster than the most likely trends in national residential rents.

[31] Rev. David Davies, The Case of Labourers in Husbandry (Bath, 1795) and Sir Frederick Morton Eden, The State of the Poor (1797), II and III. Phelps Brown and Hopkins also used budget weights from Eden, though without house rents (Phelps Brown and Hopkins, 'Seven Centuries', pp. 296-314).

[32] Five urban budgets for 1795-1845 are presented by J. Burnett, A History of the Cost of Living (Harmondsworth, 1969). Neale (Bath, pp. 597-9) gives a labourer's household budget for Bath in 1831. Tucker ('Real Wages of Artisans in London', p. 75) ventured two non-farm household budgets as averages of some underlying studies' budgets.

10   PETER H. LINDERT AND JEFFREY G. WILLIAMSON

Choosing the most appropriate set of budget weights could matter a great deal. Goods and services are consumed in different proportions by northern and southern households, by the rural and urban, or by the poor and rich. Cost of living trends could differ across classes simply because of differences in budget weights, as happened often in American experience.[33] This possibility was pursued with four separate cost-of-living indices using weights from the rural north, rural south, urban north and urban south. The reason is that the net rise in the price of food relative to manufactures, which would have impoverished the rural poor more than the better-paid urban workers, was offset by the equally impressive relative rise in house rents, which took a greater toll on urban households. The analysis below continues to use southern urban weights, but we now know that the choice makes little difference.

The resulting "best-guess" cost of living index is displayed in Table 3 by the cost of living index in Table 4. From 1788/92 to 1820/26, our index falls midway between optimists (GRS, Rousseaux, Silberling) and pessimists (Phelps Brown and Hopkins, Tucker). Between 1820/26 and 1846/50, our index is more optimistic, showing a somewhat bigger drop in living costs than any of the past indices.[34] For the century as a whole, the "best-guess" index supports the middle ground between the optimist and pessimist extremes.

IV

Deflating the nominal full-time wage series from Table 3 by the cost of living index in Table 4 yields the real wage trends in Table 5 and Figure 1 below. The results support Michael Flinn's conclusion that "there are relatively few indications of significant change in levels of real wages either way before 1810/14".[35] For later years, however, Table 5 offers some revisions. Flinn was

	Per cent change in prices		
	1788-92 to 1809-15	1809-15 to 1820-26	1820-26 to 1846-50
Silberling	74.1	−31.2	−16.7
Tucker	85.2	−24.5	−10.0
Rousseaux		−34.8	−16.4
Gayer-Rostow-Schwarz	65.7	−30.7	−19.4
Phelps Brown-Hopkins	84.6	−23.5	−10.5
Table 4, 'Best Guess'	72.5	−27.3	−26.0

[33] Jeffrey G. Williamson, 'American Prices and Urban Inequality since 1820', J. Econ. Hist., XXXVI (1976), pp. 303-33. See also Jeffrey G. Williamson and Peter H. Lindert, American Inequality; A Macroeconomic History (New York, 1980), ch. 5.

[34] To wit:

(See Flinn, 'Trends in Real Wages', p. 404.)

[35] Ibid., p. 408. There would be clearer signs of deterioration between about 1800 and 1820 if the earnings of weavers and other non-spinning cotton workers were added to the overall averages, as could be done from 1806 on. Using our "best-guess" deflator, the Bowley-Wood wage rates for all cotton workers yield the following real wage indices: 1806, 78-62; 1810, 66-57; 1815, 75-43; 1819, 54-67; 1827, 66-96; 1835, 78-62; and 1851, 100-00. Compared with blue collar earnings in Table 5, these real earnings of all cotton workers fell sharply from 1806 to 1819, but kept pace thereafter. Even the famous handloom weavers may not have suffered any further net losses after 1820. Bowley's data on piece rates for handloom weavers in the Manchester area (Wages in the Nineteenth Century), opp. p.

struck by the concentration of all real wage improvements into a period of only a dozen years of deflation beginning around 1813. Table 5 does not conform with Flinn's view.[36] There was general real wage improvement

Table 4. A "Best-Guess" Cost-of-Living Index, 1781-1850, Using Southern Urban Expenditure Weights

(1850 = 100)

Year	COL Index	Year	COL Index	Year	COL Index
1781	118.8	1805	186.7	1828	143.2
1782	119.3	1806	178.5	1829	143.9
1783	121.9	1807	169.1	1830	141.3
1784	118.4	1808	180.5	1831	141.3
1785	112.3	1809	204.9	1832	133.9
		1810	215.4		
1786	109.6			1833	124.7
1787	112.5	1811	204.5	1834	117.6
1788	115.9	1812	235.7	1835	112.8
1789	122.3	1813	230.0	1836	126.4
1790	125.9	1814	203.3	1837	129.2
1791	121.2	1815	182.6	1838	138.3
1792	118.3	1816	192.1	1839	142.3
1793	127.3	1817	197.5	1840	138.4
1794	130.7	1818	192.4	1841	133.3
1795	153.8	1819	182.9	1842	123.4
1796	159.5	1820	170.1	1843	109.6
1797	138.8	1821	155.5	1844	114.5
1798	136.9	1822	139.8	1845	112.0
1799	155.7	1823	146.0	1846	116.4
1800	207.1	1824	154.6	1847	138.0
1801	218.2	1825	162.3	1848	110.9
1802	160.9	1826	144.4	1849	101.2
1803	156.8	1827	140.9	1850	100.0
1804	160.2				

Source: DP, Appendix B.

between 1810 and 1815, and a decline between 1815 and 1819, after which there was continuous growth. After prolonged wage stagnation, real wages, measured by the evidence presented here, nearly doubled between 1820 and 1850. This is a far larger increase than even past "optimists" had announced.[37]

119) imply a real wage gain of 15.3 per cent between 1819 and 1846, with most of the gain achieved by 1832. All cotton weavers, handloom plus power loom, gained an apparent 58.0 per cent from 1819 to 1850. Even the piece rate series probably have a pessimistic trend bias. They fail to reflect rising productivity of weavers of given age and sex, and the dwindling group of handloom weavers whose pay seemed to plummet before 1820 appears to have been increasingly dominated by women and children, as adult males fled to better-paying trades (Duncan Bythell, *The Handloom Weavers* (Cambridge, 1969), pp. 50-1, 60-1). On women and children's earning, see Section VII below.

[36] Flinn's dating of the real-wage upturn has also been questioned by G. N. von Tunzelmann, 'Trends in Real Wages, 1750-1850, Revisited', *Econ. Hist. Rev.*, 2nd ser. XXXII (1979), pp. 33-49, esp. p. 48.

[37] The closest approach to the present finding for the first half of the nineteenth century is the guarded conjecture by Deane and Cole that "real wages [improved by] about 25 per cent between 1800 and 1824 and over 40 per cent between 1824 and 1850" (*British Economic Growth*, pp. 26-7.)

Some readers of an earlier draft have wondered whether the apparent upturn after 1820 is not dependent on our use of the 1827 and 1835 benchmarks instead of nearby years. Some prefer to follow pessimist tradition by stressing the depression of 1842-3, while others choose the peak-price year 1839. Yet even these

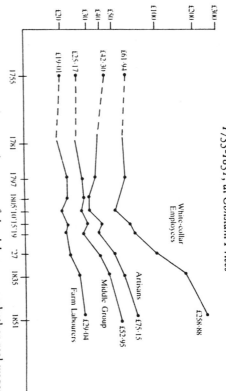

12   PETER H. LINDERT AND JEFFREY G. WILLIAMSON

Figure 1. *Adult Male Average Full-Time Earnings for Selected Groups of Workers, 1755–1851, at Constant Prices*

It is also large enough to resolve most of the debate over whether real wages improved during the Industrial Revolution. Unless new errors are discovered or a host of new declining wage series are added, it seems reasonable to conclude that the average worker was much better off in any decade from the 1830s on than in any decade before 1820. The same is true of any class of worker in Table 5.

Why has this announcement not been made before? One might have expected it from any of several devout optimists. The answer lies partly in the steady accumulation of data. Yet past findings have also been muted by the belief that trends in real full-time earnings of adult males failed to measure trends in workers' true "living standards". Each time a recent writer has come close to announcing the post-1820 improvement, the report has been disarmed by a confession of ignorance regarding trends in unemployment and in "qualitative" dimensions to life: perhaps health became poorer, work discipline more harsh and degrading, housing more crowded, and social injustice more outrageous, and perhaps these more than cancelled any improvement workers might have gained from rising real wages. These important issues dominate the remainder of this paper.

V

Time and again the unemployment issue has brought discussion of trends

extreme choices do not remove the post-1820 gains, as evident from these available real-wage data and unemployment estimates:

	1819	1835	1839	1843	1851
Real wage index, farm labourers:	73·52	91·67	80·04	103·91	100·00
Real wage index, middle group:	54·35	85·97	68·17	88·50	100·00
Estimated EMS unemployment rate (Section VI below):	n.a.	3·9%	2·2%	10·0%	3·9%

In the real-wage trough year 1839 fewer workers were denied income by unemployment. The depression year 1843 was a time of high real wages, thanks to cheap provisions. Neither of these extreme benchmarks looks as bad as 1819.

in workers' living standards to a halt: lacking national unemployment data before 1851, how can the real wage series be trusted as indicators of annual

Table 5. *Trends in Real Adult-male Full-Time Earnings for Selected Groups of Workers, 1755-1851*

Benchmark Year	Farm labourers	Middle Group	Artisans	All Blue Collar	White Collar	All Workers
1755	65·46	47·54	56·29	56·50	23·93	42·74
1781	61·12	46·19	48·30	50·19	22·24	39·24
1797	74·50	52·54	46·73	53·61	23·45	42·48
1805	74·51	52·96	42·55	51·73	20·82	40·64
1810	67·21	51·54	42·73	50·04	19·97	39·41
1815	75·51	57·81	52·18	58·15	25·49	46·71
1819	73·52	54·35	50·26	55·68	27·76	46·13
1827	75·86	70·18	66·39	69·25	39·10	58·99
1835	91·67	85·97	78·62	83·43	66·52	78·69
1851	100·00	100·00	100·00	100·00	100·00	100·00

Sources and Notes: The indices in the upper panel use the data in Tables 3 and 4, as does the row of "best guess" estimates in the lower panel. The most pessimistic and most optimistic variants are based on relatively unrealistic cost of living indices, selected as extreme cases from 16 alternatives. The most pessimistic used a cost of living index combining northern urban expenditure weights with Tucker's institutional clothing prices and Trentham cottage rents, while the most optimistic used an index combining northern rural weights with export clothing prices and no rents. Again, we prefer the "best guess" index, combining southern urban weights with export clothing prices and Trentham rents.

The 1755 figures are derived by relying on the Phelps Brown-Hopkins index to extend our 1781-1850 series (Table 4) backwards.

Percentage Change, 1781-1851, under three sets of cost-of-living weights and price assumptions:

Most pessimistic	31·6%	75·1%	68·0%	61·8%	294·5%	103·7%
"Best guess"	63·6%	116·5%	107·0%	99·2%	349·6%	154·8%
Most optimistic	107·0%	175·3%	164·2%	154·4%	520·3%	220·3%

earnings? Into this empirical vacuum Hobsbawm has injected fragmentary hints about unemployment in the industrial north, suggesting that the depression of 1841-3 was "almost certainly the worst of the century".[38]

Yet no conceivable level of unemployment could have cancelled the near-doubling of full-time wages and left the workers of the 1840s with less than their grandfathers had had. Such a cancellation of gains would require that the national unemployment rate would have had to rise from zero to 50 per cent, or from 10 per cent to 55 per cent—jumps which even the most ardent pessimist would dismiss as inconceivable. Even in the 1930s, unemployment was less than a quarter of the labour force. The 1840s lacked the availability of unemployment compensation, the sharp drop in output, wages and prices, as

[38] Hobsbawm, *Labouring Men*, p. 74. We have checked Hobsbawm's discussion of unemployment against the materials he drew from Finch, Adshead, *Facts and Figures*, Ashworth, and the Leeds Town Council. In all cases we found the primary materials shaky enough to make them unreliable even as testimony on purely local unemployment, let alone as national averages. The sources repeatedly counted persons not fully employed in a particular trade as unemployed, a procedure that ignores the widespread shifting of individual workers between sectors over the year. Thus a worker employed 40% of the time as a carpenter and 50% of the time in harvesting and assorted odd jobs is simply counted as a carpenter who can find work only 40% of the time (and who may also be counted as an underemployed harvest worker). Many of the sources include as unemployed those who have left for other towns or America. Some, especially Ashworth, ignore newcomers who came to town recently and found jobs, while taking a very generous definition of the unemployment of those previously at work. In one case, Hobsbawm (p. 75) cites figures showing that about 11% of the town of Leeds had *average* weekly incomes of 11¼ pence as evidence that "15-20 per cent of the population of Leeds had an income of less than *one shilling* per head per week", a conclusion that ignores the obvious difference between a group average and a group upper bound. Two final difficulties: all of the sources were designed to influence Parliament with pleas of special distress, and at no time does Hobsbawm compare these scraps from the 1840s with similar materials for earlier periods.

LIVING STANDARDS

Time = the year minus 1851.

The regression results on annual data for the United Kingdom are (with standard errors of coefficients in parentheses):[41]

$$U_{EMS} = 32 \cdot 96 - 16 \cdot 15 \text{ (GNP Ratio)} - 168 \cdot 02 \text{ (I/GNP)} - 71 \cdot 37 \overset{*}{w}$$
$$(7 \cdot 85) \qquad (63 \cdot 81) \qquad (21 \cdot 83)$$
$$- 288 \cdot 45 (\overset{*}{w})^2 - 0 \cdot 0032 \text{ (Time)} + 0 \cdot 148 \text{ (Time)}^2$$
$$(121 \cdot 80) \qquad (0 \cdot 0036) \qquad (0 \cdot 151)$$
$$\bar{U}_{EMS} = 5 \cdot 78, \text{ SEE} = 2 \cdot 50, R^2 = \cdot 543, F = 9 \cdot 11, \text{ d.f.} = 35.$$

The results confirm that EMS unemployment was lower when GNP was on the rise, when investment was a higher share of national product, and when engineering and shipbuilding wage rates were rising. The results also fail to reveal any other structural drift over the second half of the century: the coefficients on the time variables are statistically insignificant.

The regression can now predict EMS unemployment rates for the 1840s and late 1830s.[42] It would be unwise to make any predictions earlier than this, given the Poor Law reform of 1834 and other structural changes in the earlier years. For the period 1837-50, the equation generates the following estimates:

Period	Point Estimate of U_{EMS}	Bounds for U_{EMS} = estimate ± two standard errors
1837-1839	2·70%	0-7·70%
1840-1850	4·41%	0-9·41%
(two worst years: 1842-1843)	(9·44%)	(4·44-14·44%)

The overall rate of non-agricultural unemployment was probably lower than these estimates. Of the different sectoral output series available for the 1830s and 1840s,[43] only brick output showed as bad a slump in the early forties as did shipbuilding, the latter reflected in the EMS unemployment figures. It is not at all clear that the slump of the early forties was the "worst of the century". The available evidence make it no worse than the slumps of the late 1870s or mid-1880s. More important to the standard of living debate, industrial depression might have been as bad in the immediate post-war years (1814-19)

[41] The EMS unemployment rates are from ibid., pp. 64-5; the GNP ratio and I/GNP are from Phyllis Deane, 'New Estimates of Gross National Product for the United Kingdom, 1830-1914', Review of Income and Wealth, XIV (1968), pp. 104-5; the rate of nominal wage increase in engineering and shipbuilding is the Bowley-Wood series from Mitchell and Deane, Abstract, pp. 348-51.

[42] Serial correlation would imply that the text is too generous in setting an upper bound on unemployment in the 1840s and late 1830s. The Durbin-Watson statistic was 1·40, suggesting the possibility of serial correlation. A first-order Cochran-Orcutt transformation was performed (rho = 0·30). The altered regression had a lower standard error of estimate (2·33), but still had a Durbin-Watson statistic of only 1·59, far enough from 2·00 to encourage the suspicion of continuing serial correlation.

In the spirit of seeking overestimates of likely unemployment, we have reverted to the original equation, unadjusted for serial correlation, instead of pursuing successive iterations to push the Durbin-Watson statistic up toward 2·00. This yields inefficient estimates, overstating the standard error of the unbiased estimates presented here. (The fact that serial correlation also causes underestimation of the standard errors of the coefficients has little bearing here, since we seek accurate predictions rather than significance tests on coefficients.)

[43] For sectoral output series, see Mitchell and Deane, Abstract, passim, and Sidney Pollard, 'A New Estimate of British Coal Production, 1750-1850', Econ. Hist. Rev., 2nd ser. XXXIII (1980), pp. 212-35.

16 PETER H. LINDERT AND JEFFREY G. WILLIAMSON

as in the early forties, given that the earlier wage-price deflation was far more severe. We conclude that non-agricultural unemployment was not exceptionally high in either the 1840s or the 1850s, and even if it did rise after 1820, that unlikely event could have had only a trivial impact on workers' real earnings gains.

How might employment conditions in *agriculture* have affected the unemployment trends for the economy as a whole? Darkness is nearly total on this front. Seasonal unemployment was, of course, a serious problem throughout the eighteenth and nineteenth centuries.[44] To guess when under-employment reached crisis proportions, we can be guided by literary evidence, grain yields, and the terms of trade. The literary signs of distress were strongest during the harvest failures of the 1790s and in the twenty years after Waterloo.[45] Post-Napoleonic wheat yields were trendless from 1815 to 1840, and then rose.[46] The terms of trade shifted drastically against agriculture only twice in the century surveyed here—by about 20 per cent against agricultural products from c.1770 to c.1780 and by about 10 per cent against agricultural products from 1812-14 to 1822-24.[47] The common denominator emerging from this evidence is that the early postwar period, especially the decade 1815-24, probably witnessed exceptional unemployment in agriculture, followed by overall improvement to 1850.

All of this evidence suggests two plausible inferences: first, that unemployment among workers listing non-agricultural occupations was less than 9.41 per cent in the 1840s and 1850s; and second that unemployment among agricultural workers was no worse in the 1840s or 1850s than around 1820. We also know that the share of the British labour force engaged in agriculture dropped from 28.4 per cent for 1821 to 21.7 per cent for 1851.[48] This information is sufficient to demonstrate that the (alleged) net rise in unemployment could not have exceeded 7.37 per cent, and it may well have fallen.[49] The trend in unemployment thus could not have detracted greatly from the improvement in workers' real wages, and it may even have contributed to their improvement. Furthermore, even a pessimist's reckoning of the influence of unemployment overstates its relevance by assuming that time spent unemployed has no value as either leisure or non-market work.

[44] C. Peter Timmer, 'The Turnip, The New Husbandry, and the English Agricultural Revolution', *Quarterly Journal of Economics*, LXXXIII (1969), pp. 375-95; E. J. T. Collins, 'Migrant Labour in British Agriculture in the Nineteenth Century', *Econ. Hist. Rev.*, 2nd ser. XXIX (1976), pp. 38-59.

[45] E. L. Jones, *Agriculture and the Industrial Revolution* (New York, 1974), ch. 10; T. L. Richardson, 'The Agricultural Labourer's Standard of Living in Kent, 1790-1840', in D. Oddy and D. Miller eds. *The Making of the Modern British Diet* (1976), pp. 103-16; and E. J. Hobsbawm and G. Rudé, *Captain Swing* (New York, 1969).

[46] Jones, *Agriculture*, ch. 8.

[47] Deane and Cole, *British Economic Growth*, p. 91; Mitchell and Deane, *Abstract*, ch. xiv.

[48] Deane and Cole, *British Economic Growth*, p. 142.

[49] The proof runs as follows. Let the ^{0} superscript denote 1820, and the ^{1} superscript denote 1850. Further, let the $_a$ subscript refer to agriculture and $_n$ subscript to the rest of the economy. Let 'a' be the share of the labour force in agriculture, and U the rate of unemployment. The national unemployment rate (no sectoral subscript) is linked to the sectoral rates by definition as follows:

$$U^0 = a^0 U^0_a + (1 - a^0) U^0_n \text{ and } U^1 = a^1 U^1_a + (1 - a^1) U^1_n.$$

Since a^0 is .284 and a^1 is .217, the net change in the unemployment rate becomes

$$U^1 - U^0 = (.217 U^1_a - .284 U^0_a) + .783 U^1_n - .716 U^0_n.$$

Given that $U^1_a < .0941$, and that $U^1_a \geqslant U^1_n$, it follows that only the second of these right-hand terms can be positive, and its value must be below $.783 \times .0941 = 7.37\%$. This exercise for Britain can be repeated with the same results for England and Wales.

VI

Thus far we have taken the orthodox path by focusing solely on adult male purchasing power. Yet questions about work and earnings by women and children have always been lurking in the wings throughout the standard of living debate. The rise of their employment in mills and mines is deplored as much today as it was during the public outcry prior to the Factory Acts. The increasing dependence of working-class families on the earnings of children, and the shifting of both children and single young women from the authority of fathers to the discipline of capitalists, are thought to have undermined traditional family roles and fathers' self-esteem.[50] Such social side-effects will be treated as part of the larger issue of urban and industrial disamenities in Section VIII below. This section will address the prior question of how trends in the earning power of women and children compared with those in men's real wages.

What data there are suggest the tentative conclusion that the earning power of women and children marched roughly in step with the real wage of unskilled labouring men, a group with whom women and children tended to compete as substitutes. The evidence for this view begins with data on the ratios of women's and children's pay relative to that of adult male labourers, both within sectors and overall. The best single indicator of the relative earning power of a woman's or a child's time is the ratio of their hourly rate to that of men, averaged over all seasons and including home commodity production. Yet such hourly rates are seldom given in historical sources before 1850. We therefore gather clues on some close substitute measures.

Table 6 presents the best available evidence on two measures that should serve to bracket trends in the value of women's and children's time. One is the weekly earnings ratio. The other is the ratio of hourly hired-labour wage rates, based on data that do not reflect differences in hours worked per week.

Working women may have gained ground on unskilled men during the century from 1750 to 1850. Our gleanings of data on relative *weekly earnings* hint as much, both for women within rural areas and for a shifting rural-urban average. Yet hints about relative *hourly wages* (the second column in Table 6) warn that we cannot be sure that there was any upward trend in the true relative value of women's time. It may simply be that the relative weekly hours of those working rose, though this seems unlikely. Our tentative conclusion is that the relative earning power of women did not decline. It may have stayed the same, or it may have risen.

The relative earning power of children probably stayed the same above the age of fifteen or thereabouts, while declining slightly for younger children. This conclusion is derived mainly from the data on relative weekly earnings in Table 6. These data again may differ in trend from the true average time values because of changes in relative weekly hours, but relative hours would have had to have risen at an implausibly high rate to reverse the main conclusions advanced here.

Thus, it appears that an employment-weighted average of the wage rates of

[50] N. J. Smelser, *Social Change in the Industrial Revolution* (Chicago, 1959), chs. IX–XI; Thompson, *English Working Class*, ch. 10.

18   PETER H. LINDERT AND JEFFREY G. WILLIAMSON

Table 6. *Relative Earnings of English Working-Class Women and Children, as Fractions of those for Full-Time Adult Male Labourers, 1742-1890*

(1·000 = earnings or wage rate of full-time adult male labourers)

Data context	Employed wives/women			Employed Children (unweighted boy-girl averages)	
	Weekly earnings	*Hourly wage rate*	*Ages*	*Weekly earnings*	*Hourly wage rate*
(a) *18th-century rural:*					
Brandsby, Yorkshire, 1742-51:	<.488*	<.488	not given	<.495*	<.495
Corfe Castle, Dorset, 1790:	.202	>.202	age 13/age 17	.253/.330	>.253/>.330
English rural poor, 1787-1796:	.134	>.134	age 13/age 17	.196/.214	>.196/>.214
(b) *19th-century rural:*					
Rural England and Wales, 1833:	.224	>.224-.365	9-15 yrs.	.130	.130-.253
Norfolk-Suffolk, 1838:	.284	>.284	over 10 yrs.	.172	.172
(c) *19th-century town:*					
Textiles in towns, England and Wales, 1833:	.471	>.471	age 13/age 17	.233/.413	>.233/>.413
Birmingham, 1839:	.327^b	>.327	age 13/age 17	.153/.230	>.153/>.230
Manchester, 1839:	—	>.350	14-18 yrs.	—	>.230
Industrial workers' wives and children, England and Wales, 1889-1890:	.407	>.407	age 13/age 17	.185/.345	>.185/>.345

Sources and Notes:

* Relative daily wages, not weekly. For this reason, and because the hired-labour data are in this case biased toward the peak-demand season more for women and children than for men, the "Weekly" (here, daily) wage ratio overestimates the hourly ratio more than for later observations.
^b 63 working women, ages 21-70.

Two different concepts of an "employed" state are being applied here. The averages for weekly earnings are for persons employed either at or away from home for a significant part of the year. This concept of employment is close to the broad definition of labour force participation. The average hourly wage rates refer to persons when hired outside the home, thus excluding any unemployment.

Brandsby hired women and children: J. E. Thorold Rogers, *History of Agriculture and Prices in England*, VII, pp. 499-509. Men: 10,657 days at 9.779d., all seasons; women, 2,061·5 days at 4.772d.; boys: 1,948 days at 5·194d.; girls, 122·5 days at 4.486d. Similar ratios for womens' earnings are given for 1770 in Arthur Young, *A Six Month's Tour of the North of England* (1771).

Corfe Castle, Dorset: all wives, 20-59, and children with stated occupations including outwork; from the detailed 1790 census at the Dorset Record Office. 261 families.

English rural poor: 172 poor families with children, calculated from Davies and Eden data as described in Peter H. Lindert, 'Child Costs and Economic Development', in Richard A. Easterlin, ed. *Population and Economic Change in Developing Countries* (Chicago, 1980), pp. 5-79.

Rural England and Wales, 1833: Poor Law Commission, *Rural Queries*, in House of Commons, *Sessional Papers*, 1833, drawing on parishes giving explicit answers to questions about earnings. Similar wage rates for women and children are quoted for 1843 in House of Commons, Special Assistant Poor Law Commissioners, *Reports on the Employment of Women and Children in Agriculture* (1843).

Norfolk-Suffolk farms, 1838: 64 couples without children, 120 families with one child over 10, from J. P. Kay, 'Earnings of Agricultural Labourers in Norfolk and Suffolk', *Journal of the Royal Statistical Society*, 1 (1838), pp. 179-80.

Textiles in towns, England and Wales, 1833: weekly earnings for 1,864 children at age 13, 1,434 children at age 17, and 972 women at ages 26-30 from Dr James Mitchell's report in Factory Inquiry Commission, *Supplementary Report of the Central Board . . . as to the Employment of Children in Factories*, in House of Commons, *Sessional Papers*, 1834, vol. XIX. The other factory inquiry volumes of that era are also a rich source for earnings profiles by age and sex.

Birmingham, 1838: 'Contributions to the Economic Statistics of Birmingham', by a local Subcommittee, *Journal of the Royal Statistical Society*, 2 (1840), p. 441.

Textiles in towns, England and Wales, 1833: hourly wage rates from several industries, in David Chadwick, 'On the Rate of Wages in Manchester and Salford . . . 1839-59', *Quarterly Journal of the Statistical Society*, XXIII (1860), pp. 1-36. The comparisons used here were biased against our argument somewhat by choosing lower-paid groups of women and children and better-paid adult male labourers. The 1849 ratios from the same source are similar.

Industrial workers' wives and children, 1889-1890: 857 industrial workers' wives and 159 families with one child over 10, from US Commissioner of Labor, *Sixth and Seventh Annual Reports*, pt. III (Washington, 1891 and 1892).

women and children together would have advanced about as fast as those for adult male farm labourers in the course of the century 1750–1850. This conclusion would not be overturned by noting the decline in overall labour-force participation of both women and children.[51] An optimist might interpret this decline as voluntary, that is as showing that the implicit purchasing power (the "shadow price") of time spent away from work rose faster than the observed wage rates. A pessimist might counter that the trend was involuntary, that women and children were being thrown into involuntary unemployment faster than adult males. The latter position is hard to sustain. Aside from "protective" hours legislation from 1833 on, no institutions compelled employers to pay women and children wage rates that were increasingly above the opportunity cost of their time out of work. The real wage gains documented for men in Table 5 were not achieved at the expense of women and children. As for the perceived disamenities of having women and children shift their work from home toward factories, these become part of the net disamenities appraised in Section IX below.

Since wage rates differ between occupations, migration from low-paid to high-paid employment can raise average wages for the working class as a whole, even if wage rates do not change for any one occupation. How much of the wage gains up to 1850 were due to such mobility-induced wage drift? The "blue collar" and the "all worker" wage series in Tables 3 and 5 already capture this mobility effect. It can be factored back out by applying fixed wage rates to shifting employment numbers. Detailed calculations described elsewhere show that occupational mobility contributed less than 5·3 per cent to the rise in average full-time earnings of all blue-collar workers between 1781 and 1851, using either Laspeyres or Paasche weights.[52] Virtually all of the apparent wage gains were gains within occupations, not wage drifts due to changing occupational weights.

Migration from low-wage to high-wage regions can also raise wages for the average worker even if wages fail to rise in any one region. That nominal wages varied widely across English counties well into the nineteenth century has been well known at least since Arthur Young's late eighteenth-century tours. Elsewhere we have analyzed the causes of the regional differences in wage rates for agricultural labour.[53] It appears that *real* wage gaps persist even after regional adjustments for variation in cost of living and disamenities are made. Furthermore, it has long been appreciated that labour drifted from the low-wage south to the high-wage north during the Industrial Revolution.[54]

[51] On rates of labour-force participation, see DP, Section 3,4, and the sources cited in Table 6.

[52] For all workers, the Paasche measure of the mobility effect was as high as 17·2 per cent between 1781 and 1851, but this was again a very small share of the overall real wage gains. These are improvements over the estimates discussed in DP, Section 6, due to slight revisions in the employment weights.

Some additional shift toward higher-paying occupations after 1811 has eluded our measures. We could include only those occupations that supplied pay proxies, and the excluded groups (about a third of the labour force) shifted from a low-skill mix dominated by domestic servants to a high-skill mix dominated by new occupations created by the Industrial Revolution. More complete measures would show faster average wage gains between 1811 and 1851.

[53] See DP, Section 7.

[54] In this section, 'migration' is defined as changes in the labour force distribution across regions. There is, of course, an extensive literature which debates the demographic source of the population and labour force shift to high-wage areas over the period which bounds the standard of living debate. This section is not concerned with whether the observed shift can be attributed to natural increase (and whether to birth or death rate differences) or to actual migration.

20   PETER H. LINDERT AND JEFFREY G. WILLIAMSON

Since the average "blue collar" and "all worker" wage series in Tables 3 and 5 already include most of these regional migration effects, it is now a simple matter to explore their quantitative impact on real wage gains up to 1850.

It appears that regional migration contributed very little to the real wage gains for the average English worker after the 1780s. True, some periods registered far larger regional migration gains than others: 1841-51 was a decade of impressive gains through migration to high-wage regions; and the late eighteenth century records some small positive gains.[55] But over the period 1781-1851 as a whole, regional migration contributed less than 3·6 per cent to the observed real wage gains. It was real wage gains within regions that mattered most.

VII

Most of us care more about people's consumption *per lifetime*, rather than just per year. Conclusions based on trends in real earnings per annum risk grave error if the workers' length of life deteriorated. Alternatively, any improvements in the workers' length of life implies that standard of living gains are understated in Table 5, especially if sickness and longevity are inversely correlated. The standard of living debate commonly fails to confront the issue of lifetime incomes. There are exceptions to this characterization of the debate, and surely the most famous is Engels' original broadside on *The Condition of the Working Class in England*, which indicted industrial capitalism for killing workers with unhealthy conditions:

. . . society in England daily and hourly commits what the working-men's organs, with perfect correctness, characterise as social murder . . . its deed is murder just as surely as the deed of the single individual; disguised, malicious murder against which none can defend himself, which does not seem what it is, because no man sees the murderer . . . .[56]

To link workers' early deaths with rising capitalism, Engels drew on several available estimates showing that mortality was worse in the cities than the countryside, appalling in Liverpool and Manchester, and worst in the most crowded neighbourhoods of the same cities. A host of studies has since confirmed this spatial pattern of mortality.

Two pitfalls await anyone trying, as Engels did, to infer from such patterns that working-class longevity diminished as the Industrial Revolution progressed. First, it is important to remember that the working classes were not neatly segregated from the upper classes by place of residence. Liverpool was no closer to being purely working-class than was England in the aggregate. On the contrary, census figures show that the socio-occupational group most concentrated in the unhealthy cities was the bourgeoisie, although most bought their way out of the worst sections by paying higher rents in the more salubrious sections of the same unhealthy cities. The rise of centres of bad health gives no more support to the pessimists' view of working-class conditions

55 But hardly of the size suggested by the qualitative literature. See, for example, Deane and Cole, *British Economic Growth*, ch. III.
56 F. Engels, *The Condition of the Working Class in England*, translated from the 1845 German edition, with an introduction by E. J. Hobsbawm (St. Albans, 1974), pp. 126, 127.

than the nineteenth-century decline in national mortality gives to the optimists' position.

Thanks to the energies of William Farr and a few other scholars, a fairly clear picture of adult male working-class life expectancy can be put together towards the end of the Industrial Revolution. As we have shown elsewhere, life expectancies did not differ dramatically across occupations for England and Wales as a whole. The occupational differences were far smaller than the spatial differences, though the estimates may be slightly biased toward uniformity by migration effects and by the omission of paupers from the available figures.[57] We are warned that occupational differentials were unlikely to have been as great as stark contrasts between Manchester and rural Norfolk would suggest.

The other pitfall is mistaking a snapshot for a motion picture. Past observers have inferred that mortality must have worsened for city-dwellers (and for the working class) since mortality was higher in fast-growing cities. Such inferences are unwarranted. In fact, mortality improved (receded) in the countryside *and* most cities, and did so by enough to improve national life expectancy from about 1800 on. The exceptional cities were Liverpool and Manchester, where crude death rates stayed about the same from 1801 to 1851, while age-adjusted death rates appear to have risen only slightly up to 1820 and declined slightly to mid-century.[58]

In short, while we cannot yet determine trends in working-class infant and child mortality, it can be shown that any tendency of the rising industrial centres to lure adult workers to an early death was fully offset, or more than offset, by the lengthening of life both in the cities and the countryside.[59]

VIII

Where in our measures is the degradation and demoralization associated with the long rigid hours spent at mind-numbing work for an insensitive avaricious capitalist? The disruption of traditional family roles? The noise, filth, crime, and crowding of urban slums? Until we can devise ways of weighing these varied dimensions against material gains, we cannot answer questions about living standards, but rather only questions about real earnings.

In judging the importance of these quality of life factors, we must avoid imposing twentieth-century values on early nineteenth-century workers. We must avoid both facile indifference to past suffering and excessive indignation at conditions that seem much more intolerable now. The workers of that era

[57] See DP, Table 20. 'Migration effects' could bias the life expectancy measures toward uniformity because persons whose health had been damaged by high-mortality environments (e.g., mining or Manchester) may have migrated to healthier environments to no avail, dying there (e.g., recorded rural labourers) and raising rural mortality rates for misleading reasons.

[58] On national life expectancy, see E. A. Wrigley and R. Schofield, *The Population History of England, 1541–1871: A Reconstruction* (Cambridge, 1981), esp. Table A3.1. For crude death rates by county and city, see Deane and Cole, *British Economic Growth*, p. 131; and House of Commons, *Sessional Papers*, 1801–02, vols. VI and VII, 1849; vol. XXI, and 1865, vol. XIII, pp. 14ff. For London, we have calculated the following infant mortality rates as percentages of live births, using the bills of mortality plus the third English life table up to 1830 and annual reports of the Registrar General thereafter: 1729–39 – 3746, 1750–9 – 3322, 1780–9 – 2406, 1800–09 – 1864, 1820–30 – 1428, 1851–60 – 1548.

[59] See DP, Table 21 and the accompanying text.

22   PETER H. LINDERT AND JEFFREY G. WILLIAMSON

must themselves be allowed to reveal how much a "good" quality of life was worth to them.

How is their voice to be heard? Most of them lacked the right to vote. Some protested violently, while most remained silent, but we cannot infer a majority view from either the outcries or the silence. The most satisfactory clue to a worker's view is his response to living and working conditions that offered different rates of pay and different qualities of life.

Employers in the rising industries and cities had to pay workers more to attract a growing share of the labour force. How *much* more is a valuable clue to the importance which the workers attached to quality of life. To err on the side of exaggeration on so sensitive an issue, let us contrast the pay of unskilled common labourers in two extreme settings in the late 1830s: cotton and metal mills in Manchester in 1839 versus year-round farm labour in Norfolk and Suffolk in 1837.[60] Among the better paid unskilled in Manchester were labourers in metal mills and adult male warehousemen in cotton mills. These groups received 18 shillings a week, or £41·4 for a normal 46-week year. Other common labourers generally got less. In healthy East Anglia, a single adult male farm labourer averaged £25·1 in 1837. The extreme Faustian "Satanic mill" wage premium was thus 65 per cent.

At some human cost of moving, labourers could choose to suffer the disamenities of Manchester work, even if it looks like a Hobson's choice to us today. And choose they did, in significant numbers. The census of 1851 shows that every county in England, and even the rural districts of every county, attracted persons born in every other county. Workers also shuttled between the industrial and agricultural sectors on a seasonal basis.[61] They were free to move, and many of them knew enough about conditions in other sectors if they cared to consider moving.

The possibility of migration implies that the wage premium offered in Manchester cannot understate the importance of urban-industrial disamenities and living costs to those workers who were actually near the margin in choosing between Manchester and East Anglia. Indeed, it may well overstate this importance not only because the continued flow toward the cities implied a true gain for movers, but also because we have selected two extreme cases for contrast. Manchester was as "bad" a city as any (except perhaps Liverpool), and farm workers in East Anglia were paid a good deal less than their counterparts in the rural north.

The Manchester-East Anglia "wage gap" must be viewed as an upper bound on what it took to induce rural labour to modern industry in the second quarter of the nineteenth century. This gap can be viewed as compensation for two closely related costs: the payment necessary to compensate workers (in their own eyes) for a lower quality of life, and the payment necessary to compensate workers for the higher urban cost of living (e.g. expensive housing).

[60] The earnings data come from David Chadwick, 'On the Rate of Wages in Manchester and Salford, and the Manufacturing Districts of Lancashire, 1839-1859', *Journal of the Royal Statistical Society*, Series A, XXIII (1860), pp. 1-36, and J. P. Kay, 'Earnings of Agricultural Labourers in Norfolk and Suffolk', *J. Royal. Stat. Soc.*, 1 (1838), pp. 179-83. Both estimates posit some partial unemployment. This took the form of lower winter earnings in the Norfolk-Suffolk farm data and a 46-week year for Manchester.

[61] On migration countercurrents, see also E. G. Ravenstein, 'The Laws of Migration', *J. Royal Stat. Soc.*, Series A, XLVIII (1885), pp. 167-235, esp. pp. 187-9.

The 65 per cent gap in the 1830s and 1850s is wide, but how much long-run deterioration does it reveal? Very little, as it turns out. First, it is a contemporaneous comparison between sectors. Workers did not choose between the living conditions of 1780 and those of 1850. Yet workers' migration behaviour in the nineteenth and twentieth centuries shows that they would have chosen the conditions of 1850 overwhelmingly, not only because real wages rose over time but also because the quality of life was *improving* within both the urban and the rural sectors over time. We infer this mainly from trends in mortality, the best single proxy for the disamenities associated with demoralization, bad health, and low resistance to disease. As we have seen in Section VII, mortality was declining within the countryside and within the cities (though it was only stable in Liverpool and Manchester). Thus, disamenities were declining within both sectors, an improvement we have not measured in monetary terms.

What of the impact of population shift from low-density rural areas of high quality of life to high-density urban areas with unpleasant disamenities? For this implicit spatial migration taking place between generations, the full 65 per cent gap might be applied. But it could apply only to that share of the population making the implicit move. An overestimate of this fraction is the rise in the share living in urban places, a measure that generously assumes that all cities were as bad as Manchester. This fractional shift is only 14·89 per cent from 1781 to 1851,[62] making the disamenities and living-cost increases for the average worker only ·1489×65 = 9·7 per cent. To repeat, even this is a generous overestimate. Elsewhere, one of the present authors has analyzed the urban-industrial disamenities and cost of living effects in greater detail, and found that the former was probably under 2·5 per cent and the latter was probably under 3·3 per cent around the 1840s.[63]

Many workers did suffer from the higher disamenities and living costs in the rising industrial centres, and many others resisted them by resolving to live and work elsewhere. Yet the value implicitly put on these human costs by the marginal workers, who actually moved into the urban-industrial centres, was not large enough to cancel even a tenth of blue collar workers' real wage gains. Nor should this surprise us. The development process inevitably finds workers and policymakers more intent on basic purchasing power in the hungry early phases of development, as the history of environmental quality in Manchester, Pittsburgh, Manila, and São Paulo clearly shows.

IX

We now have a much broader empirical basis for inferring how workers fared in the century between 1750 and 1850. Our tentative findings can be summarized most easily by focusing on the relatively data-rich Industrial Revolution era from 1781 to 1851.

[62] Urban populations for 1801-51 were taken from Mitchell and Deane, *Abstract*, pp. 24-7. Deane and Cole (*British Economic Growth*, p. 7) suggested that the urban population share in the mid-eighteenth century was about 15-16 per cent, and we extrapolated between 1751 and 1801 using this figure for the former date.

[63] See Jeffrey G. Williamson, 'Urban Disamenities, Dark Satanic Mills, and the British Standard of Living Debate', *J. Econ. Hist.* XLI (1981), and 'Was the Industrial Revolution Worth It? Disamenities and Death in 19th Century British Towns', *Explorations in Economic History*, 19 (1982), pp. 221-45.

24

PETER H. LINDERT AND JEFFREY G. WILLIAMSON

Table 7 collects our best estimates of workers' experiences, beginning with our "best-guess" real wage trends and proceeding through several long-needed adjustments. Table 7 suggests impressive net gains in the standard of life: over 60 per cent for farm labourers, over 86 per cent for blue-collar workers, and over 140 per cent for all workers. The hardships faced by workers at the end of the Industrial Revolution cannot have been nearly as great as those of their grandparents.

The great majority of these human gains came after 1820. Pessimists must retreat to the pre-1820 era, where workers' net gains look as elusive in this paper as in past studies of single occupations. Optimists might feel a temptation to proclaim victory by shifting attention away from the classic Industrial Revolution era, but this inference seems premature. After all, the best measures of industrialization are still so uncertain for the years before 1831 that the timing of the Revolution itself is debatable. Furthermore, the separate influence of the French Wars has yet to be factored out of the longer-run development experience.

Pessimists in tune with larger intellectual currents of the 1960s have called for less attention to conventional measures of real income and more to the environmental aspects of the Industrial Revolution—all of those appalling health conditions and social injustices with which workers were affronted. The shift is certainly welcome. Yet the results presented here suggest that nineteenth-century environmental influences on health—such as crowding, infection, and pollution—could hardly have lowered average quality of life over time.

Research inspired by the pessimists' allegations about the Industrial Rev-

Table 7. *Revised Measures of English Workers' Standard-of-Living Gains, 1781–1851*

Source of Improvement	Overall improvement, 1781–1851		
	Farm Labourers	All Blue Collar Workers	All Workers
1. Real full-time earnings ("Best guess", Table 5)	63.6%	99.2%	154.8%
1a. Due to occupational change (DP, Section 6)	(o)	(<5·3%)	(<17·2%)
1b. Due to regional migration (DP, Section 7)	(<3·6%)	(<3·6%)	(<3·6%)
1c. Residual: real wage gains within occupations and regions	(>60·0%)	(>90·3%)	(>134·0%)
2. Diminished by an "upper-bound" rise in unemployment, or <7·4% (Section VI above)	63·6%	>91·8%	>147·4%
3. Diminished by the shift toward higher urban living costs, or <3·3%*	63·6%	>88·5%	>144·1%
4. Diminished by urban-industrial disamenities, or <2·5%*	63·6%	>86·0%	>141·6%
5. Augmented by adult mortality gains, which were not negative (Section VIII)	>63·6%	>86·0%	>141·6%

Notes: *These figures are taken from DP, Section 8. Readers preferring the estimates in Section IX above may wish to substitute the 9·7 per cent figure for Rows 3 and 4 together in the "blue collar" and "all workers" columns.

olution will now have to shift to social injustice and social disorder. Reported crime, alcoholism, protest, and illegitimacy appear to have been on the rise in the first half of the nineteenth century. In addition, rising material inequality seems to characterize the period, and these trends were likely to have influenced social disorder. We know from related research, for example, that common labourers failed to experience gains as rapid as those for better-paid employees, as even Table 7 shows in comparing three working-class aggregates. Earnings inequality statistics suggest the same between the 1820s and the 1880s. Our preliminary results on probated wealth and land rents also suggest rising inequality between upper and lower-middle classes in the course of the first half of the nineteenth century. Inequality between workers and the very poor may also have widened: we need far better information on the material condition of those below the working classes—vagrants and disabled paupers—than the large literature on poor relief has yet been able to supply. These issues, not trends in absolute living standards, are likely to mark the future battleground between optimists and pessimists about how workers fared under nineteenth-century British capitalism.

University of California, Davis
University of Wisconsin, Madison

EXPLORATIONS IN ECONOMIC HISTORY 19, 221–245 (1982)

Was the Industrial Revolution Worth It? Disamenities and Death in 19th Century British Towns*

JEFFREY G. WILLIAMSON

The University of Wisconsin

I. DISAMENITIES, DEATH, AND THE STANDARD-OF-LIVING DEBATE

The quality of urban life has always played a key role in the debate over British living standards during the Industrial Revolution. It certainly attracted the attention of Chadwick, Kay, and other social reformers in the 1830s and 1840s, but for hot rhetoric it is hard to beat Frederick Engels who viewed the migration of rural labor to British cities as "social murder."[1] The early Victorian perception persists in academic debate even today, and the "pessimists" have made much of the issue. While even the most ardent pessimist would acknowledge the ghastly environment *outside* the towns in early 19th century England,[2] urban disamenities in the Dark Satanic Mills have, nonetheless, been viewed as important negative determinants of working class living standards up to the 1840s and beyond.

* This paper is a companion to one which was read before the Economic History Association meetings in Boston, Massachusetts (September 11–13, 1980) and subsequently published in the *Journal of Economic History* (Williamson, 1981a). Analysis of the 1905 data underlying that paper has since been revised and extended. The results appearing here take precedence. Analysis of the 1834 data (on which this paper dwells) and the 1905 data is described in greater detail in a working paper which is available on request from the author (Williamson, 1981b). This paper is part of the *British Inequality Since 1680* project in collaboration with Peter H. Lindert. The project has been supported by the National Science Foundation and the National Endowment for the Humanities. The research assistance of George Boyer, Howard Metzenberg, and Kenneth Snowden is gratefully acknowledged. In addition, the paper has been greatly improved by the comments of John Bishop, Sir Henry Phelps Brown, Stanley Engerman, Claudia Goldin, Michael Haines, Jonathan Hughes, William Kennedy, Peter Lindert, Robert Margo, Paul Mc-Gouldrick, Joel Mokyr, Larry Neal, Nick von Tunzelmann, Dan Usher, Richard Vedder, Gavin Wright, and Wisconsin Economic History Workshop participants.

[1] Engels, *The Condition of the Working Class*, W. O. Henderson and W. H. Chaloner edition (1971).

[2] See, for example, the classic survey by M. C. Buer (1926, pp. 249–252).

What did the common laborer forgo by leaving some rural "Sweet Auburn"[3] for some ugly urban "Sheffield" during the Industrial Revolution? Are quantitative answers to such questions possible? A. J. Taylor (1975, p. liv) certainly didn't think so when surveying the debate some six years ago:

> How . . . can a just comparison be made between [that] which removal from a rural to urban environment entailed, and the social amenities which town and factory, however squalid, offered . . . ?

Elsewhere I have shown that the answers can be found by applying methods suggested by recent research on 20th-century urbanization and economic growth. Application of those methods to the standard-of-living debate is especially attractive since it makes it possible for the workers themselves to reveal their preferences. And it's about time! For more than a century, our perceptions have been colored by the more verbal Victorian middle-class observer who wrote books and pamphlets which—as it turns out—reveal far stronger preferences for urban amenities than did the workers themselves.

The British standard-of-living debate has its contemporary analogy. Twentieth-century pessimists and neo-Malthusians have spent the past decade or so attacking the optimists' premise that economic growth is a Good Thing. These modern pessimists—Ehrlich, Meadows, Forrester, and the Club of Rome—prodded the modern optimists to action. Among the first economists to respond, William Nordhaus and James Tobin (1972, pp. 49, 50) rose to the challenge in *Is Growth Obsolete?*

> The disamenities of urban life come to mind: pollution, litter, congestion, noise, insecurity, ... Failure to allow for these consumption items overstates not only the level but very possibly the growth of consumption. The fraction of the population exposed to these disamenities has increased, and the disamenities themselves may have worsened.

How did they propose to estimate these disamenities? Pay has always tended to be higher in cities, and this fact suggested to Nordhaus and Tobin a path to measurement:

> . . . some portion of the higher earnings of urban residents may simply be compensation for the disamenities of urban life and work. If so we should not count as a gain in welfare the full increments of NNP that result from moving a man from farm or small town to city. The persistent association of higher wages with

---

[3] "Sweet Auburn, loveliest village of the plain," a poetic image coined in 1770 by Goldsmith, refers to a deserted village. See J. R. T. Hughes (mimeo., n.d., p. 9). In contrast with Engels, Marx had a more pragmatic view of "Sweet Auburn." Marx said that the Industrial Revolution eliminated the "idiocy of rural life" in *Das Kapital*.

14   PETER H. LINDERT AND JEFFREY G. WILLIAMSON

well as the fall in the investment share that accompanied record jobless rates ninety years later.

We can be more precise about the extent to which the unemployment issue has been overstated in the standard of living debate. We have a number of clues about early nineteenth-century unemployment in Britain that have yet to be exploited. Let us examine these, focusing on the controversial period 1820–50, beginning with the non-agricultural sector before tackling the knottier problem of agricultural underemployment.

We can put an upper limit on non-agricultural unemployment in the 1850s by starting with the share of engineering, metal and shipbuilding union membership who were out of work: in 1851, 3·9 per cent were out at any one time, and the average was 5·2 per cent for 1851-9. This sector had all the attributes to suggest that unemployment would exceed economy-wide rates: early unionization, an unemployment insurance scheme, and business cycle sensitivity typical of all capital-goods industries. Indeed, from 1851 to World War I the unemployment rate in the engineering-metals-shipbuilding sector (EMS) fell below overall unemployment for insured workers in only two years, both of them boom years. Between 1923 and 1939, the EMS unemployment rate exceeded that of all insured workers by far.[39] Thus, the 3·9 and 5·2 per cent EMS figures clearly overstate unemployment for the non-agricultural sector as a whole. These figures establish upper bounds on the extent to which non-agricultural unemployment could have worsened.

How much worse could non-agricultural unemployment have been in the "hungry forties" than in the 1850s? That unemployment history can be approximated by appealing to the behaviour of other variables. We know that unemployment varies inversely with output over the business cycle. Furthermore, EMS unemployment must have been closely tied to the share of capital formation in national product. There was also a tight nonlinear relationship between unemployment and wage rate increases in Britain between 1862 and 1957, according to A. W. Phillips's classic study of the Phillips Curve.[40] Aside from the influence of these three variables, one might also suspect that the unemployment rates in engineering-metals-shipbuilding (1851-1892) drifted over time in a way that shifted the unemployment rate.

These propositions can all be tested for the second half of the nineteenth century. If they are successful, then they can be used to predict non-agricultural unemployment back into the 1830s. Regression analysis can sort out the determinants of the unemployment rates in engineering-metals-shipbuilding (1851-1892) where

U_{EMS} = the EMS unemployment rate (a 1 per cent rate measured as "1·0");

GNP Ratio = the ratio of current nominal gross national product at factor cost to its average level over the immediately preceding five years;

I/GNP = the share of gross domestic capital formation in gross national product at factor cost;

$\dot{w}$ = the rate of change from the previous year in the wage rate for shipbuilding and engineering (a 1 per cent rise is "·01"); and

39 Mitchell and Deane, *Abstract*, pp. 64-7.
40 A. W. Phillips, 'The Relationship between Unemployment and the Rate of Change in Money Wage Rates in the United Kingdom, 1862-1957', *Economica*, XXV (1958), pp. 283-99.

JEFFREY G. WILLIAMSON

pact on the real wage. Thus, a 10% change in the infant mortality rate implied a 2% change in the real wage across the 72 Board of Trade towns. It does indeed appear that urban disamenities—at least in the form of high infant mortality rates—*did* require a pecuniary bribe to induce the low-wage working-class family to locate in the cities with the lowest quality of life. The opposite was true of *SUN*; it appears that towns in sunny regions were able to pay lower wages.[7] Second, *DEN* and *POP* did *not* have a consistent, statistically significant impact on real wages.[8] If real wages rose with city size, then it must have been the association of *INFM* and the quality of labor that produced the relationship. Density and population size did not have any other independent, statistically significant influence. Third, regions did not matter. For unskilled common labor, regional influences—independent of the influences already identified which may be correlated with region—did not play a statistically significant role in accounting for the variance in wages across towns. This clearly suggests that the British regional labor market was quite efficient by the turn of the century, and real wages (where nonpecuniary rewards are included) tended to equate themselves across towns.[9]

The second step involved the selection of some small market towns with low density and high quality of life and ask by how much workers had to be bribed to move into the large, industrial, dark satanic mill towns. Thirty-two towns were selected which fell at least one standard deviation away from mean values of the explanatory variables. The towns with high quality of life were called "Sweet Auburn" and the dark satanic

---

but also on the proportions of the sexes and the population at different ages
. . . The infant mortality rate is free from this source of error.

Board of Trade (1908, p. lii). While Farr, Buer, and other students of the problem concur with the view that *INFM* is an excellent proxy for the quality or "value" of 19th-century urban life, *INFM* had far higher rural–urban variance than did death rates at other ages. In *Health, Wealth and Population* (1926), Buer tells us that between 1813 and 1830, *INFM* in the "six great towns" (London, Manchester, Liverpool, Birmingham, Bristol, and Leeds) was 1.73 times the average for England and Wales. Over all ages, the figure for the six great towns was only 1.39 times that for England and Wales. The relative sensitivity of infant mortality rates to environmental conditions has also been established for the early 20th century by Titmuss (1943) and the 39th Annual Report of the Local Government Board (House of Commons, Accounts and Papers, 1910).
[7] These regressions were also run using rain and temperature as explanatory weather variables. The sunshine (*SUN*) variable was most successful.
[8] Since town density and population size were thought to be highly correlated, the wage regressions were all recomputed eliminating first density and then population size. The result varied but little since the density–size correlation was quite imperfect.
[9] The attentive reader may argue that weather variables like *SUN* are highly correlated with our regions, ensuring that neither variable would have a significant impact on wages. It turns out that regions do not matter even if *SUN* is omitted from the regression.

milltowns were called "Sheffield." The difference (Δ) between Sweet Auburn and Sheffield was then calculated for density (*DEN*), population (*POP*), and infant mortality rates (*INFM*). Given the estimated coefficients in Eq. (1), I then calculated the cost of the marginal urban disamenities package as

$$COST = \hat{\beta}_1 \Delta DEN + \hat{\beta}_2 \Delta POP + \hat{\beta}_3 \Delta INFM. \qquad (2)$$

This estimate of *COST* was then taken as a share of the predicted unskilled wage in Sweet Auburn. The result is an estimate of the *percentage premium* offered to potential migrants considering the move from Sweet Auburn to Sheffield.

The results of this calculation compared with 1905 nominal wage differentials are as follows (a revision of an earlier, tentative calculation reported in Williamson, 1981a; see Williamson, 1981b):

Intraregional migration within	1905 urban disamenities wage premium (%)	1905 actual nominal wage differential (%)
North	+ 3.12	+ 18.83
York	+ 2.79	− .71
Lancs-Cheshire	+ 5.09	− 7.57
Midlands	+ 7.00	+ 12.36
East	− 12.13	+ 22.23
South	− 9.50	+ 8.58

Note the contrast between North and South. In the northern counties, the worker required a 3–7% bribe over his current wage to induce him to move from Sweet Auburn to Sheffield. In the southern and eastern counties, in contrast, no such bribe was required. Indeed, the unskilled worker was "taxed" when moving to London! Now obviously nominal wages were much higher in London than in the rural eastern and southern counties at the turn of the century, but so too was the cost of living. Furthermore, London's infant mortality rates (in 1905!) were not much larger so that urban disamenities in this form required little compensation.

The final step uses these estimates to test the pessimists' hypothesis regarding trends in the standard of living up to 1850. Suppose the disamenities "bribe" prevailing in the 1830s and 1840s was pretty much like that estimated for the North of England in 1905. Presumably, it is the higher disamenity bribes up North that are most relevant, since 19th-century industrialization was centered in those regions. So, what difference would the 3–7% disamenities correction make to our estimates of common labor's standard of living gains up to 1850? Even inflating the correction up to 15% made little difference. I concluded that the pessimist's stress on the worker's declining quality of life was misplaced.

The finding is controversial and the critics have been vociferous (e.g., Pollard, 1981). This paper attempts to add fresh evidence and novel argument to the debate. Section II explores the extent to which the disamenity differentials between "Sweet Auburn" and "Sheffield" were far higher in the early 19th century. Section III asks whether the workers actually required larger disamenity bribes in the 1830s than in 1905. These two sections thus offer new evidence, in particular, evidence embedded in the 1834 *Poor Law Reports* which has been relatively ignored by labor and social historians. The central issue here is whether urban disamenities have played different quantitative roles at various points in British experience with Modern Economic Growth. The punch line is offered in Section V. Section V offers new argument. From the 1830s onward, social reformers urged Britain to clean up her cities and, indeed, Britain did so over the century which followed. The most ghastly disamenities slowly fled the urban scene, and London became the "queen of Europe." Who paid? Who would have paid had the Dark Satanic Mills been cleaned up even earlier? Would real wage growth have suffered?

II. WRITING HISTORY BACKWARD FROM 1905 TO THE INDUSTRIAL REVOLUTION

What is the relevance of a 1905 disamenities calculation to the early 19th century, the battleground for the standard-of-living debate? At first sight, the relevance may indeed appear limited.

The most important contrast between the 1830s and 1905 must surely lie with the disamenities indexes themselves. Mortality evidence suggests that quality-of-life differences between Sweet Auburn and Sheffield were greater early in the 19th century than late. The issue is *not* that British quality of life was lower a century before 1905. Surely that was so. Rather, the issue is the extent to which quality of life differentials across locations changed over the 19th century. The largest and nastiest cities underwent enormous improvements in sanitation after the 1840s, suggesting that 1905 differences in infant mortality across towns seriously understate the differences in the 1840s. If true, then we have understated the disamenities premium for the early-mid 19th century by using 1905 intratown differences in INFM.

Table 1 presents infant mortality rates back as far as the earliest *Annual Reports* of the Registrar General. Not only were infant mortality rates higher in the 1840s then in 1905, but the cities had especially high rates. Thus, the difference in the quality-of-life index between Sweet Auburn and Sheffield was far greater in 1841. Replacing the 1902–1906 intraregional INFM differences with those for 1841 in Table 1, let us now use our 1905 estimated parameters in Eq. (2) to recompute the percentage premium that should have been offered potential migrants considering

TABLE I

Infant Mortality Rates in England: 1841, 1871, and 1906 (deaths per 1000)

Region	1906	1871	1841
North			
Sweet Auburn	145.3	156.1	114.8
Sheffield	148.8	212.1	174.5
Difference	+3.5	+56.0	+59.7
York			
Sweet Auburn	138.9	163.5	138.3
Sheffield	149.5	189.4	171.7
Difference	+10.6	+25.9	+33.4
Lancs-Cheshire			
Sweet Auburn	143.4	172.3	154.7
Sheffield	164.1	195.6	198.2
Difference	+20.7	+23.3	+43.5
Midlands			
Sweet Auburn	116.8	124.9	137.0
Sheffield	145.4	193.2	190.2
Difference	+28.6	+68.3	+53.2
East & South			
Sweet Auburn	110.5	154.3	129.8
Sheffield	133.0	170.9	173.2
Difference	+22.5	+16.6	+43.4

Sources and Notes. All data calculated from various issues of the *Annual Reports of the Registrar General,* "Births, Deaths and Marriages." The aggregations used to calculate "Sweet Auburn" and "Sheffield" are given in Appendix D.

the move from "Sweet Auburn" to "Sheffield" in 1841. The results of this calculation are as follows:

Intraregional migration within:	Urban disamenities wage premium (%)
North	+8.50
York	+4.88
Lancs-Cheshire	+4.59
Midlands	+6.16
East and South	-5.47

Compared with the 1905 urban disamenity premium estimates, these for 1841 are somewhat larger; if we ignore the eastern and southern counties, the 1841 urban disamenity premium ranges from 4.5 to 8.5%.

JEFFREY G. WILLIAMSON

III. URBAN POOR LAW PARISHES IN THE 1830s

Sidney Pollard (1981) and other critics have complained that the worker in the 1830s may have had quite different attitudes toward urban disamenities, presumably placing a higher value on the good life they left behind in "Sweet Auburn," thereby requiring a larger bribe to incur urban disamenities than his grandchildren who, in 1905, were hardened to "Sheffield's" ghastly urban environment and were not even aware of the world they had lost. The argument seems highly plausible. Was the elasticity of workers' earnings with respect to urban disamenities higher during the "first" Industrial Revolution than around 1905? Did urban workers in the 1830s—with lower standards of life—attach higher premia to the ghastly disamenities in which they lived and worked than did their grandchildren in 1905?

While the data are far more fragile than those supplied by the 1908 Board of Trade Inquiry, the 1834 *Poor Law Report* did include the kind of information necessary to repeat the 1905 regressions, and thus to test the hypothesis that the workers' earnings/disamenities elasticity fell over time. Appendix B supplies the details, but we might note here that the 1834 *Report* published "Answers to Town Questions," which included average wages of urban laborers (in "normal" weeks), town parish expenditures on poor relief, parish area, and parish population. When this information is augmented by 1831 Census data and the Registrar General's early estimates on mortality rates in urban districts, we have all the information we need to estimate the earnings equations in Table 2, *except* cost of living in the towns. This is clearly a tougher task, but with the help of Craft's recent estimates based on Poor Law Union records,[10] we are at least able to apply *regional* price deflators to the parish nominal wage estimates. In a world of primitive transportation, wide cost-of-living differentials are to be expected and thus the regional deflators are unlikely to capture parish price variance completely. Our hope is that the cost-of-living deflators are good enough to supply an effective test of the central hypothesis.

Table 2 presents the results based on 66 urban parishes which supplied the necessary data.[11] These parishes are sprinkled all over England and

---

[10] That these results would hold for England before 1850 seems unlikely based on the traditional literature. See, especially, Hunt (1973) who makes much of segmented regional labor markets and regional wage differentials. The issue is taken up again in Section III below. The basic data are taken from N. F. R. Crafts (1982, Tables 8 and 9). A description of the data can be found in Appendix B.

[11] Actually, there are 116 urban parishes in our sample, but 42 of these only supply annual earnings (rather than weekly wages). Since number of weeks worked is an unobservable, the parishes with annual earnings could not be pooled with those quoting weekly wages. Furthermore, some of the parishes did not supply evidence on POOREX, expenditure on poor relief per capita. We are left with the 66 observations utilized in Table 2, a complete

TABLE 2

Explaining Real Wages: 1834 Poor Law Commissioners' Laborers in Urban Parishes and 1905 Board of Trade Town Laborers Compared

Variable: linear regression	1834 Poor Law Parishes			1905 Board of Trade Towns		
	β	t statistic	Elasticity (at mean)	β	t statistic	Elasticity (at mean)
CONSTANT	11.0880	2.2541*	—	1.0327	3.5360*	—
DEN	−.0130	1.3773***	−.0233	−.0006	.8303	−.0129
POP	−.0138/10³	.1184	−.0010	−.0000	.2812	−.0032
INFM	.0171	2.2842*	.2962	.0015	3.1223*	.2149
SUN	−.1145	.1107	−.0382	−.0355	1.4388***	−.1329
POOREX	−.0795	1.3029***	—	—	—	—
PIRISH	5.1859	.5873	—	—	—	—
North	−1.5058	.7575	—	−.1276	.4585	—
York	−.7200	.3562	—	−.0868	.3193	—
Lancs-Cheshire	.1566	.0780	—	−.0855	.3130	—
Midlands	−2.8329	1.5895***	—	−.0146	.0535	—
East	.5677	.2661	—	−.1486	.5312	—
South	−1.9479	1.0657	—	−.1418	.5152	—
Wales	−2.3916	.9994	—	−.1331	.4798	—
R²	.387			.559		
N	66			72		

Sources and Notes. Dependent variable for the 1834 sample is the parish unskilled weekly wage in shillings, deflated by regional cost-of-living indexes, the latter constructed primarily from parish union records on food purchases in the early 1840s. See Appendix B for data documentation. Mean real wage RWAGEC = 12.016. Dependent variable for the 1905 sample is the town unskilled weekly wage, deflated by town cost of living, relative to London. Mean real wage RWAGEC = 1.009. See Williamson (1981b, Table 1B, p. 12) and Appendix A below.

* Denotes 5% significance levels.

** Denotes 10% significance levels.

*** Denotes 20% significance levels.

listing of which can be found in Williamson (1981b, pp. 57, 58). Tentative analysis of the larger sample suggests similar results, however. Table 3, which explains variance in parish infant mortality rates, uses 109 parish observations since the regressions reported there demand documentation on fewer variables. The two 1834 samples have the following average attributes.

Variable	N = 66	N = 109
Real wage, weekly (RWAGEC)	12.0s	na
Population (POP)	315,706	226,862
Density per acre (DEN)	21.6	18.4
Infant mortality per 1,000 (INFM)	208.1	201.0
Poor relief expenditure per capita (POOREX)	8.7s	na
SATMIL index	.301	na

Wales, and were located in very small industrial villages and market towns as well as in the biggest cities—London and Liverpool. The range on infant mortality is also extensive, from 344 and 304 per 1000 in Oldham and Toxteth Park (Liverpool), to 110 and 125 in Totnes and Townstall, both in rural Devon. Thus, the sample is well represented by "Sweet Auburns" and "Sheffields," the latter including Oldham, Huddersfield, Preston, Sheffield, Wakefield, Toxteth Park, South Shields, Stockport, the City of London, and nine others from the London Metropolitan area. The nominal wage varied considerably in the 1834 sample: six parishes reported 6–8 shillings per week and four reported wages in excess of 15 shillings per week. Finally, it should be emphasized that data supplied by *parish* should please critics like Sidney Pollard (1981, p. 903), who rightly point out that the 1905 town averages for infant mortality "offer but a poor guide [to disamenities], since they hide the enormous intra-urban dispersion."[12] As Appendix B points out, the infant mortality data for the 1830s analysis are given at the district level.

The reader will note that the 1834 and 1905 models estimated in Table 2 differ. The 1834 version contains two additional variables reflecting a social and demographic environment unique to early 19th-century labor markets. The first of these reflects the potential influence of the Old Poor Laws, where POOREX measures the impact of parish poor relief expenditures per capita on market wages. The second reflects the alleged attributes of labor market segmentation and/or short-run disequilibrium. Pollard (1959) and others have argued that the Irish immigrants served as the industrial revolution's "shock troops," flooding urban labor markets, especially in the northwest, thus depressing wages there. To the extent that labor markets were truly segmented, then the Irish would have been excluded from labor markets in the less industrial towns to the east and south. Thus, cities dominated by Irish labor would have had low wages. Pollard has recently recast his position in the language of the Todaro hypothesis (Todaro, 1969), a thesis popular in the development literature of the early 1970s: "many migrants did not even come

[12] Pollard (1959, p. 99) offers the following example from Sheffield's urban districts (average infant mortality rates per 1000 births, 1867–87):

Sheffield West	204
Sheffield	199
Sheffield South	188
Sheffield Park	185
Attercliffe	173
Brightside	172
Heeley-Nether Hallam	161
Ecclesall	155
Upper Hallam	113

Inner City Districts

for jobs, but for the expected opportunity of finding jobs'' (Pollard, 1981, p. 903), migration behavior which clearly would have swollen the urban labor force in the recipient cities even more, lowering wages as a result. Whether short-run expectations or more permanent segmentation, Irish immigrants should have depressed wages. If disamenities were highest in the industrial towns in which the Irish clustered, then our regressions would understate the disamenity premium that potential *British* in-migrants required to suffer the nasty life of the worst towns. The PIRISH variable (percentage born in Ireland among those above age 20) should help confront Pollard's Irish ''shock troops'' thesis.

Table 2 makes it quite apparent that we have been somewhat less successful in explaining real wage variance in the 1830s than in 1905. In both cases, the linear specification reported here does as well or better than the log linear. No doubt, one key reason for the difference is our inability to secure parish-level cost-of-living data, and we already know, based on 1905 results (Williamson, 1981a, Table 1; 1981b, Table 1A), that the cost of living was one of the prime determinants of nominal wage variance across urban locations. In any case, since the t statistics in Table 2 are so low for most independent variables in the 1834 sample, one must take care not to infer more than the data will support. However, the 1834 results are quite suggestive.

First, high poor relief expenditures per capita (POOREX) are associated with low market wages, a result which certainly fails to support the view that relief tended to cause a diminution in labor supply and local labor scarcity. Second, the evidence fails to support Pollard's ''Irish shock troops'' thesis. Not only is the estimated coefficient on PIRISH statistically insignificant, but the sign is *positive*! Either the Irish were more discriminating than their competitors or, equally absurd, the British were the minority suffering from labor market segmentation. I believe the explanation is simpler: the Irish had the good fortune to locate closest (in terms of migration costs) to the source of British industrial expansion and thus could best exploit the relative labor scarcity and high wages prevailing there. Third, there is the interesting suggestion that in the 1830s wages were *not* lower in the ''depressed'' east of England, and some ''high wage'' regions to the North become much more ordinary when disamenity and cost-of-living adjustments are performed. Furthermore, when disamenity and cost-of-living deflators are applied. This is certainly a finding worth pursuing if our cost-of-living indicators can be improved.

More to the point, however, is that INFM was a highly significant determinant of nominal wages in 1834, repeating the 1905 finding. Yet, Pollard is right. It does indeed appear that the elasticity of real wages with respect to the infant mortality rate was higher in the 1830s—.215 for 1905 and .296 for 1834—although significance tests suggest that this conclusion should not be pushed too hard.

Do the higher urban disamenity elasticities for 1834 matter much in accounting for wage differentials between "Sheffield" and "Sweet Auburn"? The pessimists' stress on urban disamenities gains support from two sources: we have already seen in Section II that the large, dense and nasty towns were—compared to "Sweet Auburn",—more ghastly in 1841 than in 1905 (the Δ effect in Eq. (2)); and we now find that workers placed higher weight on disamenity differentials in the 1830s than in 1905 (the β effect in Eq. (2)). Both served to raise the urban disamenities wage premium. A summary of the impact of these influences follows:

Urban disamenities wage premium (%)

Intraregional migration within	1905 β's and 1905 Δ's	1905 β's and 1841 Δ's	1834 β's and 1841 Δ's
North	+ 3.12%	+ 8.50%	+ 12.72%
York	+ 2.79	+ 4.88	+ 7.08
Lancs-Cheshire	+ 5.09	+ 4.59	+ 7.55
Midlands	+ 7.00	+ 6.16	+ 9.84
East	− 12.13		
South	− 9.50		
East and South		− 5.47	− 2.49

Whether infant mortality rates served as a proxy for all urban disamenities or whether they were the key component of the total disamenity "package," the fact remains that INFM had a very important impact on the location decisions of low-wage families. Density and population, on the other hand, appear to have offered no added influence either in 1905 or in 1834.

Well then, what role did density, city size, and industrial specialization play in accounting for the wide variance in town INFM either in 1834 or in 1905? Since we are dealing with homogeneous occupations in our data, we can ignore Ratcliffe's (1850) work of a century ago which emphasized occupations as a key determinant of variance in mortality and morbidity. In addition, weather variables may have affected infant mortality rates, although such variables were hardly urban-specific; thus, the inclusion of *TEMP*[13] in Table 3. Finally, even before Edwin Chadwick's 1842 *Sanitary Report*, it was felt that crowded housing conditions were a key contributor to high urban mortality rates, especially among infants. Thus, the inclusion of CROWD in the 1905 regressions in Table 3. Indeed, crowded housing and health were the hypothesized correlates which motivated the 1908 Board of Trade inquiry in the first place.

[13] The temperature variable (*TEMP*) works far better than sunshine (*SUN*) in the infant mortality regressions.

TABLE 3
Explaining Infant Mortality Rates (INFM): 1834 Poor Law Commissioners' Urban Parishes and 1905 Board of Trade Towns Compared

Variable: log-linear regression	1834 Poor Law Parishes		1905 Board of Trade Towns	
	β	t statistic	β	t statistic
CONSTANT	6.8509	1.2313***	14.432	3.830*
DEN	.0280	1.7024*	.068	2.413*
POP	.0726	3.6174*	.043	2.218*
SATMIL	.0382	1.1744***	.043	1.212
TEMP	−.5007	.3520	−2.670	2.759*
CROWD	—	—	.061	2.430*
North	.1902	1.3887**	.086	.580
York	.2728	2.1258*	.161	1.132
Lancs-Cheshire	.2191	2.0424*	.325	2.430*
Midlands	.3129	2.8812*	.259	1.888*
East	.2850	2.1555*	.352	2.375*
South	.1438	1.4455**	.269	1.915*
Wales	.0923	.6793	.294	2.000*
R²	.449		.508	
N	109		72	
Mean INFM	200.997		144.569	

Sources and Notes. All variables are defined in Appendices A and B. The 1834 sample here of 109 parishes is larger than that used in Table 2, since the POOREX variable is unavailable for the remainder. In addition, the CROWD variable is unavailable for the 1834 sample. See Table 2 for definition of significance levels.

Unfortunately, neither the *Poor Law Report* nor the Registrar General's *Annual Reports* supplies the necessary data to compute a "crowded living conditions" variable for 1834.

Table 3 reports our attempt to explain the variance in infant mortality rates across urban locations in both the 1830s (where the sample of urban parishes is now augmented to 109) as well as 1905. The results are very similar, but with some notable differences. Density (*DEN*) and city size (*POP*) both play a consistent and significant role, confirming the conventional wisdom that urbanization bred high mortality in the 19th century. In contrast, the "Dark Satanic Mill" index—measuring the share employed in manufacturing, mining and other nonservice/nonagricultural occupations—only plays a barely significant role early in the century! It was not industrialization which generated the disamenities associated with high INFM, but rather urbanization.[14] It also appears that the south

This finding is consistent with the conventional wisdom that most of the evils associated with industrialization are really attributable to urban density and crowding. The results in Table 3, while confirming that thesis, should not be pressed too hard since a linear regression (Williamson, 1981b, Table 7) for 1834 shows POP insignificant and SAT-MIL highly significant. For these two variables at least, functional form of the regression matters. Similar ambiguities appear in the 1905 regressions as well (Williamson, 1981b, Table 4).

JEFFREY G. WILLIAMSON

of England and Wales were regions of very high quality of life in 1834, even after controlling for regional urban and industrial attributes. By 1905, Wales and the South of England had lost that advantage. The really nasty regions stay nasty over the seven decades—Lancashire, Cheshire, Yorkshire, the Midlands, and the eastern counties. Thus, while there are some changes in the relative ranking of regional disamenity levels between 1834 and 1905, these are less notable than is the remarkable consistency in the determinants of INFM over these seven decades. Yet, average temperature appears to have played a significant role only late in the period—towns in warm regions having lower infant mortality in 1905. Finally, we note that crowding—thought to be an index of low housing quality and unhealthy conditions by the Board of Trade and others since Kay's work on Manchester[15]—does indeed have a significant impact on infant mortality rates in the log-linear regression reported here, although it does not in the linear regressions reported elsewhere (Williamson 1981b, Table 4, p. 20).

The results in Table 3 suggest that we must qualify our statement that density and city size do not matter much in accounting for wage levels across British towns in the 19th century: large, dense cities tended to have higher infant mortality rates (confirming Farr's "Law")[16] and thus unskilled workers required a wage premium to work there. Apart from this strictly urban influence, "dark satanic mill" towns did not have an independent impact on INFM at the turn of the century, and its impact in 1834 was of questionable significance.

IV. WAS THE INDUSTRIAL REVOLUTION WORTH IT? THE WORKERS' VIEW

Drawing on this new evidence drawn from the 1830s and 1840s, our estimates suggest that the urban disamenities premium in the early 19th century ranged from 7 to 13% in the North of England. These are only tentative estimates, to be sure, but would a large error matter in forming inferences for the standard-of-living debate? Would such disamenities seriously deflate the measured real wage gains of the British worker after the Napoleonic Wars? I think not.

Suppose, for example, that the "true" disamenities premium was 30% in all of Britain during the decades prior to 1850—surely a gross exaggeration. Suppose further that the relative shift of employment from "Sweet Auburn" to "Sheffield" was at the same rate as the measured decline in the agricultural employment share, that is, from 36 to 22% of the labor force between 1801 and 1851 (Deane and Cole, 1967, Table 30,

[15] J. P. Kay-Shuttleworth (1832). Engels leans heavily on Kay in describing "social murder" in the great towns of early 19th-century England.

[16] Farr actually estimated a mortality-density function to give empirical content to his "Law." See W. F. Farr (1885, pp. 172–176).

p. 142). These figures would imply that the average wage of common labor would have increased by about 4% over the full half-century due solely to the premium paid for urban disamenities (e.g. [.36 – .22] × [.30] = .042). Alternatively, consider the rise in the population urbanized. Based on Mitchell and Deane's estimates for the United Kingdom (1962, pp. 8, 9 and 24–27), the share living in urban places rose from 25.7 to 35.8% between 1805 and 1851, implying that the average wage of common labor would have increased by about 3% due solely to the premium paid for urban disamenities (e.g. [.358 – .257] × [.30] = .030). Either calculation implies a trivial downward adjustment in the measured improvement in the standard of life. Based on some recent estimates of the real wage gains accruing to urban common labor (Lindert and Williamson, forthcoming, Table 5, "best guess," middle group), real wage improvements over the 1810–1851 period might be reduced from the measured increase of 94% to an adjusted increase of 90%, a trivial disamenities correction indeed.

The pessimists' hypothesis has not yet been fully tested since they have raised *two* disamenity issues, not just one: (i) that the process of urbanization involved a move into ghastly towns, a move implying a spurious rise in nominal wages measured by the size of the disamenity premium; and (ii) that there was a steady deterioration in the quality of urban life in all cities and towns, implying a spurious rise in nominal wages due to an increase in the disamenity premium everywhere in British urban life. The first effect has been found to be trivial. What about the second?

Was there a steady deterioration in the quality of urban life from the late 18th century up to 1848 and the Public Reform Era? E. P. Thompson (1975, pp. 149, 150) would surely have us believe so: "This deterioration of the urban environment strikes us today . . . as one of the most disastrous of the consequences of the Industrial Revolution. . . ." How do we reconcile such statements with the evidence—admittedly weak—of improved mortality conditions in Britain, especially in the cities?[17] While the towns were notoriously less healthy than the countryside in the late 18th century, what evidence we do have suggests unambiguously that death rates fell throughout the late 18th century up to the early 1820s?[18] We also know that death rates fell most precipitously in the cities over

[17] While nationwide mortality did drift upward over the period, the rise was relatively minor. In any case, since urban in-migration implied movement into locations of high mortality, a nationwide upward drift is fully consistent with stability or even improvement in urban mortality. William Farr certainly understood this version of the fallacy of composition when writing a century ago, but some modern pessimists seem to have forgotten.

[18] Buer (1926, pp. 3, 29–30, 31–34, 59–60, and the table on p. 267). Both Thomas Bateman and William Farr concur. For the modern evidence, see Wrigley and Schofield (forthcoming, Chap. 6).

the same period, and especially so in London (Farr, 1885, p. 195; Buer, 1926, pp. 33, 34). In addition, we know that the nationwide fall in the death rate reversed between the 1820s and the 1840s, but given the much higher mortality rates in the towns, and given the very rapid rate of urbanization over the period, it is hard to avoid the inference that urban mortality rates either stabilized or continued to decline before the Era of Public Reform, an inference reached long ago by Bateman, Farr, Buer, and other analysts of 19th-century urban life (Buer, 1926, pp. 225, 226).

Inference is one thing, evidence another, and the urban mortality data are much too crude to confirm a rise in the quality of city life up to 1850. Barbara Hammond (1928, p. 428) was quite right when some 50 years ago she stated:

A close examination of the figures for Manchester does not lead to confidence in statistical proof of *improved* urban conditions in the early nineteenth century.

But *improvement* is not the issue. The issue is whether the evidence supports the view of urban *deterioration*, and Hammond—a pessimist— agrees that it does not. Furthermore, many observers sympathetic with the condition of the working class, and who were caught up in the great public debates of the 1830s and 1840s, cautioned members of the House of Commons from inferring trends in the quality of urban life from a single town inquiry. The first such inquiry was a blockbuster—James Kay's graphic description of Manchester's ghastly environment in his *Moral and Physical Conditions of the Working Classes* (1835), used later by Engels with such great effect. While an accurate account of Manchester in 1835, Kay's work fails to point out that things may have been even worse previously! Speaking before a House of Commons committee, Francis Place noted:

. . . I believe that what he [Kay] says is correct; but he gives the matter as it now stands, knowing nothing of former times; his picture is a very deplorable one [but] many Manchester operatives . . . inform me . . . that the condition of a vast number of the people was as bad some years ago, as he describes the worst portion of them to be now."

Obviously, Kay, Chadwick and their followers were not interested in writing accurate economic history; they were intent on developing the

<hr>

19 The reference is to Francis Place in House of Commons, Accounts and Papers (1835, p. 838) who is commenting on James P. Kay-Shuttleworth's *The Moral and Physical Condition of the Working Class* (1832). The qualitative evidence on urban water supply, pollution, sanitation, and dwelling quality does not unambiguously support the deterioration thesis, at least within cities. In addition to Buer's work, Dorothy George (1930) and Kitson Clark (1962) found conditions in the 18th century as bad or worse than those documented in the sanitary, municipal, and mortality reports of the 1830s and 1840s.

higher population densities offers one method of estimating the costs of urban life as they are valued by people making residential and occupational decisions.[4]

In short, Nordhaus and Tobin suggested that we ignore the subjective environmental pleas of the pessimists and ask the workers who were involved in the urbanization process to speak. But how is the voice of the 19th-century British worker to be heard? Most were silent. Most lacked the right to vote. But all of them could vote with their feet. And vote they did, their response having left its mark on rates of pay, high wages compensating workers in locations with ghastly environments, disamenities, and high mortality rates—at least in 1905 (Williamson, 1981a).

Relying on a Board of Trade (1908) inquiry into 72 British towns in 1905, my previous findings suggested that the pessimists have greatly overstated the role of declining quality of life in assessing the "trickling down" effects of the Industrial Revolution from 1790 to 1850. The conclusion was reached in three steps.

First, 1905 town data were used to estimate hedonic wage regressions of the following sort (reported here in linear form for convenience):

$$W_j = \beta_0 + \beta_1 DEN_j + \beta_2 POP_j + \beta_3 INFM_j + \beta_4 SUN_j + \varepsilon_{ji} \quad (1)$$

where W_j is the average nominal weekly wage of unskilled labor deflated the town's cost of living index, DEN_j is the town's density, POP_j is the town's size, $INFM_j$ is the infant mortality rate, and SUN_j is a "sunshine" amenities variable. Regional dummy variables were also introduced into the estimation.

A revised version of the results of this exercise can be found in Table 2 below.[5] The key findings can be quickly summarized. First, our proxy for disamenities—the infant mortality rate[6]—had a highly significant im-

[4] Nordhaus and Tobin (1972, p. 13). For more elaborate, recent extensions of urban disamenities measurement see the following: Hoch (1977) or his earlier 1976 paper; Tolley (1974); Smith (1978); Getz and Huang (1978); Izraeli (1979); Rosen (1979), and Henderson (forthcoming). Changes in life expectancy have obvious economic value and Dan Usher (1973) has offered an interesting index for economic growth imputations.

[5] While these 1905 results are very similar to those reported in Williamson (1981a), they differ by the addition of some new explanatory variables. The basic findings are left unchanged.

[6] As we shall see below, mortality rates appear to be excellent proxies for urban disamenities, a result consistent with Farr's rule that two persons were seriously ill for each that died (R. Wall, 1974, p. iv). Furthermore, the *infant* mortality rate is a far more effective index than the overall mortality rate, a point well appreciated by the Registrar General long ago:

. . . it should be remembered that there is often considerable uncertainty in estimating the population of a rapidly growing urban district . . . Further, the death-rate in any district is dependent not only on the sanitary conditions of the locality,

real and the Reformist Debate much more subtle than first meets the eye.

Can we estimate the trade-off? Surely any useful evaluation will require an explicit general equilibrium system which confronts two competing outputs—commodities and amenities, supplied by four inputs—labor, urban land (or "space"), "productive" capital with strong job-creating capacity, and "unproductive" social overhead (e.g., city drains) with weak job-creating capacity. What was the optimal mix of "productive" and "unproductive" capital in the 1830s and the 1840s? What about optimal land use and crowding? Optimal in terms of what objective? Whose preferences were dominant? Would history have been different if another classes' preferences had been imposed on the choice? How were those preferences constrained by the institutional realities of fragmented capital markets and regressive tax systems?

So far, neither the pessimists *nor* the optimists have confronted these issues. The jury is still out on British capitalism's trial.

APPENDIX A

The sources of the data utilized for the analysis of the 1905 Board of Trade towns are as follows:

Wages. Average weekly wages for unskilled workers in the building trades (common laborers), taken from the October 1905 inquiry. Town wages are expressed relative to London ($=100$). Source: Board of Trade (1908, pp. xxxiv–xxxv).

Cost of living. The cost-of-living index includes rents, the latter carefully adjusted to standardize by quality. The house rent index was constructed in three steps. The inquiry first identified housing types most frequently rented in the town, grouped by number of rooms. Then the inquiry computed rents relative to London ($=100$) for each of the housing types. A simple average of these percentages yielded the town rent index. The commodity price information was gathered by surveying shopkeepers who, in October 1905, were asked what prices they charged for a standard basket of commodities (e.g., tea, sugar, bacon, eggs, cheese, butter, potatoes, flour, bread, milk, meat, and coal). A working class family budget was used to generate the aggregate index, the same fixed weights applied to all towns. Source: Board of Trade (1908, Table A, pp. xliv–xlv), London $= 100$, column labeled "rents and prices combined."

Population (POP). 1901 Census figures in thousands reported in Board of Trade (1908, Table B, pp. xlvi).

Density (DEN). Population (in thousands) divided by acres (in thousands). Town acreage was taken from the 1911 Census.

Infant mortality rate (INFM). Infant mortality per 1000 births, averaged over the period 1902–1906. Source: Board of Trade (1908), various pages.

Occupational index (SATMIL). The "dark satanic mill" index is constructed as the percent of males, 10 and older, who were employed in the following occupational categories:

IX	Mines and Quarries,
X	Metals, etc.,
XIII	Woodworking, etc.,
XIV	Brick, etc.,
XV	Chemicals, etc.,
XVI	Skins and Hides, etc.,
XVIII	Textiles,
XXII	Mechanics and Labourers, not accounted for elsewhere.

1901 Census data were used to construct the above. *Regional code.* The following code is used:

0—London,
1—Northern Counties and Cleveland (NORTH),
2—Yorkshire, except Cleveland (YORK),
3—Lancashire and Cheshire (LANCS-CHESIRE),
4—Midlands (MIDLANDS),
5—Eastern Counties (EAST),
6—Southern Counties (SOUTH),
7—Wales and Monmouth (WALES).

Weather data (TEMP and SUN). Observations on two climate variables, temperature (TEMP) and sunshine (SUN) were obtained from *The Book of Normals, 1881–1915* (1919). TEMP records mean annual temperature in degrees Farenheit to the nearest 0.1°. Sunshine normals refer to duration of bright sunshine observed by the Campbell–Stokes sunshine-recorder, annual mean. While the Meteorological Office had weather stations dispersed all over the British Islands, many of the 72 Board of Trade cities had no weather stations. In such cases, representative stations were chosen to reflect the climate characteristics of each city: its latitude, elevation, and distance from the sea. In most cases it was possible to choose a weather station within a few miles of the actual town or city. Proximity to large urban centers, said to affect both temperature and sunshine, was also considered.

Crowded living conditions (CROWD). The "percentage of population living in overcrowded tenements in 1901" (i.e., greater than 2 per room) reported by the Board of Trade was used as an index of crowded living conditions and housing quality. Source: Board of Trade (1908, pp. xlvii–xlviii).

JEFFREY G. WILLIAMSON

APPENDIX B

The source of the data utilized for the analysis of the 1834 Poor Law urban districts are as follows:

Wages and earnings. The 1834 *Report from the Commissioners for the Inquiry into the Administration and Practical Operation of the Poor Laws*, XXX–XXXVI, Appendix B2, "Answers to Town Questions," includes a number of parish responses with earnings and/or weekly wage data (in shillings) for laborers in various nonfarm occupations. Some of the parishes are aggregated in the analysis in the text (e.g., there are 12 parishes underlying our City of London observation, 4 underlying York, 3 underlying Shrewsbury, etc.), but most are sole parish observations. The sample has also been augmented by seven urban observations supplied by A. L. Bowley (1900a, p. 60 and 1900b, pp. 297–315). These are for "labourers in the building trades": Manchester (1834), Kidderminster (1836), Newcastle (1840), Macclesfield (1832), Bath (1831), Worcester (1839), and Bedfont (1830).

Density (DEN). Population (in thousands) of the parish divided by acres (in thousands).

Population (POP). Population size (in thousands) of the town (or city) in the 1831 Census of which the parish was a part, or to which the parish was contiguous, or of the parish itself, whichever was bigger. All figures taken from the 1831 Census.

Infant mortality rate (INFM). Infant mortality rate per 1000 births, averaged over the period 1838–1844. These are district-level figures. Source: Appendix to the *Ninth Annual Report of the Registrar-General* (1849).

Weather data (TEMP and SUN). Observations on these two climate variables were taken from *The Book of Normals* as in Appendix A for 1905. See Appendix A also for a description of the assignment of weather stations to, in this case, parish locations.

POOREX. Total annual parish poor relief expenditures (in shillings) per capita in 1831, also contained in the 1834 *Report*.

Cost of living. The cost-of-living data are *not* available by parish, nor do they include information for clothing or rents. However, reasonable assumptions can be made about both of these latter items so that they might have an influence on cost-of-living variation across urban areas. We have not done so here.

The basic data are taken from N. F. R. Crafts (1980). Crafts utilized the 1843 published reports on prices paid for provisions by Poor Law Unions all over England. With price data for 12 food, fuel, and light items, Crafts constructs regional cost-of-living indexes for "provisions" using various weights. We favor his flexible-weight indices (the "Economiser," in Table 8). In Table 9, Crafts expands the index to include guesses about rents, and under rural and urban weights (the "rural and urban perspective"). These guesses on rents are too tentative for our tastes, so we use his Table 8 data.

Each of the urban parishes is then assigned the cost-of-living index of one of Crafts' 10 regions: e.g., London, Northern Industrial, North Midlands, South Midlands, North, North West, East, West, Home Counties, and South East.

Occupational index (SATMIL). The "dark satanic mill" index is constructed as the share of adult males who were employed in the following occupational categories:

(i) those employed in manufacturing or in making machines;

(ii) all other (common) labor, nonagricultural.

PIRISH. Number of persons greater than 20 years of age born in Ireland as a percentage of all persons greater than 20 in the registration district of which the urban parish was part.

1831 parish-level Census data were used to construct the index.

APPENDIX C

In calculating the percent wage premium associated with migration between the various locations listed in Section I, the following towns compose "Sweet Auburn" and "Sheffield":

Region	Towns composing "Sweet Auburn"	Towns composing "Sheffield"
North	Carlisle	Gateshead Middlesbrough Newcastle-on-Tyne
York	York	Bradford Castleford Leeds Sheffield
Lancs-Cheshire	Barrow-in-Furness Chester	Burnley Liverpool Macclesfield Manchester Preston Stockport Wigan
Midlands	Burton-on-Trent Gloucester	Birmingham Hanley
East	Bedford Ipswich Luton Peterborough	London
South	Croydon Dover Reading Southampton Taunton	London

APPENDIX D

In constructing the regional infant mortality rates for "Sweet Auburn" and "Sheffield" in Table 1, the following aggregations were applied (using population weights):

Region	Area composing "Sweet Auburn"	Towns composing "Sheffield"	
North	All four counties minus five "Sheffields"	Gateshead Newcastle-on-Tyne Stockton-on-Tees	South Shields Sunderland
York	All three counties minus eight "Sheffields"	Keighley Bradford Leeds Halifax	Huddersfield Hull York Sheffield
Lancs-Cheshire	Both counties minus fourteen "Sheffields"	Burnley Blackburn Preston Wigan Warrington Macclesfield Birkenhead	Rochdale Bolton Oldham Stockport Manchester & Salford Liverpool & Bootle Chester
Midlands	All thirteen counties minus ten "Sheffields"	Nottingham Derby Burton-on-Trent Stoke-on-Trent	Leicester Northampton Birmingham Bristol Walsall Wolverhampton
East & South	All nineteen counties plus city of London minus London	London Metropolis	

REFERENCES

Board of Trade (1908), "Cost of Living of the Working Class." *House of Commons, Accounts and Papers 107.*

Bowley, A. L. (1900a), *Wages in the United Kingdom in the Nineteenth Century.* Cambridge: Cambridge Univ. Press.

Bowley, A. L. (1900b), "The Statistics of Wages in the United Kingdom During the Last 100 Years." *Journal of the Royal Statistical Association* **63**, 297–315.

Buer, M. C. (1926), *Health, Wealth and Population in the Early Days of the Industrial Revolution.* London: Routledge and Sons.

Clark, K. (1962), *The Making of Victorian England.* London: Methuen.

Crafts, N. F. R. (1982), "Regional Price Variations in England in 1843: An Aspect of the Standard of Living Debate." *Explorations in Economic History,* **19**(January).

Deane, P., and Cole, W. A. (1967), *British Economic Growth, 1688–1959.* Cambridge: Cambridge Univ. Press. 2nd ed.

Engels, F. (1971), *The Condition of the Working Class in England.* Edited and translated by W. O. Henderson and W. H. Chaloner. 2nd ed.

Farr, W. (1885), *Vital Statistics.* London: Sanitary Institute.

Getz, M., and Huang, Y. (1978), "Consumer Revealed Preference for Environmental Goods." *Review of Economics and Statistics* **60**, 449–458.

George, D. (1930), *London Life in the 18th Century*. London: Kegan Paul.

Hammond, B. (1928), "Urban Death-Rates in the Early Nineteenth Century." *Economic History* No. 3 (January).

Henderson, J. V. (forthcoming), "Evaluating Consumer Amenities and Interregional Welfare Differences." *Journal of Urban Economics*.

Hoch, I. (1977), "Climate, Wages, and Quality of Life." In L. Wingo and A. Evans (Eds.), *Public Economics and the Quality of Life*. Baltimore: The Johns Hopkins Press.

House of Commons, Accounts and Papers (1910). 39th Annual Report of the Local Government Board, "Report by the Medical Officer on Infant and Child Mortality." Vol. 39.

House of Commons, Accounts and Papers (1835). Vol. 7, No. 465.

Hughes, J. R. T. (n.d.), "The Cadre Adonis—A Bourgeois Reactionary View." Department of Economics, Northwestern University (mimeo).

Hunt, E. H. (1973), *Regional Wage Variations in Britain, 1850–1914*. Oxford: Clarendon Press.

Izraeli, O. (1979), "Externalities and Intercity Wage and Price Differentials." In G. Tolley (Ed.), *Urban Growth Policy in a Market Economy*. New York: Academic Press.

Kay-Shuttleworth, J. P. (1832), *The Moral and Physical Condition of the Working Class Employed in the Cotton Manufactures in Manchester*. London: Ridgeway.

Lindert, P. H., and Williamson, J. G. (forthcoming), "English Workers' Living Standards During the Industrial Revolution: A New Look." *Economic History Review*.

Marx, K. (1930), *Das Kapital*. London: Everyman's Edition.

Mitchell, B. R., and Deane, P. (1962), *Abstract of British Historical Statistics*. Cambridge: Cambridge Univ. Press.

Nordhaus, W., and Tobin, J. (1972), "Is Growth Obsolete?" In National Bureau of Economic Research, *Economic Growth: Fiftieth Anniversary Colloquim V*. New York: Columbia Univ. Press.

Pollard, S. (1959), *A History of Labour in Sheffield*. Liverpool.

Pollard, S. (1981), "Sheffield and Sweet Auburn—Amenities and Living Standards in the British Industrial Revolution." *Journal of Economic History* **41**, 902–904.

Ratcliffe, H. (1850), *Observations on the Rate of Mortality and Sickness*. Manchester: George Falkner.

Report from the Commissioners for the Inquiry into the Administration and Practical Operation of the Poor Laws (1834). Vols. XXX–XXXVI.

Report from the Poor Law Commissioners on an Inquiry into the Sanitary Condition of the Labouring Population of Great Britain (1842).

Registrar General (1849), *Ninth Annual Report of the Registrar General*. "Deaths and Marriages." Vol. 21.

Rosen, S. (1979), "Wage-Based Indexes of Urban Quality of Life." In P. Miewzkowski and M. Straszheim (Eds.), *Current Issues in Urban Economics*. Baltimore: The Johns Hopkins Press.

Smith, B. (1978), "Measuring the Value of Urban Amenities." *Journal of Urban Economics* **5**, 370–387.

Taylor, A. J. (1975), "Editor's Introduction." In A. J. Taylor (Ed.), *The Standard of Living in Britain in the Industrial Revolution*. London: Methuen.

Thompson, E. P. (1975), "The Making of the Working Class." In A. J. Taylor (Ed.), *The Standard of Living in Britain in the Industrial Revolution*. London: Methuen.

Titmuss, R. M. (1943), *Birth, Poverty, and Wealth: A Study of Infant Mortality*. London: Hamish Hamilton Medical Books.

Todaro, M. P. (1969), "A Model of Labor Migration and Urban Unemployment in Less Developed Countries." *American Economic Review* **59** (March), 138–148.

WAS THE INDUSTRIAL REVOLUTION WORTH IT?   245

Tolley, G. (1974), "The Welfare Economics of City Bigness." *Journal of Urban Economics* 1(July), 324–345.

Usher, D. (1973), "An Imputation to the Measure of Economic Growth for Changes in Life Expectancy." In M. Ross (Ed.), *The Measurement of Economic and Social Performance.* New York: Columbia Univ. Press.

Wall, R. (1974), *Mortality in Mid 19th Century Britain.* London: Greggs International.

Williamson, J. G. (1981a), "Some Myths Die Hard—Urban Disamenities One More Time: A Reply." *Journal of Economic History* 41, 905–907.

Williamson, J. G. (1981b), "Was the Industrial Revolution Worth It? Disamenities and Death in 19th Century British Towns." Discussion Paper, Graduate Program in Economic History, The University of Wisconsin (April).

Wrigley, E. A., and Schofield, R. S. (1981), *The Population History of England, 1541–1871: A Reconstruction.* Cambridge: Harvard Univ. Press.

The Historical Content of the Classical Labor Surplus Model

Jeffrey G. Williamson

Writing in the first half of the nineteenth century, post-Smithian economists developed their dynamic models to deal with economic and demographic events they thought they saw going on around them after the 1780s. The evidence that underlay those models was mostly anecdotal—it has taken historians more than a century to establish something approximating a hard data base for the First Industrial Revolution. But based on street-level observations, expert witnesses before Parliamentary Committees, foreign trade data, incomplete tax returns, and scraps of demographic information, the classical economists thought they saw the dimensions of the First Industrial Revolution clearly. The phenomenon that struck them as most notable was stable real wages. How was it possible for rapid industrialization to occur while at the same time the standards of living of the working classes changed but little?

Marx tried to explain these events by appealing to technological forces. Labor-saving technological change in industry and enclosures pushing labor off the land in agriculture both served to augment the reserve army, keeping the lid on common unskilled labor's real wage. Thus, Marx's model offered a derived labor demand explanation, technologically driven. Although Malthus appears to have been unaware that an industrial revolution was taking place around him, his model could explain these events by appealing to a demographic response. Any improvement in real wages in the short run served to foster early marriage, greater fertility within marriages, as well as an elastic Irish emigration response. Malthus's elegant (but pessimistic) demographic-economic model implied a labor supply explanation, an elastic labor supply ensuring a long-run subsistence wage floor, and no standard of living improvement for common unskilled labor. Others appealed to conditions in agriculture. For them, "disguised unemployment" in the Irish and English countryside ensured an elastic labor supply to the rapidly growing industrial sector, and, as a result, no standard of living improvement for common unskilled labor. In these classical labor surplus models of stable real wages, rapid capital accumulation goes hand in hand with an absence of capital-deepening, since any increase in the capital stock will induce an equal increase in employment along an elastic labor supply function.

In contrast, Ricardo seems to have appealed to capital-scarcity and *slow* industrialization to get stable real wages and labor surplus. In the Ricardian model, the causation seems to go from slow capital-deepening to labor surplus, not vice versa. Given the inelastic supply of land, rents increase their share in national income, a savings shortfall results from landlords' lack of thrift, and accumulation slows down. As capital-deepening comes to a halt, labor's marginal product stabilizes at subsistence wages.

The classical labor surplus model carried into the twentieth century

As the British economy passed through a "turning point" (the term used by Fei and Ranis, 1964: ch. 6) in the middle of the nineteenth century, and real wages began to rise markedly, British economists lost interest in these classical growth paradigms. Instead they adopted the more optimistic neoclassical paradigm, which became the dominant interpretation of economic growth for almost a century. But as Third World development attracted economists' attention in the 1950s, W. Arthur Lewis (1954) asked us to take another look at those discarded classical models, the "non-Ricardian" paradigms in particular. The implication was that the Third World in the 1950s closely resembled Britain in the late eighteenth and early nineteenth century, and thus if the classical models worked well then, they should work well for the Third World too. Lewis's celebrated "labor surplus" model emerged as a result.

Figure 1 repeats the key relationships of the Lewis model. Here we have the modern industrial sector, where the supply of labor (represented by the curve S_L) is perfectly elastic (at least up to some turning point) and the derived demand for labor (represented by the marginal product curves D_L) has the usual downward slope indicating that lower wages would encourage firms to increase employment at any given level of capital stock. The classical dynamics are apparent. The wage bill (W) plus profits (P) associated with employment L, exhausts total output. Upon reinvestment of those profits, the derived demand for labor shifts to the right (to D'_L), employment increases (to L'), industrial output rises, but the real wage remains unchanged. The model implies, of course, rising inequality. Indeed, the rising inequality is necessary to get the increase in savings and accumulation. Accelerating growth is therefore assured in early stages of growth before the turning point.

Lewis's model underwent extensive refinement and elaboration after it first appeared in 1954. In the early 1960s, John Fei and Gustav Ranis (1964) formally extended the model and applied it to Japan and South Asia. In 1966, A. K. Sen showed us exactly what assumptions were required to make the labor surplus model operational, and shortly thereafter Avinash Dixit (1973)

FIGURE 1   The labor surplus model of the
industrial sector

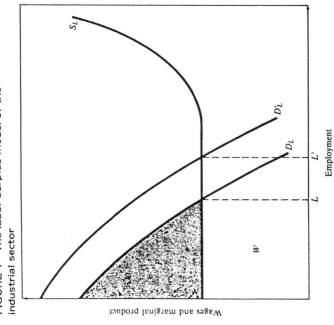

placed it within the mainstream of growth theory. It remained for Lance Taylor
(see, for example, Taylor et al., 1980) to embed the fixed-real-wage paradigm
into large-scale macro models of Third World economies. The model has not
been without its critics, of course, since neoclassical alternatives have competed
with the classical model every inch of the way (Jorgenson, 1961; Kelley,
Williamson, and Cheetham, 1972; Adelman and Robinson, 1978; Dervis, de
Melo, and Robinson, 1982; Kelley and Williamson, 1984a and 1984b).

The point of this recitation is simply to remind us that the labor surplus
model has its roots with the classical (non-Ricardian) economists, and that the
classical economists developed their paradigms to account for the economic
and demographic events they *thought* were taking place around them in the
late eighteenth and early nineteenth century. Were they right?

Were real wages stable?

Were real wages stable during the British industrial revolution? Debate over
this question is as old as the revolution itself. The controversy begins with

Friedrich Engels, who alleged in 1845 that the workers' standard of living was worse than before. Three years later *The Communist Manifesto* (Marx and Engels, 1848: 34–35) made the same claim. The Victorian apologists for British capitalism rose to the challenge, but somehow even Alfred Marshall's (1910: 687) weighty addition to the optimists' camp failed to erode the dominant view that common labor gained little during the early decades of the industrial revolution.

The debate over real wages and the standard of living heated up again in the 1920s with the appearance of John H. Clapham's *An Economic History of Modern Britain* (1926), which found far more evidence of real wage gains. Clapham's contribution was to introduce quantification where anecdotal evidence had served before. For every optimist there seems to be a pessimist, and in this case it was J. L. Hammond (1930), who led the counterattack. The intensity of this debate diminished a bit until the appearance of the more recent exchange between Max Hartwell (1959, 1961), an optimist who saw evidence of real wage gains, and Eric Hobsbawm (1957), who did not. The timing of the Hartwell–Hobsbawm exchange should occasion no surprise, for it was in the late 1950s that social scientists began to confront the problem of Third World industrialization, turning to historical evidence for guidance.

Thanks to the computer, archival collaboration, and liberal research funding, we now know far more about what happened to real wages during the First Industrial Revolution than did the classical economists or even Hartwell and Hobsbawm. Figure 2 summarizes that experience (based on Lindert and Williamson, 1983, and Williamson, 1985). The figure shows clearly that real wages were indeed stable up to about 1820. It also shows that unskilled common labor lagged behind when the real wages of more skilled workers began to exhibit dramatic growth after 1820 (farm labor and urban unskilled— the "middle group"—enjoying much slower improvements in living stan-

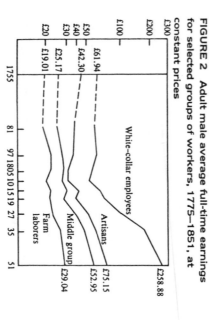

FIGURE 2   Adult male average full-time earnings for selected groups of workers, 1775–1851, at constant prices

dards). Income inequality rose across the century following 1760 as well (Williamson, 1985: ch. 4), tracing out the familiar Kuznets Curve.

It appears that the classical economists were right after all. Real wages were stable up to 1820, and when real wages rise afterward the unskilled wage lags far behind.

Was the British industrial revolution "revolutionary"?

Were the classical economists also right in assuming that British industrialization was "revolutionary"? If they were wrong on this second point, then what we need are explanations of slow growth, not labor surplus models of rapid growth with stable real wages. That is, we would need more Ricardian thinking and less Malthusian and Marxian thinking on early industrialization up to 1820.

The classical economists did not have the evidence to make that assessment, but we do now, much of it collected over the past two decades. Charles Feinstein (1978) has presented pioneering estimates of accumulation rates from 1760 to 1860, and E. A. Wrigley and Roger Schofield (1981) have offered a brilliant reconstruction of demographic events at that time. The early estimates of national income by Phyllis Deane and W. A. Cole (1962) have been augmented by a steady revisionist stream, and informed guesses on the rate of total factor productivity growth are now available.

The new evidence confirms that somewhere around the 1820s Britain passed through a secular turning point. Growth in national income was much lower before than after: for example, C. Knick Harley (1982) estimates the growth in per capita income at 0.33 percent per year for 1770–1815 and 0.86 percent per year for 1815–41. The growth rate doubling is apparent, too, in the indexes of industrial production, which grow annually at 1.5 or 1.6 percent before 1815 and at 3.0 or 3.2 percent afterward. And as we have seen in Figure 2, the turning point is equally dramatic for real wages.

British growth before the 1820s, then, was modest at best. By the standards of the many industrial revolutions to follow, Britain's per capita income growth of 0.33 percent per annum before 1815 is hardly impressive. Even during the uneven 1970s the developing countries managed an average per capita income growth rate of 3.2 percent per year, ten times the British rate before the 1820s (IBRD, 1980: 372; the figure cited is for 1970–77).

British growth before the 1820s looks odd when set beside the conventional dating of the industrial revolution. Consistent with the labor surplus model, there is no evidence of improvement in the standard of living among the working classes until the 1820s. But inconsistent with the labor surplus model, growth of income and the rate of industrialization were both surprisingly slow. Industrial output grew at only 1.5 or 1.6 percent per year up to the 1820s, a rate that hardly exceeded the national income growth rate of 1.3 percent. Furthermore, Britain was a low saver (Table 1, col. 8). A gross

best possible case for reform. Perhaps the pessimists have had their perception of the Industrial Revolution distorted ever since?

Unless one believes that mortality (and sickness) poorly reflects quality of life—a position I certainly do not adopt here—it is hard to take the pessimists' urban-quality-of-life-deterioration thesis very seriously. As a final concession in their argument, however, suppose that the infant mortality rate *rose* by as much as a third in *all* British cities and towns between 1790 and 1850. While the evidence certainly does not support such a premise, what would it imply for trends in the real standard of living of the working class? Using the 1834 elasticity of real wages to INFM (Table 2, .2962), a 33% rise in INFM implies an 11 percent fall in the quality of life for *urban* workers. But only 36% of the population was living in "urban places" even as late as 1851. Thus, the impact of the hypothetical deterioration in the quality of urban life would have been to lower the standard of living of the British working class by 4% (e.g., $[.33 \times .2962] \times [.36] = .0352$), a trivial amount.

So much for the pessimist's view that early nineteenth century urban-industrial development produced a "significant" deterioration in the workers' quality of life. Certainly the workers did not see it that way.

V. TRADING OFF ENVIRONMENT FOR COMMODITIES: TOWARD A MORE COMPREHENSIVE ASSESSMENT

None of the above confronts the question: What should have been? Was British capitalism's dark-satanic-mill and environmental-ugliness solution to the problem of Modern Economic Growth the most efficient way? Could the discounted value of the workers' stream of annual living standards have been improved with an earlier victory by the Reformists?

Since the British tax system appears to have been highly regressive at this time, the working class would have borne most of the cost of cleaning up the cities earlier in the 19th century. To the extent that the incidence would have fallen on the working class through indirect tax-ation of necessities and rising rents on now-greater-taxed urban property, then their real consumption levels might well have been eroded. Efforts to legislate higher residential health standards and lower levels of ten-ement crowding would also have inflated rents. So too would have space-intensive "urban renewal" municipal schemes. If the reader believes the contrary, and that urban landlords, merchants, and capitalists would have carried the burden, how would they have responded? Surely they would have responded in part by diminished saving as their disposable incomes contracted. If "productive" accumulation and capacity creation would have been forgone, some future urban jobs would also have been forgone. Fewer urban jobs imply a lower absorption of low-wage rural workers into high-wage city employment. Thus, workers' nominal in-comes would have diminished on that score, too. The trade-off was very

domestic saving rate of 9 or 10 percent is certainly low compared with the contemporary developing country average of 20.1 percent in 1977 or Meiji Japan (14.8 percent, 1910–16) or late nineteenth century America (28 percent, 1890–1905).[2] In addition, the saving rate only rises from 9 to 13 percent up to 1820, hardly the dramatic increase predicted by the labor surplus model and certainly well below the 5 to 12 percentage point increase thought by Arthur Lewis (1954: 155) to characterize the "central problem in the theory of development." In fact, the rate of accumulation was very modest. Between 1760 and 1830—the "heroic" age of the First Industrial Revolution—the rate of capital stock growth was only 1.2 percent per annum. Since the employed labor force grew at only 1 percent per annum, the capital–labor ratio drifted upward at the leisurely pace of 0.2 percent per annum. In short, hardly any capital-deepening took place during the classic period of "labor surplus," in Britain, and the rate of capital-widening wasn't very impressive either. The absence of capital-deepening has suggested to some that the new technologies sweeping England were capital-saving. This suggestion is certainly anti-Marxian. The suggestion is also remarkable when set beside the voluminous work on labor-saving in nineteenth-century America and in the contemporary Third World. The First Industrial Revolution looks very odd indeed, and it doesn't seem to support the labor surplus model very well. In spite of stable real wages, the saving rate remained low and the rate of accumulation was modest.

Why was British growth so slow in the six decades before the 1820s? One answer might be that Britain tried to do two things at once—industrialize *and* fight expensive wars, and she simply did not have the resources to do both.

During the 60 years following 1760, Britain was at war for 36; in the three decades following the late 1780s Britain went from a peacetime economy to a level of wartime commitment that had no parallel until World War I. The war mobilized a good share of the labor force, suggesting that the civilian economy faced labor scarcity. The war debt grew rapidly, suggesting that civilian capital accumulation was suppressed by crowding-out. Tax revenues surged to one-fifth of national income, implying that real private incomes after tax were eroded. Meanwhile, war, blockades, and embargoes diminished international trade, inflating the relative prices of agricultural and raw material importables in the home market while lowering the price of manufactured exportables deflected from world markets.

Could the modest rate of accumulation during most of the First Industrial Revolution have been the result of limited saving, constrained by war? That is the way many contemporary observers saw it, and it sounds like Ricardian capital-scarcity. New war debt crowded out private debt, and the usury laws were seen to deflect saving to government borrowing, much as funds in Third World financial markets are diverted to state-backed projects and government borrowing (McKinnon, 1973). Indeed, John Stuart Mill (1909 [1848]: 481 and 483) had a view of crowding-out in which new war debt issues displaced private capital accumulation, one-for-one: "the government, by draining away a great part of annual accumulations . . . subtracted just so much [capital] while the war lasted." And Mill (1824: 40) thought crowding-out was large enough to warrant the belief that the counterfactual peacetime rate of capital accumulation would have been "enormous":

The accumulation going on in the hands of individuals was sufficient to counteract the effect of that wasteful [military] expenditure, and to prevent capital from being diminished. The same accumulation would have sufficed, but for the government expenditure, to produce an enormous increase.

A century later, T.S. Ashton (1955, 1959) affirmed the crowding-out hypothesis, whose main victims were building and construction.

The first step in testing the Mill–Ashton hypothesis is to compute the size of the war debt. Table 1 shows that it was vast.[3] Net additions to the war debt were 3.6 percent of national income as early as the 1760s (Table 1, col. 7), about the same as the 3.7 percent the United States achieved during 1980–82, when crowding-out and capital scarcity began to attract attention. The share had risen to 6.5 percent by the 1780s, a near doubling. It reached a peak of 11.5 percent in the 1790s. Net additions to the British war debt continued at high levels through the first two decades of the nineteenth century, holding at 6.6 percent of national income in the 1800s and 7.4 percent in the 1810s. The average burden of these net additions to the war debt was 6.8 percent between 1761 and 1820, and 8.5 percent between 1791 and 1820.

To get an estimate of the gross private saving rate, new public war debt should be added to civilian reproducible capital formation. When it is, Britain's private saving rates during the First Industrial Revolution no longer seem so modest. Indeed, while domestic investment in reproducible capital averaged only around 11.4 percent of national income from 1761 to 1820 (Table 1, col. 8), the gross private saving rate averaged 18.1 percent (Table 1, col. 9). Furthermore, while the investment share only rises from 9.1 to 13 percent in the six decades following the 1760s, the gross private saving rate rises from 12.7 to 20.4 percent, an increase more in tune with Arthur Lewis's dictum.

It appears that Britain was not a "modest" saver during the First Industrial Revolution after all. What makes Britain unusual is that much of the potential saving went into financing war.

What are the implications of the crowding-out when it is posed in its strongest, one-for-one form? The most awkward part of the exercise involves the redistributive effect of the war debt. Since the war debt was held by high-income savers, and since taxes fell primarily on low-income nonsavers, a redistribution from nonsavers to savers is implied. The redistributive effect would have had an unfavorable impact on the living standards of workers, but nonetheless would have served to augment the gross private saving rate. In other words, the redistributive effect might have offset the crowding-out effect, raising investment, so we must include it in what follows.

The set of assumptions underlying Table 2 can be stated briefly. Assume that taxes on income and wealth fell on the top half of the income distribution, while all other taxes were regressive, falling on the bottom half of the income distribution. Also assume that the average saving rate out of incomes in the lower half of the distribution was zero, and define the average saving rate out of the top half to be s_H. A counterfactual investment share can now be evaluated in the absence of the wars. The counterfactual rise in I/Y is calculated as:

$$d[I/Y]_{CF} = [\Delta D - s_H (1 - \phi_t) iD]/Y,$$

where ϕ_t is the share of income and wealth taxes in total tax revenue, ΔD is the deflated deficit, iD is the deflated interest charge on the debt outstanding, and Y is total real income. Using Harrod's identity (the rate of capital accumulation, K^*, equals the investment share divided by the capital/income ratio), it is a simple matter to compute the counterfactual change in the accumulation rate, dependent on the change in the investment share just calculated:

$$d[K^*]_{CF} = (Y/K) \cdot d[I/Y]_{CF} \quad ,$$

where Y/K is the income/capital ratio.

If the crowding-out assumptions are anywhere near correct, Table 2 suggests that war debt issue explains much of the peculiarities of the First Industrial Revolution. Between 1761 and 1820 the capital formation share would have been 4.84 percent higher in the absence of war, and the rate of accumulation would have been 1.74 percent per year higher. Assuming an output elasticity of 0.35, national income would have grown some 0.6 percent per year faster. The counterfactual calculations are even more striking for the decades in which the wars were most important, 1791–1820: the capital formation share would have been higher by 6.38 percent, the rate of accumulation would have been higher by 2.42 percent per year, and the rate of output growth would have been some 0.8 or 0.9 percent per year faster.

What have we learned? First, the classical economists were right that real wages were stable up to 1820. Second, they were wrong in treating the

TABLE 2 Conjectures on the impact of war debt issue on civilian sector accumulation and growth, 1761–1820

Period	Counterfactual rise in share of investment in national income I/Y (percent) (1)	Capital's productivity Y/K (2)	Counterfactual rise in the rate of accumulation, dK^* (percent) (3)	Counterfactual rise in the aggregate growth rate, dY^* (percent) (4)
1761–1820	4.84	0.36	1.74	0.61
1791–1820	6.38	0.38	2.42	0.85

SOURCE: See text.

economic performance as "revolutionary." On the contrary, growth and accumulation were slow. Third, one plausible explanation for the slow growth performance was the war debt, which crowded-out conventional accumulation.

Why were real wages stable up to 1820?

While the counterfactual conjectures reported in Table 2 are useful, they are not enough. They offer insight into the impact at the aggregate level, but they tell us nothing directly about real wages or industrialization, although they imply that low rates of capital formation produced low rates of capital-deepening and thus little increase in labor's marginal product and real wage. Perhaps more importantly, Table 2 ignores the potential impact of other war-induced influences—such as mobilization and labor scarcity, or food and resource scarcity induced by blockades and embargoes. The latter sounds Ricardian. In the closed Ricardian model, inelastic land supplies imply eventual food scarcity. By choking off trade, the war may have had the same effect.

Major wars create unskilled labor scarcity, and the French Wars were no exception. In fact, the share of the total labor force mobilized rose from about 2 to 10 percent, a rate that begins to approximate twentieth century wars. Furthermore, the relative price of agricultural goods rose sharply across the period, implying a deterioration in Britain's terms of trade, an erosion in aggregate real income, and a fall in the real wage. The critical question is how much of this relative price drift was due to war. Glenn Hueckel (1973) has estimated that the hostilities and blockades inflated 1812 wheat prices by some 24–40 percent due solely to higher freight and insurance costs. For the 1790–1815 period as a whole, he estimates that the wars raised the relative price of grains by 28 percent.

How can we assess the impact of these three influences on British economic performance up to 1820? One way is to develop a general equilibrium model that would allow us to explore the impact on the British economy had the labor mobilization, the relative price twists, and the crowding-out not taken place. One such model has been developed (Williamson, 1984a; 1985); it contains six factors of production: farm land, capital, unskilled labor, skills, domestically produced intermediate inputs (e.g., coal), and imported intermediate inputs (e.g., raw cotton). These factor inputs are used to produce outputs in four domestic sectors: agriculture, manufacturing, services, and mining. The civilian economy is open to trade in all final consumption and investment goods, save the nontraded services. The model conforms to the reality that Britain was a net importer of agricultural goods and a net exporter of manufactures. The small country assumption takes the prices of all tradeables as determined exogenously by commercial policy and events outside of Britain, such as blockades, embargoes, and international transport costs. In other words, demands for exportables and supplies of importables are assumed to be highly price elastic. In short, the model is a simple computable general equilibrium (CGE) model. As such, it is a member of a growing family of such models used by development economists (Adelman and Robinson, 1978; Dervis, de Melo, and Robinson, 1982; Kelley and Williamson, 1984a), public finance and trade economists (Shoven and Whalley, 1984), and even economic historians (Williamson and Lindert, 1980; James, 1984).

Of the many exogenous variables driving our CGE model of the British industrial revolution, only five attract attention here: the impact of wars, embargoes, and blockades on the prices of the three tradeables (which we shall call "war-distorted price effects" in what follows); the impact of mobilization on civilian labor supplies (which we shall call "mobilization effects"); and the influence of crowding-out on civilian capital accumulation (which we shall call "war debt crowding-out"). The endogenous variables that the previous discussion has stressed are: the real wage of unskilled common labor; real national income; output growth of the four sectors; industrialization, as measured by the difference in growth rates between manufacturing and agriculture; and exports. Since the debate over the First Industrial Revolution hinges on trends and growth performance, rather than on levels, the model is converted into per annum rates of change.

All economic interpretations of history are fiction, of course, but some fictions are better than others. This one has been estimated with data drawn from the early 1820s. The model was then used to predict British trends between 1821 and 1861, a far better documented epoch than 1760 to 1820. It performed extremely well (Williamson, 1985: ch. 9). Thus encouraged, we can proceed with more confidence to the period before 1820.

One could imagine two counterfactuals, either of which would serve to factor out the wars from the industrial revolution. On the one hand, we could ask how the British economy would have performed in the absence of the wars. On the other, we could ask how Britain's performance would have differed in the absence of the wars. The second counterfactual is used here. Table 3 reports the counterfactual. The last column supplies the total impact, while the first three columns break the total into its three parts—war debt crowding-out effects on capital formation; mobilization effects on the unskilled labor force; and trade disruptions affecting relative prices at home. The counterfactual is reported separately for 1790–1815 (the worst of the war years) and for the 1760s–1810s. Each panel reports the impact on growth rates of the seven endogenous variables of interest: aggregate real income, output in four sectors, an industrialization index (the difference between the growth of industry and of agriculture), and, our main focus here, the real wage of common labor.

The effects on capital accumulation (the war debt crowding-out effects) were the most important source of slow growth (0.67/0.96 = 60 percent of the combined effects of war from the 1760s to the 1810s). Yet the war-induced

TABLE 3 By how much would Britain's growth have changed under counterfactual peacetime conditions?

Indicator	Annual growth rates (percent) of selected economic indicators during two periods of the industrial revolution			
	No war debt crowding-out effects	No mobilization effects	No war-distorted price effects	All effects combined
The 1790–1815 period				
Real wage	.94	−0.27	0.59	1.27
Real income	.93	0.13	0.46	1.51
Sector outputs				
Agriculture	.40	0.34	−2.76	−2.05
Manufacturing	1.14	0.02	2.93	4.09
Services	1.13	0.09	0.70	1.93
Mining	1.14	0.02	2.82	3.98
Industrialization index: growth in manufacturing output less growth in agricultural output	.74	−0.32	5.69	6.14
The 1760s–1810s period				
Real wage	.68	−0.13	0.30	.84
Real income	.67	0.06	0.23	.96
Sector outputs				
Agriculture	.29	0.15	−1.38	−.94
Manufacturing	.82	0.01	1.47	2.30
Services	.81	0.05	0.35	1.21
Mining	.82	0.01	1.41	2.24
Industrialization index: growth in manufacturing output less growth in agricultural output	.53	−0.14	2.85	3.24

SOURCE: Williamson (1984a, Table 6: 709).

decline in the terms of trade (the war-distorted price effects) and mobilization were both sufficiently important that the effects of war in total exceeded the accumulation effects themselves. It appears that Britain's aggregate real income growth would have been higher by 1.51 percent per year from 1790 to 1815, and higher by 0.96 percent per year from the 1760s to the 1810s, had peace prevailed.

If these calculations are even close to the mark, they have important implications for our interpretations of the British industrial revolution. Table 3 suggests that almost all of the acceleration in growth after around 1820 was caused by the return to peace, having little to do with the underlying forces of capitalist development. The table also implies that the doubling in the growth of industrial output after 1815 or 1820 can be explained entirely by the return to peace.

But the most striking result appearing in Table 3 has to do with the real wage. The classical economists believed that elastic labor supplies accounted for stable real wages during the First Industrial Revolution. Table 3 suggests instead that most of the dismal real wage performance before the 1820s can be attributed to the wars and their financing. Peace would have raised the growth in real wages by 0.84 percent per annum, or by 65 percent for the six decades as a whole. Crowding-out appears to have been the dominant influence (0.68/0.84 = 81 percent of the total over the six decades as a whole). Slow accumulation and thus slow rates of job creation (especially in the cities) account for most of the poor performance in real wages up to the 1820s. War-induced trade distortions, raising the relative price of foodstuffs and raw materials, played a major supporting role (0.30/0.84 = 36 percent of the total).

In short, a classical model of labor surplus is not required to explain stable real wages during the industrial revolution. A neoclassical model that takes into account the historical reality of war will do equally well, or even better. Paradoxically, the neoclassical analysis supports Ricardo's stress on capital-scarcity and food constraints, but for different reasons.

Can elastic labor supplies explain lagging wages up to 1860?

What happened after the wars when trade opened up and government debt no longer crowded out investment and accumulation? Did labor surplus conditions play a more critical role during Pax Britannica? After all, qualitative accounts suggest that Irish immigration into Britain became very important after the French Wars. At the same time, unskilled wages lagged behind and inequality was on the rise (Williamson, 1985: chs. 3 and 4). Did the emergence of an Irish glut at the bottom of the distribution play an important role in accounting for these two events after 1820?

The gross correlation is seductive—lagging wages and rising inequality coinciding with Irish immigration—but a clear assessment is clouded by the difficulty of controlling for everything else. Yet, economic historians writing about the British industrial revolution have always thought the Irish mattered. In Arthur Redford's (1926: 159) classic study, for example, we are told that "the main social significance of the Irish influx lay with its tendency to lower wages and the standard of living of the English wage-earning classes." And while Redford thought this tendency was obvious during the Irish Famine of the late 1840s, "the disastrous social effect of the Irish influx was, however, already apparent in the 'thirties'" (p. 159). This view has been carried into the present. I suspect it played a key role in motivating Lewis's model of elastic labor supplies, and it certainly plays a key role in Sidney Pollard's (1978) influential survey of British labor markets during the industrial revolution.

The roots of this view seem to lie solely with the opinions of contemporary observers, rather than with any explicit test of the proposition. Fear of an Irish glut was already apparent in the 1825 Select Committee on Disturbances in Ireland and the 1827 Select Committee on Emigration. Indeed, the classical economists viewed an elastic Irish labor supply as a real threat to British living standards. So said J. R. McCulloch before the 1825 Select Committee (Poor Inquiry, *Parliamentary Papers*, 1836: xxxiii). And during the 1827 Emigration Inquiry, the House called none other than the Reverend Thomas R. Malthus to serve as witness to the Irish threat to British living standards. Malthus stated that "the wages of labour have been lowered essentially by the coming over of the Irish," and that in the future the Irish immigration "might have the pernicious effect of introducing the habit of living almost entirely on potatoes" (quoted in Poor Inquiry, *Parliamentary Papers*, 1836: xxxiii).

If the Irish had an impact on real wages, surely they must also have discouraged the migration of the native-born to the booming cities. There are three categories of rates indicative of the discouraged native-born would-be migrant: low emigration rates from the poor South to the booming North, low emigration rates from British agriculture to urban employment, and rising rates of native-born emigration to the New World. On the two internal migration issues there has been abundant comment since the 1830s (see the references in Pollard, 1978, and Williamson, 1984b). The problem is posed quite simply in Figure 3, where there are two sectors, agriculture and industry. Prior to the Irish influx, we assume a labor market equilibrium where *AB* of the native-born labor force is employed in agriculture and the remainder, *BD*, is employed in industry. Assume the Irish immigrants augment the total British labor force by *DE*. These immigrants will be absorbed only if the economywide wage declines to a new equilibrium at *w*(*t* + 1). Note also that in this example all of the Irish are employed in industry—their point of entry into the British labor market—and that *BC* of the native-born are pushed out of industrial employment, presumably migrating back to agriculture since overt unemployment is ignored in this simple model.

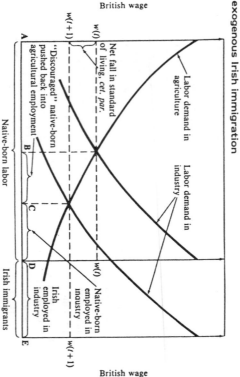

FIGURE 3 Labor absorption in British industry with exogenous Irish immigration

Were the classical economists right? Does an elastic Irish labor supply explain lagging real wages up to 1860?

In the classical labor surplus model, an elastic labor supply favors industrialization. If the Irish immigrants were sufficiently important to hold down wages in Britain, then they should also have served to favor British industrialization. The argument evolves along the following lines: disguised unemployment in Irish agriculture ensured an elastic labor supply for Britain; the elastic labor supply held wages down, which favored the expansion of labor-intensive sectors (like textiles), and which also shifted the distribution of income away from labor and toward capital, making more investment and accumulation possible. Pollard and other economic historians believe that there is historical support for the classical labor surplus model:

> There is thus an impressive degree of agreement among observers of the British industrial revolution that it was characterized by low wages and abundant labour, and that the cheap and elastic labour supply itself played an instrumental part in the progress of industrialization. (Pollard, 1978: 102)

> . . . Ireland functioned predominantly as a labour reservoir, and this role was not lost on contemporaries. . . . Disguised unemployment on Irish soil corresponds to the agricultural sector in the Lewis model, and Irish labour became an integral part of British industrialization. (Pollard, 1978: 115)

So far, the thesis has not been confronted with any quantitative evidence. Did Irish immigration foster British industrialization?

One way to answer these questions is to imagine how the British economy would have performed in the absence of the Irish. When this counterfactual question is asked of the CGE model already used in the previous section, we get the answers shown in Table 4.

The key message emerging from the table is that the Irish immigrations mattered little to British wages and industrialization over the four decades 1820–60. The counterfactual decline in the labor force growth rate, from 1.40 to 1.25 percent per annum, would not have been trivial, and it would have exceeded that of population since the Irish had far higher labor participation rates (migration self-selecting young adults). Furthermore, all of the labor force decline would have taken place among the unskilled, since the Irish immigrant was primarily illiterate and came with few urban skills. The unskilled real wage clearly would have risen in the absence of the Irish, the model suggesting that it would have grown at 1.04 rather than 0.92 percent per annum. The counterfactual experiment does confirm the view that part of the relatively slow rise in incomes at the bottom of the British distribution up to 1860 was due to an Irish glut from below. But the magnitudes hardly seem large enough to justify assigning a major role to the Irish in accounting for lagging real wages during the First Industrial Revolution.

If the reader is not persuaded by the results in Table 4, perhaps the following argument may be decisive. The "Britain without the Irish" counterfactual performs a strictly comparative static experiment with the CGE

TABLE 4 The British industrial revolution without Irish immigration

Indicator	Annual growth rates (percent) of selected economic and demographic indicators, 1821–61	
	Actual: with the Irish	Counterfactual: without the Irish
Labor force	1.40	1.25
Population	1.23	1.12
Unskilled real wage	0.92	1.04
Manufacturing output	3.17	3.14
Agricultural output	1.37	1.24
Industrialization index: manufacturing output less growth in agricultural output	1.80	1.90
Agricultural employment	0.93	0.70
Nonagricultural employment	1.58	1.46
Emigration rate from agriculture	−0.84	−1.07

SOURCE: Williamson (1984b, Table 12).

model. In other words, we assume that the rate of technological progress and its bias would not have been altered in an economy with no Irish and greater unskilled labor scarcity; we assume that the rate of capital accumulation and skill formation would have remained unchanged as well; and we assume that the native-born labor supply would have stayed the same too. These are unreasonable assumptions, but any plausible effort to endogenize capital accumulation, native-born labor force growth, and technological change would strengthen the findings in Table 4. Why so? Consider capital formation. The Lewis model stresses the connection between elastic labor supply, stable real wages, rising profit shares, and, thus, saving and accumulation. In the absence of the Irish, wages would have risen, profits would have been choked off, and the rate of accumulation would have declined. The lower rate of accumulation that rising wages induce (according to the classical labor surplus model) implies lower rates of capital-deepening and offsetting downward pressures on the real wage. Table 4 ignores such accumulation responses and thus overstates the impact of the Irish on the real wage. Consider technology. In the absence of the Irish, wouldn't rising labor scarcity induce a more active search for technologies that saved on labor, thus offsetting the rise in the real wage? Table 4 ignores such induced technological responses and thus overstates the impact of the Irish on the real wage. Consider the native-born labor supply. Surely the native-born labor supply would have been larger in the absence of the Irish. After all, the Irish immigrations encouraged native-born emigrations to the New World and discouraged non-Irish foreign immigrations into Britain. Table 4 ignores such non-Irish labor supply responses and thus overstates the impact of the Irish on the real wage.

What about industrialization? Since the labor force would have grown at a slower rate without the Irish, output, including manufacturing, would have grown slower too. But which sectors would have been hardest hit? The answer must be those sectors that were most unskilled-labor intensive. Since agriculture was more unskilled-labor intensive than industry, output would have shifted toward industry in the absence of the Irish. In other words, Table 4 rejects the hypothesis that the Irish fostered industrialization. Had there been no Irish in Britain, agriculture would have suffered far more than industry. Only if we are concerned with industrial employment and output in isolation can we conclude that the Irish fostered industrialization. If instead we focus on industry's relative share of total output and employment, then it appears that the Irish inhibited British industrialization.

The finding that Irish immigration tended to favor the expansion of agriculture more than manufacturing may seem odd to readers familiar with the fact that the Irish were never employed in agriculture with the same frequency as in industry (although seasonal Irish employment in agriculture was important). The resolution of this apparent anomaly is close at hand: in the absence of the Irish (whose point of entry was urban employment), British farm labor would have been encouraged to emigrate from agriculture at a more rapid rate. This can be seen at the bottom of Table 4, where the emigration rate rises sharply from -0.84 to -1.07 percent per annum in a counterfactual Britain without the Irish. Had there been no Irish, agricultural employment growth would have declined (from 0.93 to 0.70 percent per annum)—in part due to a decline in agricultural output growth and in part due to the rise in labor scarcity encouraging farmers to use less unskilled labor. And with the decline in agricultural employment growth, the rate of emigration from agriculture would have risen, thus filling the jobs vacated by the Irish. It appears from Table 4 that the Irish had a far bigger impact on rural–urban migration in Britain than they did on overall labor scarcity.

In short, "elastic Irish labor supplies" in Britain after 1820 did not seriously retard the rise in the real wage. It rose anyway, but it would not have risen much faster had there been no Irish glut in the British labor market.

Accumulation, inequality, and the labor surplus model

For me, the most challenging aspect of the labor surplus model is its effort to confront what Lewis argues is the central problem of development theory, namely:

. . . to understand the process by which a community which was previously saving and investing 4 or 5 per cent of its national income or less, converts itself into an economy where voluntary saving is running at about 12 to 15 per cent of national income or more. . . . We cannot explain any "industrial" revolution . . . until we can explain why saving increased relatively to national income. (Lewis, 1954: 155)

The labor surplus model confronts this central problem by adopting the classical tradeoff view of inequality and accumulation: stable real wages imply greater inequality, and inequality breeds higher saving rates, a surge in accumulation, and thus the industrial revolution.

The British historical evidence has not been kind to the labor surplus model. Although the real wage was certainly stable up to 1820, the investment rate only rose by about 4 percentage points from 1761/71 to 1811/21 (Table 1)—far below the 7 to 11 percentage points embedded in Lewis's assertion. And while inequality was sharply on the rise after 1820 as Britain passed through the upswing of the Kuznets Curve (Williamson, 1985), Feinstein (1978, Table 28: 91) has shown that the investment share in gross domestic product failed to rise at all up to the 1850s.

The lack of correlation between inequality and accumulation during the British industrial revolution does not bode well for the labor surplus model, or the classical tradeoff thinking upon which it is based. For the period prior to 1820, I have offered an alternative explanation consistent with the simultaneous appearance of the low investment rates, the slow rates of accumulation, the lack of capital-deepening, and, of course, stable real wages. The explanation lies with war and its impact on the civilian economy. It appears that a neoclassical, full employment model which captures the impact of war debt crowding-out, labor mobilization, and food scarcity due to trade deflection can adequately account for all of the peculiarities of the British industrial revolution up to 1820. To repeat, a classical model of labor surplus is not required to explain stable real wages during the First Industrial Revolution. A neoclassical model with Ricardian overtones can do better.

The period after the French Wars also fails to support the labor surplus model. The critical evidence, of course, is that the real wage begins a significant rise after 1820. Stable real wages are simply not a characteristic of the British industrial revolution during those four decades of dramatic industrialization up to the 1850s. Inequality is on the rise, however, and much of it is attributable to the fact that unskilled wages lag behind. Why the lag in unskilled wages? While much has been made of "elastic Irish labor supplies," it appears that they played only a marginal role in keeping the lid on real wages. Of course, this is also a period when the demographic transition generates a peak rate of population growth (Wrigley and Schofield, 1981); but if the labor supply was glutted by such Malthusian forces, why is there no evidence of an accumulation response? As we have seen, the investment share in gross domestic product shows no rise at all after 1820. We may not have very good explanations for this puzzle, but it is clear that the rise in inequality after 1820 did not induce a rise in the investment share.[5] Another central premise of the labor supply model seems to fail the test of history.

Assessing the classical labor surplus model

Lewis (1954: 142) insisted that "whether marginal productivity is zero or negligible is not . . . of fundamental importance to the labor surplus model." All that matters is that the "price of labour . . . is a wage at the subsistence level." Much of the profession disagreed, apparently, since a good share of the critical response that emerged after 1954 focused primarily on that issue. This paper has taken a different tack. It has, instead, raised two questions: Is the historical evidence drawn from the British industrial revolution consistent with the macro implications of the classical labor surplus model? Can a neo-classical model more adequately account for the British industrial revolution? The answer to the first question is no, while the answer to the second is yes.

It appears that there is very little historical content to the classical labor surplus model, a paradoxical result since the British classical economists developed their dynamic models to explain the events they thought they saw going on around them. Is this historical evidence from the First Industrial Revolution fatal to the labor surplus model? After all, the First Industrial Revolution is only a sample of one in a large population of industrial revolutions, the most numerous of which have taken place since 1945. Whether the evidence drawn from the Third World is any more supportive of the labor surplus model than that drawn from Britain is a question that takes us too far afield in this paper. It is true, of course, that population pressure is far greater in the Third World than it ever was in Britain. On the other hand, Britain never had the advantage of technological transfer and capital inflows that the Third World had in abundance during much of the 1960s and 1970s. The question is still open and awaiting empirical assessment.

Notes

This paper, stimulated by debate with faculty and students at Williams College, has benefited from discussions with Robert Dorfman.

1 This section and the one following draw liberally on my paper "Why was British growth so slow during the industrial revolution?" (Williamson, 1984a).

2 The Third World estimates are taken from the World Bank (IBRD, 1980: 421), the figures for Japan from Kelley and Williamson (1974: 233), and the American figures from Williamson (1979: 233).

3 The real impact of the war debt can be assessed by using one of two concepts. Most economists use the Department of Commerce National Income Accounts approach, deflating the increase in the nominal debt outstanding. Others have argued that we should use instead

Real Accrual Accounting, computing the real debt at the beginning and the end of the period, before the increase is calculated. The accrual concept includes the impact of inflation on the stock of old debt, whereas the national accounts concept does not. The national income approach is used commonly in the literature, so I apply it here too. Use of the accrual concept, however, would yield the same conclusion as what follows.

4 This section draws heavily on my unpublished paper "Irish immigration, elastic labor supplies and crowding-out during the British industrial revolution, 1821–1861" (1984b).

5 British evidence is not unique in rejecting this basic premise of the classical labor surplus model. America also underwent a sharp rise in inequality across the nineteenth

TABLE 1   Public debt issue, gross domestic saving in reproducible capital, and gross private saving: levels and shares in national income: England, 1761–1821

Year	Nominal government debt outstanding (£ million) D (1)	National income price deflator (1851/61 = 1.0) P_Y (2)	Real debt outstanding D/P_Y (3)	Decade	Increase per year in government debt (£m)			Shares in real national income (percent)		Gross private saving rate (percent) $S/P_I + \Delta D/P_Y$ (9)
					P_Y (4)	Nominal: ΔD (5)	Real: $\Delta D/P_Y$ (6)	Debt increase $\Delta D/P_Y$ (7)	Savings and investment S/P_I (8)	
1761	103.2	.77	134.7							
1771	130.2	.90	144.9	1761–1771	.83	.2.7	3.3	3.6	9.1	12.7
1781	173.7	.95	183.2	1771–1781	.92	4.4	4.7	4.9	10.5	15.4
1791	243.6	1.00	244.9	1781–1791	.97	7.0	7.2	6.5	13.3	19.8
1801	443.1	1.50	295.6	1791–1801	1.25	20.0	16.0	11.5	13.5	24.9
1811	618.9	1.60	387.3	1801–1811	1.55	17.6	11.4	6.6	9.0	15.6
1821	838.0	1.19	703.6	1811–1821	1.40	21.9	15.7	7.4	13.0	20.4

SOURCE: Williamson (1984a, Table 3: 697).

[8]

Essays in Exploration

Growth, Equality, and History*

PETER H. LINDERT

University of California–Davis

AND

JEFFREY G. WILLIAMSON

Harvard University

Complex policy issues deserve frequent reassessment, and the relationship between economic growth and equality is undeniably complex. Policymakers who care about trade-offs between the two goals continue to press the scientific limits of empirical economics. It takes an enormous sample of long-term national experiences to approximate the data base necessary to move debate from allegation to evidence. Fortunately, the sample continues to expand. Since the 1950s dozens of countries have produced evidence on income distribution and growth, and the records of some currently developed countries have been extended back into the 17th century. This article assesses the empirical harvest. Most of our inferences, however, are based on American and British history.   © 1985 Academic Press, Inc.

I. TWO HYPOTHESES

A. *Growth versus Equality*

Must policymakers choose between growth and equality? Certainly the British classical economists thought so. For at least two centuries, mainstream economists and government officials were guided by the belief that the national product could not be raised while at the same time giving the poor a larger share. After all, did not redistribution to the poor cut the surplus for saving and accumulation? This view of the trade-off was not based on firm evidence or policy

* The authors are grateful to the National Science Foundation for financial support, and thank Moses Abramovitz, Larry Neal, and two anonymous referees for helpful criticisms of earlier drafts. Please address requests for reprints to Jeffrey G. Williamson, Department of Economics, 216 Littauer Center, Harvard University, Cambridge, Mass. 02138.

341

experimentation, but rather on theory, allegation, and perhaps spurious correlation. And since income, wealth, and political clout have always gone together, policies left untested in the past were more likely to have been those which might have produced egalitarian growth. Indeed, since only the top economic classes had political voice and literacy in 18th and early 19th century Britain, policy tended to be regressive, and the conventional trade-off view reigned supreme. Not surprisingly, from Adam Smith onwards, English economic thought eulogized saving and decried generous poor relief. The trade-off made its way into the 20th century where, for example, in the 1920s the British "treasury view" alleged that job programs and the dole would crowd out productive investment; and in the 1980s, Reagan and Thatcher both appear to believe that "scarce savings" is at the heart of the productivity slowdown, and that generous welfare programs somehow account for both. Even such critics of capitalism as Marx, Hobson, and Kaldor accepted the classical or Smithian assumption that the rich save a lot more at the margin.

With the spread of suffrage and national independence in the Third World, rejection of the Smithian trade-off gained momentum under the leadership of Robert McNamara and some World Bank economists (e.g., Adelman and Morris, 1973; Chenery et al., 1974; Ahluwalia, 1976, 1980). Their competing view is that the Third World has overlooked a vast range of policy options that would enhance growth by raising the value of the poor's assets: investments in public health, mass education, rural infrastructure, and staple foods. These prescriptions are backed by evidence from the Virtuous Asian Nations (South Korea, Sri Lanka, and Taiwan) and the Bad Latins (Brazil, Mexico, Panama, and Peru) (see especially Chenery et al., 1974, pp. 42, 273–290; Cline, 1975; Adelman and Robinson, 1978; Bacha, 1979, p. 56; Fei et al., 1979; Fields, 1980; Ahluwalia, 1980).

The debate is hardly over, and there are at least two reasons why the controversy is likely to persist over the next two centuries as well. First, highly politicized debates tend to have long lives. Government policies which involve a possible redistribution of income create opposing self-interests, and each side can be counted on to promote its cause by economic arguments that are hard to falsify. Second, the issue is exceedingly difficult to resolve with evidence. Certainly the trade-off cannot be assessed by simple correlations between growth and inequality. Nor can the trade-off be assessed by correlations between inequality, aggregate saving rates, and accumulation, although the 19th century certainly offers convenient examples. For example, as we shall see below, American inequality rose sharply between the two epochs 1800–1835 and 1855–1871, the gross saving rate in gross national product doubled, and the rate of growth in reproducible capital per man-hour quadrupled. It is exactly this kind of correlation—rising inequality coinciding with rising saving and accumulation rates during Industrial Revolutions, that encouraged the trade-off belief among classical economists who developed their growth models while the process was underway in England. Could it be that such correlations were spurious? After all, 20th century histories fail to confirm the correlation. Indeed, the correlation seems to have disappeared even from British and American experience: inequality and the growth rate rose together from the 18th to the late 19th century, but while the growth rate held up thereafter, inequality declined. The same appears to have been true for almost all current members of the OECD.

To move beyond simple correlations to true policy options, we must first note that the term "growth" is misleading. One cannot eat growth rates, although they do imply something about present and future consumption. "Growth" seems to have replaced "efficiency" in much of the trade-off debate (but see Okun, 1975) not only because it is a shorter word, but also because many of the efficiencies in question relate to the process of accumulation. It is a common fear that society accumulates too little, both because saving is overtaxed and because many social benefits from investment fail to accrue to the private investor. Attention has focused on these accumulation issues to such an extent that growth has displaced efficiency in the trade-off debate. We shall follow the literature in this regard, but remind readers of the crucial underlying distinction.

B. The Kuznets Curve

If the growth–equality debate reflects theory in search of fact, then the Kuznets Curve—the second hypothesis to be surveyed here—reflects facts in search of a theory.

Simon Kuznets (1955, 1966, pp. 206–217) was among the first to note that income inequality seemed to have declined in several nations across the mid-20th century, and cautiously ventured the guess that it had risen earlier. Others took up the hypothesis and found cross-section evidence supporting the Kuznets Curve, showing that income inequality first rises and then declines with development (Paukert, 1973; Adelman and Morris, 1973, Appendix C; Chenery *et al.*, 1974, pp. 27–29; Ahluwalia, 1976; Bacha, 1979; Fields, 1980, pp. 59–71).

The Kuznets Curve is illustrated in Fig. 1, based on Ahluwalia's data (Ahluwalia, 1976, Table 8, pp. 340–341). A quadratic fits this 60-country World Bank sample fairly well, where the inequality statistic is simply the income share of the top 20%.[1] The underlying data can and have

---

[1] Limitations of space prevent our comparing the wide range of useful inequality measures already discussed by others (e.g., Atkinson, 1970). Our examination of historical and contemporary data shows that the most significant inequality trends are revealed by almost any conventional measure. Situations in which the gaps between top and median incomes widen (narrow) are normally situations in which the median either holds its own or gains (loses) ground relative to the poorest. Subtleties of Lorenz-curve intersections rarely play

LINDERT AND WILLIAMSON

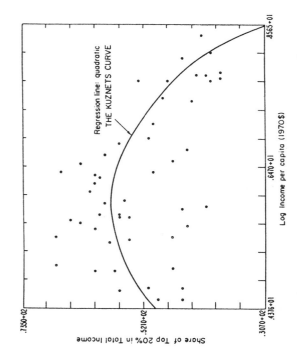

FIG. 1. The Kuznets curve: international 60-country cross-section from the 1960s and 1970s (*source:* Ahluwalia, 1976, Table 8, pp. 340, 341).

been criticized, but one thing is clear: the variance around the estimated Kuznets Curve is greatest from low to middle levels of development. Figure 1 thus dramatizes a point worth recalling whenever the Kuznets Curve is debated: inequality is unlikely to rise systematically across a pooled cross-section of early Industrial Revolutions; even if most countries undergo increasing inequality during early modern economic growth, such correlations are bound to be poor since history and geography have given less developed countries very different starting points. The more robust portion of the Kuznets Curve lies to the right: income inequality falls with the advance of per capita income at higher levels of development.

Historical research reinforces these inferences. For example, the British experience since 1688 (Fig. 2) looks like an excellent advertisement for the Kuznets Curve, with income inequality rising across the Industrial Revolution, followed by a prolonged leveling in the last quarter of the nineteenth century. Since these figures are "pre-fisc," and since the

a major role. Space also prevents a treatment of distribution trends in the socialist bloc. We can only note here that most countries in Eastern Europe seem to have had postwar income distributions much like the pre-fisc distributions of most northwest European nations in Figs. 1 or 2. An exception is Czechoslovakia, which, like Finland, has had far greater income equality than the rest of the Continent. The available estimates show a slight trend toward equality in the Soviet Union, Poland, and the GDR, but perhaps an inegalitarian trend in Bulgaria, Czechoslovakia, and Yugoslavia, since the 1950s. See McAuley (1979); Berry *et al.* (1983), and the appendices of the 1981 working paper cited there.

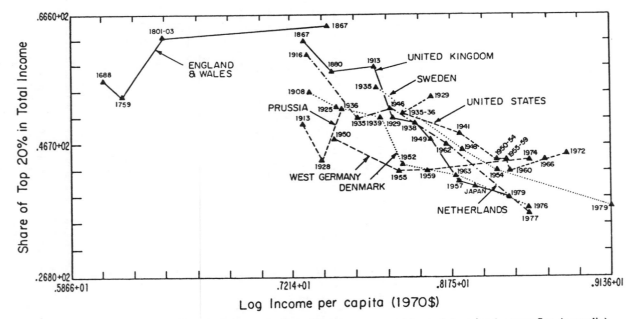

Fig. 2. The Kuznets curve: historical time series from five European countries and America (*source:* See Appendix).

leveling predates progressive fiscal policy, union strength, and the rise of the welfare state, it follows that the British Kuznets Curve reflects something more than changes in labor's political power.

But what is most striking about Fig. 2 is the extraordinary similarity in the downswing of the Kuznets Curve across the 20th century. The figure collects time series for six nations: the United States (1929–1972), the United Kingdom (1688–1979), Germany (1913–1974), Denmark (1908–1976), the Netherlands (1916–1977) and Sweden (1935–1979). What Arthur Burns (1954) saw in America as a "revolutionary leveling" after 1929 apparently was shared by most of Europe, whose experience is documented in Fig. 2. The one possible exception is Germany, whose inequality history is complicated by the income leveling that accompanied wartime defeat. Nor is the historical pattern in Fig. 2 statistically unique. When these 20th-century time series are pooled with the contemporary cross-section in Fig. 1, neither the levels nor the trends show significantly different patterns from those already summarized in Fig. 1. Thus, 20th-century history agrees with the international cross-sections and with Kuznets' original conjecture: while the early stages of development may have seen widening gaps more often than not, the clearer trend is an equality downswing in the later stages. We must try to explain this regularity, drawing on the information now available for two well-documented histories, those of America and Britain.

The current status of the Kuznets Curve is thus analogous to that of the Phillips Curve around 1970 (Bacha, 1979, p. 52). It is familiar yet fragile: now you see it, now you don't. Yet, the Kuznets Curve is rife with theoretical possibilities, especially if the theory explains exceptions, as well as the general rule.

C. Inequality of What?

As we have made clear, the standard approach to inequality measurement is the pragmatic one which uses conventional annual income data. Such data certainly have their flaws when it comes to inequality measurement. Three need to be emphasized here. First, we would prefer a measure of "full-time" income, with its earnings component adjusted to some conventional full-time work year. Time not spent generating earnings has some opportunity cost, at or below the individual's market wage. Income inequality should be adjusted to include home time, just as it should be included in any assessment about economic growth (Nordhaus and Tobin, 1972).

Second, the distribution of resources should be defined so as to include items that are hard to value because they are not traded in a conventional marketplace. In particular, political voice is unequally distributed. Omitting it from our measures implies that a one-dollar-one-vote rule governs the political marketplace. This may be nearer the mark in electoral democracies than we care to admit, but it is an issue worth including in future debates over inequality. How political voice is distributed under other forms of government, and how it correlates with the distribution of conventional income, remains central to any comparative judgment about inequality across nations or over time.

Third, a basic component of the inequality of lifetime resources has been seriously neglected. What about inequality in the length of life? Even studies that have extended the income concept across the full life cycle (e.g., Lillard, 1977) have assumed an identical life span for all individuals. Yet modern economic growth has brought striking changes in the inequality of length of life. Where average life expectancies are short, as in earlier centuries for all countries or in the poorest countries today, life expectancies are also very unequally distributed. Where average life expectancies are long, they tend to be more equally distributed. Thus, 20th-century improvements in life expectancy have favored the poor more than the rich, although just how much has been subject to debate. (See Antonovsky's 1967 survey of life expectancy by social class over time.) To the extent that these class-specific mortality trends are correct, 20th-century improvements in life expectancy must have equalized the distribution of lifetime resources in America and Europe even more than the equalization of annual incomes shown in Fig. 2. In current international cross-sections, the rise in average life expectancy between the poorest nations and those with middling income means that inequality in lifetime incomes within the poorest nations is understated perhaps enough that the lifetime income inequality there is just as high as in Latin nations whose annual incomes look so unequal (Preston, 1980). Clearly, here is another inequality dimension awaiting further empirical work.

This essay, however, uses the more conventional data. The variant used here is *pre-fisc* annual income, income before the effects of taxes, transfers, or government purchases of goods and services. There are three reasons for the choice. First, it makes it far easier to perform a comparative assessment of a literature which is dominated by similar measures. Second, while well-being at any point in time is certainly better gauged by *post-fisc* income, it is not at all clear that inequality differences across time or across nations can be explained by differences in the "fisc." Indeed, there is considerable evidence from the Great Depression and the post-World War II period that fiscal redistribution explains only part of the timing of the leveling in post-fisc incomes among the industrialized countries or with differences in the level of inequality between them (Nicholson, 1974, p. 79; Reynolds and Smolensky, 1977, p. 71; Smolensky et al., 1978, p. 74; O'Higgins and Ruggles, 1981; Renaghan, 1984, p. 60). The same is true of today's international cross-sections: the contrast in post-fisc gini coefficients between egalitarian Britain and inegalitarian Brazil owes less to fiscal redistribution and more to pre-fisc inequalities as they are generated in the marketplace. Third, the economist is presented with a greater challenge in explaining pre-fisc inequality since it is the complex outcome of a whole range of macroeconomic forces which influence factor rewards, forces which the economist is better equipped to analyze.

Section II will elaborate on the various forces which seem to be highly correlated with long-run inequality, and thus have been seen by economic historians and development economists as likely "prime movers" of both growth and inequality. Section III moves from theorizing about the growth–inequality causal direction, to the inequality–growth causal direction and to the heart of the trade-off debate. Section IV confronts these theoretical propositions with the historical evidence, leaning heavily on American and British experience. Section V concludes with a suggested reinterpretation of the Kuznets Curve and the Trade-Off.

II. WORKING PARTS: LEADING VARIABLES DRIVING INEQUALITY

A. Focus on Factor Markets

Can inequality trends be explained without reference to changes in factor returns? Were this possible, then the nasty complexity of modeling the entire macroeconomic structure of factor returns could be avoided. Unfortunately, most of the observed movements in measured inequality appear to stem from changes in the relative rates of factor returns, so that the macromodeling cannot be avoided. Classical economists knew this well enough so that their dynamic models of growth and distribution focused on factor incomes accruing to labor, land, and capital. Modern human capital theory implies the same, with focus on the structure of pay by skill.

Kuznets himself wondered if the Kuznets Curve might not be the result of shifts in the structure of occupations alone (Kuznets, 1955; also Robinson, 1976). Perhaps the inequality patterns of Figs. 1 and 2 are merely by-products of the diffusion of jobs rewarded with a uniform but higher level of income. Imagine that a society begins with perfect equality, with everybody earning an income of 5. Let some modernizing influence introduce a job rewarded by an income of 10, which is first enjoyed by just one individual and then diffuses through society until everybody is earning 10. Any conventional inequality measure will rise from the initial perfect equality and then return to it later, tracing out the Kuznets Curve. This diffusion mechanism is potentially important, since we know that modernization does indeed involve the diffusion of higher-paying jobs.

Yet there are limits to any inequality explanation that relies solely on such compositional shifts. It is not true that the inequality histories underlying Fig. 2 are just shifts between fixed relative income positions as in the example just given. The pay advantages themselves have the same tendency to rise and fall. Even though the unskilled typically enjoy gains in absolute real income in the early stages of development, skilled occupations typically enjoy far greater gains (Morley and Williamson, 1977; Williamson and Lindert, 1980; Morley, 1982; Lindert and Williamson, 1983; Williamson, 1985). Indeed, over half the observed rise in aggregate earnings inequality in 19th-century Britain stemmed from movements in intraoccupational inequalities rather than from occupational shifts or movements in pay ratios (Williamson, 1985). These pay ratios then decline in the later stages of development (Lydall, 1968; Brown, 1977, Chap. 3; Williamson and Lindert, 1980, Chap. 4; Williamson, 1985, Chap. 3), in harmony with the 20th-century leveling in the size distributions in Fig. 2. Pay-ratio leveling also accounted for more than half the drop in American earnings inequality following 1939 (after controlling for unemployment and macroinstability; see Chiswick and Mincer, 1972).

This pattern of rising and falling pay ratios is sufficiently widespread, and so closely parallel with overall inequality trends, to require that any theory of the Kuznets Curve explain why the rates of pay themselves first diverge and then converge during modern economic growth.

What about the distribution of non-human wealth? In principle, one might imagine that changes in the distribution of wealth might be an independent determinant of changes in income inequality. Although changes in wealth distribution associated with slave emancipation, war losses, land reform, and nationalization may be loosely associated with the stresses of modern economic growth, they are too sporadic to offer a coherent explanation of the Kuznets Curve. It seems better to view changes in the distribution of wealth either as a result of previous changes in the distribution of income or as a simultaneous outcome, since those forces driving returns on assets surely also govern the aggregate value and distribution of wealth.

We are led, then, back to factor markets in searching for the sources of inequality, and labor markets in particular. So it is that economic historians and development economists have pondered at length how labor markets work in economies shocked by the disequilibrium of Industrial Revolutions and Demographic Transitions. And so it is that Jan Tinbergen (1975) has focused on a "demand and supply" model of labor markets to account for the mid-20th-century leveling of income and earnings in advanced industrialized economies. What follows is in that tradition: we look for the microeconomic foundations of what appears to be a macroevent—the Kuznets Curve. Furthermore, the task of explaining long-run distribution trends thus rejoins the search for the explanations of growth itself. That is, we seek the factor-demand and factor-supply forces that can account for both distributional trends and the pattern and rate of economic growth. Growth and distribution require a simultaneous attack whether or not we end up believing that a policy trade-off exists between them, a subject still waiting in the wings.

How might factor demand and supply forces have operated in the past to produce the Kuznets Curve?

B. Final Product Demand

Exogenous shifts in final-product demand can affect the overall inequality of income through derived factor demands. Such factor-demand influences must be assessed in two steps. The first is to find large shifts in final-product demand that could reasonably be called exogenous to the growth and distribution process. The outstanding possibility in recent times is the 20th-century rise in government purchases of goods and services as a share of national product. Since the rise of government occurred during periods of economic leveling, especially during the two World Wars and the Great Depression, one may suspect that the rise of government has shifted aggregate demand toward goods and services making intensive use of low-paid unskilled labor.

To quantify the effects of the rise of government purchases on demand factors, one must take the second step: employing input-output data to decompose government purchases and other final-product demands into implied demands for unskilled labor versus other factors. Calculations on the U.S. input-output table for 1963 (Williamson and Lindert, 1980, pp. 186–188) tentatively suggest a pattern. Purchases of "general government" services, both civilian and military, are noticeably unskilled-labor intensive, simply because they consist mostly of direct labor services by government employees. By contrast, government purchase of other services and of goods do not differ from the rest of the economy in their unskilled-labor intensity. This pattern suggests that one could sketch the factor-demand implications of the rise of government simply by plotting over time the share of government employees in the labor force. If future research confirms the 1963 pattern, then the rise of government purchases will indeed emerge as an egalitarian force shifting demand toward the unskilled, with most of its impact coming during wars.

C: Labor-Saving Technological Change

A potentially powerful factor-demand force behind the distribution of income is the degree to which technological progress tends to economize on some factors of production while favoring the use of others. A bias toward unskilled-labor saving can widen income gaps by worsening job prospects and relative wages for the unskilled while bidding up the returns to skills and property. This idea is hardly novel, since it reappears with each issue of our journals. Yet the empirical evidence on longer-run and systematic movements in the factor demand bias needs to be established. We *do* know that American growth in the 19th century was heavily unskilled-labor saving in the aggregate (Abramovitz and David, 1973); the same appears to have been true of Britain in the first half of the 19th century (Williamson, 1985, pp. 86–91), and of the Third World since 1950 (Eckhaus, 1955; Fei and Ranis, 1963; Williamson, 1971; Turnham, 1971; Morawetz, 1974; Cline, 1975; Kelley and Williamson, 1984, Chaps. 4–6). Is there any evidence suggesting that these high rates of unskilled-labor saving abate as industrializing nations approach maturity? The Third World development record is, of course, too short to offer any guidance, but Britain's experience with productivity slowdown around the turn of the century appears to be consistent with a sharp retardation, if not reversal, in the rate of unskilled-labor saving (Floud and McCloskey, 1981, Vol. 2, Chaps. 1 and 5). But America offers the most complete evidence by far. for the economy as a whole, each of several studies has found a strong aggregate labor-saving bias from about the start of this century to 1929, followed by a switch to either neutrality or a labor-using bias up to the Korean War. There was considerable debate in the 1960s as to whether a strong labor-saving bias had in fact resumed in the postwar period (David and van de Klunder, 1965; Brown, 1966, Chap. 10; Morishima and Saito, 1968). None of these studies actually distinguished between unskilled and skilled labor, making inferences about the distribution of income somewhat difficult, but it may be surmised that any era of labor saving was likely to have been especially unskilled-labor saving.

The econometric literature from the 1960s thus suggests that the equalization of incomes in America following 1929 may have been due to a switch in the bias of aggregate technological progress from unskilled-labor saving patterns.

However, we must take care to identify the truly *exogenous* role of technological progress, and not be content with measures of aggregate unskilled-labor saving alone. An aggregate labor-saving bias can be decomposed into the following four components:

(i) an aggregate bias due to *endogenous* labor-saving within industries induced by a rise in labor's relative scarcity;

(ii) an aggregate bias due to *endogenous* shifts in industrial activity, in response to shifts in the structure of product demand or factor-supply forces;

(iii) an aggregate bias due to *exogenous* differences in the rate of neutral technological advance between industries with different labor intensities; and

(iv) an aggregate bias due to the introduction of labor-saving technologies within industries, independent of labor scarcities and thus *exogenous*.

The first source of labor saving is not a source at all, but simply a response to relative factor scarcities. That is, an apparent bias towards labor saving that is simply a response to rising labor scarcities induced by long-run development can hardly be counted as an exogenous technological force driving wage rates and other factor incomes. On the contrary, this kind of labor saving is no more than conventional factor substitution which serves to minimize any leveling in earnings and income which the initial labor scarcity generated in the first place.

The second source might appear more promising. Development economists agree that changes in output mix have been a critical determinant of aggregate labor saving and rising inequality in the Third World since 1950 (Morawetz, 1974; Cline, 1975). While numerically important, this second source of aggregate labor saving may, nevertheless, fail to offer an independent explanation of the Kuznets Curve. The expansion of manufacturing at agriculture's expense may look like aggregate unskilled-labor saving technological change, since the favored sector uses unskilled labor far less intensively than does agriculture, but we must dig deeper for causes.

This point deserves stress. it is certainly true that one of the documented "stylized facts of development" is the nonlinear shift in output and employment mix as economies undergo long-run development from an agrarian base to advanced industrialization (Chenery and Syrquin, 1975; Morris and Adelman, 1980). Thus, the rate at which agriculture declines as a share of aggregate output or employment begins slowly, then quickens, reaches a peak as the Industrial Revolution hits full stride, and then drops off as the transformation is completed at late stages of development. To the extent that agriculture is relatively unskilled-labor intensive, high adn rising aggregate unskilled-labor saving early in the Industrial Revolution should be followed by a fall in the rate of aggregate unskilled-labor saving late in the development process. If these derived labor demand forces are strong enough, the Kuznets Curve is assured.

Convenient and elegant, this explanation does not go quite far enough. Unbalanced output growth such as this cannot be viewed as an exogenous force driving inequality across the Kuznets Curve if endogenous domestic demand forces—like Engel Effects—account for it. How much of the spectacular shift in output mix in the Third World can be explained by the rapid rate of technological progress outside of unskilled-labor intensive agriculture? How much of the shift can be explained by import substitution policies which favor capital/skill-intensive activities, and how much by favorable world market conditions? How much of it is due to changes in the structure of domestic demand, as households respond to higher incomes? These are important questions, and we need answers. The key point here is simply that the sectoral shift itself is not an independent influence on inequality unless it can be shown that it comes from exogenous forces, like policies, world markets, and what we shall call (below) unbalanced productivity advance.

What do we know about the third and fourth forces listed above? Labor saving at the industry level—item (iv) above—has frequently been estimated in the econometric production-function literature. The results

century. In contrast with British experience between 1820 and 1850, the American investment rate increased by two and a half times. However, the correlation between inequality and the investment rate turns out to be mostly spurious (Williamson, 1979).

References

Adelman, Irma, and Sherman Robinson. 1978. *Income Distribution Policy in Developing Countries: A Case Study of Korea.* Stanford, Calif.: Stanford University Press.

Ashton, T. S. 1955. *An Economic History of England: The 18th Century.* London: Methuen.

———. 1959. *Economic Fluctuations in England, 1700–1800.* Oxford: The Clarendon Press.

Clapham, John H. 1926. *An Economic History of Modern Britain.* Cambridge, England: Cambridge University Press.

Deane, Phyllis, and W. A. Cole. 1962. *British Economic Growth, 1688–1959.* Cambridge, England: Cambridge University Press.

Dervis, Kemal, Jaime de Melo, and Sherman Robinson. 1982. *General Equilibrium Models for Development Policy.* Cambridge, England: Cambridge University Press.

Dixit, Avinash. 1973. "Models of dual economies," in *Models of Economic Growth*, ed. James A. Mirrlees and Nicholas H. Stern. New York: Wiley.

Engels, Friedrich. 1845. *The Condition of the Working Class in England.* Translated from the German edition with an introduction by E. J. Hobsbawm. St. Albans, Herts.: Panther, 1974.

Fei, John C. H., and Gustav Ranis. 1964. *Development of the Labor Surplus Economy: Theory and Policy.* Homewood, Ill.: Richard D. Irwin.

Feinstein, Charles. 1978. "Capital formation in Great Britain," in *The Cambridge Economic History of Europe: Volume VII: The Industrial Economies: Capital, Labour, and Enterprise*, ed. Peter Mathias and Michael Postan. Cambridge, England: Cambridge University Press.

Hammond, J. L. 1930. "The industrial revolution and discontent," *Economic History Review*, 1st series, no. 2: 215–228.

Harley, C. Knick. 1982. "British industrialization before 1841: Evidence of slower growth during the industrial revolution," *Journal of Economic History* 42 (June): 267–289.

Hartwell, R. M. 1959. "Interpretations of the industrial revolution in England: A methodological inquiry," *Journal of Economic History*, no. 19: 229–249.

———. 1961. "The rising standard of living in England, 1800–1850," *Economic History Review*, 2nd series, no. 13 (April): 397–416.

Hobsbawm, Eric J. 1957. "The British standard of living, 1790–1850," *Economic History Review*, 2nd series, no. 10 (August): 46–68.

Hueckle, Glenn. 1973. "War and the British economy, 1793–1815: A general equilibrium analysis," *Explorations in Economic History* 10 (Summer): 365–396.

International Bank for Reconstruction and Development. 1980. *World Tables*, 2nd ed. Baltimore: Johns Hopkins University Press.

James, John A. 1984. "The use of general equilibrium analysis in economic history," *Explorations in Economic History* 21 (July): 231–253.

Jorgenson, Dale W. 1961. "The development of a dual economy," *Economic Journal*, no. 71 (June): 309–334.

Kelley, Allen C., Jeffrey G. Williamson, and Russell J. Cheetham. 1972. *Dualistic Economic Development: Theory and History.* Chicago: University of Chicago Press.

———, and Jeffrey G. Williamson. 1974. *Lessons from Japanese Development: An Analytical History.* Chicago: University of Chicago Press.

———, and Jeffrey G. Williamson. 1984a. *What Drives Third World City Growth? A Dynamic General Equilibrium Approach.* Princeton, N.J.: Princeton University Press.

are too scattered and miscellaneous to cite here. Suffice it to say that nothing in them establishes any historic pattern, Kuznetsian or otherwise. A more rewarding path is to follow the literature on technological imbalance between sectors, item (iii) above.

An extensive literature has sketched the sectoral patterns of total factor productivity growth over the last 150 years in the United States. While the estimates require the usual caveats about possible mismeasurement, they leave strong suggestions. The secular movements do trace out a 19th-century drift toward labor-sparing sectors, largely because productivity advance was rapid in capital/skill-intensive manufacturing and transportation while large and labor-intensive agriculture lagged far behind (see the literature surveyed in Williamson and Lindert, 1980, Chap. 7). Early in this century the same labor-saving imbalance between sectors continued up to World War I and across the 1920s (Kendrick, 1961; Keller, 1973; Williamson, 1976). From 1929 to about 1953 the sectoral pattern was much more balanced. In particular, agriculture caught up with the rest of the economy in its rate of productivity growth and its capital intensity (Kendrick, 1961, 1973). An imbalance favoring labor-spring sectors tended to reemerge in the early postwar period, but the more recent energy shock and subsequent slowdown have again brought balanced productivity advance, perhaps because energy-capital complementarity has dampened productivity advance in the capital-intensive sectors (Gollop and Jorgenson, 1980; Berndt and Wood, 1975; Hoffman and Jorgenson, 1977; Nadiri, 1980; Pindyck and Rotemberg, 1983). The rise and fall in the rate of labor-saving associated with unbalanced productivity growth seems to match the timing of the Kuznets Curve for the United States.

A similar pattern may have characterized British experience. In the Industrial Revolution era 1780–1860, technological progress was very unbalanced in favor of the capital/skills-intensive sectors, shifting factor demand away from unskilled labor (Floud and McCloskey, 1981, Vol. 1, Chap. 6). Since 1860, the sectoral pattern of British productivity advance has been more balanced in its factor-demand effects (Matthews *et al.*, 1982, pp. 222–229). Again agriculture switched from a large, unskilled-labor-intensive sector with relatively slow productivity change to a small sector with average capital intensity and productivity performance. Here again, the timing of the switch to more balanced productivity growth coincided with a historic peak in the Kuznets Curve.

The sectoral patterns of total factor productivity growth are intriguing, both in their own right and for their correspondence with trends in income distribution. Should we expect to find an early rise and later abatement of the labor-saving bias implied by sectoral productivity growth in other countries? Would their data also show agriculture evolving over time from a lagging sector to a dynamic modern sector? Or should such a pattern be expected only in countries that in fact pass through a Kuznets Curve?[2] This subject is ripe for further historical research. Here we can note only that American and British experience underlines the possible causal role of imbalance in the rates of total factor productivity advance across sectors. If product demands are elastic,[3] technological imbalance can be a prime source of secular inequality trends.

D. Demographic Change and Labor Supply

It has become commonplace in the historical literature to associate demographic transition with labor surplus and inequality. The argument develops along the following lines: modern economic growth begins on a traditional agrarian base characterized by elastic labor supplies, better known as "surplus" unskilled labor. Accelerating rates of capital accumulation associated with early industrialization thus fail to generate rising real wages among the unskilled until the surplus labor pool is exhausted. This turning point can be postponed for some time if demographic forces are right and Malthusian population pressures or immigration continually replenish the initial pool whether in contemporary Asia (Fei and Ranis, 1964), in Japan since the 1880s, (Minami, 1973), in America before World War I (Lindert, 1978, Chap. 7; Williamson, 1982), or even in early postwar Europe (Kindleberger, 1967). Under such conditions stable real wages for the unskilled could coincide with rising per capita incomes, tending to create more inequality.

This classical model of capitalist growth was built by British economists surrounded by the poverty and pauperism of early 19th-century Britain. W. Arthur Lewis (1954) carried the classical labor surplus model into the 20th century. Although the model has had its critics, it has become the dominant paradigm used by Third World observers to analyze exactly the same set of problems which attracted the British classical economists. The application of the labor surplus model to Britain was encouraged in part by the forces of demographic transition there: primarily increases in fertility (Wrigley and Schofield, 1981, Chap. 7), but also improvements in infant mortality and Irish immigration into England's industrial North.

[2] What little is known about her sectoral productivity advance seems to make Japan an exception which confirms the rule. There is no clear drift in the rate of labor-saving implied by the intersectoral pattern of Japanese productivity advance. See Ohkawa and Rosovsky (1973, pp. 73, 110, 264). Japan also avoided the Kuznets Curve. Thus, Japan's economic history supports the correlation between technological imbalance and inequality, since neither appeared in Japan's long-run experience.

[3] If product demands are inelastic, it is theoretically possible for neutral productivity advance in the capital/skills-intensive sectors to depress the returns on capital and skills and raise the unskilled wage rate, by shifting the terms of trade against those sectors. We ignore this possibility in the text since it is not likely to occur. Product demand elasticities should be high enough for the arguments in the text to hold, especially in very open economies.

The model seems even more pertinent to the Third World after World War II, where population growth has been more than twice as fast as in 19th-century Britain. The rise in fertility and the fall in infant mortality in the Third World have served first to raise the dependency rate (Coale and Hoover, 1958; Leff, 1969), while later tending to glut labor markets with impecunious and unskilled new entrants. Such massive changes in the age distribution can create inequality even if factor prices are unaffected, as Simon Kuznets and others have noted (Kuznets, 1976, 1979; Morley, 1981).

Theory favors the argument that higher fertility and immigration should indeed lower wages, raise returns to capital, and foster income inequality. Since fertility increases subsequently produce an expansion of the labor force at young ages, the wage rate for unskilled labor (new, young entrants) should undergo an especially large decline, thus raising skill premia and earnings inequality as well. What is true for previous fertility increases will be even more true for current immigrations, if young unskilled males dominate the immigrants, just as they did in the century between the 1820s and the 1920s. If it can be shown that immigration and fertility are both primarily exogenous forces in American development—rather than simply an endogenous response to rising real wages—then we have an influence on inequality which certainly warrants careful attention.[4]

The American immigration–inequality literature has relied largely on raw correlations between inequality and labor supply. The correlations are not hard to document. For example, the period of highest labor force growth, from 1820 to 1860, was also one of rising skill premiums and sharply rising wage inequality, while the period of lowest labor force growth, 1929 to 1948, was one of dramatic leveling in earnings and total income. The intervening observations reveal a fairly tight positive correlation as well. In terms of immigrations, new arrivals from abroad had their biggest impact on the growth of the American labor force in 1846–1855, and between the turn of the century and World War I. These two periods of peak influx were also ones in which immigrants seemed to have had the lowest skills relative to the indigenous labor force. The migrants in the 1840s and 1850s were coming from countries with per capita incomes quite a bit lower than those found in America. This was also true after 1890, when again the flood began to feature people from the lower-income countries, this time largely from southern and eastern Europe. Immigrants from much lower-income countries continued to

[4] On the long run dominance of "push" forces in governing the rate of U.S. immigration in the 19th century, and thus the exogeneity of labor-supply growth, see Easterlin (1961), Williamson (1974, Chap. 1; 1982), and Neal (1976). American "pull" forces were more visible in the short and medium term. The state of the labor market dominated the timing of immigration over the U.S. business cycle and long swing. See Kuznets (1958) and Easterlin (1968).

dominate after World War I, but after the mid-1920s and the imposition of immigrant restrictions, the flows became such a low share of the American labor force that they were unlikely to have suppressed average skills growth by much. As a result, the rate of skills deepening accelerated after 1929 (Lindert, 1978, Chaps. 6 and 7). Things seem to have changed in recent decades as immigrations, this time from Latin America, have tended to raise unskilled labor force growth rates once more (Easterlin, 1980b, pp. 301–305).

Thus the history of pay and the history of the rate and quality of labor-force expansion correlate remarkably well in American experience. The widespread belief in a causal link from labor supply to income inequality has been strengthened, though further tests are in order.

E. Human Capital Accumulation and Skills Deepening

As early as 1848, John Stuart Mill predicted that industrialization would eventually match its own bias toward skills scarcity with a faster diffusion of the same skills:

> The general relaxation of barriers, and the increased facilities of education which are already . . . within the reach of all, tend to . . . bring down the wages of skilled labor (Mill, 1848, II, xiv, p. 2).

But it wasn't until the 1960s that economists systematically quantified human capital formation, led by Gary Becker (1962, 1964) and Theodore Schultz (1961, 1963). Since then, there has been a veritable flood of empirical work documenting trends in labor force quality, most of which have dealt with 20th-century trends (Denison, 1962, 1967, 1974; Denison and Chung, 1976; Christensen et al., 1978; Gollop and Jorgenson, 1980). Recently, similar estimates have been constructed for both 19th century America (Williamson and Lindert, 1980, Chaps. 9 and 10, Appendix J) and Britain (Williamson, 1985, Chap. 7).

These estimates suggest that the rate of skills deepening (the rise in skills per member of the labor force) correlates well with skills scarcity and earnings inequality. The rate of skills deepening was exceedingly low in Britain during her early period of rising wage inequality; the pace quickened around the mid-19th century, about a decade after Mills observation; and the rate of skills deepening reached impressive levels in the era following the educational reforms of the 1870s, coinciding with the first drop down Britain's Kuznets Curve. The American correlation looks similar, though the turning points come later, well into the 20th century, both for the rate of skills deepening and for the leveling of incomes. While the underlying estimates are necessarily crude, they do seem to suggest a slow equilibrating process, whereby one generation's skilled-wage gap promotes the next generation's faster accumulation of skills.

Thus far we have kept the accumulation of nonhuman capital waiting in the wings, not because it is unimportant but because its link with inequality is so complicated. It now enters center stage, first as a proximate source of inequality and then as a possible consequence of inequality.

III. BEHIND ACCUMULATION

A. *The Distributional Effects of Capital Deepening*

The income distributional effects of shifts in the supply of capital must be assessed with special care, both in theory and in empirical analysis. To do the issue justice, one must start with at least three factors of production, not just the conventional capital and labor: unskilled labor (earning a wage rate w_u), skilled labor (earning a wage rate w_s), and nonhuman capital (earning a rental rate R).

If our view of inequality could be confined to movements in the earnings distribution and the skilled-wage ratio w_s/w_u, it would be a simple matter to predict the effects of more capital. Since capital tends to be complementary with skills and a substitute for unskilled labor (Griliches, 1969; Berndt and Christensen, 1974; Fallon and Layard, 1975), a rise in the supply of capital should raise w_s/w_u and earnings inequality. Furthermore, a rise in the supply of capital implies a shift in the output mix favoring capital goods. Since the capital goods sector tends to use skilled labor intensively (Williamson and Lindert, 1980, pp. 194, 197), the demand for skills is driven up and we have another force tending to raise w_s/w_u and earnings inequality.

However, theoretical prediction is a lot easier than empirical testing since *ceteris paribus* rarely holds in history. Not all capital deepening was exogenous to the process determining the distribution of income; and any effect hinging on the gap between two substitution elasticities (capital/skills and capital/unskilled labor) may have been small in any case. Accordingly, not all historical experiences reveal a raw correlation between the rate of capital-deepening and trends in w_s/w_u. The correlation emerges from American experience since both variables accelerate across the middle of the 19th century and decelerate across the middle of the 20th. But for the United Kingdom, there is no clear correlation across the last two centuries (on the rates of capital deepening in the U.K., see Feinstein, 1978; Matthews, *et al.*, 1982, pp. 77, 501).

And the impact of capital supply on inequality becomes more difficult to identify when we move from the earnings distribution to overall income inequality. Suppose an outward shift in the supply of savings, due to a rise in thrift, creates capital deepening. The augmented supply of capital will raise w_s/w_u for the reasons already offered, but it is also likely to depress R, and r, the return to equity. Capital's relative return is eroded while earnings inequality is augmented. Thus, extra savings have an ambiguous impact on overall inequality. Suppose instead that the source of the capital deepening is an improvement in capital goods supply revealed by a decline in the relative price of capital goods, P_K. In this case, the impact on overall inequality is unambiguous. Not only should wage widening take place (a rise in w_s/w_u), but r should rise as well, both absolutely and relative to the unskilled wage rate (w_u). This latter prediction, however, still awaits a clear historical test. If we focus only on periods where the relative price of capital goods declined, we do indeed find income inequality on the rise. Capital cheapening was accompanied by rising inequality in mid-19th century America, although w_s/w_u did not rise when capital goods cheapened across the Civil War era and again across the 1890s (Gallman, 1966, pp. 26, 34). Inequality obligingly fell on two occasions when the relative price of capital goods clearly rose: in the United States from 1929 to 1948 (Gordon, 1961; U.S. Dept. of Commerce, 1975, pp. 229–331) and in the United Kingdom from 1938 to 1948 (Matthews, *et al.*, 1982, pp. 586–588).

The link between capital supply and income inequality is complex, and the source of the augmented capital supply is important to any understanding of the relationship.

B. Redistribution and the Supply of Saving

Support for the growth and equality trade-off has always rested on the belief that redistribution from the poor to the rich augments the supply of private saving and thus raises the rate of accumulation. This belief was central to 19th-century models of growth and distribution developed by British classical economists to explain the Industrial Revolution. It is also central to recent debates over productivity slowdown in the most advanced countries.

Changes in the distribution of income have long been thought to change saving through three channels: (1) Kaldorian redistribution toward high-saving classes, (2) fiscal policies shifting the saving function for any given rate of return, and (3) the saving disincentives of taxation on capital income.

The first channel is governed by marginal propensities to save (mps). Any force redistributing income may raise aggregate saving and accumulation if those benefitting have higher mps's than the rest of society. Since higher income classes were always thought to have higher mps's, as in Kaldor's famous model, it seemed natural to conclude that any redistribution toward the rich would raise saving and capital formation. This argument should apply equally to 18th- or 19th-century redistributions through market forces and to 20th-century redistributions through government fiscal action.

The second and third channels have been explored more in the 20th century, when redistribution has been more frequently initiated by government fiscal action. The expansion of taxation and government expenditure clearly contributed to the egalitarian trend within this century, especially in the industrialized countries since World War II. Many economists suspect that the fiscal redistribution has retarded capital formation and productivity growth. Others argue that egalitarian social insurance programs have reduced the flow of conventional saving to productive investment. Still others insist that capital income taxation has discouraged aggregate private saving. None of these arguments turns out to be very persuasive.

1. Kaldorian redistribution. While intuitively plausible and a staple in political economy since Adam Smith, pure Kaldorian redistribution from low to high savers appears in fact to have little quantitative impact on the aggregate saving rate. So say studies on aggregate United States data (Husby, 1971; Blinder, 1975), on Latin American data (Cline, 1972, Chap. 4), and from international cross-sections (Della Valle and Ogushi, 1976; Musgrove, 1980). Rough calculations for 19th-century America agree (Williamson, 1979; Williamson and Lindert, 1980, Chap. 12). Such results should come as no surprise. After all, the increased saving as a percentage of national income is the product of two small fractions: the share of national income that can be taken from the poor and the difference between class mps's. The resulting percentage increases in the saving rate are too small to suggest much trade-off between equality and accumulation.

2. The impact of saving supply shifts on accumulation. Even those redistributions that have a large effect on the supply of saving may have only a limited impact on capital formation. This impact is more limited the more elastic is saving, and the more inelastic is investment, with respect to the rate of return.

To illustrate the key dependence of any capital-formation effects on these elasticities, consider the simplest (flow or stock) model of the interaction between saving, investment and the rate of return. Let the pretax rate of return, R, govern equilibrium in the following way:

$$I = I_0 R^\varepsilon$$

$$S = S_0 (R/T)^\eta \text{ and } I = S, \text{ where}$$

I = capital formation, S = saving flow, null subscripts denote exogenous shift terms, and $\varepsilon \leqslant 0$ and $\eta \geqslant 0$ are elasticities. The tax multiple is denoted by $T = 1/(1 - \text{tax rate on savings})$, so that saving is written as a function of the after-tax rate of return, R/T. Using lower-case letters to denote percentage rates of change, we can derive

$$i = s = \frac{\varepsilon s_0 - \eta (i_0 + \varepsilon t)}{\varepsilon - \eta}, \text{ so that}$$

$$\frac{di}{dt} = \frac{-\eta \varepsilon}{\varepsilon - \eta} \leqslant 0,$$

$$\frac{di}{ds} = \frac{\varepsilon}{\varepsilon - \eta} \geq 0,$$

$$\frac{di}{di_o} = \frac{-\eta}{\varepsilon - \eta} \geq 0.$$

The derivatives tell us which elasticities are central to which issues and why. Consider *shifts* in the saving function, ds_o, and their impact on the capital formation share, di. The saving elasticity (η) matters. The more elastic is the saving response to after-tax returns, the less important is *any* horizontal shift in the saving function (i.e., higher η implies lower di/ds_o). So the more elastic is the saving response to the rate of return, the less important are all those saving-supply-driven forces which receive so much attention in the literature, such as social security, Kaldorian redistribution, demographic change (through the dependency effect: Leff, 1969; Lewis, 1983), and the like. What do we know about η? Our quantitative impressions about the elasticity of domestic saving with respect to the after-tax rate of return are generally higher now than they were even a decade ago, either for 20th century America (von Furstenberg and Malkiel, 1977; Boskin, 1978), or for 19th century Britain (Edelstein, 1977; 1982, Chap. 8). And if *domestic* saving is responsive to the rate of return, *total* saving will be even more so in a world of international capital markets.

The expression for (di/di_o) also shows that the more elastic is saving behavior, the more important is the investment-demand side. This point deserves stress. It may seem easier to explain capital formation from the saving-supply side, given the well-developed literature on consumption functions and the life-cycle hypothesis. But the approach depends critically on the assumptions that the saving supply function is inelastic and that the investment demand function is elastic. The direct link between shifts in the saving function and capital accumulation is seriously weakened in those historical circumstances where these assumptions were violated.

This simple model is also relevant to a heated contemporary debate. The recent supply-side wave in America has seen a resurgence of the view that a reduction in the taxation of capital incomes would yield large welfare gains, especially if it were to yield large increases in saving and investment (von Furstenberg and Malkiel, 1977; Feldstein, 1977a, 1978a; Boskin, 1978; Howrey and Hymans, 1978; Summers, 1981; Evans, 1983). While there is merit to the point that the decision to save is distorted by the presence of capital-income taxation, this position does not necessarily support the growth-equality trade-off view. After all, the estimates of large welfare losses from capital income taxation reported in the literature (Boskin, 1978; Summers, 1981) depend critically on the elasticities of saving and investment with respect to rates of return. We can see this clearly in the expression di/dt above. The key role which these elasticities play has been masked in the recent literature by the fact that Feldstein's welfare formula implicitly assumes that the pretax rate of return (the ρ in Feldstein, 1978a, p. S34; used also in Baskin, 1978, p. S19) is unaffected by taxation. This implies that investment demand is infinitely elastic, an assumption that is at odds with any theoretical or empirical literature. If a downward sloping investment demand schedule is assumed instead, then the rightward shift in the savings schedule would induce some fall in the rate of return, and only a fraction of the previous tax burden on savers' capital returns would end up as an addition to their after-tax return. Once again, the case for emphasizing saving–supply shifts is undercut by the elasticity of saving itself.

In our view, the impact of fiscal redistributions on saving and capital formation cannot be assessed in the absence of evidence on the most elusive elasticity of all, the response of investment to the rate of return (ε). Everything hinges on that Achilles heel of macroeconomics, the investment function.

C. Competing Assets and Portfolios

The direct link between redistribution, domestic private saving, and conventional capital formation is further weakened by the availability of competing forms of wealth. The motivation for extra saving can be served equally well by accumulating government debt, foreign debt, irreproducible assets (e.g. land, antiques), slaves (Ransom and Sutch, 1982), and property rights (e.g., restrictive licenses), as well as by capital gains on any of these. The larger and more elastic are these alternative asset supplies, the stronger are the points just made in the previous section, since conventional domestic capital formation will depend less on shifts in the supply of domestic private saving, and more on investment demand.

Of these competing assets, the supply of net foreign debt is likely to be most elastic. The more open a nation becomes to international capital flows, the less relevant is the supply of domestic saving to the rate of capital formation. If a nation is a price taker in international financial markets and faces no credit rationing, then domestic capital formation is determined solely by investment demand at home. Capital formation is determined on the production side in such cases, and domestic saving is irrelevant. As national financial markets become more open, the more crucial are good estimates of the true elasticity of net foreign investment to domestic rates of return.

Investment in land adds another surprising twist to the question of how fiscal redistribution affects private saving and accumulation. Taxing land site rents can easily *raise* the rate of accumulation, in addition to being efficient and egalitarian. If one believes that different kinds of wealth compete for shares of household portfolios tied to desired wealth-income ratios, as in the life-cycle and permanent-income models, then it seems clear that taxes on pure site rents would induce households to accumulate more claims on reproducible capital (Feldstein, 1977; Lindert, 1983). The revenues could be used to reduce other taxes falling on capital formation, yielding the sought-after efficiency gains emphasized by Boskin, Summers and others. The relevance of site taxation for the larger growth-equality debate is especially clear in countries where landownership is concentrated among families with the highest incomes and net worth. Although they were never tried in Henry George's time, equality could be promoted by efficient site taxes of the sorts that have proved workable in more recent years (Bahl, 1979).

Recent history suggests that the amount of saving that might be shifted from the pursuit of capital gains on site ownership into conventional accumulation is large. Through much of the postwar era real capital gains on land sites in Britain and America yielded a respectable *ex post* rate of return and a significant percentage of national product (Colin Clark, 1965; Lindert, 1974). Real capital gains on land sites have been very large in postwar Japan, running at 16% per annum between 1955 and 1974. These capital gains added 60% to GNP around 1955, and 27% around 1972 (Mills and Ohta, 1976, pp. 697–705). Even more spectacular examples can be found in Third World experience since the late 1950s (Mills and Song, 1977; Kelley and Williamson, 1984, Chaps. 2,3).

While there are notable exceptions (Nichols, 1970), why has so little been written about the possible impact of capital gains in land on ac-cumulation in other forms? Certainly there are some historical examples which support the link between trends in land values and accumulation in competing assets. For example, did the invasion of New World grains in late 19th century Britain induce some portion of the massive capital outflow between 1880 and 1914? One would think so if the decline in grain prices created significant capital losses on farmland held by the English rich.

D. Summary

This section of our survey has urged that the links between inequality and accumulation are weak in both causal directions. First, accumulation is unlikely to have a strong impact on income inequality, except in cases where the underlying source of change is an exogenous shift in the supply of capital goods. Shifts in the supply of saving do not have clear inequality consequences. Second, egalitarian redistributions short of wholesale con-fiscation are not likely to lower capital formation very much. They have little effect through Kaldorian differences in class marginal propensities to save. Even a large shift in saving has its impact on capital formation dampened by elasticities and the availability of competing assets. In the case of egalitarian taxation on site rents concentrated into high-income hands, there are even good reasons to believe that capital formation could be enhanced.

IV. UNDERSTANDING INEQUALITY TRENDS: PUTTING THE PARTS TOGETHER

A. *Accounting for Inequality Trends*

Thus far, we have followed Montek Ahluwalia's (1976, p. 307) advice in pursuing the growth-equality issue: "Ideally, such processes should be examined in an explicitly historical context for particular countries." We shall continue to follow his advice, drawing on long-run macroeconomic models to quantify the determinants of income distribution trends. The exercise is hardly trivial, however. Any such model must be complex, but some simplification can be achieved by eliminating some contending explanations right at the start.

We begin by setting aside two contenders that lack good *prima facie* historical support: unionization and inflation. Unionization can affect the income distribution in obvious ways, and Freeman has plausibly argued that it could have contributed to the American leveling in this century (Freeman, 1980). But the Kuznets Curve in America and Britain transcends the possible impact of unions (Hildebrand and Delahanty, 1966; Evans 1971; Williamson and Lindert, 1980, pp. 139–140). In particular, the onset of earnings equalization in Britain in the late 19th century clearly antedated any union influence on behalf of more equal pay scales. A correlation between leveling and inflation is also absent from historical time series, despite individual episodes where the link might have held. While the literature on inflation in America's Civil War and Britain's French Wars has favored a wage-lag-and-profit-inflation view (Mitchell, 1903, 1908; DeCanio and Mokyr, 1977; Mokyr and Savin, 1976) both wars induced a modest wage leveling which may have offset any (still-unmeasured) inegalitarian trends induced by a rising profit share. And the two World Wars brought dramatic leveling by an measure, enough to encourage the view that wartime inflations leveled incomes. By contrast, the post-OPEC inflation has not been accompanied by any egalitarian trend. The variety can doubtless be explained by the source of these inflations. The point remains, however, that inflation cannot be viewed as a proximate force driving income distributions, especially over longer periods where the temporary effects of unexpected inflation has had plenty of time to dissipate.

Our view of inequality history, particularly in Britain and America, leads us to concentrate on basic trends in factor demands and supplies (see also Freeman, 1979; Tinbergen, 1975). To quantify these influences, we favor the use of computable general equilibrium (CGE) models. A multisector and multifactor CGE model is especially useful for analysis of the long run, where neoclassical assumptions do least damage to the macroeconomic facts, and where the determinants of output mix, input use, and factor incomes are the prime focus. It has become a familiar tool in modern public finance (Shoven and Whalley, 1972, 1974, 1984;

Fullerton *et al.*, 1981), where tax incidence and other income distribution issues have been addressed. CGEs have been used at least as often in the development literature to assess industrialization, trade, urbanization, and distribution issues (Kelley *et al.*, 1972; Adelman and Robinson, 1978; Dervis *et al.*, 1982; Kelley and Williamson, 1984). CGE models have an equally long tradition in economic history, although the cliometrician usually deals with models containing less detail, given that data constraints often dictate parsimonious modeling.[5] More to the point, CGEs have been used to quantify the sources of the American (Williamson, 1976; Williamson and Lindert, 1980, Chaps. 10–11) and British (Williamson, 1985) Kuznets Curves.

When these CGE models are applied to American and British inequality history, what do we find?

B. American Experience

The past. The surge in wage inequality before the Civil War seems to have been due primarily to the extraordinary rates of capital accumulation obtained during those decades. Rapid accumulation favored skilled and high-wage workers in two ways. First, a greater proportion of unskilled labor (a substitute for capital) than skilled labor (a complement to capital) was replaced by mechanization. Second, accumulation helped raise income per capita, and this rise, through Engel's Law, caused agriculture to contract as a share in national income, a process that released more unskilled than skilled labor. Unbalanced technological progress centered on manufacturing also favored the expansion of the more capital-cum-skill-using sectors, thus reinforcing the rise in earnings inequality.

What, then, explains the high and rising rate of antebellum capital accumulation? Contrary to the so-called "classical" saving and accumulation model, rising inequality seems to have contributed little. Rather, most of this accumulation experience can be explained by the sectoral imbalance of antebellum technological progress and rapid labor force growth on the investment demand side (Williamson and Lindert, 1980, Chap. 12; Williamson, 1979), and demographic-life-cycle forces on the saving supply side (Lewis, 1983). Rapid labor force growth raised in-

[5] Following the early suggestions of Ronald Jones (1965), economic historians have used CGEs to assess the impact of U.S. tariffs on antebellum income distribution and regional conflict (Pope, 1972; James, 1978, 1981), American federal land policy and the congressional slave debates (Passell and Wright, 1972; Kotlikoff and Pinera, 1977; Schmitz and Schaefer, 1981), the railroads and American growth (Williamson, 1974, Chap. 9), American land scarcity and immigration (Lindert, 1974; Williamson, 1974, Chap. 11 and 1982), Anglo-American differences in the choice of technique (Temin, 1966; Fogel, 1967; Clarke and Summers, 1980), the British standard of living debate (von Tunzlemann, 1982; Williamson, 1984), the sources of slow British growth during the industrial revolution (Williamson, 1984, 1985, Chap. 11), the distributional impact of the French Wars in Britain (Hueckel, 1973), and many others. For a survey, see James (1984).

vestment demand in conventional growth-theoretic ways, although the long-swing literature of the 1950s and 1960s preferred to call it a "population-sensitive investment response" (Kuznets, 1958; Abramovitz, 1961). Unbalanced technological progress raised investment demand, and thus the rate of accumulation, in two ways. First, total factor productivity growth was particularly rapid in those sectors supplying producers' equipment. This served to cut the (quality-adjusted) supply price of producer durables, encouraging the purchase of more equipment out of the same stream of income. Second, total factor productivity growth was also biased toward those sectors which tended to be capital-cum-skill intensive. As these sectors enjoyed relative expansion, the demands for capital and skills were both raised economy wide, checking part of the supply-induced decline in the relative price of capital goods, further raising capital accumulation rates, and buoying up still further the premium on skills and earnings inequality. It thus appears that the explanation of the 19th-century rise in wage inequality owes quite a bit to technological imbalance, much of this influence being transmitted through the rate of capital accumulation.

In the late 19th century, capital accumulation became a bit less rapid, and productivity growth a bit less unbalanced. These changes explain about half of the observed shift from sharply rising wage inequality on the upswing of the Kuznets Curve, to relative stability in the inequality trends along the Kuznets Curve's high plateau. Demographic events explain much of the remainder. Skills per man-hour appear to have grown significantly in the late 19th century after having remained stable for much of the antebellum period. The apparent "cause" of this acceleration was the decline in the share of the labor force consisting of unskilled immigrants: the resulting rise in the rate of skills deepening helped prevent a continuation of the surge in earnings inequality started earlier in the century.

The first decade of this century brought a resumption in wage stretching. This time, however, the rising trend owed nothing to capital accumulation or to demographic shifts. Rather, the explanation for the return to widening gaps seems to rest on a resumption of the more unbalanced technological progress, centered in skill-intensive utilities and some service sectors.

Across the 1910s and 1920s, earnings inequality first compressed during the war and then bounced right back in the immediate postwar period, leaving no net change. There are two interesting attributes of this net stability over the two decades as a whole. First, sectoral capital intensities converged. As a result, rapid capital accumulation after 1909 came to mean accumulation of a factor widely spread across all sectors rather than one concentrated in relatively skill-intensive sectors. It turns out that this "convergence-in-factor-intensity" helps in understanding much about U.S. 20th-century experience with structural change. Second, if the only kind of growth from 1909 to 1929 had been growth in factor supplies, the era of income leveling would have been ushered in two decades earlier. This would have happened since immigration and fertility were making smaller contributions to labor force growth, especially during World War I and after the immigration restrictions took effect in 1924–1925. The slower labor force growth and faster growth in skills per worker tended to depress the pay advantage of the more skilled. But in fact there was no net compression in the pay structure. Why? The answer will sit well with most historians of the Roaring Twenties: the 1909–1929 era was again one of very unbalanced technological progress, this time centered on autos, tires, consumer appliances, petrochemicals, and electric utilities. The locus of faster total factor productivity growth was close enough to the locus of skill intensity to create disproportionately heavy demands for skills. This offset the leveling effect of the demographic forces, and net stability in earnings inequality resulted.

When the downswing of the American Kuznets Curve finally arrived following 1929, it was largely the result of a synchronization between technological and demographic forces. Total factor productivity growth was more evenly balanced across sectors than in any other era since 1840, accelerating in agriculture and some services. This change seems to have accounted for about half of the observed wage leveling between 1929 and 1948. Most of the remainder is explained by demographic forces: by having fewer babies and by shutting out potential immigrants from the Old World, America achieved a "revolutionary" (Burns, 1954) distribution leveling between 1929 and the post-World War II era. If the rise of government played a role in contributing to the "revolutionary" leveling, it did so only in indirect ways—contributing to skills deepening and more balanced productivity growth in the private sector. Government's *direct* impact via long-run changes in the structure of final demand cannot have been great. That is, while government purchases were somewhat more unskilled-labor intensive than private purchases in 1963, as we noted above, this "pro-poor government bias" ends up making only a small contribution in the CGE accounting.

Why did the "income revolution" cease around the Korean War years? Why has the *pre-fisc* income distribution remained so stable since (Blinder, 1980)? First, there was the impressive acceleration in the growth of skills, due primarily to changes in the age–sex distribution of the labor force. The rise of women of ages 35–64 in the labor force tended to glut the market in jobs a little below the average of all employees. Although the postwar influx of wives into the labor force was steady and impressive (Cain, 1966; Easterlin, 1980a, Chap. 4), it was no match for the earlier surges of immigration from southern and eastern Europe. Nonetheless, it, and the baby boom cohort (Freeman, 1979; Welch, 1979; Grant and Hamermesh, 1981), did serve to depress the growth in skills per worker

———, and Jeffrey G. Williamson. 1984b. "Population growth, industrial revolutions, and the urban transition." *Population and Development Review* 10, no. 3 (September): 419–441.

Lewis, W. Arthur. 1954. "Economic development with unlimited supplies of labour," *Manchester School of Economic and Social Studies*, no. 22 (May): 139–191.

Lindert, Peter H., and Jeffrey G. Williamson. 1983. "English workers' living standards during the industrial revolution: A new look," *Economic History Review*, 2nd series, no. 36 (February): 1–25.

Marshall, Alfred. 1910. *Principles of Economics*, 6th ed. London: Macmillan.

Marx, Karl. Originally published in 1848. *Capital*. Volume I. New York: International Publishers, 1947.

———, and Friedrich Engels. Originally published in 1848. *The Communist Manifesto*. New York: International Publishers, 1930.

McKinnon, Ronald. 1973. *Money and Capital in Economic Development*. Washington, D.C.: The Brookings Institution.

Mill, John Stuart. 1824. "Observations on the effects produced by the expenditure of government during the restriction of cash payments," *The Westminster Review* II (July), Art. II: 27–48.

———. 1909. *Principles of Political Economy*. 5th ed., vol. II. New York: D. Appleton and Company.

Pollard, Sidney. 1978. "Labour in Great Britain," in *The Cambridge Economic History of Europe: Volume VII: The Industrial Economies: Capital, Labour, and Enterprise*, Part I, ed. Peter Mathias and Michael Postan. Cambridge, England: Cambridge University Press.

Poor Inquiry (Ireland), Appendix G, *Report on the State of the Irish Poor in Great Britain*. 1836. *Parliamentary Papers*, vol. 34.

Redford, Arthur. 1926. *Labour Migration in England, 1800–1850*. Manchester, England: Manchester University Press.

Sen, A. K. 1966. "Peasants and dualism with or without surplus labor," *Journal of Political Economy*, no. 74 (October): 425–450.

Shoven, John B., and John Whalley. 1984. "Applied general-equilibrium models of taxation and international trade: An introduction and survey," *Journal of Economic Literature* 22 (September): 1007–1051.

Taylor, Lance, Edmar L. Bacha, Eliana A. Cardoso, and Frank J. Lysy. 1980. *Models of Growth and Distribution for Brazil*. New York: Oxford University Press.

Williamson, Jeffrey G. 1979. "Inequality, accumulation and technological imbalance: A growth-equity conflict in American history?," *Economic Development and Cultural Change* 27 (January): 231–253.

———. 1984a. "Why was British growth so slow during the industrial revolution?," *Journal of Economic History*, no. 3 (September): 687–712.

———. 1984b. "Irish immigration, elastic labor supplies and crowding-out during the British industrial revolution, 1821–1861," *Harvard Institue for Economic Research*, Discussion Paper No. 1085 (September).

———. 1985. *Did British Capitalism Breed Inequality?* London: Allen and Unwin.

———, and Peter H. Lindert. 1980. *American Inequality: A Macro-Economic History*. New York: Academic Press.

Wrigley, E. A., and Roger S. Schofield. 1981. *The Population History of England, 1541–1871: A Reconstruction*. Cambridge, England: Cambridge University Press.

LINDERT AND WILLIAMSON

As with America, changes in the rate of unbalanced productivity advance and changes in the rate of skills deepening are two critical forces driving the British Kuznets Curve across the 19th century. The pay gaps and earnings inequality set in motion by unbalanced productivity advance—favoring relatively rapid expansion in the derived demand for skills, served to offer great and increasing incentive to investment in human capital much like John Stuart Mill alleged in 1848. However, the slow and inelastic supply response in skills per worker (Williamson, 1985, Chap. 7) made it possible for inequality to persist for many decades before the demand-side disequilibrium began to be rectified in the late 19th century and earnings inequality began to settle down.

One of the reasons Britain underwent a leveling on the downside of the Kuznets Curve before America did appears to be because Britain suffered a late 19th-century and early 20th-century productivity slowdown (Matthews *et al.*, 1982, p. 501) while America did not. A second explanation can be found on the factor-supply side: Britain never had to absorb increasing unskilled labor supplies from abroad—although she had her share of Irish early in the century—so that she could accelerate the rate of skills deepening earlier than could America.

V. REINTERPRETATIONS

A. A Theory of the Kuznets Curve

A clearer understanding of the Kuznets Curve in Britain and America is now emerging. While the underlying theory avoids claiming any firm laws, it does suggest those conditions under which inequality trends are likely to trace out a Kuznets Curve, conditions which need not hold for all nations undergoing modern economic growth.

Over the long sweep of modern development, the three prime movers of income inequality are those listed on the left of the following schematic diagram (Scheme 1).

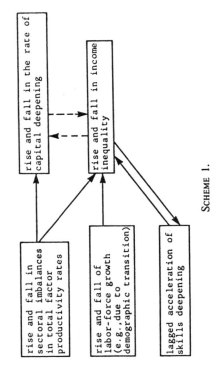

SCHEME 1.

The early-versus-late differences in the rates of productivity-growth imbalance, labor-force growth, and the growth of skills per member of the labor force seem crucial. The early rise in unbalanced productivity growth and in labor-force growth might seem to imply an inevitable rise in inequality, but no such inference can be drawn. Magnitudes matter, and these early technological and demographic forces may not be strong enough in some historic cases to outweigh the effects of human capital accumulation or the tendency of Engel's Law to undercut rural landed wealth. In some cases, the schematic summary above may be more effective in explaining the absence of a rise in income inequality or a delay in the income leveling. Among Third World countries, the early rise is most likely for countries with rapid population growth, potential for rapid industrialization, and a large initial share of small-owner staple-crop cultivators in the population (e.g., the northern United States before 1860, postwar Brazil, or Mexico). It is least likely under the opposite conditions.

This view of the past suggests conditional predictions about inequality trends in the already advanced countries. Continued deceleration of labor-force growth should favor further income leveling, though immigration may arrest any leveling trend in the United States. Our discussion of technology and skills suggests two opposing views of the current computer-electronics revolution. To the extent that it demands high skills, it may tend to create a new high-earnings elite. On the other hand, there is evidence that the newly demanded skills diffuse more rapidly than the industrial skills that were crucial in the past. This diffusion should be as egalitarian in the future as its analogs from the past. The forces on which future leveling should depend are now at least better understood, thanks to the recent literature on distribution and development.

B. Growth, Inequality, and Policy Choice

This survey urges that an old lesson should be unlearned. American and British history suggests that more inequality does not raise accumulation by much, and that more accumulation contributes little to inequality. This important moral has two implications, one dealing with research strategy and one dealing with policy debate.

What about research strategy? Economists should, in the future, model the accumulation process more as a response to technological change and to other determinants of investment demand. They should be far less enthusiastic about those models which dwell on shifts in the saving function.

What about the policy trade-off debate? American and British history suggests that the "growth-equality trade-off" should be redirected to the more fundamental debate on the efficiency and equality trade-off. Where policy improvements which move the national economy toward its efficiency frontier happen to reward high-income groups more than (or at the expense of) low-income groups, we can continue to speak of specific trade-offs between efficiency and equality. But there is no sound basis for presuming that the policy opportunities that enhance efficiency are wholly or even predominantly inegalitarian. Indeed, the past political dominance of higher-income groups would suggest the opposite. Their political power should have caused a near exhaustion of such efficient inegalitarian policies, leaving a menu of potential reforms that promote equality while undoing past inefficiencies. As the World Bank group has rightly insisted, the "growth-versus-equality" view is in retreat, and a previously closed debate remains open.

APPENDIX: NOTES TO FIGURE 2

Each observation is subject to errors in the underlying estimates, and the definitions of income and household units differ somewhat from country to country.

The inequality data for England and Wales, 1688–1867, are based on size distributions among aggregated economic classes, as described in Lindert and Williamson (1982, 1983).

The inequality data for the United Kingdom refer to the years 1867, 1880, 1913, 1929, 1938, 1947, 1957, and 1979, and are from Lindert and Williamson (1983). Kuznets (1966), and the World Bank (1982).

The U.S. inequality data refer to 1929, 1935/1936, 1941, 1950–1954, 1955–1959, 1960, 1966, and 1972. The source for 1929 through 1955–1959 is Kuznets (1966), and for 1960–1972 is Jain (1975). The underlying postwar figures include some receipts of transfer payments in the measure of household income.

The inequality data for Germany (1913, 1928, and 1936) and West Germany (1950, 1955, 1959, and 1974) are taken from Kuznets (1966) augmented by the World Bank (1982). The inequality data for Denmark (1908, 1925, 1939, 1952, 1963, and 1976) and Sweden (1935, 1948, 1954, and 1979) are taken from Tinbergen (1975, Table 2.I.A., p. 15) augmented by the World Bank (1982). The inequality data for the Netherlands (1916, 1924, 1929, 1935, 1950, 1955, 1960, 1965, 1970, 1972, and 1977) are taken from Hartog and Veenbergen (1978).

REFERENCES

Abramovitz, M. (1961), "The Nature and Significance of Kuznets Cycles." *Economic Development and Cultural Change* 9(3), 225–248.

Abramovitz, M., and David, P. (1973), "Reinterpreting Economic Growth: Parables and Realities." *American Economic Review* 63(2), 428–439.

Adelman, I., and Robinson, S. (1978), *Income Distribution Policies in Developing Countries: A Case Study of Korea.* Stanford: Stanford Univ. Press.

Ahluwalia, M. S. (1976), "Inequality, Poverty and Development." *Journal of Development Economics* 3(4), 307–342.

Ahluwalia, M. S. (1980), "Growth and Poverty in Developing Countries." In H. Chenery (Ed.), *Structural Change and Development Policy*. New York: Oxford Univ. Press, pp. 456–495.

Antonovsky, A. (1967), "Social Class, Life Expectancy and Overall Mortality." *The Millbank Memorial Fund Quarterly* 45(2), 31–73.

Atkinson, A. B. (1970), "On the Measurement of Inequality." *Journal of Economic Theory* 2, 244–263.

Bacha, E. L. (1979), "The Kuznets Curve and Beyond: Growth and Changes in Inequalities." In Ed. Malinvaud (Ed.), *Economic Growth and Resources*, Vol. 1, *Major Issues*. New York: St. Martin's Press.

Bahl, R. W. (Ed.) 1979), *The Taxation of Urban Property in Less Developed Countries*, Madison: Univ. of Wisconsin Press.

Barro, R. J. (1974), "Are Government Bonds Net Wealth?" *Journal of Political Economy* 82(6), 1095–1117.

Becker, G. (1962), "Investment in Human Capital: A Theoretical Analysis." *Journal of Political Economy* 70(5), 9–49.

Becker, G. (1964), *Human Capital*. New York: Nat. Bureau of Econ. Res.

Berndt, E., Christensen, L. (1974), "Testing for the Existence of a Consistant Aggregate Index of Labor Inputs." *American Economic Review* 64(3), 391–404.

Berndt, E., and Wood, D. (1975), "Technology, Prices and the Derived Demand for Energy." *Review of Economics and Statistics* 57(3) 259–268.

Berry, A., Bourguignon, F., and Morrison, C., (1983), "Changes in the World Distribution of Income." *Economic Journal* 93(370), 331–350.

Blinder, A. S. (1975), "Distribution Effects and the Aggregate Consumption Function." *Journal of Political Economy* 83(3), 447–475.

Blinder, A. S. (1980), "The Level and Distribution of Economic Well-Being." In M. Feldstein (Ed.), *The American Economy in Transition*. Chicago: Univ. of Chicago Press.

Boskin, M. (1978), "Taxation, Saving, and the Rate of Interest." *Journal of Political Economy* 86(2), S3–S27.

Brown, E. H. P. (1977), *the Inequality of Pay*. Oxford: Oxford Univ. Press.

Brown, M. (1966), *On the Theory and Measurement of Technological Change*. Cambridge: Cambridge Univ. Press.

Burns, A. (1954), *The Frontiers of Economic Knowledge*, Princeton, N.J: Princeton Univ. Press.

Cain, G. (1966) *Married Women in the Labor Force: An Economic Analysis*, Chicago: Univ. of Chicago Press.

Chenery, H., *et al.*, (1974), *Redistribution with Growth*, London: Oxford Univ. Press.

Chenery, H., and Syrquin, J. (1975), *Patterns of Development, 1950–1970*. London: Oxford Univ. Press.

Chiswick, B. and Mincer, J. (1972), "Time-Series Changes in Personal Income Inequality in the United States from 1939, with Projections to 1985." *Journal of Political Economy* 80(3), S34–S66.

Christensen, L., Cummings, D., and Jorgenson, D. (1978), "Productivity Growth, 1947–1973: An International Comparison." In W. Dewald (Ed.), *The Impact of International Trade and Investment on Employment*. Washington, D.C.: U.S. Govt. Printing Office.

Clark, C. (1965), "Land Taxation: Lessons from International Experience." In P. Hall (Ed.), *Land Values*. London: Sweet & Maxwell, pp. 126–146.

Clarke, R. N., and Summers, L. H. (1980), "The Labor Scarcity Controversy Reconsidered." *Economic Journal* 90(357), 129–139.

Cline, W. R. (1972), *Potential Effects of Income Redistribution on Economic Growth: Latin American Cases*. New York: Praeger.

Cline, W. R. (1975), "Distribution and Development: A Survey of the Literature." *Journal of Development Economics* **1**(4), 359–400.

Coale, A., and Hoover, E. (1958), *Population Growth and Economic Development in Low-Income Countries*, Princeton, N.J.: Princeton Univ. Press.

David, P. A., and van de Klundert, Th. (1965), "Biased Efficiency Growth and Capital-Labor Substitution in the U.S., 1899–1960." *American Economic Review* **55**(3), 357–394.

DeCanio, S. and Mokyr, J. (1977), "Inflation and Wage Lag During the American Civil War." *Explorations in Economic History* **14** (4), 311–36.

Della Valle, P. A., and Ogushi, N. (1976), "Distribution, the Aggregate Consumption Function and the Level of Economic Development: Some Cross-Country Results." *Journal of Political Economy* **84**(6), 1325–1334.

Denison, E. (1962), *The Sources of Economic Growth in the United States*. New York: Committee for Econ. Dev.

Denison, E. (1967), *Why Growth Rates Differ: Postwar Experiences in Nine Western Countries*. Washington, D.C.: Brookings Inst.

Denison, E. (1974), *Accounting for United States Economic Growth, 1929–1969*. Washington, D.C.: Brookings Inst.

Dervis, K., DeMelo, J., and Robinson, S. (1982), *General Equilibrium Models for Development Policy*. New York: Cambridge Univ. Press.

Easterlin, R. (1961), "Influences in European Overseas Emigration Before World War I." *Economic Development and Cultural Change* **9**(3), 331–351.

Easterlin, R. (1968), *Population, Labor Force, and Long Swings in Economic Growth*. New York: Nat. Bureau of Econ. Res.

Easterlin, R. (1980a), *Birth and Fortune: The Impact of Numbers on Personal Welfare*. New York: Basic Books.

Easterlin, R. (1980b), "American Population Since 1940." In M. Feldstein (Ed.), *The American Economy in Transition*. Chicago: Nat. Bureau of Econ. Res.

Eckaus, R. (1955), "The Factor Proportions Problem in Underdeveloped Areas." *American Economic Review* **45**(4), 539–565.

Edelstein, M. (1977), "UK Savings in the Age of High Imperialism and After." *American Economic Review* **67**(1), 288–294.

Edelstein, M. (1982), *Overseas Investment in the Age of High Imperialism: The United Kingdom, 1850–1914*. New York: Columbia Univ. Press.

Evans, O. J. (1983), "Tax Policy, the Interest Elasticity of Saving, and Capital Accumulation: Numerical Analysis of Theoretical Models." *American Economic Review* **73**(3), 398–410.

Evans, R. (1971), *The Labor Economics of Japan and the United States*. New York: Praeger.

Fallon, P. R., and Layard, P. R. G. (1975), "Capital-Skill Complementarity, Income Distribution, and Output Accounting." *Journal of Political Economy* **83**(2), 279–301.

Fei, J., and Ranis, G. (1963), "Innovation, Capital Accumulation, and Economic Development." *American Economic Review* **53**(3), 282–313.

Fei, J., and Ranis, G. (1964), *Development of the Labor Surplus Economy: Theory and Policy*. Homewood, Ill.: Irwin.

Fei, J. C. H., Ranis, G., and Kur, S. W. Y. (1979), *Growth with Equity: The Taiwan Case*. New York: Oxford Univ. Press.

Feinstein, C. (1978), "Capital Formation in Great Britain." In P. Mathias and M. Postan (Eds.), *The Cambridge Economic History of Europe*, Volume VII, *The Industrial Economies: Capital, Labour, and Enterprise*. Cambridge: Cambridge Univ. Press.

Feldstein, M. S. (1977a), "Does the United States Save Too Little?" *American Economic Review* **67**(1), 116–121.

Feldstein, M. S. (1977b), "The Surprising Incidence of a Tax on Pure Rent: A New Answer to an Old Question." *Journal of Political Economy* **85**(2), 349–360.

Feldstein, M. S. (1978a), "The Welfare Costs of Capital Income Taxes." *Journal of Political Economy* **86**(2), S29–S51.

Feldstein, M. S. (1978b), "The Rate of Return, Taxation and Personal Savings." *Economic Journal* **88**(3), 482–487.

Fields, G. S. (1980), *Poverty, Inequality and Development*. Cambridge: Cambridge Univ. Press.

Floud, R., and McCloskey, D. (1981), *The Economic History of Britain Since 1700*. Cambridge: Cambridge Univ. Press.

Fogel, R. W. (1967), "The Specification Problem in Economic History." *Journal of Economic History* **27**(3), 283–308.

Freeman, R. (1979), "The Effect of Demographic Factors on Age—Earnings Profiles." *Journal of Human Resources* **14**(3), 289–318.

Freeman, R. B. (1980), "Unionism and the Dispersion of Wages." *Industrial and Labor Relations Review* **34**(1), 3–23.

Fullerton, D. A., King, T., Shoven, J., and Whalley, J. (1981), "Corporate Tax Integration in the United States: A General Equilibrium Approach." *American Economic Review* **71**(4), 677–691.

Gallman, R. (1966), "Gross National Product in the United States 1834–1909." In *Output, Employment, and Productivity in the United States after 1800*. New York: Nat. Bureau of Econ. Res.

Gollop, F., and Jorgenson, D. (1980), "U.S. Productivity Growth by Industry." In J. Kendrick and B. Vaccara (Eds.), *Studies in Income and Wealth*. Chicago: Univ. of Chicago Press. Vol. 44.

Gordon, R. A. (1961), "Differential Changes in the Prices of Consumers' and Capital Goods." *American Economic Review* **51**(5), 937–957.

Grant, J., and Hamermesh, D. (1981), "Labor Market Competition Among Youths, White Women and Others." *Review of Economics and Statistics* **63**(3), 354–360.

Griliches, Z. (1969), "Capital-Skill Complementarity." *Review of Economics and Statistics* **51**(4), 465–468.

Hartog, J., and Veenbergen, J. G. (1978), "Dutch Treat: Long-Run Changes in Personal Income Distribution." *De Economist* **126**(4), 521–549.

Hildebrand, G., and Delahanty, G. (1966), "Wage Levels and Differentials." In R. Gordon and M. Gordon (Eds.), *Prosperity and Unemployment*. New York: Wiley.

Hillman, A., and Clark, B. (1978), "Energy, the Heckscher-Ohlin Theorem, and U.S. International Trade." *American Economic Review* **68**(1), 96–106.

Hoffman, K., and Jorgenson, D. (1977), "Economic and Technological Models for Evaluation of Energy Policy." *Bell Journal of Economics* **8**(2), 444–466.

Howrey, E., and Hymans, S. H. (1978), "The Measurement and Determination of Loanable-Funds Saving." *Brookings Papers on Economic Activity* **3**, 665–685.

Hueckel, G. (1973), "War and the British Economy, 1793–1815: A General Equilibrium Analysis." *Explorations in Economic History* **10**, 365–396.

Husby, R. D. (1971), "A Nonlinear Consumption Function Estimated from Time-Series and Cross-Section Data." *Review of Economics and Statistics* **53**(1), 76–79.

Jain, S. (1975), *Size Distribution of Income: A Compilation of Data*. Washington: World Bank.

James, J. (1978), "The Welfare Effects of the Antebellum Tariff." *Explorations Economic History* **15**(3), 231–256.

James, J. (1981), "The Optimal Tariff in the Antebellum United States." *American Economic Review* **71**(4), 726–734.

James, J. (1984), "The Use of General Equilibrium Analysis in Economic History." *Explorations in Economic History* **21**(3), 231–253.

Jones, R. (1965), "The Structure of Simple General Equilibrium Models." *Journal of Political Economy* 73(6), 557–572.

Kaldor, N. (1956), "Alternative Theories of Distribution." *Review of Economic Studies* 23(2), 83–100.

Keller, R. (1973), "Factor Income Distribution in the United States During the 1920s: A Re-examination of Fact and Theory." *Journal of Economic History* 33(1), 252–273.

Kelley, A. C., Williamson, J. G., and Cheetham, R. J. (1972), *Dualistic Economic Development: Theory and History*. Chicago: Univ. of Chicago Press.

Kelley, A. C., and Williamson, J. G. (1984), *What Drives Third World City Growth? A Dynamic General Equilibrium Approach*. Princeton, N.J.: Princeton Univ. Press.

Kendrick, J. (1961), *Productivity Trends in the United States*. New York: Nat. Bureau of Econ. Res.

Kendrick, J. (1973), *Postwar Productivity Trends in the United States, 1948–1969*. New York: Nat. Bureau of Econ. Res.

Kindleberger, C. (1967), *Europe's Postwar Growth: The Role of Labor Supply*. Cambridge, Mass.: Harvard Univ. Press.

Kotlikoff, L., and Pinera, S. (1977), "The Old South's Stake in the Interregional Movement of Slaves." *Journal of Economic History* 37(2), 434–450.

Kuznets, S. (1955), "Economic Growth and Income Inequality." *American Economic Review* 45(1), 1–28.

Kuznets, S. (1958), "Long Swings in the Growth of Population and in Related Economic Variables." *Proceedings of the American Philosophical Society* CII(1), 25–52.

Kuznets, S. (1966), *Modern Economic Growth*. New Haven: Yale Univ. Press.

Kuznets, S. (1976), "Demographic Aspects of the Size Distribution of Income: An Exploratory Essay." *Economic Development and Cultural Change* 25(1), 1–94.

Kuznets, S. (1979), *Growth, Population and Income Distribution: Selected Essays*. New York: Norton.

Leff, N. (1969), "Dependency Rates and Savings Rates." *American Economic Review* 59(5), 886–896.

Leimer, D. R., and Lesnoy, S. D. (1982), "Social Security and Private Saving: New Time-Series Evidence." *Journal of Political Economy* 90(3), 606–629.

Lewis, W. A. (1954), "Economic Development with Unlimited Supplies of Labour." *Manchester School of Economic and Social Studies* 22(2), 139–191.

Lillard, L. A. (1977), "Inequality: Earnings vs. Human Wealth." *American Economic Review* 67(2), 42–53.

Lindert, P. H. (1974), "Land Scarcity and American Growth." *Journal of Economic History* 34(4), 851–884.

Lindert, P. H. (1983), "Who Owned Victorian England?" Agricultural History Working Paper 14, Davis Calif.: Univ. of Calif.

Lindert, P. H., and Williamson, J. G. (1982), "Revising England's Social Tables, 1688–1812." *Explorations in Economic History* 19(4), 385–408.

Lindert, P. H., and Williamson, J. G. (1983), "Reinterpreting Britain's Social Tables, 1688–1913." *Explorations in Economic History* 20(1), 94–109.

Lydall, H. B. (1968), *The Structure of Earnings*. Oxford: Oxford Univ. Press.

Matthews, R. C. O., Feinstein, C. H., and Odling-Smee, J. C. (1982), *British Economic Growth, 1856–1973*. Stanford: Stanford Univ. Press.

McAuley, A. (1979), *Economic Welfare in the Soviet Union*. Madison: Univ. of Wisconsin Press.

Mill, J. St. (1848), *Principles of Political Economy*. London: 1st edition.

Mills, E. S., and Ohta, K. (1976), "Urbanization and Urban Problems." In H. Patrick and H. Rosovsky (Eds.), *Asia's New Giant*. Washington: Brookings Inst. pp. 696–751.

Mills, E. S., and Song, B. N. (1977), "Korea's Urbanization and Urban Problems, 1945–1975," "Working Paper No. 7701. Seoul: Korea Dev. Inst.

Minami, R. (1973), *The Turning Point in Economic Development: Japan's Experience.* Tokyo: Kinokuniya Bookstore.

Mitchell, W. C. (1903), *A History of the Greenbacks.* Chicago: Univ. of Chicago Press.

Mitchell, W. C. (1908), *Gold, Prices and Wages under the Greenback Standard.* Berkeley: Univ. of California Press.

Mokyr, J., and Savin, E. (1976), "Stagflation in Historical Perspective." In P. Uselding (Ed.) *Research in Economic History*, Vol. I. Greenwich, Conn.: Johnson Associates.

Morawetz, D. (1974), "Employment Implications of Industrialization in Developing Countries: A Survey." *Economic Journal* 84(335), 491–542.

Morishima, M., and Saito, M. (1968), "An Economic Test of Hicks' Theory of Biased Induced Inventions." In J. Wolfe (Ed.), *Value, Capital and Growth.* Chicago: Aldine.

Morley, S. A. (1981), "The Effect of Changes in the Population on Several Measures of Income Distribution." *American Economic Review* 71(3), 285–294.

Morley, S. A. (1982), *Labor Markets and Inequitable Growth: The Case of Authoritarian Capitalism in Brazil.* Cambridge: Cambridge Univ. Press.

Morley, S. A. and Williamson, J. G. (1977) "Class Pay Differentials, Wage Stretching and Early Capitalist Development." In M. Nash (Ed.), *Essays on Economic Development and Cultural Change.* Chicago: Univ. of Chicago Press.

Morris, C. T., and Adelman, I. (1980), "Patterns of Industrialization in the Nineteenth and Early Twentieth Centuries." In P. Uselding (Ed.), *Research in Economic History*, Vol. 5. Greenwich, Conn.: Johnson Associates.

Musgrove, P. (1980), "Income Distribution and the Aggregate Consumption Function." *Journal of Political Economy* 88(3), 504–525.

Nadiri, M. (1980), "Sectoral Productivity Slow-Down." *American Economic Review* 70(2), 349–352.

Neal, L. (1976), "Cross-Spectral Analysis of Long Swings in Atlantic Migration." In P. Uselding (Ed.), *Research in Economic History*, Vol. I. Greenwich, Conn.: Johnson Associates.

Nichols, D. A. (1970), "Land and Economic Growth." *American Economic Review* 60(3), 332–340.

Nicholson, J. L. (1974), "The Distribution and Redistribution of Income in the United Kingdom." In D. Wedderburn (Ed.), *Poverty, Inequality and Class Structure.* Cambridge: Cambridge Univ. Press.

Nordhaus, W. (1972), "The Recent Productivity Slowdown." *Brookings Papers on Economic Activity* 73, 493–546.

Nordhaus, W., and Tobin, J. (1972), "Is Growth Obsolete?" In *Economic Growth: Fiftieth Anniversary Colloquium V.* New York: Nat. Bureau of Econ. Res.

O'Higgins, M., and Ruggles, P. (1981), "The Distribution of Public Expenditures and Taxes Among Households in the United Kingdom." *Review of Income and Wealth* 27(3), 298–326.

Ohkawa, K., and Rosovsky, H. (1973), *Japanese Economic Growth: Trend Acceleration in the Twentieth Century.* Stanford: Stanford Univ. Press.

Passell, P., and Wright, G. (1972), "The Effects of the Pre-Civil War Territorial Expansion on the Price of Slaves." *Journal of Political Economy* 80(6), 1188–1202.

Paukert, F. (1973), "Income Distribution at Different Levels of Development: A Survey of Evidence." *International Labour Review* 108(2–3), 97–125.

Pindyck, R. S., and Rotemberg, J. J. (1983), "Dynamic Factor Demands and the Effects of Energy Shocks." *American Economic Review* 73(5), 1066–1079.

Pope, C. (1972), "The Impact of the Ante-Bellum Tariff on Income Distribution." *Explorations in Economic History* 9(4), 375–422.

376 LINDERT AND WILLIAMSON

Preston, S. H. (1980), "Causes and Consequences of Mortality Decline in Less Developed Countries during the Twentieth Century." In R. A. Easterlin (Ed.), *Population and Economic Change in Developing Countries.* Chicago: Univ. of Chicago Press.

Ransom, R., and Sutch, R. (1982), "The Long-Run Implications of Capital Absorption in Slave Labor." Univ. of California, Berkeley, Calif., December 20, 1982.

Renaghan, T. M. (1984), "Distributional Effects of Federal Tax Policy 1929–1939." *Explorations in Economic History* 21(1), 40–64.

Reynolds, M., and Smolensky, E. (1977), *Public Expenditures, Taxes, and the Distribution of Income in the United States, 1950, 1961, 1970.* New York: Academic Press.

Robinson, S. (1976), "A Note on the U Hypothesis Relating Income Inequality and Economic Development." *American Economic Review* 66(3), 437–440.

Schmitz, M., and Schaefer, D. (1981), "Paradox Lost: Westward Expansion and Slave Prices before the Civil War." *Journal of Economic History* 41(2), 402–407.

Schultz, T. (1961), "Education and Economic Growth." In N. Henry (Ed.), *Social Forces Influencing American Education.* Chicago: Univ. of Chicago Press.

Schultz, T. (1963), *The Economic Value of Education.* New York: Columbia Univ. Press.

Shoven, J., and Whalley, J. (1972), "A General Equilibrium Calculation of the Effects of Differential Taxation of Income from Capital in the U.S." *Journal of Public Economics* I(3/4), 281–321.

Shoven, J., and Whalley, J. (1974), "On the Computation of Competitive Equilibria in International Markets with Tariffs." *Journal of International Economics* 4(4), 341–354.

Shoven, J., and Whalley, J. (1984), "Applied General-Equilibrium Models of Taxation and International Trade." *Journal of Economic Literature* 22(3), 1007–1051.

Temin, P. (1966), "Labor Scarcity and the Problem of American Industrial Efficiency in the 1850s." *Journal of Economic History* 26(3), 277–298.

Tinbergen, J. (1975), *Income Distribution: Analysis and Policies.* Amsterdam: North-Holland.

Tunzelmann, G. N. (1982), "The Standard of Living, Investment, and Economic Growth in England and Wales, 1760–1850." In L. Jorberg and N. Rosenberg (Eds.), *Technical Change, Employment and Investment.* Lund: Lund Univ.

Turnham, D. (1971), *The Employment Problem in Less-Developed Countries: A Review of the Evidence.* Paris: OECD Dev. Center.

U.S. Department of Commerce, Bureau of the Census (1975), *Historical Statistics of the United States, Part I.* Washington, D.C.: U.S. Govt. Printing Office.

von Furstenberg, G. M., and Malkiel, B. G. (1977), "The Government and Capital Formation: A Survey of Recent Issues." *Journal of Economic Literature* 15(3), 835–878.

Welch, F. (1979), "Effects of Cohort Size on Earnings: The Baby Boom Babies' Financial Bust." *Journal of Political Economy* 87(5), S65–S97.

Williamson, J. G. (1971), "Capital Accumulation, Labor Saving, and Labor Absorption Once More." *Quarterly Journal of Economics* 85(1), 40–65.

Williamson, J. G. (1974), *Late Nineteenth Century American Development.* Cambridge: Cambridge Univ. Press.

Williamson, J. G. (1976), "The Sources of American Inequality, 1896–1948." *Review of Economics and Statistics* 58(4), 387–397.

Williamson, J. G. (1979), "Inequality, Accumulation and Technological Imbalance: A Growth-Equity Conflict in American History?" *Economic Development and Cultural Change* 27(2), 231–254.

Williamson, J. G. (1980), "Earnings Inequality in Nineteenth-Century Britain," *Journal of Economic History* **40**(3), 457–476.

Williamson, J. G. (1982), "Immigrant-Inequality Trade-Offs in the Promised Land: Income Distribution and Absorptive Capacity Prior to the Quotas." In B. Chiswick (Ed.), *The Gateway: U.S. Immigration Issues and Policies.* Washington, D.C.: Amer. Enterprise Inst.

Williamson, J. G. (1984), "Why Was British Growth So Slow During the Industrial Revolution?" *Journal of Economic History* **44**(3), 687–712.

Williamson, J. G. (1985), *Did British Capitalism Breed Inequality?* London: Allen & Unwin.

Williamson, J. G., and Lindert, P. (1980), *American Inequality: A Macroeconomic History*, New York: Academic Press.

World Bank (1982), *World Development Report, 1982.* New York: Oxford Univ. Press.

Wrigley, E., and Schofield, R. (1981), *The Population History of England, 1541–1871: A Reconstruction.* Cambridge: Cambridge Univ. Press.

PART III

INDUSTRIALIZATION, URBANIZATION AND MIGRATION OFF THE FARM

[9]

Population Growth, Industrial Revolutions, and the Urban Transition

Allen C. Kelley

Jeffrey G. Williamson

While many demographers have been preoccupied with problems of aggregate population growth, another drama has been unfolding in the Third World: the growth of cities and the shift of population to urban centers at unprecedented rates. At the beginning of the last century, world urban population numbered 25 million; today it exceeds 1.6 billion, and the United Nations predicts a figure of 3.1 billion by the year 2000. Not only have recent rates of urban growth been three times those of rural areas in many parts of the world, but also some Third World cities are predicted to reach extremely large sizes by the end of the century: Mexico City, 31 million; São Paulo, 25.8 million; Rio de Janeiro, Bombay, Calcutta, and Jakarta each exceeding 16 million; Seoul, 14.2 million; Cairo, 13.1 million; and Manila, 12.3 million (World Bank, 1984).

Modeling the urban transition

What explains the timing and extent of the urban transition? Why does city growth speed up in early development and slow down in later stages? While the urban transition is certainly part of the industrial revolution and the demographic transition, exactly how do these forces link together? Speculation has never been in short supply. Friedrich Engels (1845) thought that Manchester's booming growth in the early nineteenth century—and the urban decay associated with "overcrowding"—could be easily explained by the development of manufacturing under capitalism. Ravenstein (1885, 1889) and Redford (1926) thought that rural–urban migration, and thus town growth, was conditioned by Malthusian forces, agricultural land scarcity, and enclosure. In short, Engels favored "pull," whereas Ravenstein and Redford favored "push." Some time after the appearance of Adna Weber's (1899) book, academic battles over "push" and "pull" shifted from internal migration and the urban transition to external migration from the old to the new world. With the post–World War II development of the Third World, the academic debate shifted back again to internal migration and the urban transition.

In spite of a century and a half of debate, social scientists are still uncertain about the quantitative importance of the sources of the urban transition. The two principal hypotheses advanced in the literature are that rapid city growth and urbanization can be explained primarily by: (1) unusually rapid rates of population growth pressing on limited farm acreage, pushing landless labor into the cities; and (2) economic forces pulling migrants into the cities. In the contemporary developing world these forces include: domestic policies that distort prices to favor cities (e.g., the domestic terms of trade have been twisted to "squeeze" agriculture); cheap energy prior to OPEC favoring the growth of energy-using sectors, most of which are located in the cities, thus creating urban jobs; the diffusion of technology from the developed world, which favors modern, large-scale urban industries; foreign capital flows into city infrastructure, urban housing, power, transportation, and large-scale manufacturing—further augmenting Third World city growth; and the liberalization of world trade since the late 1950s, which has stimulated demand for manufacturing exports produced in Third World cities.

Most population specialists favor the first hypothesis. Exploding numbers of people must be employed, and a marginal agriculture with quasi-fixed arable land cannot offer sufficient employment for the Malthusian glut created by the demographic transition. Marginal survival by hawking urban services may be the only way a social system can absorb the population glut, and squalid urban living conditions have been an attribute of early stages of industrialization since Engels wrote of Manchester in the 1840s. The demographer (writing under the shadow of Malthus) is likely, therefore, to favor causation running from population boom, to push off the land, to city immigration, and thus to rapid urban growth under abysmal living conditions. This view has also had a profound influence on economists' thinking about development. It is central to W. Arthur Lewis's (1954) "labor surplus" model—a model that also worked well for the classical economists developing their paradigms of growth during the British industrial revolution. It is also central to the Todaro (1969) thesis that rising immigration to the city can be associated with high and even increasing rates of urban unemployment. On the other hand, most economists tend to favor the second principal hypothesis, that is, those economic forces contributing to urban pull. It makes little difference, however, which social science perspective is adopted: a quantitative assessment of these "sources" of urban change has yet to be performed.

Why should we care about the sources of the urban transition? Primarily because we cannot be very confident in projections to the year 2000, let alone projections into the twenty-first century, if we do not understand the economic and demographic forces that have driven Third World city growth in the past two or three decades. And future city growth projections are essential to formulating proper economic and social policies.

What is required, then, is a credible model of the urbanization process. Without such a model, we cannot identify what city growth might be like under different policies, under different fertility rates, or under different world market conditions. Nor can we determine what the sources of past Third World city growth have been without a model to do the appropriate accounting. Two key features must be incorporated into such a model.

First, we require a model of the urban transition in which rural–urban migration is endogenous and responsive to various macroeconomic and macrodemographic forces. This perspective is quite different from that which forms the basis of most projections of urban Third World populations to the year 2000.[1] Some of these projections assume a constant migration rate and some allow it to vary, but all take the rural–urban migration rate to be exogenous to, or at least independent of economic forces. That is, the projections are made in the absence of a model in which economic forces are allowed to have an impact on rates of rural to urban migration. In the absence of endogenous forces driving rural outmigration or urban immigration, city growth and the urban transition must be viewed as exogenous in such projections.

The second feature that a long-run model of the urbanization process must possess is "closure," a property loosely defined by the requirement that the model exhibit feedback and interaction between sectors (most notably, price endogeneity), as well as flexibility in production and consumption. These attributes have not been stressed in most economic/demographic modeling efforts, even those in which disaggregation is a feature. A model in which scarcity is not allowed to trigger economies in consumption and production would not serve well any effort to account for long-run urbanization. What is required is a framework in which urban land scarcity can create a rise in residential density and other land-saving responses; in which rising fuel prices are allowed to provoke fuel-saving responses; and in which rising urban costs of living and disamenities can discourage inmigration to the city.

The objective of this article is to present some of the insights that have emerged from the authors' efforts to construct such a model.[2] We attempt to provide the reader with enough information about the model, its empirical representation, and its use in counterfactual, policy, and impact-multiplier analysis to serve as an overview of our research design. The model's technical detail, which we present in brief, has been relegated to an appendix. This format provides sufficient material for the specialist to assess the model's underlying structure, without burdening the text with technical jargon and with formal presentation of somewhat marginal interest to most nonspecialists.

Before summarizing what we have learned about the urban transition in the Third World, we need to go through some preliminaries. In particular, does our model replicate the recent past?

Does the model replicate the recent past?

The model has been given empirical content by relying on the fictional construct of a "representative developing country." This is simply the average experience of a large group of developing countries that broadly satisfy the conditions that underly the model's theoretical structure.[3] These conditions are: low per capita income in 1960; some per capita income growth over the past two decades; primary reliance on domestic saving for accumulation; and being a "price taker" in world markets. The last condition required exclusion of a number of countries that have an impact on world prices of key resource-intensive products (most notably, the OPEC countries). Fairly extensive historical documentation on economic and demographic variables back to 1960 was necessary for a country to be included in the sample. The 40 countries that met these requirements accounted for about 80 percent of the Third World's population (excluding China).[4]

Using this data base, we documented initial conditions, estimated parameters, and then used the model to simulate the urbanization process over the period 1960–80. Five groups of variables are taken as exogenous, each one central to debates regarding the sources of the urban transition. The first group is the prices of three main types of commodities that enter world trade—imported fuels and raw materials; manufactured goods; and primary products. (While there are eight sectors and thus eight output prices in the model, only the prices of the three main types of commodities that enter world trade are determined exogenously.) By comparing simulations based on pre-OPEC fuel price trends with those based on post-OPEC fuel price trends, for example, we can assess the influence of fuel scarcity on the rate and character of the urban transition. The second exogenous variable is land stock growth. The model splits up land into urban and farm use, both of which grow at exogenous rates, making it possible to assess the impact of urban land scarcity as a source of "push" to the cities as well as to assess the impact of urban land scarcity on increasing density, on increasing rents, and, thus, on the rising cost of city life. Third, the level of foreign capital inflow is exogenous, permitting us to explore the hypothesis that foreign capital has been an essential ingredient in Third World city-building and thus in the urban transition. Fourth, rates of productivity growth by sector are determined exogenously and are held to be "unbalanced" in favor of the modern sectors. It has long been believed that rapid technological progress in the modern urban-based sectors has been a central ingredient to rapid urban job creation, to city immigration, and thus to the urban transition. This hypothesis can be tested by varying the rates of sectoral technological change. Finally, with respect to demographic change, the aggregate rates of population and labor force growth are exogenous in the model, making it possible to vary the Malthusian burden so as to assess its importance in contributing to the urban transition in the Third World.

Given historical trends in these five sets of exogenous variables, the model determines the rate of capital accumulation, investment in dwellings, and training and skill development; the patterns of resource allocation and income distribution; the rate of industrialization; and, of course, trends in rural to urban immigration and urbanization. All told, the model yields predictions on over 100 endogenous variables. Although historical documentation is not available for many of these variables, we did assess the validity of the model's predictions on all those for which data were available for the 1960s and 1970s.

Table 1 offers a glimpse of the ability of the model to replicate the recent observed trends in the Third World. Space permits presentation of only a small sample of our results, but those in Table 1 cover some of the most important aspects of economic growth and of the urban transition in particular. The validation of the model in Table 1 focuses on 1960–73, partly to control for the impact of OPEC and partly to reflect the fact that detailed census data around 1980 for most of the countries in our sample are not yet available. And, while the model generates annual predictions for each variable for all 13 years from 1960 to 1973, Table 1 summarizes that experience by means of decade averages and end-of-period observations.

TABLE 1   Economic growth, economic structure, and urbanization in the "Representative Developing Country" group: model predictions and the observed historical record, 1960–73

Variable	Predicted by model	Observed
Aggregate real GDP growth (percent per annum)		
1960–65	5.9	5.8
1965–73	6.6	6.1
1960–73	6.3	5.8
Sectoral shares in GDP in 1973 (percent)		
Manufacturing and mining	20.9	20.8
Services	50.9	50.6
Agriculture	28.2	28.6
Aspects of urban population growth (1960–70)		
Urban population growth (percent per annum)	4.7	4.6
Increase in share urban (percent per annum)	0.7	0.5
Net urban immigration rate (decade average)	2.0	1.8
Net rural outmigration rate (decade average)	1.1	1.0
Net immigrant share of urban population increase (percent)	45.0	39.3

SOURCE: The observed figures for aggregate GDP growth, sectoral shares in GDP, urban growth, and the urban share are taken from the *World Tables 1976* (IBRD, 1976). The United Nations (1980), p. 198, supplies the estimate of the net immigrant share based on 29 developing countries, some of which are not part of our Representative Developing Country group. The migration rates are based on the other figures, taking 1970 as the base; see Kelley and Williamson (1984), Chapter 3. For composition of the RDC group, see note 4 and discussion in the text.

The model is a rather fast grower, averaging 6.3 percent per annum in constant price gross domestic product. This is somewhat higher than the observed Third World growth, but note that the model does capture a trend acceleration over the period—a phenomenon much discussed and widely documented with reference to the concepts of the "take-off" or the "industrial revolution." Overall, aggregate growth experience generated by the model seems to conform to recent Third World history.

More importantly, the model accurately captures unbalanced output growth and industrialization. Since urbanization and city growth are the central issues in the present analysis, the close conformity of sectoral output share predictions to the historical record is especially satisfying since those shares are key determinants of the spatial distribution of jobs and thus of rural–urban migration and city growth.

Most important, however, is the model's performance in capturing characteristics of the urban transition. Growth rates of the urban population averaged 4.6 percent per annum over the 1960s in our 40-country sample, and the model prediction is almost exactly the same rate, 4.7 percent per annum. Although it is not reported in Table 1, the model also predicts an accelerating rate of urban growth across the 1960s and early 1970s, conforming to the pre-inflexion point phase along logistic urbanization curves found so commonly in time series. Migration experience is also closely replicated by the model. The rural outmigration rate is predicted at 1.1 percent per annum, while Preston (1979), using a sample of 29 developing countries, has estimated the outmigration rate to have been about 1 percent. Similarly, the per annum urban immigration rates are 2.0 in the model and 1.8 percent in Preston's estimates. Finally, the model predicts that 45 percent of the urban population increase can be attributed to immigration, a prediction that lies midway between Preston's estimate of 39.3 percent and Keyfitz's (1980) estimate of 49 percent.

Scores of other predictions are generated by the model, some of which provide even closer replication of the historical experience than those shown in Table 1, and some of which are worse. (Many other predictions cannot be evaluated except by qualitative guesses.) Evidence like that presented in Table 1 has convinced us that our model replicates history sufficiently well to make further analysis worthwhile. It might be suggested that since the model was parameterized on data drawn from the 1960s, its ability to replicate the pre-OPEC past is in a sense inevitable. Such a suggestion would miss two points. First, parameterization itself is demanding: there are over 100 parameters and initial conditions that had to be estimated, and errors in estimation or data can lead to flaws in predictions. Second, while predictions are based on parameters, the model structure plays the greater role. What distinguishes the present research effort from earlier efforts is the use of an explicit economywide model of the process.

Projecting the urban transition

How urbanized will the Third World be by the year 2000? Demographers have certainly supplied answers to this question; but as we have already noted, demographic projections take the rural to urban migration rate to be exogenous, with the result that city growth and the urban transition must also be viewed as exogenous.[5]

Since rural–urban migration flows are endogenous in our model, we are in a position to learn more about the future, although our predictions for the year 2000 may not be any more accurate than those of demographers. First, we can explore long-run patterns of migration, urban growth, and urbanization

Allen C. Kelley / Jeffrey G. Williamson

in a "stable" economic/demographic environment in which exogenous prices, technological change, labor force growth, land expansion rates, and foreign capital inflows all exhibit smooth trends and are shielded from the disturbances of demographic transition, oil price shocks, productivity slowdowns, and increasing foreign capital scarcity due to financial austerity in the lending North. We are able, in effect, to explore a counterfactual world in which endogenous forces of growth and development are allowed to have their unfettered impact on the spatial redistribution of population. What would our model predict under such conditions? A smooth logistic curve? If so, where would the point of inflexion be? The year 1970? The year 2000? Second, we can explore long-run patterns of migration and urban growth in an economic/demographic environment that experts think is likely to prevail over the next two decades. This "Baseline" projection can then be compared with the "Stable" projection to examine the impact of a changing economic/demographic environment over the next two decades. The gap between the two projections should yield insights into the role of these expected changes in the economic/demographic environment, especially since we can use the model to isolate the impact of each event separately by means of the appropriate counterfactual assumptions.

Defining the "Baseline"

What are the characteristics of the most likely economic/demographic environment in the Third World over the next two decades? Table 2 summarizes that environment and reports the values of the exogenous variables underlying the model's Baseline projections. It also reiterates the "actual" conditions that prevailed in the period immediately preceding 1980, and during the pre-OPEC price rise phase discussed in the previous section. It also reports the Baseline

TABLE 2 Selected economic and demographic variables characterizing a representative Third World country: Stable and Baseline projections, 1960–2000

Variable	Estimated		Baseline projection		Stable projection	
	1960–73	1974–80	1981–90	1991–2000	1981–2000	
Relative price of fuels and raw materials. growth per annum. percent	0.0	5.2	1.5	1.5	0.0	
Relative price of manufactures. growth per annum. percent	−0.7	−1.6	−0.6	−0.6	−0.7	
Agricultural land stock. growth per annum. percent	1.0	0.5	0.0	0.0	1.0	
Urban land stock. growth per annum. percent	1.0	1.0	1.0	1.0	1.0	
Labor force. growth per annum. percent	2.54	2.68	2.79	2.84	2.54	
Foreign capital inflow per annum as percent share in GDP	3.0	3.0	Declines linearly from 3.0 to 2.4		3.0	
Economywide total factor productivity, growth per annum. percent	1.8	1.8	1.8	1.8	1.8	

and Stable values assumed for the two decades following 1980. The Stable values simply assume that the pre-OPEC conditions persisted throughout the 1970s and continue to hold for the next two decades. We do not view such post-1980 trends as very likely, but that is not the point of the exercise. Rather, the Stable values simply offer a useful benchmark for exploration of the urban transition in a typical developing country.

The Baseline values are a different matter entirely. Consider in turn each of the key assumptions (on labor force growth, relative price changes, foreign capital inflows, total factor productivity growth, and the expansion of land) that enter into the Baseline projections.

Relative price projections are, needless to say, hazardous. Table 2 reports what experts at the World Bank believed in 1982 to be the most likely trends up to 2000. They did not foresee a dramatic increase in the relative price of fuels and raw materials like that of the 1970s, but they did project an upward drift at the brisk rate of 1.5 percent per annum relative to primary product exports. They also predicted a persistent decline in the relative price of manufactures at the rate of 0.6 percent per annum, much like the trends typical of the pre-OPEC period. The reader should be reminded that we are far less interested in what will actually happen to relative prices between 1980 and the year 2000 than in what might happen under alternative relative price scenarios. Given that qualification, the experts' guesses will serve to establish a Baseline around which counterfactual alternatives can be evaluated.

Foreign capital inflows are even more difficult to project. They certainly will depend on real income growth and fiscal austerity in the lending countries of the industrialized North. They will also depend on OPEC price policy and the financial surpluses thereby generated in the oil-exporting countries. Nonetheless, the World Bank has projected the most likely "resource gaps" in the oil-importing Third World, and these provide the Baseline trends in the foreign capital inflow/GDP ratio reported in Table 2—a steady decline from an average of 3 percent in the 1970s to 2.4 percent by the year 2000. The projected time series in this ratio are, incidentally, quite similar to the Chenery and Syrquin (1975, Table 3, pp. 20–21) cross-section estimates for low-income countries.

Apparently, there are no expert opinions on the likely future trends in total factor productivity growth and in the land stock. The qualitative literature suggests the complete disappearance of an extensive margin in agriculture, thus our Baseline assumption of zero growth in arable land. The assumption of urban land growing at 1 percent per annum is reasonable but purely guesswork. Since we have no research on total factor productivity growth in the late 1970s, let alone for the next two decades, we assumed that the 1.8 percent estimated for the pre-OPEC period will continue to the year 2000. There has, of course, been a productivity slowdown in the industrialized North for some time, but we do not have any hard evidence of similar long-run trends in the Third World. Those Third World countries that do offer some scraps of evidence fail to suggest any unambiguous slow-down in the late 1970s, much less whether the measured productivity trends are dominated by short-run structural adjustment to external shocks.

427

Allen C. Kelley / Jeffrey G. Williamson

The long-run urban transition

Table 3 covers six aspects of the urban transition: the population share urban, the labor force share in manufacturing as a ratio of the share of population urban, the growth rate of the urban population, the net rural outmigration rate (as a percent of the rural population), the net urban inmigration rate (as a percent of the urban population), and the share of urban population increase accounted for by rural to urban migration. Figure 1 plots the percent urban,

FIGURE 1 Urbanization, urban growth, and inmigration in the Third World: "Baseline" and "Stable" projections, 1960–2000

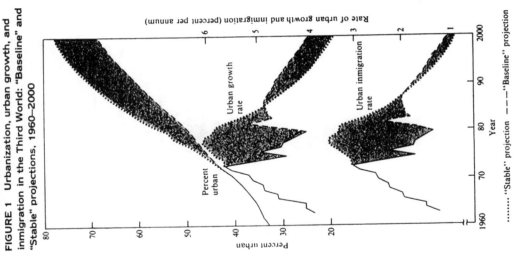

.... "Stable" projection — — "Baseline" projection

the urban growth rate, and the city immigration rate for both the Baseline and the Stable case. The comparison between these two cases is informative.

Consider Figure 1 first. The Stable projection yields the model's prediction assuming the pre-OPEC environment holds for 40 years. Thus, the Stable environment illustrates the stylized patterns of urban change in the absence of shifting macroeconomic/demographic conditions. The model appears to replicate the standard logistic curve. Indeed, rates of urban growth and urban immigration rise sharply through the 1960s and 1970s, peak in the late 1970s, and decline sharply thereafter, following Zelinsky's (1971: 233) hypothesis of mobility transition.[6] Thus, the Stable projection predicts a pronounced decline in urban growth rates from a high of about 6 percent per annum in 1980 to the much more modest annual rate of about 3.5 percent by the year 2000.

Under the Stable projection, the urban transition would have largely been completed by the year 2000. This can be seen most clearly in Figure 2, where the Stable projection is extended to cover a full century, from 1960 to 2060. The equilibrium urban share approximates 85 percent (America's current "urban limit," from which it now appears to be retreating). The representative Third World economy almost reaches that level by 2020; the urban immigration rate is near zero by 2030; and the urban growth rate matches the national rate of population growth in that year as well. Between 1960 and the end of the urban transition, the urban share increases by 52.4 percentage points (from 32.6 percent in 1960 to 85 percent in equilibrium). By the year 2000, the Stable projection has already generated an increase of 45.3 percentage points.

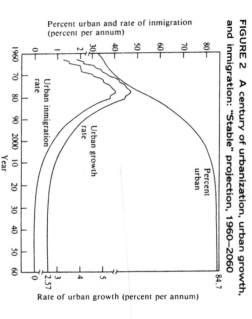

FIGURE 2 A century of urbanization, urban growth, and inmigration: "Stable" projection, 1960–2060.

In short, the economy has passed through about 85 percent of the urban transition by the year 2000.

Figure 1 also plots trends according to the Baseline projection. Urban growth rates reach an earlier peak in the Baseline projection, due to the urban growth slowdown induced by post-OPEC conditions. Furthermore, the gap between the Baseline and the Stable projection (indicated by the shaded area in Figure 1) is large. But note that urban growth rates, at least in part, tend to make up the lagging performance through the late 1980s and 1990s. Nevertheless, the Baseline projection also predicts the same long-run decline in urban growth rates—from 5.15 percent per annum in 1970 to less than 4 percent per annum in the year 2000.

In short, whether we focus on the Baseline or the Stable predictions, the model produces the conventional logistic curve with rising then falling urban population growth and immigration rates. Based on the model, problems of urban growth will be less severe by the end of the century, even though there will be no serious diminution of Malthusian population pressure in the Third World over the remainder of the century. Presumably, we will hear fewer complaints from urban planners, the much-abused term "overurbanization" may disappear from our lexicon, and pessimists' stress on urban environmental decay might lose some of its urgency. Far slower urban growth rates by the year 2000 will make it easier to cope with the accumulated problems associated with decades of rapid urban expansion.

Table 3 offers more information of interest to the urban analyst. Consider, for example, the debate on overurbanization that was initiated by Bert Hoselitz in the 1950s. His thesis was that urbanization was outpacing industrialization in developing countries in the sense that urban population shares were large in relation to industrial employment shares, at least when compared with the historical performance of currently developed countries. While Hoselitz (1955, 1957) and others found support for this thesis in data from the 1950s, it has been rejected on more recent evidence of trends in such statistics as the percent of the labor force in industry relative to the percent of the population in urban areas (United Nations, 1980; Preston, 1979). This statistic is also produced by the model in the second column of Table 3, although "industry" is limited to manufacturing. Comparing the 1970 with the 1950 statistics, the United Nations (1980: 13) concluded that "urban growth is no longer outpacing industrial growth: if anything, a slight reversal of the over-urbanization tendency has appeared." The model's predictions are consistent with the UN finding since the statistic rises, although at a declining rate, throughout the four decades. According to the UN, industrialization (or manufacturing employment growth) has served as the "engine of urbanization" over the past two decades in the Third World, and according to both the Baseline and the Stable projections, it will continue to do so in the future.

When demographers discuss the sources of urban growth, they focus on the statistical decomposition of that growth into its two parts—the natural

TABLE 3 Urbanization, urban growth, and immigration in the Third World: Baseline and Stable projections, 1960–2000

Year	Population urban (percent)	Ratio of percent labor force in mfg. to percent urban	Urban population growth rate (percent)	Net rural outmigration rate (percent)	Net urban immigration rate (percent)	Net immigrant share of urban population increase (percent)
Baseline						
1960	32.6	.374	5.56	1.41	2.91	
1965	35.8	.394	4.11	0.82	1.50	45.1
1970	39.9	.406	5.15	1.60	2.51	
1975	45.2	.420	4.48	1.38	1.72	48.1
1980	49.2	.435	4.10	1.28	1.35	
1985	54.3	.450	4.84	2.23	1.96	44.7
1990	59.7	.466	4.67	2.53	1.79	
1995	64.4	.478	4.33	2.45	1.41	35.6
2000	68.4	.486	3.97	2.21	1.05	
Stable						
1960	32.6	.374	5.56	1.41	2.91	
1965	35.8	.394	4.11	0.82	1.50	45.1
1970	39.9	.406	5.15	1.60	2.51	
1975	46.2	.427	5.94	2.67	3.29	60.6
1980	54.8	.454	5.97	3.74	3.31	
1985	62.9	.480	4.98	3.75	2.35	53.0
1990	69.3	.493	4.32	3.64	1.70	
1995	74.2	.499	3.79	3.26	1.18	34.7
2000	77.9	.501	3.43	2.85	0.84	

increase in the urban population and net migration. Thus a recent article by Nathan Keyfitz (1980) is entitled "Do cities grow by natural increase or by migration?" The question is of interest to an economist because the net migration rate is determined endogenously in any serious general equilibrium model of development and urban growth. The last column of Table 3 offers the relevant statistic, the net immigrant share of urban population increase. For the 1960s, the model yields the estimate of 45.1 percent, a figure that we have already shown replicates the findings of the demographers for that period. More to the point, the model predicts a long-run decline in the relative importance of migration as a source of urban population growth, from about 45 percent in the 1960s to about 35 percent in the 1990s (and close to zero in the year 2020). These findings are consistent with the work of Andrei Rogers (1982) and others. Yet, Table 3 illustrates that the share rises to a peak in the 1970s before embarking on the long-run decline, a temporal pattern consistent with an immigration rate that remains at high levels until late in the 1970s in the Baseline case, or until the early 1980s in the Stable case.

Comparisons with purely demographic projections

The endogenous treatment of urban immigration endows our model with a significant advantage over purely demographic models. Even the most elaborate demographic models were never developed to show how Third World urban experience over the next two decades might behave under alternative world market conditions, altered technical progress, unforeseen acceleration in demographic transition, new policy regimes, and the like. Although they were developed for somewhat different purposes, it might be interesting to compare our model's Baseline projections to the year 2000 with the projections of some purely demographic models.

Table 4 summarizes the projections of five demographic models. The key elements of the first model, a recent effort by Robert Schmidt (1981), are a roughly constant rate of total population growth (2.7 percent per annum) very close to that assumed in the Baseline and a constant net rate of rural outmigration (call it the crude migration rate) equal to 1.13 percent per annum. Thus, not only is migration exogenous, but it is held fixed at a rate far below that predicted by the Baseline projection. In the Baseline, the crude migration rate surges from 1.41 percent in 1960 to a peak of 2.53 percent in 1990, declining modestly to 2.21 percent in the year 2000 (Table 3). The second demographic projection reported in Table 4, by Jacques Ledent (1982), like all the demographic models reviewed here, takes migration rates as exogenous, although the crude migration rate in Ledent's projections is allowed to vary. In this case, the rate passes through phases predicted by Zelinsky's mobility transition hypothesis, and much like those predicted endogenously by the Baseline—namely, a rising rate is observed during the first two decades and a falling rate during the last two decades. The timing is unlike that of the Baseline projection. but the general configuration is similar. The third demographic projection, by Andrei Rogers (1978), uses a spatial variant of Ansley Coale's (1969) classic analysis of Third World demographic trends. In Rogers's model, the exogenous crude migration rate is allowed to rise over time. The fourth and fifth demographic projections have been generated by the United Nations (1980) under the guidance of Samuel Preston. These projections rely on gravity-type migration flows and natural urban/rural increase differentials, both declining linearly with the urban share. The UN projection treats the crude migration rate as exogenous. but in contrast with the other demographic models the crude migration rate declines throughout the projection period. We report two UN projections: one covers the "less developed region" as a whole, while the other is limited to the countries comprising our "representative developing country," group.

How does the Baseline projection with endogenous migration rates stack up against the demographers' projections with exogenous migration rates? First, the urban transformation is more dramatic in the Baseline. The average annual increase in the percent urban is 0.9 percent in the Baseline; only Rogers's projection matches that performance, while the others yield lower rates of urbanization over the four decades. With respect to urban growth rates, the Baseline records 4.7 percent per annum over the four decades, while the demographic projections range from 4.0 to 4.5 percent per annum. Second, all but one of the demographic projections reveal a much earlier and more pronounced slowdown in urban growth than the Baseline. The key explanation

TABLE 4 Comparison of the Baseline projection with selected demographic projections, incorporating exogenous crude rural outmigration rates (CMRs), 1960–2000

Year	Kelley–Williamson Baseline (Endogenous CMR)		Schmidt (Exogenous, fixed CMR)		Ledent (Exogenous, variable CMR)		Rogers (Exogenous, variable CMR)		UN–Preston (LDCs) (Exogenous, variable CMR)		UN–Preston (40 RDCs) (Exogenous, variable CMR)	
	Percent urban	Urban growth rate (percent)	Percent urban	Urban growth rate (percent)	Percent urban	Urban growth rate (percent)	Percent urban	Urban growth rate (percent)	Percent urban	Urban growth rate (percent)	Percent urban	Urban growth rate (percent)
1960	32.6		31.9		32.6		30.9		21.9		27.4	
		4.7		4.7		4.8		5.5		4.0		4.4
1970	39.9		38.9		40.5		40.9		25.8		32.8	
		4.8		4.3		4.7		4.6		4.1		4.3
1980	49.2		45.5		49.2		51.7		30.5		38.3	
		4.8		3.9		4.4		3.7		4.1		4.4
1990	59.7		51.0		57.2		61.0		36.5		44.4	
		4.3		na		3.9		2.8		3.8		4.3
2000	68.4		na		63.2		67.8		43.5		50.9	
Avg. per annum increase	0.9		0.6		0.8		0.9		0.5		0.6	
Avg. per annum growth		4 7		4.3		4.5		4.1		4.0		4.3

SOURCES: Schmidt: R. M. Schmidt (1981), Table 3, "Medium" projection, and based on our 40-country RDC group for aggregate population growth projection. Ledent: J. Ledent (1982), equation (20), p. 532, used to project the urban share based on the "Baseline's" per capita GNP; city growth rates are derived by applying the percent urban to the "Baseline's" population trends. Rogers: A. Rogers (1978), Table 10.11, p. 182, "scenario Bb," from his year 15 (yielding the percent urban figure closest to our "Baseline's" 1960 figure) to 55, 40 years hence. This gives us the percent urban projections. The city growth rates are derived from the same table, starting with the same year. UN–Preston (LDCs): United Nations (1980), Tables 4 and 8, pp. 11 and 16, where LDCs include all less developed regions; CMRs are exogenous but variable (UN, 1980, p. 10). UN–Preston (40 RDCs): United Nations (1980), Table 50, pp. 159–161.

Allen C. Kelley / Jeffrey G. Williamson

for these differences lies, of course, with the predicted behavior of migration in our model. Our model suggests that Third World economic development embodies forces that are far more favorable to rural–urban migration than the purely demographic model would suggest. Since the endogenous forces of economic development tend to generate increasing city "pull" in the early stages of growth, the demographers' models may not fully capture the forces driving the mobility transition. In contrast, our model offers an endogenous explanation for both the urban and the mobility transition.

What else have we learned about the urban transition?

Experiments with our general equilibrium model of urban transition have generated additional insights other than those described above. What follows is a brief summary of some of those findings.

Exogenous shocks and departures from smooth urban transitions

What happens when the "representative developing country" experiences abrupt changes in the macroeconomic/demographic environment? It turns out that the urban transition can be sharply retarded, halted, or accelerated by changes in the economic/demographic environment over which most Third World countries have little or no control.

Conditions prior to the 1973–74 OPEC price shocks were unusually favorable to rapid Third World city growth. While urban inmigration and urban growth would have been high and rising in the absence of these favorable conditions, they were even higher due to their presence. Furthermore, the modest urban growth slowdown in the Third World during the remainder of the 1970s was initiated entirely by the appearance of unfavorable exogenous conditions. Had the favorable pre-OPEC conditions prevailed after 1973, urban growth rates would have risen still further, making Third World urban problems even more severe than in fact was the case. Which of these two sets of conditions will prevail over the next two decades? The answer will have important implications for Third World urban growth up to the year 2000, although the long-run urban transition will have similar dimensions in both cases.

Which exogenous shocks matter most?

Our research has explored the impact of various "shocks" to the macroeconomic/demographic environment of the Third World economies: (1) population pressure and demographic transition; (2) unbalanced productivity advance; (3) adverse terms of trade between primary products and manufactures; (4) the relative scarcity of imported fuels and raw materials; (5) the increasing scarcity of arable land; and (6) the relative austerity of international capital markets and limits on the availability of foreign capital. Some of these have a predictable

sufficiently so that the "revolutionary" leveling would have slowed down on that score alone. Third, the "revolutionary" leveling stopped entirely because in addition an imbalance of productivity growth reappeared. Once more the industrial sector emerged as the locus of fastest productivity improvement, out-pacing such unskilled-labor-intensive sectors as agriculture and private services.

The Future. There are two reasons for expecting a resumption of the downswing of the American Kuznets Curve across the 1980s and beyond. First, more balanced patterns of productivity growth are likely to emerge in the wake of the jump in the relative price of fuels, and the shift out of fuel-intensive outputs appears to favor the demand for relatively unskilled, low-wage labor (Berndt and Wood, 1975; Hillman and Bullard, 1978). In any case, the overall productivity slowdown since the 1960s (Nordhaus, 1972; Denison, 1979; Nadiri, 1980) would encourage the belief of a diminution in the sectoral imbalance in rates of total factor productivity growth if the past century and a half is any guide. Second, labor force growth rates are expected to drop off and remain low in the late 1980s as the postwar baby boom peters out (Easterlin, 1980b), and if illegal immigration is kept in check. More to the point, the ratio of young, low-wage, new entrants into the labor force to older, high-wage members should decline sharply in the 1980s, causing a leveling even in the age-adjusted distribution of earnings and income.

C. *British 19th-Century Experience*

One can view the increase in inequality that appears to accompany early industrialization as a manifestation of disequilibrium which all capitalist countries must pass through as they emerge from a backward agrarian past. While the inequality which typically accompanies early experience with the Industrial Revolution has been documented for many Third World economies, we were never really sure about 19th century capitalist development, in spite of the allegations by classical economists and the hot debate among contemporaries of that time. Nor were we really sure how much of the alleged early inequality experience might have been purely demographic, associated with the demographic transition.

It now appears evident that America and Britain both experienced the Kuznets Curve of first rising, then falling, inequality. Nonetheless, the timing of the Kuznets Curve differed. As we have seen in Section I, British inequality seems to have peaked in the middle of the 19th century while American inequality remained at a plateau from Civil War to the 1920s before starting its downswing. Why does the leveling start a half-century sooner in Britain? Apart from this difference, were the forces driving the British Kuznets Curve across the 19th century quantitatively similar to those which we have already documented for America? It seems so.

impact on urban growth. Others offer surprises. In any case, our objective from the start has been to sort out the influence of each of these forces in the past as well as their likely influence in the future.

Our technique for identifying the impact of various exogenous events on Third World urban growth has been to employ counterfactual assumptions— what if conditions were different from those that "actually" prevailed during the OPEC watershed period of 1973–79? Table 5 presents some illustrative results. The assumptions underlying the counterfactual simulations are shown in the lower panel of the table, where the boxed figures indicate a departure in the assumptions from the actual 1973–79 experience. For example, column 1 represents urban growth rates for the actual set of conditions during this period; column 2 represents rates based on conditions during the pre-OPEC period. A comparison of these two columns provides the basis for the conclusions reached above relating to the significant impact of the favorable pre-OPEC conditions on urban growth, while columns 3 through 6 break that total effect into its component parts. In addition, columns 7 through 10 explore the implications of some additional counterfactual assumptions that are relevant to the debate about Third World urban growth. Column 7 shows the impact of reducing the rate of foreign capital inflows to zero; column 8 shows the impact of reducing population growth rates to the levels prevailing in the industrialized countries during the 1960s; column 9 shows the impact of substantially reducing the terms of trade between manufacturing and agriculture; and column 10 shows the impact of technological slowdown (the size of which is comparable to the slowdown in industrialized countries since the late 1960s). Each of these counterfactual cases should be compared with the "actual" 1973–79 performance reproduced in column 1. For example, the "fuel abundance" counterfactual projection in column 3 maintains all of the exogenous conditions underlying the "actual" of column 1 *except* fuel price behavior; while the OPEC-augmented relative increase in fuel prices was actually 5.2 per annum during 1973–79, the counterfactual calculation assumes the absence of any shift in relative fuel prices, as was approximately the case up to 1973. The table presents the results for the period 1973–79, for urban growth only. We have explored other scenarios over longer periods of time and for many economic and demographic variables. Most of the conclusions emerging from Table 5 hold when longer periods are considered in the counterfactual analysis.

It is commonly believed that the scarcity of agricultural land has played an important role in pushing labor into Third World cities. While the qualitative argument is certainly correct, has rural land scarcity been an important quantitative ingredient of Third World urban growth? The answer is unambiguously no. First, arable land stock growth is a relatively insignificant determinant of urban growth. (A comparison of the results of column 1 with those of column 5 indicates that urban growth would have been 4.61 percent per annum under counterfactual land abundance conditions, a figure only slightly below the 4.65 percent that actually obtained between 1973 and 1979.) Second, declining growth in the stock of arable land in the Third World should have tended to raise the rate of urban growth in the 1970s above that of the 1960s. Since

TABLE 5 Sources of deceleration in urban growth: some counterfactual analyses applied to 1973—79

Growth of the urban population per annum (percent)	"Actual" 1973–79 (1)	"OPEC watershed" counterfactuals					Other counterfactuals			
		Total pre-OPEC environment (2)	Pre-OPEC fuel abundance only (3)	Pre-OPEC world markets only (4)	Pre-OPEC land expansion only (5)	Pre-OPEC population pressure only (6)	Foreign capital austerity (7)	Population growth rate = developed country rate (8)	Stable world markets (9)	Technological slowdown (10)
1973	5.72	5.72	5.72	5.72	5.72	5.72	5.72	5.72	5.72	5.72
1974	5.10	5.75	5.35	5.59	5.09	5.06	5.21	4.46	5.95	5.10
1975	4.48	5.92	4.91	5.67	4.51	4.50	5.66	4.03	6.46	4.27
1976	5.03	6.03	5.28	5.90	4.95	4.96	4.37	4.37	6.51	4.60
1977	4.52	6.14	5.13	5.91	4.47	4.48	4.33	3.72	6.64	4.22
1978	4.47	6.23	5.05	5.96	4.36	4.36	4.21	3.68	6.63	3.93
1979	4.29	6.16	4.83	5.79	4.27	4.28	4.24	3.57	6.76	3.82
Average	4.65	6.04	5.09	5.80	4.61	4.60	4.67	3.97	6.49	4.32

Assumptions on underlying exogenous variables

	(1)	(2)	(3)	(4)	(5)	(6)	(7)	(8)	(9)	(10)
Relative price of fuels and raw materials, growth per annum, percent	5.2	0	0	5.2	5.2	5.2	5.2	5.2	5.2	5.2
Relative price of manufactures, growth per annum, percent	−1.6	−0.7	−1.6	−0.7	−1.6	−1.6	−1.6	−1.6	0	−1.6
Agricultural land stock, growth per annum, percent	0.5	1.0	0.5	0.5	1.0	0.5	0.5	0.5	0.5	0.5
Labor force, growth per annum, percent	2.68	2.54	2.68	2.68	2.68	2.54	2.68	0.9	2.68	2.68
Foreign capital inflow per annum as percent share in GDP	3.0	3.0	3.0	3.0	3.0	3.0	0.0	3.0	3.0	3.0
Economywide total factor productivity, growth per annum, percent	1.8	1.8	1.8	1.8	1.8	1.8	1.8	1.8	1.8	1.0

urban growth typically slowed down in the 1970s, trends in land stock growth cannot account for trends in city growth. Finally, Third World urban growth rates in the pre-OPEC period would have been only slightly higher had the arable land stock failed to grow at all over the period.

In view of the relative capital-intensity of city economies, W. Arthur Lewis (1977) has suggested that urban growth breeds foreign capital dependence and that the relative abundance of foreign capital must therefore be a significant determinant of urban growth. This hypothesis encourages the view that foreign capital inflows to the Third World must have played a critical role in accounting for the rapid urban growth up to 1973–74. After all, the Third World was a heavy recipient of foreign capital during the 1960s and 1970s, reaching an average of 3 percent of gross domestic product for the 40 countries underlying our analysis. Yet, in our model urban growth rates between 1960 and 1973 would have been approximately the same had there been no net foreign capital inflows into the Third World (see column 7 of Table 5). Thus, conditions in foreign capital markets simply will not matter much for long-run urban growth up to the year 2000.

The remaining four forces appear to be far more crucial to past, present, and future urban growth in the Third World. But even here we have some surprises: the Malthusian "bomb" plays a smaller role than conventional wisdom would suggest; the terms of trade between primary products and manufactures are more important than is the relative scarcity of imported fuels and raw materials; the unbalanced character of productivity advance across sectors is more important than the overall economywide productivity rate. Consider each of these findings in detail.

Popular accounts of Third World urban growth and urbanization suggest that high rates of population growth lie at the core of the problem. Indeed, a World Bank team recently reported that "the increase in population growth of the 20th century is the single most important factor distinguishing present and past urbanization" (Beier et al., 1976: 365). While the argument seems plausible, this conventional wisdom may have to be qualified. Rapid population growth does foster rural to urban migration and urban growth; however, it does not offer an explanation for Third World urbanization experience since it has precisely the opposite effect. While the simulation results for urbanization (i.e., percent of population in urban areas) are not presented here, the rationale of this somewhat counterintuitive result can be easily explained. Classical international trade theory has shown that a decline in the price of a factor due to an expansion of its supply (in this case labor) will result in the relative expansion of the sector in which it is used most intensively (in this case agriculture). According to such reasoning, more rapid population growth leads to slower urbanization rates. Also, contrary to conventional wisdom, "the increase in population growth in the 20th century" is not "the single most important factor." Had the Third World experienced the much lower population growth rates that prevailed in the industrialized countries in the 1960s, the rate of immigration and urban growth would still have been very high (compare

437

Allen C. Kelley / Jeffrey G. Williamson

columns 1 and 8 of Table 5). In short, it appears that population pressure has been overdrawn as a source of Third World urban growth in the recent past. Furthermore, the forces of "demographic transition" over the next two decades are unlikely to play a major role in urban growth in the future.

What about world markets, domestic price policy, natural resource scarcity, and the cost of imported fuel? Here we appear to have found one of the key determinants of Third World urban growth. Not only is our general equilibrium model very sensitive to the terms of trade between primary products and manufactures as well as to the relative price of imported raw materials and fuels, but it appears that past, present, and future trends in those prices matter a great deal. Almost all of the slowdown in urban growth after 1973 can be attributed to price trends, and the "unusually favorable" urban growth conditions in the 1960s and early 1970s are almost entirely due to "unusually favorable" price trends. Indeed, were post-OPEC price trends in the late 1970s to prevail in the future, the rate of urbanization would slow down sharply during the 1980s and stop entirely by the year 1990.

But which relative price trends matter most? Here we have some surprises. It turns out that the terms of trade between urban-based manufactures and rural-based primary products have been and will be a more important determinant of Third World urban growth performance than the relative price of imported fuels and natural resources, in spite of the fact that urban-based activities are more fuel and natural resource intensive than are rural-based primary product activities.

Finally, what about the pace and character of technological progress? The conventional wisdom has it that "the income elasticity of demand for goods provides clues as to why cities and economic growth invariably seem to accompany each other" (Mohan, 1979: 6–7). As an economy grows, the proportion spent on food declines, increasing the relative demand for urban-based nonfood products. Presumably, the faster the growth—induced by rapid rates of economywide total factor productivity advance—the more rapid the demand shifts toward urban-based activities. While this conventional argument certainly makes sense, it is not so much the overall rate of productivity advance—helping to drive per capita income improvement—that counts; rather, it is the unbalanced character of that growth which has done and will likely do most of the work.

By unbalanced total factor productivity advance we simply mean that technological change is usually much more rapid in the modern, urban-based manufacturing sectors than in the traditional, rural-based primary product sectors. Traditional service sectors, of course, also tend to lag behind. The size of the bias and the magnitude of the unbalancedness vary across countries, but they have been a technological fact of life since Britain's First Industrial Revolution, and in spite of past agricultural revolutions and the contemporary Green Revolution. The unbalanced rate of technological progress in the Third World was the key condition accounting for the unusually rapid rates of urban growth in the 1960s and 1970s. It follows that if the productivity slowdown currently characterizing the industrialized nations spills over into the industrializing Third World during the next two decades, Third World urban growth rates will slow down as well. Finally, among the eight sectors in the model, it is the unbalancedness between agriculture and manufacturing that matters most to urban growth.

Appendix
The model: an overview

Our paradigm of Third World city growth has been presented in detail elsewhere (Kelley and Williamson, 1980, 1983), so what follows is simply an overview sufficient to indicate its salient characteristics.[7]

The model is in the neoclassical general equilibrium tradition. Prices of outputs and inputs are completely flexible, and most are endogenously determined; firms are driven by profit maximization; households are driven by utility maximization; and even government demand decisions obey well-defined rules from consumer demand theory. Mobility of capital and of labor is constrained to reflect the institutional realities of Third World factor markets, but economic agents are motivated to search for the optimal sectoral and spatial use of resources.

The model's eight sectors are summarized in Table A-1. The model distinguishes between tradeables and nontradeables, the latter including various location-specific services. This specification results in spatial cost-of-living differentials. Since migrants are assumed to move in response to improvements in expected earnings adjusted for cost of living, the latter may exert an important impact on the rate of urban growth.

The model is "savings driven," and the aggregate savings pool is generated endogenously from three sources: retained after-tax corporate and enterprise profits, government saving, and household saving. (Financial transfers from abroad serve to augment government resources and thus indirectly appear as a component of government saving.) This savings pool is allocated to three uses: investment in physical ("productive") capital, investment in human capital (training), and investment in ("unproductive") housing. These three modes of accumulation are competitive and are determined endogenously. That is, training investment in skills takes place up to

the point where rates of return are equated to the economywide rate on physical capital. Dwelling investment utilizes household saving only to the point where rates of return are equated to the economywide rate on physical capital. Of course, certain institutional and technological features seriously restrict the economy's ability to equate rates of return at the margin. For example, any of the three dwelling markets (rural, urban "squatter settlements," and urban "luxury" housing) may be starved for funds since in the absence of an intersectoral mortgage market may leave housing investment requirements in excess demand. The immobility of sector-specific capital stocks makes it likely that current investment allocations are insufficient to equalize sectoral rates of return. Furthermore, firms' demands for skills may remain unsatisfied if the stock of "potential trainables" is insufficient to meet desired training investment levels. In short, capital market disequilibrium may well be a chronic attribute of our economy.

Finally, there is the set of exogenous variables that help to drive the economy over time, and that are hypothesized to have influenced Third World urban growth as a consequence: the nominal value of foreign capital and aid available in each year to help finance the development effort and forestall balance of payments problems; the total unskilled labor force determined by previous demographic events; the sectoral rates of total factor productivity advance, favoring "modern" sectors and exhibiting labor-saving; prices of imported raw materials and fuels, influenced by the vagaries of OPEC and other world market conditions; and the terms of trade between primary exportables and manufactured importables, twisted by domestic price policy and the political economy of shifting protectionist/liberalization trends in the industrialized nations.

TABLE A-1 Sector characteristics of the Kelley-Williamson general equilibrium model of Third World economies

Model's sector	Spatial location	UN standard (ISIC) counterpart	Market price determination	Tradeability characteristics	Production inputs		Production function form
					Primary	Intermediate	
Manufacturing	Urban	Manufacturing, mining	Exogenous	Internationally and interregionally traded	Capital, skills, labor	Imported raw materials (plus fuels)	Nested CES,* constant returns
"Modern" services	Urban	Electricity, water, gas; banking; public administration; trade; commerce; construction	Endogenous	Interregionally traded	Capital, skills, labor	Imported raw materials (plus fuels)	Nested CES,* constant returns
"Informal" urban services	Urban	Personal services, some trade and commerce	Endogenous	Nontraded	Labor	None	Cobb-Douglas diminishing returns
Low-quality urban "squatter" housing services	Urban	Dwellings: rent and imputed ownership	Endogenous, owner-occupier shadow price	Nontraded	Dwellings, land	None	Cobb-Douglas constant returns
High-quality urban housing services	Urban	Dwellings: rent and imputed ownership	Endogenous, owner-occupier shadow price	Nontraded	Dwellings, land	None	Cobb-Douglas constant returns
Agriculture	Rural	Agriculture, livestock, forestry, fishing, hunting	Exogenous	Internationally and interregionally traded	Capital, land, labor	Imported raw materials (plus fuels)	Cobb-Douglas constant returns
"Informal" rural services	Rural	Personal services, some trade and commerce	Endogenous	Nontraded	Labor	None	Cobb-Douglas diminishing returns
Rural housing services	Rural	Dwellings: rent and imputed ownership	Endogenous, owner-occupier shadow price	Nontraded	Dwellings	None	Leontief

*Constant elasticity of substitution.

References

Beier, G., A. Churchill, M. Cohen, and B. Renaud. 1976. "The task ahead for the cities of the developing countries," *World Development* 4, no. 5: 363–409.

Chenery, H. B., and M. Syrquin. 1975. *Patterns of Development, 1950–1970*. London: Oxford University Press.

Coale, A. J. 1969. *Population and Economic Development*. In P. M. Hauser (ed.), *The Population Dilemma*. 2nd ed. Englewood Cliffs, N.J.: Prentice-Hall.

Engles, F. 1845. *The Condition of the Working Class in England*. Translated from the German edition, with an introduction by E. J. Hobsbawm. St. Albans, Herts.: Panther, 1974.

Hoselitz, B. F. 1955. "Generative and parasitic cities," *Economic Development and Cultural Change* 3: 278–294.

———. 1957. "Urbanization and economic growth in Asia," *Economic Development and Cultural Change* 5: 42–54.

International Bank for Reconstruction and Development (IBRD). 1976. *World Tables, 1976*. Baltimore: Johns Hopkins University Press.

Kelley, A. C., and J. G. Williamson. 1980. *Modeling Urbanization and Economic Growth*. Laxenburg, Austria: International Institute for Applied Systems Analysis, RR-80-22.

Notes

Financial support for this project was provided by the Ford Foundation, the National Science Foundation, and the International Institute for Applied Systems Analysis.

1 See, for example, Keyfitz (1980), Rogers (1978, 1982), Ledent (1980, 1982), Preston (1979), and United Nations (1980).

2 Constructing such a model has been a time-consuming effort. The six-year project was started in 1978 and will be completed with a forthcoming book, *What Drives Third World City Growth?* (Kelley and Williamson, 1984). The book presents a lengthy discussion of the construction, estimation, and validation of our computable general equilibrium model of the urban transition.

3 We have used unweighted averages to summarize data on the representative developing country (RDC). It is, after all, the record of individual countries that constitutes the unit of analysis. More important, the application of weights to construct the RDC would imply that some countries are more representative than others. We do not know enough about the development process to specify such weights on an a priori basis.

4 The sample consists of the following countries: Algeria, Bangladesh, Brazil, Cameroon, Chile, Colombia, Costa Rica, the Dominican Republic, Ecuador, Egypt, El Salvador, Ethiopia, Gambia, Guatemala, Honduras, India, Indonesia, Ivory Coast, Kenya, South Korea, Malaysia, Mexico, Morocco, Nicaragua, Nigeria, Pakistan, Panama, Paraguay, Peru, the Philippines, Portugal, Sri Lanka, Swaziland, Syria, Taiwan, Thailand, Togo, Turkey, Uganda, and Yugoslavia.

5 Demographers might take issue with this critique. Postulating that migration is a constant fraction of population (that exceeds the rate of national increase) in the rural sending region, for example, results in a diminishing number of migrants per period. Thus, some demographers might argue that an exogenous and constant rural outmigration rate implies endogenous migration flows and perhaps even an endogenous urban immigration rate. The issue, however, is the extent to which there is behavioral content in the migration specification. In the demographic models, migrants do not respond to economic events; in our model, they do.

6 See also Ledent (1980, 1982), Rogers (1978: 164–167), and United Nations (1980: 29).

7 This summary draws heavily on Kelley and Williamson (1984). The model has 128 equations.

Allen C. Kelley / Jeffrey G. Williamson

———, and J. G. Williamson. 1983. "A computable general equilibrium model of Third World urbanization and city growth," in *Modeling Growing Economies in Equilibrium and Disequilibrium*, ed. A. C. Kelley, W. C. Sanderson, and J. G. Williamson. Durham, N.C.: Duke University Press Policy Studies.

———, and J. G. Williamson. 1984. *What Drives Third World City Growth?* Princeton, New Jersey: Princeton University Press.

Keyfitz, N. 1980. "Do cities grow by natural increase or by migration?" *Geographical Analysis* 12, no. 2: 142–156.

Ledent, J. 1980. *Comparative Dynamics of Three Demographic Models of Urbanization*. Laxenburg, Austria: International Institute for Applied Systems Analysis, RR-80-1.

———. 1982. "Rural–urban migration, urbanization, and economic development," *Economic Development and Cultural Change* 30, no. 3: 507–538.

Lewis, W. A. 1954. "Development with unlimited supplies of labor," *Manchester School of Economics and Social Studies* 20: 139–192.

———. 1977. *The Evolution of the International Economic Order*. Princeton, New Jersey: Princeton University Press.

Mohan, R. 1979. *Urban Economic and Planning Models*. Baltimore: Johns Hopkins University Press.

Preston, S. H. 1979. "Urban growth in developing countries: A demographic reappraisal," *Population and Development Review* 5, no. 2 (June): 195–215.

Ravenstein, E. J. 1885. "The laws of migration," *Journal of the Royal Statistical Society* 48: 167–227.

———. 1889. "The laws of migration," *Journal of the Royal Statistical Society* 52: 214–301.

Redford, A. 1926. *Labour Migration in England 1800–1850*. Edited and revised by W. H. Chaloner. New York: Augustus Kelley, 1968.

Rogers, A. 1978. "Migration, urbanization, resources, and development," in *Alternatives for Growth: The Engineering and Economics of Natural Resources Development*, ed. H. J. McMains and L. Wilcox. Cambridge, Mass.: Ballinger Publishing Company for the National Bureau of Economic Research.

———. 1982. "Sources of urban population growth and urbanization, 1950–2000: A demographic accounting," *Economic Development and Cultural Change* 30, no. 3: 483–506.

Schmidt, R. M. 1981. "The demographic dimensions of economic–population modeling," unpublished Ph.D. dissertation, Duke University, Durham, N.C.

Todaro, M. 1969. "A model of labor migration and urban unemployment in less developed countries," *American Economic Review* 59, no. 1: 138–148.

United Nations. 1980. "Patterns of urban and rural population growth," *Population Studies*, no. 68.

Weber, A. F. 1889. *The Growth of Cities in the Nineteenth Century*. New York: Macmillan.

World Bank. 1982. *World Development Report 1982*. New York: Oxford University Press.

———. 1984. *World Development Report 1984*. New York: Oxford University Press.

Zelinsky, W. 1971. "The hypothesis of the mobility transition," *Geographic Review* 61: 219–249.

13 Coping with city growth

Jeffrey Williamson

Looking backward from the present

The past four decades have witnessed economic progress in the Third World which is unprecedented by the standards of the first industrial revolution. Economic success of that magnitude has always created problems of dislocation and structural adjustment. City growth is one such problem and, given the unprecedented progress in the Third World, their problems of city growth seem, at least to those who ignore history, unprecedented as well. Rates of Third World city growth have bordered on the spectacular, averaging between 4 and 5 per cent per annum.

Analysts and policy makers are sharply divided on the wisdom of these city-growth trends. Pessimists stress the Third World's inability to cope with the social overhead requirements of rapid urban growth and high urban densities, citing ugly squatter settlements, poverty, pollution and environmental decay as evidence of their inability to cope. Third World city growth is viewed by the pessimists as another example of the tragedy of the commons, a classic example of overuse of a collective resource. In contrast, optimists view city growth as a central force raising average living standards. They view urbanisation as the natural outcome, indeed a carrier, of economic development. Debate over public options remains intense, the optimists favouring an open-city approach and the pessimists searching for ways to close the cities down to new immigrants.

Economic success breeds problems of adjustment and they certainly seem severe in Third World cities. Development economists have spent three decades debating urban unemployment, underemployment and the alleged failure to absorb the flood of rural emigrants into city labour markets; the persistent influx of newcomers makes it extremely difficult for municipal planners to improve the quality of social overhead; the migrants crowd into densely packed urban slums, jammed into primitive dwellings with little or no social services; and the rising density and size of the city augments pollution while lowering the quality of the city environment. None of this would sound unfamiliar to Victorians coping with city

Coping with city growth

growth in the middle third of the nineteenth century. They too were overwhelmed by the same 'success', and they did not have World Bank loans and foreign technologies to help them cope. They too took innumerable surveys, held countless parliamentary hearings, published one official document after another, searched for scapegoats and struggled with reform. Thus, the debate between optimist and pessimist is hardly new, and can be found in the British Parliamentary Papers as early as the 1830s, in treatises by political economists and in the British press.

Britain's city growth in comparative perspective

During the reform debates of the 1830s and 1840s, the conventional wisdom had it that Britain was undergoing unusually rapid city growth. This characterisation is embedded in the historiography even today. To offer one example, Flinn's sublime introduction to Chadwick's *Report on the Sanitary Condition of the Labouring Population* cites census data to show that some nineteenth century towns grew at rates 'that would bring cold sweat to the brows of 20th century housing committees' (Flinn 1965: 4). Thus, Glasgow grew at 3.2 per cent per annum in the 1830s, Manchester and Salford at 3.9 per cent in the 1820s, Bradford at 5.9 per cent in the 1830s, and Dukinfield nearly trebled in the 1820s. These were fast-growing cities and towns in the industrialising north, of course, and, as it turns out, these were the decades of most rapid growth. The average British city grew at a slower 2.5 per cent per annum in the 1820s, and this rate was almost half of those for the Third World in the 1960s (Table 13.1).

But contemporary observers who lived during the first industrial revolution had reason to view their city growth as unusually fast. After all, they had no previous industrialised country with which to compare their own. They had only the evidence that city growth was far faster in the early nineteenth century than it had been in the previous one. Modern historians do not suffer the same disadvantage. So, was Britain's city growth rapid by the standards of the typical European industrial revolution? As Table 13.1 shows, there was little that was unusual about Britain's city growth during her industrial revolution, except, of course, that it was first. The rest of Europe reached its peak rate of city growth much later in the nineteenth century. Yet, the rate of city growth at their respective maxima were almost identical: 2.5 per cent per annum for England in the 1820s versus a little less than 2.6 per cent per annum for the rest of Europe between 1880 and 1900.

The level of urbanisation is quite a different story. Because urbanisation is highly correlated with per capita income, it is useful to compare levels of urbanisation between countries of comparable incomes. At roughly the

Table 13.1. *A comparative assessment of city-growth performance since 1800*

Country	Date maximum city growth reached			Maximum rate of city growth per annum (%)
	Early 1800-50	Middle 1850-1900	Late post-1900	
England and Wales	1821-31			2·50
France	1830-50			1·58
Germany	1830-50			3·43
Austria		1800-1900		2·10
Belgium		1880-1900		1·95
Denmark		1880-1900		3·22
Finland		1880-1900		4·00
Italy		1880-1900		1·86
Norway		1850-70		2·94
Sweden		1850-1900		2·91
Netherlands			1900-10	1·93
Spain			1900-10	1·82
Switzerland			1900-10	3·22
Europe (excluding England and Wales)		1880-1900		2·58
Third World (excluding China)			1960-70	4·21

Source: Williamson (1990a: Table 1.1, 3).

same per capita income, England in 1840 had a much higher share of her population urban, about 48 per cent, than did the rest of Europe in the mid-late nineteenth century or the contemporary Third World, about 26 per cent. Yet this comparison tells us far more about British comparative advantage and eighteenth-century preconditions than it does about its alleged unusual city growth in the early nineteenth century, while it is the latter which is at issue in this chapter.

Birth, death, and local labour supplies in city and countryside

Understanding the demographic dimensions of what has come to be called the urban transition should help to improve our understanding of the first industrial revolution. Certainly it is essential in searching for answers to any of the following questions. Did English cities grow more by natural increase than by migration? Did city immigration rates rise as industrialisation accelerated? Did rural emigration respond vigorously to the employment demands of rapid city growth, or were rural English men and

Table 13.2. *Crude birth rates (CBR), crude death rates (CDR) and crude rates of natural increase (CRNI) in various regions of England and Wales, 1841–66*

Region	1841			1856			1866		
	CBR	CDR	CRNI	CBR	CDR	CRNI	CBR	CDR	CRNI
England and Wales									
Total	36·24	22·29	13·95	35·73	22·17	13·56	36·22	22·42	13·80
Urban	37·86	25·96	11·90	37·22	24·82	12·40	37·58	25·10	12·48
Rural	35·41	20·39	15·02	34·86	20·62	14·24	35·39	20·77	14·62
Urban detail									
London	34·75	25·86	8·89	35·10	23·63	11·47	36·42	24·31	12·11
4 largest cities	36·55	27·34	9·21	36·12	25·17	10·95	37·06	26·00	11·06
Cities > 100,000	37·50	27·16	10·34	36·70	25·42	11·28	37·71	26·20	11·51
Cities < 100,000	38·35	24·30	14·05	37·93	24·00	13·93	37·39	23·64	13·75
Southern cities	34·39	25·23	9·16	34·58	23·36	11·22	35·87	23·82	12·05
Northern cities	41·12	26·64	14·48	39·79	26·25	13·54	39·23	26·33	12·90
All cities	37·86	25·96	11·90	37·22	24·82	12·40	37·58	25·10	12·48

Source: Williamson (1990a: Table 2.1, 12).

women more attached to their villages than has been true of other industrial revolutions since? What role did push and pull forces play in rural and urban labour markets? These questions have always been at centre stage, or at least lurking in the wings, in debates about the first industrial revolution. The answers hinge on an assessment of those forces which created and displaced jobs in the two labour markets, as well as on the migration thought to link them, assessments which can be made far better with the prior demographic information summarised in this section, which is an introduction to the demographic and economic links underlying city growth.

Table 13.2 supplies estimates of crude birth rates, crude death rates, and crude rates of natural increase across the middle third of the nineteenth century. It is important to emphasise some of the facts that emerge from the table, especially given that mid-nineteenth-century England exhibits vital rates which are in sharp contrast to those in the contemporary Third World. That is, rural birth rates exceed urban in the Third World: the opposite was true of England. Rural death rates exceed urban death rates in the Third World: the opposite was true of England. Rural rates of natural increase never exceed urban rates by much in the Third World: they exceeded urban rates by a lot in England.

The demographic dimensions of English experience a century and a half ago were thus very different from those in the Third World today, and this fact had very important implications for city immigration, rural emigration and labour market behaviour during the first industrial revolution. The higher rates of natural increase in the countryside must have placed even greater stress on rural–urban labour markets in Britain compared with the Third World, as booming labour demands in her cities were distant from booming labour supplies in the countryside. Although Third World economies have certainly grown faster than did Britain, they never had to cope with Britain's poor demographic match between excess city labour demands and excess rural labour supplies. Perhaps this is one reason why, as we shall see, city immigration and rural emigration rates were so high in England even though the rate of industrialisation was fairly modest compared with the Third World. And perhaps this is one reason why, as we shall also see, wage gaps between city and countryside were so large in England compared with the Third World. England was characterised by a demographic mismatch between city and countryside which placed an unusually heavy burden on labour market adjustment.

The key explanation for the demographic mismatch is that crude death rates were much higher in the cities. They were highest in large cities (although London was an important exception), somewhat lower in small cities, but lowest in rural areas. These death rate differentials between city and countryside declined some time after 1841 but they were still pronounced in 1866. They continued to decline during the remainder of the nineteenth century, but the switch to a regime of relatively benign city mortality environments did not take place until around the First World War.

Thus, the role of public health and sanitation reform in making the city a relatively benign mortality environment is a twentieth-century phenomenon. In nineteenth-century Britain, the cities were killers, a very important fact in understanding the operation of urban labour markets during the first industrial revolution.

Much of this differential between city and countryside in crude birth and death rates may be due to differences in age distributions between the two. Both economists and demographers have long understood that fast-growing areas which absorb immigrants tend to have large proportions of young adults since it is the young adults who migrate in large numbers; Britain in the mid-nineteenth century was no different in that regard. Thus, to the extent that the cities tended to have a higher proportion of young adults, the crude death rate differentials between city and countryside understate the true mortality experience by age, a prediction borne out, for example, by infant mortality rates. Similarly, the higher crude birth rates in the cities may be attributable in large part to the fact that young adults comprised a high proportion of urban populations.

Leaving the village to go to the city: augmenting local labour supplies

Although some cities grow without industry and some industries grow outside cities, modern industrialisation tends to be city-based. As a result, industrial revolutionary events tend to augment the demand for labour and capital in the city far more rapidly than in the countryside. Labour and capital supplies, on the other hand, tend to be abundant in rural areas, a result of centuries of gradual agrarian-based pre-industrial development. One of the fundamental problems created by industrial revolutions is, therefore, to reconcile excess factor demands in the cities with excess factor supplies in the countryside. How do labour and capital markets cope with the disequilibrium?

Rural emigration is documented in Table 13.3. With the exception of the war-induced good times for English agriculture between 1801 and 1806, rural emigration took place at every time between 1776 and 1871. Furthermore, the rate of emigration more than doubled over the period. That rural emigration rates rose while urban immigration rates fell may seem odd, but the arithmetic is almost inevitable. After all, these rates are calculated as the ratio of migration flows to a population base, and because the urban population base enjoyed fast growth (augmented by the immigrants) while the rural population base did not (depleted by the emigrants), city immigration and rural emigration rates would have moved in opposite directions solely because of the demographic arithmetic.

These measured rates of rural emigration are inconsistent with the conventional wisdom that English farm labourers were reluctant to move, and that the agricultural counties were full of 'a vast, inert mass of redundant labour' who were 'immobile' (Redford 1926: 84 and 94). On the contrary, these are quite impressive emigration rates by almost any standard. Indeed, after the 1820s they were higher than they have been in the Third World recently, and by the 1860s they were twice as large. The comparison suggests that rural English men and women were no more reluctant to leave their village parishes than were rural populations in the Third World, although that judgement should await evidence on the size of the earnings differentials between city and countryside which were necessary to induce the emigration.

Did England's cities grow more by immigration or by natural increase? This question is motivated in part by a debate over contemporary Third World experience, where city growth has been spectacular. Modern

Table 13.3. *Urban immigration and rural emigration, England and Wales, 1776–1871*

Years	Urban annual rates (%)			Urban population increase due to immigration (%)	Rural emigration rate (%)
	Population increase	Natural increase	City immigration		
1776–81	2·08	0·87	1·26	59·49	0·86
1781–6	1·81	0·21	1·62	88·99	0·50
1786–91	2·20	0·89	1·37	61·08	0·56
1791–6	2·17	1·04	1·37	53·69	0·79
1796–1801	2·08	1·03	1·10	51·87	0·83
1801–6	2·15	0·27	1·91	88·18	−0·18
1806–11	2·07	1·52	0·59	27·53	1·07
1811–16	2·40	1·10	1·37	55·55	0·59
1816–21	2·39	1·40	1·06	42·82	0·87
1821–6	2·61	1·57	1·12	41·35	1·19
1826–31	2·33	1·34	1·06	43·95	1·14
1831–6	2·08	1·10	1·04	48·66	1·01
1836–41	2·04	1·26	0·83	39·50	1·20
1841–6	2·41	1·25	1·23	49·68	1·57
1846–51	2·05	1·13	0·97	45·89	1·73
1851–6	2·06	1·34	0·77	36·39	1·54
1856–61	2·08	1·52	0·60	27·92	1·60
1861–6	2·35	1·36	1·06	43·67	2·10
1866–71	2·29	1·21	1·15	48·63	2·05

Source: Williamson (1990a: Table 2.5, 26).

demographers have shown that the answer depends where in the urban transition the assessment is made: at some intermediate point in the urban transition most countries tend to switch from migration-driven to urban-natural-increase-driven city growth. English experience during the first industrial revolution is similar. Immigration accounted for about 60 per cent of city growth 1776–1811 but for about 40 per cent 1846–71. The cross-over point – where the contribution of natural increase began to exceed immigration – appeared in the 1810s and 1820s. In any case, immigration accounted for a far higher share of city growth in England between 1776 and 1871 than it has in the Third World. Those high nineteenth-century city death rates and low rates of natural increase account for the difference.

Cities were prime movers during the industrial revolution, but how much of that dynamism was attributable to the fact that they were full of young adults, a demographic fact which had advantageous economic

Table 13.4. *Population distribution by age, immigrants and non-immigrants: Britain's cities in 1851 (%)*

Group	Less than 20	Greater than or equal to 20
Irish immigrants	25·6	74·4
Other immigrants	23·0	77·0
Non-immigrants	58·9	41·1
Total	42·8	57·2

Source: Williamson (1990a: Table 2.11, 41).

consequences? If so, was it caused by a migrant-selectivity bias, young adults favouring the cities and shunning the countryside? It turns out that cities had a significantly larger share of people in their twenties and thirties than the countryside in 1861 (33 versus 28 per cent). The opposite was true of the tails of the age distribution: the countryside had more old people and children. Furthermore, the young-adult bias during the first industrial revolution was stronger than it is today in the Third World. And since Britain's cities were full of young adults in 1861, it is not surprising to find that they had been even more full of young adults a few decades earlier. After all, the cities were absorbing immigrants at a more rapid rate in the late eighteenth century than they were in the mid-nineteenth century, and immigrants tended to be young adults.

Migrants incur costs when they move and these were sufficiently large in nineteenth-century Britain that significant returns over a number of years were necessary to motivate even short-distance moves. Older people with shorter expected productive lifetimes and bigger village commitments must have found the migration costs too high and the returns too low. Thus, migration selected young adults, those who had the greatest chance for immediate employment and who could recoup their migration costs over a longer lifetime (including the emotional pain of leaving the village). It follows that the greater the influence of urban job pull, the greater the young-adult selectivity bias. The greater the influence of rural push, the more likely migration would be a family affair.

The influence of the young-adult selectivity bias can be seen in two ways, in the stock of city immigrants enumerated in any given census and in the flow of city immigrants between any two censuses. The census figures for 1851 in Table 13.4 should be enough to illustrate the point. About 41 per cent of the non-immigrants in Britain's cities were adults, while the figures for the Irish and other immigrants (primarily from the British countryside) were almost twice that figure, about 74 and 77 per cent. The adult-selectivity bias mattered a lot in the cities.

The cities had lower dependency rates and an abundance of young adults. Partly as a result of this favourable demographic feature, the cities had higher per capita incomes than the countryside. This favourable demographic feature also helps explain why the cities had lower relief burdens than the countryside. Many historians have explored the sources and impact of the Old Poor Laws in England; all stress the fact that the Speenhamland system was an agricultural relief scheme. Yet, how much of that fact was due simply to demography – young adults selecting the cities and shunning the countryside, leaving behind dependants who were more vulnerable to pauperism? At least in 1851, the incidence of pauperism was higher in the villages than in the cities and most of the difference is explained by the young-adult bias. Furthermore, this fact may help to explain why the cities seem to have higher saving and accumulation rates than the countryside. This inference follows directly from what development economists call the dependency hypothesis: more children and elderly people per productive adult increases consumption requirements at the expense of saving. This dependency rate effect may have been manifested by a direct influence on the household saving behaviour of common labour. But it seems more likely to have had its impact indirectly, first on poor relief, then on the local tax burden and thus finally on disposable incomes of potential savers paying the taxes (who were certainly not common labourers). In any case, the inference is that the young adult bias must have favoured saving in the cities where the accumulation requirements were highest, and it did so when the city immigration rates were highest (in the late eighteenth and early nineteenth centuries), and when financial capital markets were most poorly equipped to cope with the problems of capital transfer from village to city.

The young adult bias had another favourable influence on British industrialisation. As the demand for labour boomed in the cities, village immigrants were needed to fill the new jobs. But the immigrants who arrived in large numbers were young adults who had two attributes: they were in the age groups least vulnerable to the high mortality environment, and they were in the age groups with the highest fertility rates. Thus the first generation of new immigrants generated a bigger increase in the local labour force in the next generation than would have been the case without the young-adult bias. The next generation of city growth, therefore, required less immigrants to satisfy those booming labour demands. These demographic responses would have tended to ease the pressure on labour markets linking city with countryside had not industrialisation quickened after the Napoleonic Wars, augmenting those city labour demands even

Coping with city growth

more. Alternatively, without the demographic accommodation, city immigration would have been even higher in the post-Napoleonic era, and so too would have been the pressure on labour markets linking city to countryside.

City labour demand and migrant absorption

Where were the jobs that absorbed the farm exodus? Was it rapid job creation in manufacturing that pulled the farm emigrant to the city, or was it the threat of agricultural unemployment that pushed the farm emigrant into low-wage jobs in the city service sector? These are very old questions which concerned Marx and Mayhew in the nineteenth century just as much as they concern the International Labour Organisation and the World Bank now.

Table 13.5 disaggregates non-agricultural employment growth into three sectors. Panel A makes it clear that manufacturing was hardly the leading sector driving non-agricultural employment growth during the French Wars. On the contrary, employment growth in manufacturing was a bit below that of services and far below that of mining. Rapid employment growth in a small sector may not create very many jobs, of course, so Panel B shows the share of the non-agricultural employment increase which was attributable to each sector. Panel B shows that between 1755 and 1811, manufacturing and mining job creation were about of equal importance, and services were more than twice as important as both. The service sector, not manufacturing, was the main source of new urban jobs up to 1811. Conditions changed somewhat after the wars because new jobs in manufacturing increased as a share of total new non-agricultural jobs. Even so, at least between 1841 and 1861, the service sector maintained its position as the main source of new urban jobs. City growth across the British industrial revolution cannot be understood by looking at booming labour demand in manufacturing alone; mining and the heterogeneous service sector were equally or even more important.

Figure 13.1 offers a simple characterisation of the city labour market which helps to organise the discussion for the remainder of this section. Total city employment appears on the horizontal axis and grew at 1.75 per cent per year between 1821 and 1861 (or, at least, non-agricultural employment did). The real wage facing city firms (not to be confused with workers' living standards) is on the vertical axis and grew at 0.91 per cent per year over roughly the same period. Figure 13.1 supposes that all city immigration was attributable to the combined effects of the pull of wages and employment conditions in the cities as well as to the push of conditions in Irish and British agriculture. Thus, the labour supply curves are taken to

Table 13.5. *The sources of civilian employment growth in non-agriculture, 1755–1861*

Period	Manufacturing	Mining	Services	Non-agricultural
A Percentage per annum				
1755–1811	0·70	4·31	0·79	0·92
1821–61	n.a.	n.a.	n.a.	1·56
1841–61	1·45	4·69	1·88	1·82
B Percentage of non-agricultural employment increase due to				
1755–1811	23·8	22·4	53·8	53·8
1841–61	34·6	11·5	53·8	53·8

Source: Williamson (1990a: Table 4.2, 85).

be very elastic, reflecting a powerful response of potential immigrants to rising city wages. Labour supply shifts rightward in response to the forces of natural increase which underlay the demographic behaviour of the resident labour force, as well as conditions in British and Irish agriculture which pushed labour into the cities. In equilibrium, the incremental labour supply matching the boom in labour demand comes from two sources, the natural increase in the resident labour force and immigration.

This figure makes it clear that there were four forces at work that influenced immigrant absorption and wages in this labour market. First, there was the shift in labour supplies generated by the combined effects of demographic forces in the city and by all the push forces in Ireland (like the famine) and in British agriculture (like enclosures). There is a second force at work in Figure 13.1, namely the elasticity of city labour supply which was conditioned primarily by potential farm emigrants' response to the more favourable employment conditions in the city, a force which will be considered later. The more elastic the labour supply, the cheaper will be city labour, the bigger will be city employment growth, and the smaller will be wage gaps between city and countryside. If these two forces are big enough, a glut in city labour supply can force wages down and blight otherwise dynamic urban growth with poverty. Those city demographic forces were discussed in the previous section, and immigration from the British countryside will be discussed at greater length below. What about the Irish?

To add to all the other social problems which Britain's cities had to face during the first industrial revolution, they also had to absorb the Irish. Rapid growth after the French Wars made the absorption easier, but the Irish immigrants still serve to complicate any assessment of Britain's

Coping with city growth

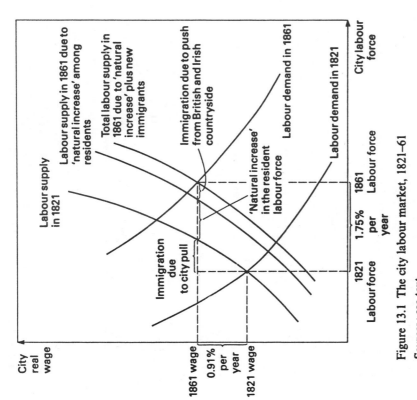

Figure 13.1 The city labour market, 1821–61
Sources: see text.

economic performance up to the 1850s. Would the cities have been able to cope with growth far more easily in their absence? Would common labour's wages and living standards in the city have risen much more rapidly? Was rural emigration from the British countryside strongly suppressed by Irish competition in the cities? Did British industrialisation receive a powerful boost from an elastic supply of cheap Irish labour? That immigration lowers the wages of comparably skilled native-born, and serves to 'crowd out' the native-born from city jobs, is obvious. What is not so obvious, however, is whether the Irish had a significant quantitative impact. Are they important to any fundamental understanding of British city growth in the four decades after 1820? Like other immigrants, the Irish were, of course, unskilled, urban and young adults, but were they really a big part of labour supplies to the cities? With the possible exception of the famine-driven 1840s, they were never more than about 8 per cent of the British labour force. In any case, when we pose the counterfactual 'What would Britain's economy have been like in the absence of Irish immigrations after 1820?', the answers are: Yes, the Irish immigrations did tend to inhibit rural emigration from the British countryside. No, they did not play a significant role in accounting for the behaviour of real wages in Britain. No, they did not foster industrialisation. (Williamson 1990a: ch. 6).

There are two other forces at work in Figure 13.1. There is the shift in city labour demand over time as technological and accumulation events associated with the industrial revolution unfolds over time. Finally, there is the elasticity of city labour demand, an issue over which opinions abound but on which evidence is slight. Debates in development economics would suggest that this fourth issue needs more of our attention.

Development economists have always stressed a technological asymmetry between modern and traditional sectors. They view the modern sector (typically manufacturing) as capital intensive in a technology where the elasticity of substitution between capital and labour is low. In contrast, they view the traditional sector (typically agriculture) as labour intensive where the elasticity of substitution is high. These conditions imply that the elasticity of demand for labour in the city is low, conditions that make the absorption of immigrant labour difficult because it takes a big drop in wages to encourage firms to expand employment very much. The elasticity of city labour demand will be even lower if the price elasticity of product demand is low, a condition typical of many Third World economies which, by hiding behind protective tariff policies, are relatively closed to trade.

So much for development economists and so much for the contemporary Third World. What about Britain during the first industrial revolution? Here there may be reason to have a more optimistic view of those labour demand elasticities. After all, real wages did rise sharply after the French Wars, and especially in the cities, so there is little evidence suggesting that British cities had unusual difficulties absorbing the immigrants.

What about the shifts in labour demand in Britain during the first industrial revolution? There are four forces that underlay that boom in city labour demand.

First, there were output price movements. If world market conditions tended to raise the relative price of manufactures (or to lower the price of raw material inputs), manufacturing should have boomed on that account, the derived demand for city labour should have shifted outward to the right, and immigrants would have been absorbed by this rapid rate of job creation. Between 1821 and 1861, however, just the opposite took place. Instead, the terms of trade moved against manufacturing. In cotton textiles, for example, the terms of trade fell by more than 30 per cent over the three decades following 1821. It has long been argued that a good share of that fall in the terms of trade was due to rapid technological advance which lowered costs in British textiles. A plausible argument can be made, however, that other world market conditions were also helping to drive down the relative price of British manufactures after the French Wars. There is the rapid expansion of competitive foreign supplies to consider. Between 1820 and 1860, Britain's share in trade between France, Germany, Italy, the United States and Britain itself declined from 27 to 25 per cent, and Britain's share in industrial production also declined, from 24 to 21 per cent. This extraordinary expansion of industrial production among Britain's competitors served to glut world markets and to drive down the relative price of manufactures. Second, the rise in protectionism on the Continent also must have weakened Britain's terms of trade. Thus, to the extent that some of those price trends were attributable to world market conditions, then they must have held back rightward shifts in city labour demand.

Second, there is capital accumulation to consider. Capital accumulation in manufacturing clearly served to augment capacity, to create jobs and to shift labour demand to the right. Although the rate of capital deepening (an increase in capital per worker) was very slow during the first industrial revolution, the rate of capital widening (an increase in employment at fixed capital per worker) was much more impressive. Indeed, the non-agricultural capital stock grew at 2.65 per cent per year between 1830 and 1860.

Third, productivity advance in manufacturing augmented labour demand there. For an economy so dependent on trade, where output demands were fairly price elastic and where manufactures could be vented on to foreign markets, rapid productivity advance in British manufacturing surely played an important role in fostering the expansion of that sector, thus causing the demand for labour to shift out to the right. Marx made the claim that capitalist development is uneven, and that unbalanced technological advance tends to breed an increasing concentration of production and employment in industrial activities. The limited evidence on sectoral rates of total factor productivity growth seems to confirm the premise that industry leads agriculture. It is certainly consistent with nineteenth-century United States evidence, and it seems to be consistent with Third World experience as well. McCloskey (1981b: Table 6.2) has argued that the evidence, such as it is, supports the view for Britain between 1780 and 1860: productivity growth rates are estimated to have been 1.8 per cent per year in industry and transport, much higher than in agriculture at 0.45 per cent per year. Lack of hard evidence, however, has kept the debate alive.

Fourth, there is the possibility of labour-saving to consider. Ever since Marx started us thinking about labour displacement and the reserve army, labour-saving has become entrenched in the lexicon of growth theorists, economic historians and development economists. Yet surprisingly little has been done to isolate its impact on the derived demand for labour during the British industrial revolution. Certainly there have been many anecdotal accounts of how certain craftsmen were displaced by modern technology (e.g. the hand-loom weavers), but a comprehensive assessment of the impact of these disequilibrating technological forces has yet to be made. Von Tunzelmann (1981: 158), however, finds no evidence to support the labour-saving hypothesis. If he is correct, then Britain would have contrasted sharply with America after 1820 and certainly with the Third World where labour-saving is generally agreed to have been pronounced. The jury is still out on labour-saving during the first industrial revolution.

There is one more influence to consider, the so-called urban bias. While it dominates the Third World, it played no role in Britain. The urban bias refers to those policies which favour city growth at the expense of the countryside. There is no shortage of policies which have that effect in the Third World: the domestic terms of trade are twisted against agriculture, thus encouraging more rapid rural emigration to the city than would have been true in the absence of such policies; tariffs and exchange-rate management also serve to protect urban industry, fostering its expansion at agriculture's expense; financial markets are manipulated by government policy to create cheap capital for favoured urban industries; and social overhead capital is allocated disproportionately to the cities (schools, health facilities, roads, water supplies and electricity), all offered at less than user cost, and all financed from general tax revenues rather than from urban land taxes.

Given the dominance of this view (Lipton 1976), it is important to stress that the urban bias played no role in Britain between 1780 and 1860, although it certainly did for post-Civil War America and the Soviet economy under Stalin. Indeed, it could be argued that a rural bias motivated British policy. The policy that mattered, of course, was the Corn Laws. At least until the repeal in 1846, tariffs favoured rural agriculture and penalised city industry. Certainly the debates from 1815 to 1846 posed the issue that way. Cobden and the Anti-Corn Law League made it absolutely clear who gained and who lost. Landlords gained from high rents and the urban working man suffered from the 'bread tax'. Manufacturers rightly complained that they had to pay higher nominal wages, that the export trade was repressed and that their profits were choked off. In short, city growth would have been faster in the absence of the Corn Laws (Williamson 1990b). Whether the great Victorian trading boom following the late 1840s was due mainly to repeal and free trade has, of course, been debated at length (ch. 12 above), but that event did not herald the replacement of a rural bias with an urban bias, but rather it implied a policy switch from rural bias to neutrality.

Debate over Third World urbanisation generates the same gloomy pessimism that characterised Britain in the early nineteenth century. Even the rhetoric is the same, Victorian and modern critics both citing urban unemployment, primitive housing, inadequate public services and poverty. Many modern analysts think the Third World has 'overurbanised', and many Victorian urban reformers thought the same was true of Britain. According to this view, the cities are too large and too many, and they got that way in part through some perverse migration behaviour. Pushed off the land by technological and institutional events in agriculture, by harvest failure and by Malthusian pressure, rural emigrants flood the cities in far greater numbers than good jobs can be created for them. Attracted by some irrational optimism that they will be selected for those scarce high-wage city jobs, the rural immigrants keep coming. Lacking high-wage jobs in the growing industrial sectors, the glut of rural immigrants spills over into low-wage service sectors, manifested by unemployment and pauper-ism, while their families crowd into inadequate housing.

Many contemporary economic historians have used this Third World paradigm in thinking about British cities during the first industrial revolution (Pollard 1981b, Williamson 1981), and many point to low-wage casual labour on the docks and in the building trades to illustrate the point. Certainly Mayhew made much of what now would be called London's informal services, and low-wage casual labour, sweat-shops and street vending have all played an important part in nineteenth-century labour histories since. Whether one adopts the view that the urban service sector was a vast holding area for the reserve army of immigrants who were pulled into the city in anticipation of getting those high-wage industrial jobs, or whether one shares Mayhew's view that London street people were pushed into those low-wage jobs, both predict the following: while the earnings of new city immigrants may have caught up eventually with those of previous residents, newcomers faced poor job prospects early on since the cities had problems absorbing them when they first arrived. Thus, if Victorian cities really had serious absorption problems, immigrants must have had lower earnings than non-immigrants.

The limited information in the 1851 census (Williamson 1990a: ch. 5) provides little evidence to support this view. Unemployment and poverty certainly blighted Britain's cities in the mid-nineteenth century, but the same was true of the countryside. There is nothing inconsistent between the well-known finding of poverty in Britain's cities during the industrial revolution and a relatively efficient city labour market that absorbed the migrants quickly into the labour force. And quick absorption it was. With the significant exception of the Irish, male immigrants into Britain's cities did not exhibit lower earnings than non-immigrants. Nor did they suffer higher unemployment rates. The evidence seems to be inconsistent with the view that migrants entered the city in response to inflated expectations of future earnings possibilities, suffering unemployment or underemployment in traditional low-wage service sector jobs while they waited for better jobs. Rather, they were motivated by current job prospects, and those prospects were confirmed. This is not to say that migrants were never unemployed or that they could not be found in large numbers in the low-wage service sectors. The evidence from the 1851 census simply confirms that city immigrants had the same earnings experience as non-immigrants.

Leaving the village to go to the city: a second look

Did farm labourers respond quickly to economic opportunities in the cities? Or, did inelastic migrant labour supplies to the city create urban–rural wage gaps and drive up the cost of city labour, thus choking off the rate of industrialisation?

Table 13.6 shows that an index of the gap between the average nominal earnings of unskilled city and farm labour (1797 = 100) rose sharply across the first half of the nineteenth century. The rise in farm wages lagged far behind the rise in city wages. The table suggests that the nominal wage gap did not begin to rise until well after the French Wars. Indeed, the index implies that wartime conditions served to erode the gap. Because the conflict caused a contraction in foreign trade (cutting back the import supply of grains and choking off the foreign export demand for manufactures), the relative price of grains rose, and domestic agriculture was favoured. It is hardly surprising, therefore, that the wage gap collapsed since wartime labour demands were unusually strong in the countryside. With the end of the wars, however, the pace of British industrialisation accelerated and agriculture resumed its long-run relative demise. Labour demand in the cities far outstripped local labour supplies. Rising wage gaps between farm and city need not imply that rural emigration was small (Table 13.3). Rather, they imply only that it was not big enough, so the relative cost of labour rose in the cities as a consequence. By the 1830s, nominal city wages were 73 per cent higher than farm wages.

Have other countries repeated the British experience? The absence of comparable data makes it impossible to say for sure, but one thing is certain: wage gaps of this magnitude have been commonly observed in the middle of industrial revolutions ever since Britain experienced the first. City wages are about 41 per cent higher than farm wages in the contemporary Third World, and they were about 51 per cent higher among

Table 13.6. *Trends in the British nominal wage gap, 1797–51 (1797 = 100)*

Year	Index
1797	100·0
1805	86·0
1810	96·7
1815	105·1
1819	99·7
1827	132·4
1835	134·7
1851	148·3

Source: Williamson (1990a: Table 7.1, 182). The gap is calculated as the difference between the unskilled earnings rate of urban labour and the farm-earnings rate, divided by the farm-earnings rate. Thus, it is the percentage differential by which city unskilled wages exceeded farm wages, the common measure used in the development literature.

late nineteenth-century industrialisers. Nor were things much different in the New World: wage gaps were about 50 per cent in America in the mid-1890s at the end of three decades of fast industrialisation after the Civil War.

Why were English farm labourers in the 1830s willing to accept much lower wages than those available in city and town? Perhaps these nominal wage gaps fail to measure the better quality of village life compared with the city. After all, these nominal wage gaps fail to take account of the fact that the cities were expensive places in which to live, that the cities were ugly places in which to live, that there were relief schemes in the countryside to ease the burden of seasonal unemployment, and that farmers made some payments in kind. While these attributes do help to explain that 73 per cent wage gap in the 1830s, an equally interesting question is whether they can help account for the rise in the wage gap after the French Wars. There are reasons to think so, especially those related to the rising cost and falling quality of city life, events which city employers must have been forced to offset with higher nominal wages if they were to attract rural workers in large numbers.

One price which increases sharply during industrial revolutions is city rents. There are three reasons for this. First, housing construction is labour intensive and per unit labour costs do rise during industrial revolutions. Second, urban housing is space intensive, and rising urban land scarcity is a fact of life during all industrial revolutions. Third, the rate of productivity advance in the building trades is slower than that of commodity production. All of these factors should serve to raise the cost of urban housing as industrialisation unfolds. It is manifested by a rise in rents, and it is manifested by families saving on rising dwelling costs by moving into smaller dwellings and by the dwellings themselves packing in closer together, events which serve to raise mortality and morbidity, while lowering the quality of city life.

The facts support this view. From the 1790s to the 1840s, real rents (nominal rents relative to the cost of living) in Leeds, Black Country towns and an industrial village in Staffordshire rose by 2.5 per cent per year, for a whopping 30 per cent per decade. Since rents accounted for about 20 per cent of the urban labourer's budget, this explosion raised the rate of city cost of living growth by perhaps as much as 0.5 per cent per year. A good share of the increase in the nominal wage gap between city and farm may simply reflect these forces.

Furthermore, what about the poor quality of urban life? Did urban employers have to pay a premium to attract potential rural emigrants to locations of poorer environmental quality, manifested most vividly by the much higher mortality and morbidity in nineteenth-century cities, so much so that Frederick Engels called it 'social murder'? The next section will discuss at greater length how to estimate the value of these ghastly urban disamenities. It turns out that the premium may have been as high as 24 per cent in England as a whole.

After adjusting for the fact that cities were expensive, that cities were environmentally unattractive and required some compensation for the 'bads' prevailing there, and that poor relief was used to augment workers' incomes in the countryside during slack seasons, the nominal wage gap drops to a true wage gap of about 33 per cent. The central fact remains: although they left their villages in large numbers, farm emigrants were slow to take advantage of better city jobs.

Did these wage gaps matter? Contemporary development economists think that they do, and they have been central to debates over development strategy since the Second World War. By appealing to sluggish migration and resulting distortions which make wages 'too high' in the city, development economists have used this evidence to support arguments for protection. Since Britain did not protect city industries with tariffs, did wage gaps in the 1830s lower rates of industrialisation well below what they should have been? If farm labour had responded to city employment opportunities robustly enough to erase the wage gap, would indus-trialisation have taken place even more rapidly than it did up to the 1860s? It can be shown that it would have. Indeed, one estimate has it that industrial employment growth might have been something like 2.7 per cent

and villages in nineteenth-century England cannot be denied (Table 13.2). But the best indicator of environmental quality is the infant mortality rate, and the Registrar General started to publish comprehensive evidence on it back as early as 1841. Not only was infant mortality higher in the 1840s than in the 1900s, but the cities had much higher rates than the countryside. Furthermore, the difference between city and countryside was far bigger in the 1840s than in the 1900s. These differentials had disappeared by the 1920s, but for nineteenth-century England, the cities were indeed the killers advertised by Engels' rhetoric.

What role did density, crowding, city size and industrialisation play in accounting for the wide variance in infant mortality rates in the 1830s? It turns out that city density and size both play a positive role, confirming the conventional wisdom that urbanisation bred high mortality. Municipal social overhead and housing simply could not or did not keep up with the requirements that were generated by population size and density, thus implying a deterioration in the mortality environment. In contrast, the industrial orientation of the city, or lack of it, played no role. It was not industrialisation that generated the disamenities associated with the high infant mortality rates, but rather urbanisation. The south of England and Wales were regions of very high quality of life, even after controlling for regional urban and industrial attributes. In summary, a very large share of the infant mortality variance across England in the 1830s can be explained by two forces: crowding within dwellings, and the density of the urban environments within which those dwellings were located.

Increasing land scarcity, rising labour costs, lagging productivity advance, more expensive resource-intensive building materials and foregone dwelling investment during the French Wars all served to generate the spectacular increase in city rents from the 1790s to the 1840s. Workers responded by economising on dwelling space and quality. Crowding resulted. Perhaps for some of the same reasons, municipal planners found it difficult to maintain the necessary social overhead capital to serve the environmental needs of a rapidly expanding city population. City environments deteriorated as a result. Both of these forces kept disamenity levels, mortality and morbidity high in the cities.

Did workers demand a premium (above the lower village wages) for that city life? It turns out that they did. The premium was higher in the north of England where the towns were environmentally worse (ranging between 12 and 30 per cent) than in the south of England (ranging between 8 and 20 per cent), and ranged between 10 and 24 per cent for England as a whole (Williamson 1990a: ch. 9). These premia were not big enough to erase the wage gains from moving from village to city. Nor were they large enough to erase the wage gains for the average Englishman between the 1800s and the 1860s. But they were large enough to confirm the views of Victorian reformers that the cities were an environmental mess which needed to be cleaned up by more active policy intervention.

Did Britain underinvest in cities?

By the standards of the contemporary Third World and the late nineteenth century, Britain recorded very modest investment shares in national income and very modest rates of accumulation. That fact has generated a long and active debate centred around the question: was the investment share low because investment requirements were modest, or was the investment share low because of a savings constraint? The first argues that investment demand in the private sector was the critical force which drove accumulation during Britain's industrial revolution, low rates of technical progress and the absence of a capital-using bias both serving to minimise private sector investment requirements. The second argues that Britain's growth was savings-constrained. Until very recently, the first view dominated the literature.

This dominant view sees early nineteenth-century Britain as so labour intensive and innovations so capital-saving that investment requirements to equip new workers could easily be fulfilled by modest amounts of domestic savings, so easily in fact that domestic savings had to look for outlets overseas. There are some odd omissions from this view. First, rarely is there any mention of housing, infrastructure and social overhead. This is a puzzling omission because there is another strand of historical literature which stresses crowding in the cities, a deteriorating urban environment and lack of public investment in infrastructure (sewers, water supplies, street paving, lighting, refuse removal and so on). It is also puzzling because such investments loom very large in typical industrial revolutions, the Third World included. Indeed, many development economists and historians have argued that such investments are essential complements to the plant and equipment set in place in modern industry. Without them, rates of return in the modern private sector may sag and industrialisation can be choked off. Dirty and unhealthy cities can serve to drive up the effective price of labour to urban firms either by producing sick workers or by requiring large nominal wage bribes to get reluctant workers to enter dirty cities. Both would serve to raise the effective cost of labour and choke off industrial profits. Thus, low rates of accumulation in industry may be induced, in part, by low rates of investment in complementary public infrastructure and private housing.

Second, discussion on this subject may have confused what actually was with what should have been. It may be a mistake to conclude that Britain's labour-intensive growth strategy was a good thing. Those modest investment requirements may reflect an attempt to achieve an industrial revolution on the cheap. If so, the strategy may have turned out to be more expensive in the longer run.

If investment requirements were really modest at the margin during the first industrial revolution, this should have been reflected in declining average capital–output ratios (ACORs) between, say, 1800 and 1860. Decline they did: Britain's economy-wide ACOR underwent a spectacular drop from about 5.2 in 1800 to about 3.6 in 1860, the biggest fall by far taking place in the first three decades of the nineteenth century. The fall is a little less spectacular outside agriculture, but big nonetheless: from 4.9 in 1800 to 3.5 in 1860. At the margin, therefore, Britain's investment requirements during the industrial revolution were far below eighteenth-century averages. Yet, one of the key reasons why investment requirements were so modest, and why the ACOR drops so steeply, is that Britain failed to commit resources to those urban infrastructure investments that, to paraphrase Sir Arthur Lewis, makes city growth in the contemporary Third World so capital intensive and thus so expensive. Investment in housing and public works simply failed to keep pace with the rest of the economy in the first half of the nineteenth century. One can see this very clearly when the ACOR outside agriculture is calculated to exclude housing and public works: then the ACOR rises over those six critical decades. One can also see it by looking at per capita growth in social overhead capital stock (residential housing plus public works and public buildings). These growth rates were negative from 1760 to 1800, and they were far below those of the rest of the economy between 1800 and 1860. Indeed, these estimates suggest that dwelling stocks per capita were lower in 1860 than they had been in 1760!

Investment requirements during the late eighteenth century were kept modest by allowing the stock of social overhead per capita to fall, contributing to a deterioration in the quality of urban life. This growth regime continued for the first three decades of the nineteenth century, although not with quite the same intensity. By 1830, therefore, Britain had accumulated an enormous deficit in her social overhead capital stocks by pursuing seventy years of industrialisation on the cheap. It cost her dearly, as the social reformers were about to point out. Between 1830 and 1860, there is some evidence of catching up in public works, in part a response to the goading of the social reformers, but the gap in growth rates between dwelling stocks and all other fixed capital per capita increased. In short, while actual investment requirements may have been modest during the first industrial revolution, they would not have been so modest had investment in social overhead kept pace. It had its price: the cities became ugly, crowded and polluted, breeding high mortality and morbidity. The reformers were moved to political agitation.

In early July 1842, during a summer of high unemployment and social protest in the cities, Edwin Chadwick, secretary to the Poor Law Commission, presented to the House of Lords his 'Report on the Sanitary Condition of the Labouring Population of Great Britain'; it has been viewed as a turning point in sanitary reform ever since. Part of a flood of public documents which were directed toward social reform in the 1830s and 1840s, Chadwick's Report is far and away the best. As a piece of pure legislative and social protest rhetoric, it is superb. The Report also contains an extraordinary amount of empirical documentation about the economic condition of the urban labour force – disease, mortality, morbidity, housing and, most important, the state of city sanitation or what we would now call the quality of public health infrastructure. It also offers engineering and cost details on sewage and water systems. The Report even goes so far as to compute benefit/cost assessments of various projects. It also contains explicit administrative and legislative proposals on how the sanitary reform could be best implemented. Although an outstanding social document, the Report also represented a turning point in another way. It reflected the fact that the public health movement now had a leader in Chadwick, who gave the reformers a well-defined legislative focus.

It is said that the Sanitary Report awakened middle-class and upper-class sensibilities to the ghastly environment of Britain's urban poor, an environment which most non-poor Victorians failed to comprehend. Most Victorians with political influence were located at a safe distance from the worst part of that environment, and their pride in Britain's economic success was based on the manifest evidence of booming industrialisation, accumulation and world trade. The Report informed them of the ugly underside of urbanisation, and it appealed to their humanitarian and economic instincts to make an investment in cleaning up the cities and thus to improve the sanitary and economic condition of the labouring poor.

Yet it is easy to make too much of the 1842 Sanitary Report. Remarkable as the document and Chadwick may have been, the fact remains that the Report was preceded by at least a century of accumulated understanding and public health experimentation. If we fail to appreciate that fact, then we will be left with the mistaken impression that a far greater commitment to cleaner cities through social overhead investment was technologically out of reach prior to 1842. We will also make the far greater error of assuming that a major commitment of public resources to sanitation and housing reform took place in the decades immediately following. In truth, Britain was well into the late nineteenth century before she made significant progress towards cleaning up her cities.

A final remark

It is appropriate to leave this chapter on coping with city growth during Britain's industrial revolution with this central policy debate, and with a question: Was Britain's environmental ugliness the most efficient path to industrialisation?

Because the British tax system was highly regressive at this time, certainly prior to Peel's tax reforms of 1842, the working class would have borne most of the cost of cleaning up the cities and improving housing earlier in the nineteenth century. To the extent that the incidence would have fallen on the working class through indirect taxation of necessities and through rising rents on now-greater-taxed urban property, then their real consumption levels might well have been eroded. Efforts to legislate higher residential health standards and lower levels of tenement crowding would also have inflated rents. So too would have space-intensive municipal urban renewal schemes. If the contrary is believed, that urban landlords, merchants and capitalists would have absorbed the tax burden, how would they have responded? Surely they would have responded in part by diminished saving as their disposable incomes contracted through the rise in taxes. If some industrial accumulation and capacity creation had been foregone as a consequence, some future urban jobs would also have been foregone. Fewer urban jobs imply a lower absorption of low-wage rural workers into high-wage urban employment. Thus workers' nominal incomes would have diminished on that score too.

The trade-off between commodities and environment was very real and the reform debates much more subtle than first meets the eye. Did the unfortunate environmental ugliness of Britain's cities reflect, nonetheless, an efficient path to industrialisation? We simply do not know.

References

Chadwick, E. 1842. *Report on the Sanitary Condition of the Labouring Population of Great Britain*, 1842. Ed. M.W. Flinn, Edinburgh.

Flinn, M.W. 1965. Introduction to Chadwick 1842.

Floud, R.C. and McCloskey, D.N., eds. 1981. *The Economic History of Britain since 1700*, vol. 1: 1700-1860. 1st edn, Cambridge.

Lipton, M. 1976. *Why Poor People Stay Poor: Urban Bias in World Development*, Cambridge.

McCloskey, D.N. 1981. The industrial revolution: a survey. In Floud and McCloskey 1981.

Pollard, S. 1981. Sheffield and sweet auburn - amenities and living standards in the British industrial revolution: a comment. *Journal of Economic History* 41: 902-4.

Redford, A. 1926. *Labour Migration in England*, 1800-1850. Manchester.

von Tunzelmann, G.N. 1981. Technical progress during the industrial revolution. In Floud and McCloskey 1981.

Williamson, J.G. 1981. Some myths die hard - urban disamenities one more time: a reply. *Journal of Economic History* 41: 905-7.

Williamson, J.G. 1990a. *Coping with City Growth during the British Industrial Revolution*, Cambridge.

Williamson, J.G. 1990b. The impact of the Corn Laws prior to repeal. *Explorations in Economic History* 27: 123-56.

[11]
What Explains Wage Gaps between Farm and City? Exploring the Todaro Model with American Evidence, 1890–1941*

Timothy J. Hatton
University of Essex

Jeffrey G. Williamson
Harvard University

I. The Problem

Nominal wage gaps between farm and city employment are one of the most pervasive aspects of modern economic growth—so much so that they have become a key stylized fact of development economics. Indeed, a good portion of the literature on the Third World has focused on this problem at length, both in terms of labor market behavior and in terms of policy formation in the face of factor market distortions. Yet, wage gaps are not simply an institutional peculiarity of newly industrializing Third World countries, since they seem to have been even greater among nineteenth- and twentieth-century western nations. While unskilled full-time nominal city wages are about 41% higher than farm wages in the contemporary Third World, they were about 51% higher among late nineteenth-century industrializers.[1] They were even higher in England in the 1830s, about 73%.[2] Furthermore, the evidence suggests that these wage gaps vary substantially over time: they rose from 29% to 41% in the American North between the antebellum and postbellum periods, and were about 50% by the mid-1890s in the United States as a whole—a figure that reached an all-time U.S. high of about 65% by the late 1930s.[3]

There are three questions that these wage gaps raise, not just one. First. Would these nominal full-time wage gaps disappear if they were properly measured? Proper measurement would include the fact that cities are more costly places to live, that cities may have greater disamenities, that farmers also make in-kind payments to their workers, and that farm laborers suffer seasonal underemployment. Elsewhere, we have shown for the 1890s[4] and for the 1920s[5] that much of these nominal wage gaps evaporate when adjusted for cost-of-living differentials and the perquisites paid farm laborers, but a residual gap still remains to be explained even for those decades, let alone the huge gaps of the 1930s. If the wage gaps survive improved measurement, then a second question becomes relevant: Are we observing equilibrium annual real earnings differentials or are they true manifestations of disequilibrium distortions? One of the most popular arguments for the equilibrium differentials view can be found in the Todaro model, a pillar of development economics for 20 years. Perhaps because of limited time series data, this model has never been adequately tested, but it makes the plausible assertion that sticky industrial wages, urban unemployment, and flexible farm wages jointly account for the wage gap. Given the dominance of the model in the Third World literature, it may come as a surprise to learn that the idea has its intellectual roots in the U.S. experience during the interwar period where the evidence to test it is abundant, but it appears that with the possible exception of Daniel Suits no one has ever done so.[6] Finally, if equilibrium models cannot fully account for these wage gaps, we can move on to the third question: What accounts for these wage distortions and for their variation over time?

This article will focus on the second and third questions during an epoch when U.S. agriculture was a major employer of labor, from 1890 when annual time series begins, to 1941. Our main objective is to explain the U.S. experience with the ratio of farm to unskilled urban weekly wages, plotted in figure 1.[7] Similar trends are documented when daily wages are used in the comparison, and all regions reported roughly comparable movements.[8] So why did the nominal farm/non-farm wage ratio rise so persistently from the relatively low levels in the mid-1890s to the end of World War I, collapse so dramatically in the intermediate postwar years, and then fall to even lower levels in the 1930s? In the 1890s, farm wages were about 50% of unskilled city wages, rising to almost 65% on the eve of World War I. By the late 1920s they had fallen below 50% of unskilled city wages, while in 1940 the figure was less than 35%. Real farm/nonfarm wage ratios are closer to parity in the 1890s and 1920s, but they too undergo the same decline after World War I.[9]

What accounts for these large swings in the wage gap over time? Were they simply a reflection of variations in urban unemployment as the equilibrium version of the Todaro model would suggest, or was there a disequilibrium component to the wage gap resulting from imperfect mobility between rural and urban labor markets? If (as we find) there was a disequilibrium component, what were the underlying forces driving labor supply and demand that gave rise to variations in the wage gap? Before answering these questions, we examine the

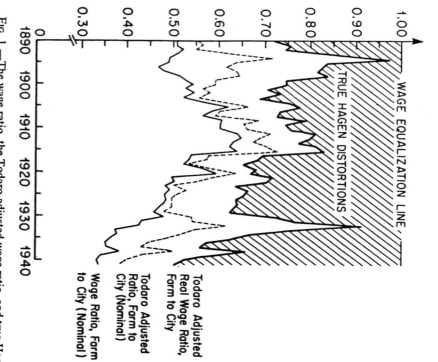

FIG. 1.—The wage ratio, the Todaro-adjusted wage ratio, and true Hagen distortions: 1890–1941.

hypotheses that emerge from an earlier literature that has dwelt on these issues at length.

II. Debates over Wage Gaps in Development Economics

Hagen's "Dynamic" Distortions. By 1958, the early pioneers in development economics had a full appreciation of wage gaps, and they were central to debates over development strategy. Everett Hagen published an influential paper in that year, "An Economic Justification of Protectionism." Based on evidence drawn both from advanced and underdeveloped countries, he concluded that "the agricultural-urban wage differential exists in underdeveloped and economically advanced countries alike; the available evidence suggests that it does not disappear, or even diminish, in the course of development. It is a persistent long-run phenomenon."[10] Hagen's priors were very strong. He felt that these wage differentials were the result of unbalanced growth in the derived demand for labor. Rapid industrialization creates an excess demand for labor in urban sectors while lagging labor demand in agriculture creates an excess supply in rural sectors. Since migration is never adequate to clear fully these two markets in any one year, and since the unbalanced growth persists year in and year out, a disequilibrium wage distortion will emerge. The more rapid the rate of unbalanced growth, the bigger the distortion. Only in advanced economies where the industrial revolution is complete do rural-urban labor markets have an opportunity to erase those gaps, but even then large terms-of-trade shocks and industrial crises (like those of the 1930s) may matter.

Establishing the argument that wage gaps reflected true wage distortions was central to Hagen's agenda since it helped support a policy of active intervention to foster industrialization. Recall that the "exports as engine of growth" thesis had been badly damaged by the interwar collapse of Third World primary product markets, and that import substitution was the favored policy of the 1950s. Hagen's arguments tended to support the new view of history offered by Ragnar Nurkse, Gunnar Myrdal, Raoul Prebisch, and Hans Singer, all of whom argued that Third World primary product exports were no longer the engine of growth that they had been up to World War I, and that industrialization through import substitution was the best policy route to follow. By appealing to wage distortions, Hagen could offer support for the infant industry argument for protection, leaning heavily on the theoretical contributions of G. Haberler and J. Viner. Since those wage distortions tended to price domestic manufacturers out of their own markets (artificially raising labor costs), government intervention to offset the distortion was warranted.

Some economists offered other explanations for the wage gaps, while still favoring the view that they were true distortions. Others were skeptical, and felt that the wage gaps were likely to be the spurious result of mismeasurement. Jagdish Bhagwati and V. K. Ramaswami expressed such skepticism in their important paper "Domestic Distortions, Tariffs and the Theory of Optimum Subsidy," but they also helped clarify the possible sources of a true distortion. In addition to Hagen's focus on "dynamic" distortions, Bhagwati and Ramaswami appealed to trade unions, government employment, and minimum wage legislation (an argument later pursued by Jacob Mincer).[11]

Distortions and Economic Dualism. While Hagen offered "dynamic" distortions that he felt accompanied every successful industrial revolution, another active group of development economists invoked more elegant explanations for these wage distortions. These explanations came to be known as models of economic dualism, and they implied that the wage distortions would persist as long as preindustrial agricultural institutions persisted well into early industrialization.

The dualistic model had its source with Sir Arthur Lewis's labor surplus model, and it came to be formalized both in a neoclassical and a classical fashion.[12] The argument supporting wage gaps in such models was based on the view that precommercial family subsistence farms in the Third World "paid" all members their average, rather than their marginal, product. As a result, capitalist industry had to pay a wage that insured a spread between sectoral marginal products. The distortion implied market failure that warranted government intervention. Note, however, that the dualistic model need not generate wage gaps but, rather, only gaps in marginal products. To get wage gaps as well, these models had to appeal to any or all of the forces already listed above.

Unemployment and Equilibrium Gaps

The dualistic model had a very optimistic view of the development process. Given elastic labor supplies from the countryside, industrialization could proceed where the only constraint was the rate of accumulation. Labor was transferred from low marginal productivity in the countryside to high marginal productivity in the city, and all of these models implied that the rate of labor absorption in city employment would be fast. As the 1960s unfolded, a more gloomy view began to emerge. The rate of labor absorption in Third World cities was far slower than the rapid rate of accumulation would have predicted and, even more alarming, urban unemployment became more and more pronounced. The appearance of overt urban unemployment created two camps that tried to explain it: there were those who argued that rural labor was being pushed by Malthusian forces into the cities at a rate too fast for its absorption in good industrial jobs, a view that implied that wage gaps and urban unemployment should have increased; and there were those who argued that urban labor market distortions could account for both the rising unemployment and the increased wage gaps.

Lewis was the first development economist to bring attention to urban unemployment in the Third World. It appears prominently in his 1965 Richard T. Ely lecture to the American Economic Association where he sketched out the following argument: attracted by an apparently irrational optimism that they will be selected for those scarce high-wage city jobs, the rural emigrants keep coming, and the glut spills over into urban unemployment.[13] By focusing on expected rather than current wage gaps, Michael Todaro developed a framework that formalized Lewis's argument. The Todaro framework and its extensions enjoyed considerable popularity over the 2 decades that followed.[14]

The Todaro hypothesis is simple and elegant.[15] While similar statements can be found sprinkled through the development literature, the most effective illustration can be found in Max Corden and Ronald

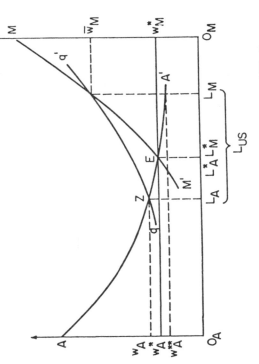

Fig. 2.—The Todaro model according to Corden and Findlay

Findlay, reproduced in figure 2. There are only two sectors analyzed in figure 2, but they are sufficient to illustrate the point. Under the extreme assumption of wage equalization through migration, and in the absence of wage rigidities, equilibrium is achieved at E (the point of intersection of the two labor demand curves, AA' and MM'). Here wages are equalized at $w_A^* = w_M^*$, and the share of the total labor force, L, employed in urban jobs is $O_M L_M^*$, where M denotes manufacturing and A denotes agriculture. Since wages are not equalized in the contemporary Third World, the Todaro model incorporates the widely held belief that the wage rate in manufacturing is pegged at artificially high levels by unions, by minimum wage legislation, or by private-sector emulation of inflated public-sector wage rates, say at w_M. If, for the moment, we ignore urban unemployment, then all those who fail to secure the favored jobs in manufacturing would accept low-wage jobs in agriculture at w_A^{**}. Now let us add the reality of unemployment. Todaro introduces an expectations hypothesis which, in its simplest form, states that the favored jobs are allocated by lottery and that the potential migrant calculates the expected value of that lottery ticket and compares it with the certain employment in the rural sector. Migration then takes place until the urban expected wage is equated to the rural wage. Given $\bar{w}_M$, at what rural wage would the migrant be indifferent between city and countryside? If the probability of getting the favored job is simply the ratio of L_M to the total urban labor force L_U, or one minus the unemployment rate, then the expression $w_A = (L_M / L_U)\bar{w}_M = (1 - U)\bar{w}_M$ indicates the agricultural wage at which the potential migrant is indifferent about employment locations. This structural equation of migration behavior is in fact the qq' curve in figure 2. The equilibrium agricultural wage is now given by w_A.[16]

The new equilibrium at Z in figure 2 offers an explanation for wage gaps observed between city and countryside which competes with the Hagen hypothesis. While Hagen views these wage gaps as a manifestation of dynamic disequilibrium, the Corden and Findlay version of the Todaro model does not. In the next section we will develop a reduced-form model that captures all the essential elements of figure 2: labor demand in the two sectors, a migration equation that links the two markets, and statements about how wages are determined in city and countryside. The exercise is important since there are three hypotheses embedded in figure 2, not just one, and they all need attention: first, that migration is driven by expected wages; second, that migrants are sufficiently responsive to market signals that expected wages are roughly equalized between the two sectors; and third, that wages are sticky in city labor markets while flexible in the countryside. We want to test each of these propositions. Furthermore, we are interested in the underlying forces that drove wage gaps and migration over time. What role did the terms of trade play? Shifts in industrial demand? Economy-wide labor supply shocks, in this case driven by the stop and go of foreign immigration?

III. Twentieth-Century American Wage Gaps: Searching for Causes

Oddly enough, these propositions have never been formally tested. Even more surprising, while the Todaro model was constructed to explain a contemporary Third World problem, the proposition has its intellectual roots with agricultural economists who were writing about the American interwar wage gap some 40 years ago. Todaro himself was aware of this when he cited U.S. experience with exceptionally large wage gaps in the 1930s.[17] He also cited Theodore Schultz's early book on U.S. agriculture, but the literature on American interwar wage gaps is far bigger than even Schultz's impressive volume would suggest.[18]

These economists writing 40 years ago focused almost exclusively on interwar wage gaps. Their interest was in farm income parity and thus compared the 1920s and 1930s with World War I benchmarks, where farm income matched up quite well with industrial income. Thus, Daniel Ahearn gives the impression that the wage gap opened up only after 1920, while in fact it appears to have returned to something like late nineteenth-century levels.[19] Similarly, Louis Ducoff decries the lack of "parity" between incomes of hired farm workers and nonfarm wage earners in the 1930s, using the far more favorable 1910–14 period as his base.[20] An excellent study by Howard Parsons adopts a similar stance, restricting his analysis solely to the years 1910–45.[21]

This interwar fixation is somewhat surprising given that in his 1930 book Paul Douglas devoted a whole chapter to the partial collapse in the wage gap from the early 1890s to World War I.[22] Furthermore, we now know that the wage gap between farm and city increased markedly over the 2 decades or so prior to 1890.[23] In short, the wage gap exhibited wide variance over the 7 decades of 1870–1941, and that variance was not solely a manifestation of interwar instability and the Great Depression.

What accounts for the variance in the wage gap? The interwar literature offers three explanations. First, in the tradition of Hagen's disequilibrium distortions, both Ahearn and Parsons stressed the role of the terms of trade in commodity markets in driving the wage gap, although their work was anticipated by G. F. Warren and F. A. Pearson some 20 years before.[24] The argument is simple enough. When world price shocks twist the commodity terms of trade against agriculture, farm wages suffer. If the decline in the terms of trade persists, and if the rate of rural emigration is sluggish, then not only will the gap persist but it will tend to increase. This disequilibrium view is supported by the gross correlation between falling wage gaps and improving farm terms of trade from the 1890s to World War I and the reversal of those trends in the 1920s and 1930s.

Second, like so many authors writing on this topic at that time, Ahearn made much of elastic rural labor supplies.[25] However, it is not at all clear how this explanation can account for the variance in wage gaps over time. After all, there is no evidence that supports a slow-down in rural labor supply growth from the 1890s to World War I and a speedup thereafter. However, there is an alternative labor supply source that might help account for the variance in wage gaps—foreign immigration into American cities. After all, there was a striking surge in American immigration from a trough in the early 1890s to a peak just prior to World War I. The impact of immigration into American urban labor markets may or may not have served to erase the wage gap, depending on the model espoused. If urban wages were relatively inflexible, as the Todaro model asserts, then the agricultural wage would have declined as potential farm emigrants faced being crowded out by the foreign immigrants in the cities. The wage gap gets bigger. If urban wages were relatively flexible, this glut in urban labor markets would have tended to diminish urban wages. The wage gap gets smaller. If we believe the latter mechanism, then it would also follow that as postwar quotas choked off foreign immigration to American cities, urban labor scarcity would have increased, augmenting the wage gaps. Like the terms-of-trade argument, both immigration arguments fall into the Hagen disequilibrium tradition, thus supporting the view that some portion of the wage gaps represent true distortions.

Third, anticipating Todaro, Ducoff dwelt at length on the role of urban unemployment, concluding that "farm wage rates have been highly vulnerable to the recurring cycles of mass urban unemployment."[26] and he offered some persuasive evidence to support the proposition for the years 1929–43.[27] Parsons built on Ducoff, extending the time series and stressing the asymmetry in the two labor markets, one with flexible and one with sticky wages: "In the industrial sector the depression tends to affect the labor market in the form of unemployment with the earnings of those still employed . . . tending to remain relatively constant in real terms. In the agricultural economy, on the other hand, wages are affected adversely while employment is not affected to an appreciable extent."[28] This theme was further extended by Willis Weatherford, who argued: "When industrial unemployment rises above its trend, farm wages fall below their trend. When unemployment is high, the farm labor force stays on the farm, youth postpones leaving the farm, the large labor supply forces farm wages to low levels."[29]

What remains to be done is to test these propositions more formally, using time series information covering the period 1890 to 1941. What drove the wage gap between city and countryside over these 5 decades?

IV. Todaro Equilibrium Wage Gaps versus Persistent Hagen Distortions: 1890–1941

We start by comparing trends in the observed wage ratio with the Todaro-adjusted wage ratio, $w_A/w_M(1 - U)$. The result is plotted in figure 1. How much of the large and rising discrepancy between the actual wage gap and counterfactual wage equalization can be explained by urban unemployment? It appears that some of the gap can be so explained, but much of it is left unexplained. When adjusted further by somewhat crude cost-of-living differentials between city and countryside, a large and variable residual persists. We call the unexplained residual the "true Hagen disequilibrium distortion." The crude cost-of-living deflators do not seem to have a significant impact on the wage-gap time series, so the remainder of this article will focus on explaining trends in the nominal wage gap.[30]

Two attributes of the nominal wage-gap time series persist even after these crude Todaro adjustments are made: first, the abrupt fall in the wage ratio after World War I, and second, the downward drift in the adjusted wage ratio throughout the interwar period. In short, there appears to be a sharp break in the wage-gap trends around World War I as well as evidence of increasing intersectoral labor-market disequilibrium across the twenties and the thirties. Do disequilibrium shocks and slow adjustment account for this break and a rise in the true Hagen distortions?

Potential migrants may, of course, have assessed the probabilities of urban unemployment or even its private costs very differently than this crude Todaro adjustment in figure 1 suggests. The next step, therefore, is to actually estimate the migration equation embedded in the Todaro model. The exercise is important for yet another reason. While our interest is in those puzzling wage gaps rather than in farm emigration itself, a skeptic might offer an alternative explanation for any Todaro-like relationship in the data. Given that urban nominal wages were far more sticky than rural nominal wages, and given that demand shocks were correlated across sectors, the skeptic would expect a more severe decline in the rural wage and a more pronounced rise in urban unemployment in a slump. This prediction would hold even if the two sectors were completely segmented. To allay such suspicions, we must first estimate a migration equation to establish that labor markets in the two sectors were directly linked, and that both the wage gap and urban unemployment mattered precisely as Todaro would have predicted.

The exercise certainly fits comfortably into the historiography of the interwar period which dwells at length on farm emigration during a period of powerful terms-of-trade shocks and extraordinary levels of urban unemployment during the Great Depression. Between 1920 and 1941, the farm population fell by 1.6 million and net farm emigration averaged 549,000 per year. While those farm emigration figures are impressive, they were not enough to eliminate or even reduce the wage gap between farm and city (fig. 1). In addition, as figure 3 indicates, farm emigration was hardly stable over the 2 decades. It was very high in the early and mid-twenties but fell steadily from a peak in 1922 to a trough a decade later. Indeed, there was net farm immigration in both 1931 and 1932. Following the trough of the Great Depression, farm emigration surged to World War II, and in 1941 it was higher than at any time during the interwar period. What explains the instability? Can the Todaro model account for these farm emigration patterns?

Todaro's familiar migration equation can be written as

$$M_A = \mu \left[\log(w_M/w_A) + \log(1 - U)\right], \qquad (1)$$

where M_A is the net farm emigration rate, while on the right-hand side we have logs of the ratio of nonfarm to farm wages and the city employment rate (or one minus the unemployment rate). The dependent variable in equation (1) is defined as annual net farm emigration divided by the agricultural population, and it has two limitations: first, it measures population migration rather than labor migration, and second, the U.S. Department of Agriculture (USDA) supplies the farm emigration estimates only starting in 1920. In spite of these data limitations, equation (1) still offers a test of Todaro's key structural equation on migration behavior.

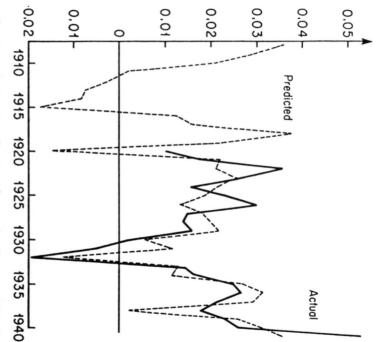

Fig. 3.—Actual and predicted net farm emigration rate, 1908–41

The results are reported in table 1, including the lagged dependent variable, making it possible to asses the importance of lags in migration adjustment to market signals. The Todaro hypothesis fares well. A rise in the nonfarm wage relative to the farm wage tends to foster emigration, and the *t*-statistic on $\log(w_M/w_A)$ is large. A rise in the urban employment rate also tends to foster farm emigration, and, once again, the *t*-statistic on $\log(1-U)$ is large. Furthermore, the coefficients on the wage ratio and the employment rate are of roughly equal magnitude, just as Todaro would have predicted. When the value of the parameters μ_1 and μ_2 are constrained to be equal (as in the regression where $\log(w_M/w_A)$ and $\log(1-U)$ are restricted to be equal, μ is about 0.06 in the short run and 0.09 in the long run. That is, the farm emigration elasticity with respect to labor-market signals was very low, suggesting an explanation for those big Hagen distortions that figure 1 documents for the interwar years.[31] Hence, it appears that the disequilibrium version of the Todaro model is appropriate. Note also that migrants in the interwar period appear to have been responsive primarily to current labor-market signals, since the coefficient on lagged mi-

TABLE 1

EXPLAINING NET FARM EMIGRATION, 1921–41: SIMPLE
STRUCTURAL MODEL
(Dependent Variable: M_A, the Off-Farm Migration Rate)

	Equation (1)	Equation (2)
Constant	.028	.031
	(.016)	(.015)
$\log(w_M/w_A)$	.069	...
	(.026)	
$\log(1 - U)$	.092	...
	(.043)	
$\log(w_M/w_A) + \log(1 - U)$	...	.063
		(.025)
M_{A-1}	.056	.323
	(.314)	(.237)
R^2	.512	.493
D-W	1.219	1.368
SE	.011	.011

NOTE.—Standard errors are in parentheses.

gration is fairly small and insignificant. That result may be explained in part by the fact that the migration data are reported from April in the current year to April in the next. In any case, we will omit the lagged dependent variable in the model development that follows.

The next step is to explore the determinants of farm wages. We start with a simple farm-labor demand function,

$$L_A^D = A (w_A/P_A)^{-\alpha} e^{rt}, \quad (2)$$

where w_A/P_A is the real wage facing employers in agriculture and r captures the combined effects of accumulation and technical change. Since we want to make this labor demand (a stock) consistent with farm emigration (a flow), we express equation (2) in rates of change:

$$\Delta \log L_A^D = -\alpha \Delta \log w_A + \alpha \Delta \log P_A + r.$$

In rates of change, farm-labor supplies are written as

$$\Delta \log L_A^S = n_A - M_A,$$

where n_A and M_A are rates of natural increase and emigration, respectively, both taken as a ratio of the agricultural labor force. Solving for the rate of change in the farm wage, we get

$$\alpha \, \Delta \log w_A = \alpha \, \Delta \log P_A + r - n_A + M_A. \quad (3)$$

Substituting the migration equation from (1) into (3), and dividing through by α, we get an expression for the rate of change in the farm wage

$$\Delta \log w_A = \Delta \log P_A + \frac{(r - n_A)}{\alpha} + \frac{\mu}{\alpha}[(\log(w_M/w_A) + \log(1 - U)]. \quad (4)$$

This equation tells us that farm wages are influenced by two forces, conditions in agriculture and conditions in industry. That is, we are treating farm wages as flexible and responsive to labor-market conditions off the farm, and the estimate μ/α tells us just how strong links between the two labor markets were. The link is expected to be weak given that we now know that migration responded only sluggishly to urban employment conditions (μ is small). It will be strong, however, to the extent that the labor-demand elasticity was low (α is low), so that small emigration-induced changes in the farm-labor supply required big changes in farm wages to clear the agricultural labor market.

Gathering all the farm-wage terms on the left-hand side, equation (4) can be rewritten as equation (5),

$$\Delta \log w_A = \frac{\alpha}{\alpha + \mu} \Delta \log P_A + \frac{(r - n_A)}{(\alpha + \mu)}$$
$$+ \frac{\mu}{\alpha + \mu}[\log(w_M/w_A - 1) + \log(1 - U)], \quad (5)$$

which is then estimated. Table 2 reports the results on annual time series for 1890–1941 where $(r - n_A)$ is treated as a constant. The results are relatively successful, but not completely so: the signs are all correct and the t-statistics are large for $\Delta \log P_A$, $\log(1 - U)$, and $\log(w_M/w_A - 1)$ but not on the restricted variable $\log(w_M/w_A - 1) + \log(1 - U)$. That is, the coefficients on the wage ratio and the employment rate are significantly different from each other. Most important, however, farm wages exhibit a strong flexible response to farm price shocks, as predicted. They exhibit a predictably weaker response to city employment conditions, but they are significant nonetheless. That is, even though farm emigration responded only sluggishly to city wage incentives ($\mu = 0.09$ from table 1), the elasticity of farm labor demand was sufficiently low ($\alpha = 0.60$ or less) so that the total impact of city employment conditions on farm wages was significant.[32]

At this stage we should consider wage determination in the non-farm sector. There are two dominant views in the literature, both of which conform to the conventional wisdom that these two sectors obey an asymmetry in wage flexibility and wage adjustment. First, because

TABLE 2

Explaining Farm Wages, 1891–1941: Partial Reduced
Form Model

(Dependent Variable: $\Delta \log w_A$, the Rate of Change
of Farm Wage)

	Equation (1)	Equation (2)
Constant	−.034	.027
	(.034)	(.032)
$\Delta \log P_A$	.539	.600
	(.059)	(.061)
$\log(w_M/w_{A-1})$	.129	...
	(.057)	
$\log(1 - U)$	.336	...
	(.100)	
$\log(w_M/w_{A-1}) + \log(1 - U)$	...	.022
		(.037)
R^2	.732	.669
D-W	1.511	1.510
SE	.058	.064

Note.—Standard errors are in parentheses.

of the relatively small size of the farm sector, city labor-market conditions have a significant influence on farm labor markets, while the influence is only very weak in the opposite direction. Second, nominal wages are very flexible in agriculture but very sticky in industry. The industrial sticky wage view has, of course, a long tradition in both macroeconomics and in American historiography. Indeed, Jeffrey Sachs has successfully bridged the two by estimating Phillips curves for the 1890–1976 period.[33] Although his goal was to show that wage rigidity was far greater after the Korean War than prior to 1929, he finds significant wage rigidity in the earlier period nonetheless. We attempted to estimate a Phillips curve for the manufacturing wage for 1892–1940 but obtained poor results. Little of the year-to-year variation in the rate of wage change was explained by the model, and the unemployment term was always insignificant.[34] Therefore, in what follows we take the urban real wage to be exogenous with respect to both the unemployment rate and conditions in agriculture, just as Todaro suggested.

The next step is to endogenize urban unemployment. To do so, we start with nonfarm labor demand

$$L_M^D = B\,(w_M/P_M)^{-\beta}\,e^{rt}$$

$$\log L_M^D = \log B - \beta \log(w_M/P_M) + vt, \tag{6}$$

where v captures the influence of accumulation and technical change. Now equation (6) can be rewritten in terms of unemployment or employment rates. First, the nonfarm employment rate is

$$(1 - U) = L_M^D / L_M^S \text{ or } \log(1 - U) = \log L_M^D - \log L_M^S.$$

Substituting for L_M from equation (6) yields

$$\log(1 - U) = \log B - \beta \log(w_M / P_M) + vt - \log L_M^S. \tag{7}$$

Due to internal migration, L_M^S is endogenous, but we can express it as

$$\log L_M^S = \frac{1}{(1 - s)} \log L - \frac{s}{(1 - s)} \log L_A,$$

where $s = L_A / L$, and L is the total labor force in both sectors combined.[35] Using the agricultural labor demand function (and assuming no "cyclical" unemployment in agriculture), we get

$$\log L_M^S = \frac{1}{(1 - s)} \log L - \frac{s}{(1 - s)} \log A$$

$$+ \frac{\alpha s}{(1 - s)} \log(w_A / P_A) - \frac{s}{(1 - s)} vt. \tag{8}$$

Finally, substitute equation (8) into equation (7) to get

$$\log(1 - U) = \log B - \beta \log(w_M / P_M) + vt - \frac{1}{(1 - s)} \log L$$

$$+ \frac{s}{(1 - s)} \log A - \frac{\alpha s}{(1 - s)} \log(w_A / P_A) + \frac{s}{(1 - s)} rt. \tag{9}$$

Thus, unemployment depends on employment demand in the urban sector, employment demand in the farm sector, and total labor supply.

We now have three equations and three endogenous variables: farm emigration (eq. [1]), farm labor-market equilibrium (eq. [3]), and urban unemployment (eq. [9]). They can be solved either for farm emigration or for the wage gap. We are interested in both. By substituting equation (9) into the migration equation (1), we obtain the quasi-reduced form farm emigration equation

$$M_A = -\mu \log(w_A / w_M) + \mu \left[\log B + \frac{s}{(1 - s)} \log A \right] - \mu \beta \log(w_M / P_M)$$

$$+ \mu_z t - \frac{\mu s \alpha}{(1 - s)} \log(w_A / P_A) - \frac{1}{(1 - s)} \log L, \tag{10}$$

TABLE 3

EXPLAINING NET FARM EMIGRATION, 1921–41: QUASI-REDUCED
FORM MODEL

(Dependent Variable: M_A, the Off-Farm Migration Rate)

	Equation (1)	Equation (2)
Constant	3.410	3.819
	(.974)	(1.056)
$\log(P_A/P_M)$	−.157	−.176
	(.052)	(.056)
$\log(w_M/P_M)$	.259	.282
	(.064)	(.068)
$\log(w_A/P_A)$	−.200	−.198
	(.048)	(.048)
$\log L$	−.322	−.356
	(.091)	(.097)
$\Delta \log(w_A/P_A)_{-1}$	. . .	−.032
		(.032)
R^2	.604	.629
D-W	1.871	1.803
SE	.010	.010

NOTE.—Standard errors are in parentheses.

which can be rearranged to get

$$M_A = -\mu \log(P_A/P_M) + \mu \left[\log B + \frac{s}{(1-s)} \log A \right]$$
$$+ \mu z t + (\mu - \mu\beta) \log(w_M/P_M)$$
$$- \left(\mu + \frac{\mu s \alpha}{(1-s)} \right) \log(w_A/P_A) - \frac{\mu}{(1-s)} \log L, \tag{11}$$

where $z = v + [s/(1-s)]r$. This is the equation estimated in table 3, both with and without the lagged variable $\Delta \log(w_A/P_A)_{-1}$, that carries over from the lagged dependent variable in table 1. The time trend is not present since it competes with the log of the total civilian labor force, log L, and is statistically insignificant.

Alternatively, substituting equation (9) into equation (4) and rearranging terms yields a reduced-form expression for the wage gap

$$\log(w_A/w_M) = \frac{[\alpha + \alpha\mu s(1-s)^{-1}]}{[*]} \log(P_A/P_M) + \frac{\alpha}{[*]} \log(w_A/P_A)_{-1}$$
$$+ \frac{(r - n_A)}{[*]} + \frac{\mu}{[*]} \left[\log B + \frac{s}{(1-s)} \log A \right]$$
$$- \frac{[\alpha + \alpha\mu s(1-s)^{-1} + \mu\beta]}{[*]} \log(w_M/P_M) + \frac{\mu z t}{[*]}$$
$$- \frac{\mu(1-s)^{-1}}{[*]} \log L, \tag{12}$$

TABLE 4

Explaining the Wage Gap, 1921–41: Reduced Form Model
(Dependent Variable: $\log(w_A/w_M)$, the Log Ratio of Farm to Nonfarm Wage)

	Equation (1)	Equation (2)
Constant	−.500	−.718
	(.885)	(.835)
$\log(P_A/P_M)$	.790	.822
	(.116)	(.106)
$\log(w_M/P_M)$	−.772	−.767
	(.087)	(.080)
$\log(w_A/P_A)_{-1}$	.496	.399
	(.115)	(.109)
$\log L$	−.028	−.028
	(.067)	(.063)
$\Delta \log(w_A/P_A)_{-1}$	...	.365
		(.122)
R^2	.851	.881
D-W	1.211	1.914
SE	.073	.067

Note.—Standard errors are in parentheses.

where $[*] = [\alpha + \mu + \alpha_M s(1 - s)^{-1}] > 0$, and, as we have already noted, s is the share of the labor force in agriculture. Equation (12) is estimated in table 4, with and without the lagged variable $\Delta \log(w_A/P_A)_{-1}$, that carries over, once again, from the lagged dependent variable in table 1.

The Corden-Findlay-Todaro diagram in figure 2 is consistent with equation (12), as it should be (though eq. [12] represents a disequilibrium version of it). A boom in agriculture's terms of trade shifts the AA' curve to the right in figure 2, thus diminishing the wage gap and raises the wage ratio on the left-hand side (thus diminishing the wage gap). A rise in the real nonfarm wage—taken here to be exogenous, just as Todaro argued—raises the farm wage in figure 2 but it also increases the wage gap and creates urban unemployment. Similarly, a rise in w_M/P_M in equation (12) lowers the wage ratio, increases the wage gap, and creates more urban unemployment. Although it is not shown in figure 2, an immigrant-augmented labor force widens the base of the diagram, yielding an increase in the wage gap. Similarly, a rise in L in equation (12) also lowers the wage ratio, raises the wage gap, and adds to urban unemployment.

The estimates of equation (12) are reported in table 4. The results are quite successful. The estimated coefficients are of the correct sign: an expansion in the labor force serves to lower the wage ratio and to raise the wage gap (and to augment the urban unemployment rate); a boom in agriculture's terms of trade serves to raise the wage ratio; and

Economic Development and Cultural Change

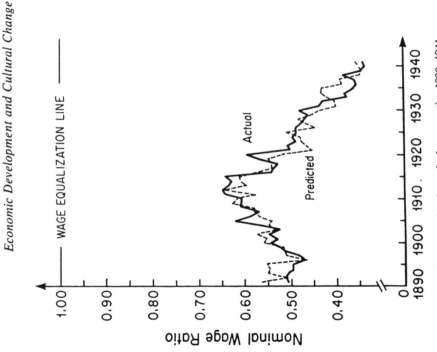

Fig. 4.—Actual and predicted nominal wage ratio, 1890–1941

an increase in the real nonfarm wage serves to lower the wage ratio. With the exception of log L, the t-statistics are favorable everywhere, and the same is true of the R^2 and the D-W statistic. In short, we seem to have captured the central forces driving the wage gap from the early 1890s to the eve of World War II.[36]

The predicted (from the equation excluding $\Delta \log[(w_A/P_A]_{-1})$ and actual wage ratio are plotted in figure 4. The model seems to perform well in all epochs. It captures the collapse in the wage ratio during the depression of the mid-1890s, the modest rise in the ratio up to World War I, the sharp postwar collapse, and the continued erosion in the ratio across the twenties and thirties. Any evidence of structural break in U.S. labor markets has now disappeared: those dramatic movements in the wage gap seem to be adequately accounted for by the magnitude of the labor-market shocks and migrant sluggishness in responding to them.

Thus far we have used the Todaro model to explain U.S. experi-

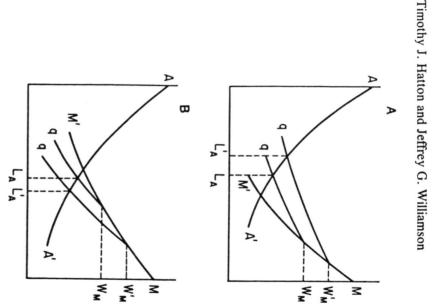

Fig. 5.—The impact of nonfarm real wages on farm emigration according to Todaro: the role of derived labor demand elasticities in the nonfarm sector.

ence with wage gaps over the half-century after 1890. However, Todaro's structural equation on wage gaps can be restated easily in terms of migration behavior, as we have seen by the quasi-reduced form equation (11). Our expectation, of course, is that an improvement both in the farm terms of trade and the farm real wage should choke off emigration. Furthermore, a rise in the labor force nationwide (assumed to originate in the nonfarm sector) should also choke off farm emigration; given the real nonfarm wage, more laborers implies more urban unemployment and thus less farm emigration. The sign on the nonfarm real wage, however, is ambiguous, hinging as it does on the elasticity of labor demand in the city. This argument can be seen clearly in figure 5. The inelastic labor demand curve MM' in figure 5A (recall that the qq curve has unitary elasticity) implies a reduction in agricultural employment in response to a rise in w_M and thus a rise in farm emigration: that is, the rise in the w_M offsets the more modest rise in urban unemployment, implying a rise in the expected real wage in the city. The elastic labor demand curve MM' in figure 5B implies an increase in agricultural employment in response to a rise in w_M and thus a fall in farm emigration: that is, the rise in w_M is offset by the more dramatic rise in urban unemployment, implying a fall in the expected real wage in the city.

Table 3 shows that the reduced-form version of the Todaro model performs very well when applied to farm emigration. Every t-statistic (with the exception of $\Delta \log[w_A/P_A]_{-1}$) is large, and the signs on the farm terms of trade, the real farm wage, and the real manufacturing wage all conform with expectations. Furthermore, the negative coefficient on the labor force supports the Todaro view. Given that industrial wages were sticky, an immigrant-swollen (urban) labor force should have served to raise urban unemployment, to lower the expected wage there, to choke off farm emigration, and to reduce the farm wage relative to industry. Table 3 shows that it does just that. Foreign immigrants did indeed crowd out farm emigrants.

The actual and the predicted farm emigration rates are plotted in figure 3. The model captures the fall in the farm emigration rate from the early twenties to the depths of the Depression and the striking resurgence thereafter. While we do not have farm emigration estimates for the years prior to 1920, the predicted values for 1908–19 seem to conform to qualitative histories. That is, the rate of farm emigration drops off sharply up to and including the early years of World War I, consistent with the bouyant conditions in agriculture that served to retain greater numbers on the farm. With the exception of the short but severe industrial depression of 1920, farm emigration achieved very high rates after 1917, consistent with the collapse in the agricultural terms of trade.

What we would like to learn now is which labor-market shocks were doing most of the work that drove farm emigration and the wage gap. Was it terms-of-trade shocks emanating from conditions in world markets, as argued by Ahearn, Parsons, and Warren and Pearson? Was it labor-supply shocks generated by foreign immigration, favored by Brinley Thomas and stressed by Sir Arthur Lewis and other "pessimistic" development economists?[37] Was it institutional forces manipulating the industrial wage, a premise that motivated the Todaro model in the first place, and one with which many macroeconomists might be comfortable? Was it always the same labor-market shocks doing all the work, or did the driving forces vary across the epochs of 1891–96, 1896–1915, and 1915–40?

Table 5 supplies the answers for the farm/nonfarm wage ratio. It is based on the parameters estimated in table 4 and the observed changes in the exogenous variables. The model should be viewed as short run, given the presence of lagged w_A/P_A, but the results that

TABLE 5

DECOMPOSING THE SOURCES OF CHANGES IN THE NOMINAL WAGE RATIO: THREE EPOCHS

	1891–96	1896–1915	1915–40
Change in actual $\log(w_A/w_M)$	–.0633	+.2202	–.5677
Contributions of change in:			
$\log(P_A/P_M)$	–.0245	+.1227	–.1420
$\log(w_M/P_M)$	–.1049	+.0839	–.4867
$\log(w_A/P_A)_{-1}$	+.0424	–.0021	+.1050
$\log L$	–.0032	–.0116	–.0094
Residual	+.0269	+.0273	–.0346

NOTE.—Each year is centered on a 3-year average, and the "contributions of change" are calculated using the estimated equation in table 4 without $\Delta(w_A/P_A)_{-1}$.

follow are similar when we look at the long-run equilibrium properties. For starters, labor-force growth always served to lower the wage ratio and raise the wage gap, ceteris paribus. Indeed, had the immigrant-induced labor-force expansion from 1896 to World War I not been so rapid, the actual rise in the farm/nonfarm wage ratio would have been even more impressive. This result may appear to be counterintuitive. Did not the influx of immigrants into American cities serve to lower the urban wage and thus to raise the wage ratio and diminish the wage gap? Not in the Todaro model (and confirmed in table 3, as we have seen): the story here is that the nonfarm wage was sticky, so a glut of immigrants tended to increase urban unemployment, to discourage potential farm emigrants, to lower the flexible farm wage, and thus to reduce the wage ratio. The terms of trade had exactly the impact that the traditional literature assigns to it, and it is large. The collapse in the farm terms of trade in the early 1890s and the interwar decades lowered the wage ratio, and it accounted for about a third of the 1891–96 decline and a quarter of the interwar decline. The boom between 1896 and World War I did just the opposite, and here the terms-of-trade shock accounted for about half of the rise in the farm/nonfarm wage ratio.

Nevertheless, the major force driving the wage gap over the period as a whole appears to have been real wages in nonfarm employment. The sharp rise in the nonfarm real wage down to 1896 accounts for most of the fall in the wage ratio; its puzzling fall between 1896 and 1915 accounts for almost a third of the improvement in the wage ratio over the same period; and the near doubling in the nonfarm real wage between 1915 and 1940 accounts for most of the fall in the wage ratio during the twenties and thirties. Todaro would have predicted as much. Indeed, his model was constructed to assess the impact of precisely such events.

Of course, we can perform a similar decomposition analysis on

TABLE 6

DECOMPOSING THE SOURCES OF FARM EMIGRATION DURING TWO
INTERWAR EPOCHS

	1921–32	1932–40
Change in actual migration, M_A	− .0245	+ .0371
Contributions of change in:		
$\log(P_A/P_M)$	+ .0311	− .0178
$\log(w_M/P_M)$	+ .0436	+ .0721
$\log(w_A/P_A)$	− .0229	+ .0056
$\log L$	− .0572	− .0335
Residual	− .0191	+ .0107

NOTE.—Each year is centered on a 3-year average, and the "contributions of change" are calculated using the estimated equation in table 3 without $\Delta \log(w_A/P_A)$.

farm emigration. What accounts for those farm emigration trends after World War I? We just concluded that it was real-wage shocks in the nonfarm sector that were doing most of the work in driving the wage gap. Do we find the same for farm emigration? Table 6 supplies the answers. The sharp and steady decline in farm emigration rates from their high in 1921 to their low in 1932 can be attributed, according to the model, entirely to the rise in the nationwide labor force and to the recovery of real wages in agriculture. The surge in farm emigration rates from 1932 to 1941, on the other hand, is explained almost entirely by the sharp rise in real nonfarm wages, although the erosion in real farm wages adds to this influence.

One might wonder whether our results would be affected by New Deal policies, particularly wage setting under the National Industrial Recovery Act (NIRA) and the expansion of relief programs. The residuals from the migration equation (fig. 3) offer no evidence of systematic deviations in the second half of the 1930s, and when we entered a dummy variable for 1933–41 it did not take on a significant coefficient. This is not as surprising as it seems when we consider the likely effect of New Deal programs. With regard to NIRA wage setting, its effects are already captured in the real-wage ratio. With regard to relief, the effects are more difficult to judge. It has been argued that the inclusion of relief workers in the unemployment count leads to a substantial exaggeration of the total.[38] In terms of the Todaro model, the deterrent effect of high urban unemployment on farm-city migration would be attenuated in the presence of city doles or work relief. However, it should be remembered that much of the emergency relief took place in rural areas, and it has been estimated that perhaps a third of outdoor relief expenditures went to assist rural families, who were about one-fifth of the population.[39] Hence, rural and urban relief programs would have had opposite effects on rural-urban migration though it is not yet possible to say whether these were approximately offsetting.

Timothy J. Hatton and Jeffrey G. Williamson

V. Labor Market Distortions, the Todaro Model and Macroeconomic Implications

As far as we know, this article represents the first attempt to address quantitatively the puzzle of the American wage gap between farm and factory during the turbulent years from 1890 to 1941. Why were the gaps so large and why did they vary so much over these 5 decades? More to the point, can they be explained by models whose intellectual tradition originates with American experience but that have until now been used principally to explain wage gaps in the Third World? If we were able to account fully for in-kind payments, seasonal underemployment in agriculture as well as components of compensating differentials, the wage gap, or what we call "true Hagen distortions," could possibly, on average, disappear. Yet this unlikely event would hardly help explain why the wage gap varied so much over time, and why it was so large in the 1930s.

When we take Todaro's migration equation and embed this in a two-sector model, can more fundamental forces like the intersectoral terms of trade, the urban real wage, and total labor supplies be shown to play an important role? In Section IV we show that they can, provided we take account of the sluggish response of migration to these shocks. Yet it is important to stress that it was not sluggish migration behavior alone that led to volatility in the wage gap. The underlying shocks would have led to roughly the same rise in the wage gap across the 1920s and 1930s even if migration had fully adjusted each year. That is, fundamental shocks to the economy served to drive the urban unemployment rate, and thus the wage gap, just as Todaro argued.

Were contemporary interwar observers and early postwar writers right in the emphasis they gave to terms-of-trade shocks and elastic intersectoral labor supplies? In part, they were. Our model suggests that the declining relative price of farm products drove down the farm wage relative to the factory wage during the Great Depression, over the longer period from 1915 to 1940, and during the early 1890s. Growth in labor supplies exacerbated these trends. Contemporary observers like Ducoff, Parsons, Schultz, and Weatherford also understood the importance of urban unemployment in conditioning farm emigration, but they failed to understand what drove the urban unemployment rate itself—urban real-wage shocks. Above all, it was these shocks that opened up such a wide wage gap in the 1920s and 1930s, both directly and indirectly through their impact on labor demand and unemployment in the cities.

As we pointed out in Section IV, a skeptic might offer an alternative explanation for the Todaro-like relationship in the data. Given that urban nominal wages are more sticky than rural nominal wages, and given that demand shocks are correlated across sectors, the skeptic would expect a more severe decline in the rural wage and a more pronounced rise in urban unemployment in a slump. This prediction would hold even if the two sectors were completely segmented. To anticipate this argument, we estimated our migration equation in Section IV. The results reinforce the view that the two sectors were linked by migration, and that both the wage gap and urban unemployment mattered precisely as Todaro would have predicted. However, while long lags in adjustment were absent in the interwar period, we found that the migration response was very inelastic, helping to account for those large "true Hagen distortions."

What are the macroeconomic implications of our results? Some contemporaries saw the rural sector as an "industrial labor reserve," such that the urban sector drew on rural labor supplies when times were good and sent them back when in a slump. They emphasized that gross migration flows went in both directions and that a flexible wage in agriculture helped absorb labor during depressions. Using the expression for urban unemployment in equation (9), we can assess the strength of such effects. Now we may ask the question: What would have happened to unemployment had the farm wage been inflexible downward and had it not collapsed relative to city wages during the 1930s? Aggregate unemployment would have been higher, of course, since agriculture would have been able to employ fewer workers. But how much higher hinges on two factors: the size of the agriculture sector and the elasticity of labor demand in agriculture. This counterfactual can be estimated given the value for $\alpha s/(1 - s)$ that appears in the expression for unemployment in equation (9). Deriving this coefficient from our estimate of equation (11), we can estimate the counterfactual unemployment rate in the 1930s had the nominal wage ratio between farm and factory remained constant at its 1931 value, 0.43.[40] The results:

	Actual *U*	Counterfactual *U*
1931–35	26.90	28.40
1936–40	19.79	23.48
Difference	7.11	4.92

These results suggest that employment recovery from the Great Depression was aided by the fall in the farm wage, and the effect was very large. There is reason to expect, furthermore, that even more powerful results would obtain for the 1890s or the 1870s, when the agricultural sector was far bigger. The larger the agricultural sector, the greater would be the observed stability in the (urban) unemployment rate over the business cycle given identical shocks to the economy overall.

This conclusion has relevance, we believe, to recent efforts to answer the question, Has the American economy become more stable over the past century? It argues that such comparisons had best be made with a macroeconomic model that pays attention to two sectors, not just one. Multisectoral models of macroinstability are needed to truly assess such questions, and we urge macroeconomists to think in those terms in the future. Development economics might be a good place to look.

Appendix
Data Sources

Nominal Farm Wage (w_A). This is defined as the weekly wage rate without board and is derived as an average of monthly and daily rates, and, following Douglas, both are adjusted to a weekly basis and weighted by 0.6 and 0.4, respectively. For 1890–1909, the series is calculated from the USDA.[42]

Nominal Nonfarm Wage (w_M). This is defined as average weekly earnings of unskilled male workers in manufacturing. For 1921–41, the series is taken from National Industrial Conference Board figures.[43] For 1890–1920, the series is taken from W. Coombs.[44]

Cost of Living Farm and Nonfarm (underlying fig. 1). The benchmark year is 1941. N. Koffsky estimates farm versus nonfarm cost of living differentials for that year, and these have been adjusted for rents by L. J. Alston and T. J. Hatton.[45] This benchmark year is then extended back in time by using farm and city cost-of-living time series for 1890–1941.[46]

Urban Unemployment Rate (U). The underlying data are taken from S. Lebergott.[47] The denominator is civilian minus farm labor force, where the latter was derived for 1890–1900 from a linear interpolation of the ratio of farm to civilian labor force. We ignore the important debate on the unemployment data between Lebergott, C. Romer, and D. R. Weir, since it is irrelevant to our reduced-form models.[48] We assume that all unemployed are nonfarm, although farm seasonal employment was, of course, quite significant.

Terms of Trade (P_A, P_M). Bureau of Labor Statistics prices are used for farm products.[49] Manufactured commodity prices are constructed from two sources.[50]

Farm Emigration Rate (MIG). Net emigration of farm population from current April 1 to next year's April 1, relative to farm population at current year's April 1.[51]

Civilian Labor Force (L). Same source as urban unemployment rate above.

Notes

* Research for this article was supported partially by a grant from the National Science Foundation, SES-84-08210. We gratefully acknowledge the research assistance of Chris Hanes and Carlos Ramirez. An earlier version of this article was presented at the Second World Congress of Cliometrics, Santander, Spain (June 24–27, 1989), the NBER/DAE workshop, Cambridge, Massachusetts (July 17–21, 1989), and the Department of Economics, University of Warwick (November 1989). We are grateful for the helpful comments offered by participants at both conferences as well as by referees of this journal.

1. L. Squire, *Employment Policy in Developing Nations: A Survey of Issues and Evidence* (New York: Oxford, 1965), p. 102, table 30; C. Clark,

The Conditions of Economic Progress, 3d ed. (London: Macmillan, 1957), pp. 526–31, table 2.

2. J. G. Williamson, "Did English Factor Markets Fail during the Industrial Revolution?" *Oxford Economic Papers* 39 (December 1987): 1–38, esp. 52, table 3.

3. J. G. Williamson, "Labor Market Failure in the New World? Wage Gaps and Labor Market Segmentation in Nineteenth-Century America" (Harvard University, Department of Economics, September 1988, mimeographed).

4. T. J. Hatton and J. G. Williamson, "Wage Gaps between Farm and City: Michigan in the 1890s," Discussion Paper no. 1449 (Harvard Institute of Economic Research, Harvard University, September 1989).

5. L. J. Alston and T. J. Hatton, "The Wage Gap between Farm and Factory: Labor Market Integration in the Interwar Years" (paper presented at the American Economic Association, New York, December 28–30, 1988).

6. D. Suits, "U.S. Farm Migration: An Application of the Harris-Todaro Model," *Economic Development and Cultural Change* 33 (July 1985): 815–28.

7. For the derivation and sources of the data used in this article, see the Appendix.

8. Farm wage rates can be broken down into broad regions, but for unskilled manufacturing wage rates only the Northeast can be isolated separately. When we take the ratio of each region's farm wage to the Northeast manufacturing wage, a similar time series emerges in each case, suggesting that interregional wage variations do not distort the picture given by the aggregate series used throughout the article.

9. Alston and Hatton; Hatton and Williamson; fig. 1 below.

10. E. E. Hagen, "An Economic Justification of Protection," *Quarterly Journal of Economics* 72 (November 1958): 496–514, quote on 503.

11. J. Bhagwati and V. K. Ramaswami, "Domestic Distortions, Tariffs, and the Theory of Optimum Subsidy," *Journal of Political Economy* 71 (February 1963): 44–50; J. Mincer, "Unemployment Effects of Minimum Wages," *Journal of Political Economy* 84 (August 1976): S87–S104.

12. W. A. Lewis, "Economic Development with Unlimited Supplies of Labour," *Manchester School of Economics and Social Studies* 20 (May 1954): 139–92; D. W. Jorgenson, "The Development of a Dual Economy," *Economic Journal* 71 (June 1961): 309–34; A. C. Kelley, R. J. Cheatham, and J. G. Williamson, *Dualistic Economic Development in Theory and History* (Chicago: University of Chicago Press, 1972); J. C. H. Fei and G. Ranis, "A Theory of Economic Development," *American Economic Review* 51 (September 1961): 533–65.

13. W. A. Lewis, "A Review of Development Theory," *American Economic Review* 55 (May 1965): 12–13.

14. M. P. Todaro, "A Model of Labor Migration and Urban Unemployment in Less Developed Countries," *American Economic Review* 59 (March 1969): 138–48; J. R. Harris and M. P. Todaro, "Migration, Unemployment, and Development: A Two-Sector Analysis," *American Economic Review* 60 (March 1970): 126–42; J. Stiglitz, "Wage Determination and Unemployment in LDCs," *Quarterly Journal of Economics* 88 (May 1974): 194–227; W. Corden and R. Findlay, "Urban Unemployment, Intersectoral Capital Mobility and Development Policy," *Economica* 42 (February 1975): 59–78; W. E. Cole and R. D. Sanders, "Internal Migration and Urban Employment in the Third World," *American Economic Review* 75 (June 1985): 481–94.

15. This and the next two paragraphs are taken from J. G. Williamson, *Coping with City Growth during the British Industrial Revolution* (Cambridge: Cambridge University Press, 1990), pp. 102–4.

16. The qq' curve is a rectangular hyperbola with unitary elasticity. The elasticity of the labor demand curve MM is assumed to be less than unity in fig. 2, an assumption that is commonly invoked by development economists and confirmed by the empirical analysis that follows below.

17. Todaro, p. 140.

18. T. W. Schultz, *Agriculture in an Unstable Economy* (New York: McGraw-Hill, 1945).

19. D. J. Ahearn, *The Wages of Farm and Factory Laborers, 1914–1944* (New York: Columbia University Press, 1944), pp. 18–21.

20. L. J. Ducoff, *Wages of Agricultural Labor in the United States*, U.S. Department of Agriculture, Bureau of Agricultural Economics (Washington, D.C.: Government Printing Office, September 1944), p. 135.

21. H. L. Parsons, *The Impact of Fluctuations in National Income on Agricultural Wages and Employment* (Cambridge, Mass.: Harvard Studies on Labor in Agriculture, June 1952).

22. P. H. Douglas, *Real Wages in the United States, 1890–1926* (Boston: Houghton Mifflin, 1930).

23. Williamson, "Labor Market Failure in the New World?" (n. 3 above).

24. Ahearn, pp. 89–179; Parsons, pp. 5–6; G. F. Warren and F. A. Pearson, *The Agricultural Situation: Economic Effects of Fluctuating Prices* (New York: Wiley, 1924).

25. Ahearn, p. 35.

26. Ducoff, p. 190.

27. Ibid., p. 187, fig. 23.

28. Parsons, p. 43.

29. W. D. Weatherford, *Geographic Differentials of Agricultural Wages in the United States* (Cambridge, Mass.: Harvard University Press, 1957), p. 66.

30. It is particularly difficult to find a reliable index for rural cost of living for the era before 1913. The only available series appears to be that for rural Vermont (see J. G. Williamson and P. H. Lindert, *Macroeconomic History* [New York: Academic Press, 1980], p. 123). Given the possible lack of representativeness of this series and the fact that deflation makes little difference to the time series movements after 1913 when we have more reliable series, the nominal wage gap is used in the analysis that follows.

31. We term this coefficient an elasticity in the sense that it represents the elasticity of the farm population with respect to the wage ratio. These results are roughly consistent with those of Suits. He finds an elasticity of farm emigration with respect to urban unemployment of .109 (Suits [n. 6 above], p. 826). Suits's paper differs from ours in two ways. First, his focus is on migration rather than wage gaps. Indeed, he takes labor productivities as proxies for wages. Second, he does not endogenize urban unemployment or deal with the issues of asymmetry in wage adjustment in the two sectors.

32. That is, $\mu/(\alpha + \mu) = 0.34$, the coefficient on $\log(1 - U)$, smaller if we use the coefficient on $\log(1 - U)$.

33. J. Sachs, "The Changing Cyclical Behavior of Wages and Prices, 1890–1976," *American Economic Review* 70 (March 1980): 78–90.

34. Our best estimate for 1892–1941 is as follows:

$$\Delta \log w_M = 0.052 + 0.225 \log (1 - U) + 0.270\, \Delta \log WPI$$
$$(0.021) \quad (0.127) \quad\quad\quad (0.124)$$

$$R^2 = 0.180,\ \text{D·W} = 1.653,\ SE = 0.088.$$

We also estimated this equation over various subperiods, obtaining coefficients on $\log(1 - v)$ between 0.03 and 0.55, but always insignificant.

35. This expression is derived as a simple log-linearization of the labor supply identity $L = L_M + L_A$.

36. A referee has pointed out that if $\log(w_A/P_A)_{-1}$ were not lagged one period, the equation would be an identity. However, it should be borne in mind that this is the true reduced form generated by the model given that the terms of trade and the real manufacturing wage are taken to be exogenous. The lag in the real farm wage arises from the labor-demand equation embedded in eq. (4). Furthermore, the coefficients on the two real-wage terms are significantly different from one (which would be expected for an identity).

37. B. Thomas, *Migration and Urban Development* (London: Methuen, 1972).

38. M. R. Darby, "Three and a Half Million U.S. Workers Have Been Mislaid: Or, An Explanation of Unemployment, 1934–1941," *Journal of Political Economy* 84 (February 1976): 1–16.

39. A. E. Geddes, *Trends in Relief Expenditures, 1910–1935*, WPA Research Monograph 10 (Washington, D.C.: Government Printing Office, 1937), p. 44.

40. From the first equation in table 3, we have estimates for the parameters $\mu = 0.16$ and $\mu + (\mu\alpha s/1 - s) = 0.2$. Hence, we can calculate $\alpha s/1 - s = 0.25$. This is the parameter we use to produce our counterfactual estimates based on eq. (9). Note that the value of μ is larger than that from our earlier structural equations in table 1 and that the implied values of α and s are 0.25 and 0.5, respectively.

41. Douglas, p. 186, table 62.

42. *Farm Wage Rates, Farm Employment, and Related Data*, U.S. Department of Agriculture, Bureau of Labor Economics (Washington, D.C.: Government Printing Office, 1943), pp. 3–4.

43. *Historical Statistics of the United States*, U.S. Department of Commerce, Bureau of the Census (Washington, D.C.: Government Printing Office, 1975), Series D-841, p. 172.

44. W. Coombs, *The Wages of Unskilled Labor in Manufacturing Industries in the United States, 1890–1924* (New York: Columbia University Press, 1926), p. 99, table 5, series 2.

45. N. Koffsky, "Farm and Urban Purchasing Power," in *Studies in Income and Wealth* (New York: National Bureau of Economic Research, 1949), 11: 170. Alston and Hatton (n. 5 above), p. 14, table 5.

46. Williamson and Lindert (n. 30 above), p. 123, table 5.12.

47. S. Lebergott, *Manpower and Economic Growth* (New York: McGraw-Hill, 1964), pp. 510, 512, 522, tables A-1, A-3, A-15.

48. Ibid.; C. Romer, "Spurious Volatility in Historical Unemployment Data," *Journal of Political Economy* 94 (February 1986): 1–37; D. R. Weir, "Unemployment Volatility, 1890–1980: A Sensitivity Analysis" (Yale University, Department of Economics, December 1985, mimeographed).

49. *Historical Statistics of the United States*, Series E-42, p. 200.

50. *Historical Statistics of the United States*, Series E-89, p. 203; *Handbook of Labor Statistics*, U.S. Department of Labor, Bureau of Labor Statistics, Bulletin no. 1016 (Washington, D.C.: Government Printing Office, 1951), D-5, p. 118, linked on 1913–15.

51. *Historical Statistics of the United States*, Series C-76 and C-78, p. 96.

Name index

Economists of the Twentieth Century

per year without those wage gaps, instead of the 2 per cent actually achieved, and manufacturing output might have grown at 3.9 per cent per year, not the 3.1 per cent it actually achieved (Williamson 1990a: ch. 7).

As Sir Arthur Lewis pointed out some time ago, the urban transition can be slowed down or choked off if inelastic urban labour supplies drive up the nominal cost of labour facing urban firms. Based on the first industrial revolution, Sir Arthur is right: the wage gaps between farm and city did indeed choke off British city growth and industrialisation between the 1820s and the 1860s.

Housing, disamenities and death

The quality of urban life has always played a key role in debates over the British industrial revolution. It certainly attracted the attention of Chadwick, Kay and other social reformers in the 1830s and 1840s, but for hot rhetoric it is hard to beat Frederick Engels, who, as we have seen, viewed the migration of rural labour to British cities as 'social murder'. High density, crowding and resulting environmental decay all contributed to high city mortality and morbidity, and immigrants entered that environment at their peril. The early Victorian perception persists in academic debates even today, and the 'pessimists' in the standard of living debate have made much of the issue. Although even the most ardent pessimist would acknowledge the dreary environment of rural England at this time, urban disamenities have, nonetheless, been viewed as seriously lowering working-class living standards up to the 1840s and beyond. Not only was this true of old residents – whose cities, it was alleged, deteriorated in quality over time – but it was true of new urban immigrants, who left more benign rural environments for employment in the ugliest districts of Bradford, Salford, Leeds, Manchester, east London and elsewhere.

What did the rural emigrant forego by leaving his village for some ugly urban district during the first industrial revolution? The answer can be found by applying methods suggested by recent research on twentieth-century urbanisation. Application of these methods to assess the perils of city life in the early nineteenth century is especially attractive because it makes it possible for the workers themselves to reveal their preferences. For more than a century, our perceptions have been coloured by the more verbal Victorian middle-class observer who wrote books and pamphlets which, as it turns out, reveal far stronger preferences for urban amenities than did the workers themselves who placed higher priority on better-paying jobs.

That there was wide variance in crude mortality rates across cities, towns